Esther Ademmer's book makes an important and timely contribution to our understanding of EU and Russian influence on policy developments in their contested common neighborhood. Against the simplistic depiction of the EU and Russia as opposing forces for and against policy reform, the book provides rich case study evidence of Russia's diverse impact, the challenges the EU faces, and the room of maneuver local elites enjoy. Highly recommended reading for anyone interested in the post-Soviet region and EU external governance.

Frank Schimmelfennig, *ETH Zurich, Switzerland*

A welcome change from simplistic geopolitical approaches, this book offers a sophisticated, theory driven analysis of the impact and the limitations of the European Union and Russia in their shared neighbourhood. The 'preferential fit' framework, applied to well-chosen case studies, yields important conclusions about the primacy of domestic elites in shaping compliance with European or Russian demands for policy change.

Antoaneta L. Dimitrova, *Leiden University, the Netherlands*

This book provides an outstanding account of the competing influence of Russia and the European Union over the European Neighborhood Countries. It shows how countries such as Armenia and Georgia cope with opposing pressures from Russia and the EU, maneuvering between their contradictory influences in ways that minimally satisfy both partners, while achieving domestic political goals. Through detailed discussion of countervailing pressures in migration and energy policy, this book provides a clear model for understanding the domestic politics of compliance with two competing behemoths. Ademmer's book is required reading for anyone seeking to understand the European Neighborhood Policy and how the competition between the EU and Russia plays out in the lands in between.

Mitchell Orenstein, *University of Pennsylvania, USA*

Russia's Impact on EU Policy Transfer to the Post-Soviet Space

Russia's impact on EU policy transfer to the post-Soviet space has not been as negative as often perceived. EU policies have traveled to countries and issue areas, in which the dependence on Russia is high and Russian foreign policy is increasingly assertive.

This book explores Russia's impact on the transfer of EU policies in the areas of Justice, Liberty, and Security, and energy policy – two policy areas in which countries in the EU's Eastern neighborhood are traditionally strongly bound to Russia. Focusing especially on Armenia and Georgia, it examines whether it is the structural condition of interdependence, the various institutional ties and similarities of neighboring countries with the EU and Russia, or their concrete foreign policy actions that have the greatest impact on domestic policy change in the region. The book also investigates how important these factors are in relation to domestic ones. It identifies conditions under which different degrees of EU policy transfer occur and the circumstances under which Russia exerts either supportive or constraining effects on this process.

This book will be of key interest to students and scholars of EU and European politics, international relations and comparative politics.

Esther Ademmer is post-doctoral researcher at the Kiel Institute for the World Economy and at Freie Universität Berlin, Germany. Her research interests include European integration and governance, and the impact of external actors on the political economy of domestic change, especially in the post-Soviet space.

Routledge/UACES Contemporary European Studies

Edited by Federica Bicchi, London School of Economics and Political Science, Tanja Börzel, Free University of Berlin, and Mark Pollack, Temple University, on behalf of the University Association for Contemporary European Studies

Editorial Board: Grainne De Búrca, European University Institute and Columbia University; Andreas Føllesdal, Norwegian Centre for Human Rights, University of Oslo; Peter Holmes, University of Sussex; Liesbet Hooghe, University of North Carolina at Chapel Hill, and Vrije Universiteit Amsterdam; David Phinnemore, Queen's University Belfast; Ben Rosamond, University of Warwick; Vivien Ann Schmidt, University of Boston; Jo Shaw, University of Edinburgh; Mike Smith, University of Loughborough and Loukas Tsoukalis, ELIAMEP, University of Athens and European University Institute.

The primary objective of the new Contemporary European Studies series is to provide a research outlet for scholars of European Studies from all disciplines. The series publishes important scholarly works and aims to forge for itself an international reputation.

A full list of titles in this series is available at: www.routledge.com. Recently published titles:

31. The Formulation of EU Foreign Policy
Socialization, negotiations and disaggregation of the state
Nicola Chelotti

32. Core-periphery Relations in the European Union
Power and conflict in a dualist political economy
Edited by José M. Magone, Brigid Laffan and Christian Schweiger

33. Russia's Impact on EU Policy Transfer to the Post-Soviet Space
The Contested Neighborhood
Esther Ademmer

34. Domestic Politics and Norm Diffusion in International Relations
Ideas do not float freely
Thomas Risse

Russia's Impact on EU Policy Transfer to the Post-Soviet Space
The Contested Neighborhood

Esther Ademmer

LONDON AND NEW YORK

First published 2017 by Routledge

2 Park Square, Milton Park, Abingdon, Oxfordshire OX14 4RN
711 Third Avenue, New York, NY 10017

Routledge is an imprint of the Taylor & Francis Group, an informa business

First issued in paperback 2018

Copyright © 2017 Esther Ademmer

The right of Esther Ademmer to be identified as author of this work has been asserted by her in accordance with sections 77 and 78 of the Copyright, Designs and Patents Act 1988.

All rights reserved. No part of this book may be reprinted or reproduced or utilised in any form or by any electronic, mechanical, or other means, now known or hereafter invented, including photocopying and recording, or in any information storage or retrieval system, without permission in writing from the publishers.

Notice:
Product or corporate names may be trademarks or registered trademarks, and are used only for identification and explanation without intent to infringe.

British Library Cataloguing in Publication Data
A catalogue record for this book is available from the British Library

Library of Congress Cataloging in Publication Data
Names: Ademmer, Esther, author.
Title: Russia's impact on EU policy transfer to the post-Soviet space : the contested neighbourhood / Esther Ademmer.
Other titles: Russia's impact on European Union policy transfer to the post-Soviet space
Description: New York, NY : Routledge, 2016. | Series: Routledge/UACES contemporary European studies series ; 33 | Includes bibliographical references and index.
Identifiers: LCCN 2016009842| ISBN 9781138944244 (hardback) | ISBN 9781315672007 (ebook)
Subjects: LCSH: European Union–Former Soviet republics. | Former Soviet republics–Politics and government. | European Union countries–Foreign relations–Russia (Federation) | Russia (Federation)–Foreign relations–European Union countries. | Former Soviet republics–Foreign relations–Russia (Federation) | Russia (Federation)–Foreign relations–Former Soviet repubics.
Classification: LCC HC240.25.F6 A34 2016 | DDC 320.60947–dc23
LC record available at https://lccn.loc.gov/2016009842

ISBN: 978-1-138-94424-4 (hbk)
ISBN: 978-1-138-36189-8 (pbk)

Typeset in Times New Roman
by Taylor & Francis Books

Contents

List of illustrations		viii
Acknowledgement		ix
List of abbreviations		x
1	Introduction	1
2	Theorizing Russia's impact on neighborhood Europeanization	14
3	Constraining EU policy transfer? A bird's-eye view	45
4	Migration management	102
5	Energy diversification	149
6	Anchoring policy change in times of crisis	185
7	Conclusion	206
	Appendix: Interviews	220
	References	226
	Index	263

List of illustrations

Figures

2.1	Aggregated Freedom House Index scores, 1999–2013	40
3.1	Estimated number of migrants from Georgia and Armenia in Russia and the EU	58
3.2	Net energy imports, in percent of energy use	61
3.3	Overview of JLS compliance patterns in Georgia and Armenia	64
3.4	Overview of energy compliance patterns in Georgia and Armenia	65
3.5	Governance Indicators, Rule of Law score	75
3.6	Comparative Economic Freedom Index score, 1999–2013	76
3.7	Governance Indicators, Regulatory Quality score	78
3.8	Governance Indicators, Government Effectiveness score	78
3.9	Governance Indicators, Control of Corruption score	79
7.1	Decision tree for neighborhood Europeanization East	210

Tables

2.1	Interaction effect of preferential fit and multiple policy conditionalities	33
2.2	Interaction effect of preferential fit and multiple external capacity building	35
3.1	Compliance coding across sectors and countries, in percent	63
3.2	BTI Status Index scores, Transformation to Market Economy	77
4.1	Overview of cases: migration management	141
5.1	Overview of cases: energy diversification	181

Acknowledgement

I have been grateful for the support and encouragement of many while working on the book and the PhD thesis upon which it is based. My first thanks go to Tanja Börzel, who was a great supervisor for my thesis at Freie Universität (FU) Berlin and has been a great mentor ever since. Her guidance and support helped me to finish my thesis and the book in every possible way.

I have also very much appreciated and profited from the intellectual and financial support of many other people and institutions. My thanks go to my colleagues, friends and staff at the DFG-Research College 'The Transformative Power of Europe' (KFG) and the Berlin Graduate School for Transnational Studies (BTS) at FU Berlin, who helped to create an inspiring academic and personal environment for my PhD research. I have also been grateful for the financial and intellectual support of the Fox Fellowship Program at Yale University, which was the perfect place to finalize my PhD thesis. As I worked on this book while being a post-doc at the Kiel Institute for the World Economy (IfW) and Kiel University (CAU), my thanks also go to my highly supportive Kiel colleagues at the IfW's Poverty Reduction, Equity and Development (PRED) research area, and the Comparative Politics, Interdependence and Globalization (CPIG) research group at CAU.

There are numerous other people who supported me intellectually and personally along the way and whom I would like to thank for their comments, advice and the fruitful discussions on the theme of this book at different points in time. In this regard, I would especially like to thank my second PhD-supervisor Timm Beichelt, as well as Laure Delcour, Julia Langbein, Anna Leupold, Imke Pente, and Kataryna Wolczuk. As this book heavily draws on interview material, I owe my gratitude to the interviewees who devoted their time and resources to make this research project possible in the first place. I am also grateful to Nino and Sophio Barbakadze, and Tamar Iakobidze for turning my research trips into an enriching experience in an academic as well as a personal way. Any remaining errors in this book are of course solely my responsibility.

My friends and especially my parents deserve a massive thank you for their unlimited support and encouragement throughout this entire endeavor. Finally, I owe Martin for his smart comments on parts and components of this book and, most importantly, for his invaluable backing in whatever I do and have done throughout the last decade. I dedicate this book to him.

List of abbreviations

AA	Association Agreements
AEI	Alliance for European Integration
AENEAS	Program for financial and technical assistance to third countries in the area of migration and asylum
AEPLAC	Armenian-European Policy and Legal Advice Center
AP	European Neighborhood Policy Action Plans
ARF	Armenian Revolutionary Federation-Dashnaktsutyun
BOMCA	Border Management Program for Central Asia
BSEC	Organization of the Black Sea Economic Cooperation
BTC	Baku–Tbilisi–Ceyhan oil pipeline
BTE	Baku–Tbilisi–Erzurum pipeline
BTI	Bertelsmann Transformation Index
CEEC	Central and Eastern European countries
CIPDD	Caucasus Institute for Peace, Democracy and Development
CIS	Commonwealth of Independent States
CNC	Caucasian neighborhood countries
CoE	Council of Europe
CRA	Civil Registry Agency
CSRDG	Center for Strategic Research and Development of Georgia
CSTO	Collective Security Treaty Organization
CU	Eurasian Customs Union
CUG	Citizen's Union of Georgia
DCFTA	Deep and Comprehensive Free Trade Area
DCI	Development Cooperation Instrument
DG	Directorate-General
DMR	Department of Migration and Refugees
DP	Democratic Party
DRC	Danish Refugee Council
EaP	Eastern Partnership
EBRD	European Bank for Reconstruction and Development
EC	European Commission
EEAS	European External Action Service
EEC	Energy Efficiency Center Georgia

List of abbreviations xi

EEU	Eurasian Economic Union
EIA	US Energy Information Administration
EIB	European Investment Bank
EIU	Economist Intelligence Unit
EKENG	e-Governance Infrastructure Implementation Unit
EMCDDA	European Monitoring Center for Drugs and Drug Addiction
ENC	European neighborhood countries
ENI	European Neighborhood Instrument
ENP	European Neighborhood Policy
ENPI	European Neighborhood and Partnership Instrument
EPC	Electric Power Council
EPRS	European Parliamentary Research Service
EU	European Union
EUAG	European Union Advisory Group
EUI	European University Institute
EurAsEc	Eurasian Economic Community
Eurojust	European Union Judicial Cooperation Unit
Europol	European Police Office
FATF	Financial Action Task Force
FDI	foreign direct investment
FMS	Federal Migration Service
FRONTEX	European Agency for the Management of Operational Cooperation at the External Borders of the Member States of the European Union
GD	Georgian Dream
GDP	gross domestic product
GEPLAC	Georgian-European Policy and Legal Advice Center
GFSIS	Georgian Foundation for Strategic and International Studies
GIZ	Deutsche Gesellschaft für Internationale Zusammenarbeit
GNI	gross national income
GRECO	Council of Europe Group of States against Corruption
GUAM	Georgia, Ukraine, Azerbaijan, Moldova
GYLA	Georgian Young Lawyers' Association
IAEA	International Atomic Energy Agency
ICAO	International Civil Aviation Organization
ICHD	International Center for Human Development
ICMPD	International Center for Migration Policy Development
IDP	internally displaced person
IEA	International Energy Agency
IFC	International Finance Corporation
ILO	International Labour Organization
IMF	International Monetary Fund
INOGATE	Interstate Oil and Gas Transportation to Europe
IO	international organization
IOM	International Organization for Migration

IRENA	International Renewable Energy Agency
JLS	Justice, Liberty and Security
KfW	German Development Bank (Kreditanstalt für Wiederaufbau)
KV	kilovolt
LDP	Liberal Democratic Party
MENR	Ministry of Energy and Natural Resources
MFA	Ministry of Foreign Affairs
MIA	Ministry of Internal Affairs
Moneyval	Council of Europe's Committee of Experts on the Evaluation of Anti-Money Laundering Measures and the Financing of Terrorism
MRA	Ministry for Refugees and Accommodation (in 2010, renamed Ministry for Internally Displaced People from the Occupied Territories, Accommodation and Refugees)
MW	megawatt
NATO	North Atlantic Treaty Organization
NGO	non-governmental organization
NIF	Neighborhood Investment Facility
NIS	Newly Independent States
NPP	nuclear power plant
ODIHR	Office for Democratic Institutions and Human Rights
OECD	Organisation for Economic Co-operation and Development
OSCE	Organization for Security and Co-operation in Europe
OSF	Open Society Foundation
PCA	Partnership and Cooperation Agreements
PEEREA	Energy Charter Protocol on Energy Efficiency and Related Environmental Aspects
R2E2	Revolving Fund for Renewable Energy
REEEP	Renewable Energy and Energy Efficiency Partnership
RFE/RL	Radio Free Europe and Radio Liberty
SCP	South Caucasus gas pipeline
SIPRI	Stockholm International Peace Research Institute
SMS	State Migration Service
SOEAI	State Office for Euro-Atlantic Integration
TACIS	Technical Assistance to the Commonwealth of Independent States
TAIEX	Technical Assistance and Information Exchange Instrument
TIG	Targeted Initiative Georgia
TRACECA	Transport Corridor Europe–Caucasus–Asia
UES	Unified Energy System
UN	United Nations
UNDP	United Nations Development Programme
UNESCAP	United Nations Economic and Social Commission for Asia and the Pacific
UNHCR	United Nations High Commissioner for Refugees

UNM	United National Movement
UNODC	United Nations Office on Drugs and Crime
USA	United States of America
USAID	United States Agency for International Development
VLAP	Visa Liberalization Action Plan
WTO	World Trade Organization

1 Introduction

> I want to see a 'ring of friends' surrounding the Union and its closest European neighbors, from Morocco to Russia and the Black Sea.
> (Romano Prodi 2002)

More than a decade after Romano Prodi's vision inspired the development of the European Neighborhood Policy (ENP)[1] in 2003, the 'ring of friends' he had hoped for had turned into a 'ring of fire' (The Economist 2014). The war in Ukraine, a political crisis in Moldova, and Armenia's decision to forego the European Union's (EU) offer of further economic integration, were among the drivers that made the EU review its neighborhood policy in 2015. To many observers, its alleged failure was not much of a surprise. The ENP had been designed on the blueprint of the EU's enlargement policy (Kelley 2006) with the central goal to make neighboring countries adopt a large amount of EU rules and policies, comprising parts of the EU's acquis communautaire, bilaterally negotiated rules, and international conventions. However, it did not provide a membership perspective to the neighbors – the incentive that had boosted Europe's transformative power in Central and Eastern European countries (CEEC) (Schimmelfennig and Sedelmeier 2005b). In addition, unlike the young democracies in Eastern Europe, the EU's new neighbors had been stuck in transition, suffered from high levels of corruption and qualified as semi-democratic countries at best – all unfavorable conditions for EU policies to travel (Börzel 2011; Schimmelfennig 2012).

The failure of the ENP in the East, however, was attributed less to the lack of a membership perspective or the neighbors' domestic politics, than to the fact that the EU was no longer 'the only game in town'. Russia had been widely perceived to actively try to reduce 'Western' influence in the post-Soviet space for a long time (Bugajski 2010; Kubicek 1999; Leonard and Popescu 2007). Unlike the EU, it reigned over strong, historically grown interdependencies in terms of trade, security, or migration flows with post-Soviet states that were likely to undermine the ENP's attempt for policy transfer to the region (Delcour and Kostanyan 2014; Dimitrova and Dragneva 2009). The competition between the EU and Russia eventually peaked when Russia started to formalize previously toothless Eurasian integration attempts.[2] It lobbied European neighborhood countries (ENC) to join the Eurasian Customs Union (CU), which was, however, incompatible with the EU's offer of closer economic integration. After intense pressure by Russia in 2013, Ukraine and Armenia rowed back from finalizing Association Agreements (AA) with the EU that foresaw the transfer of an even greater amount of EU rules to the ENC – fueling perceptions of a geopolitical rivalry in the region that the EU was not winning (Lehne 2014).

A closer look at the region, however, shows a much more puzzling picture: Moldova and Georgia signed Association Agreements with the EU despite threats and economic sanctions by Russia, and EU-demanded policy changes occurred in areas in which neighbors were more dependent on Russia and subject to its assertive foreign policy. Armenia has taken over a large portion of EU demands for migration management, even though its migration flows are primarily directed toward Russia. Georgia responded to some EU demands for energy sector reforms, despite the fact that it had been fully dependent on Russian energy supplies and subject to Russian sanctions and threats when faced with EU demands for reform. Likewise, Ukraine converged toward EU market rules under conditions of high interdependence with Russia – a process on which Russia's foreign policy and Russian non-state actors had both supportive and countervailing effects (Langbein 2015). However, while Russia's trade embargos or its involvement in the war in eastern Ukraine have generally received substantial academic and public attention, its impact on the central goal of the ENP, namely to transfer EU policies and rules to the EU's neighborhood, has rarely been analyzed.

This book sets out to explain these puzzling findings and asks whether, how and under which conditions Russia impacts EU policy transfer to the post-Soviet space. It studies EU policy transfer to Armenia and Georgia in the areas of Justice, Liberty and Security (JLS), and energy policy – two policy areas that lie at the heart of a state's sovereignty, and in which the ENC are traditionally strongly bound to Russia. In the realm of JLS, the book provides for in-depth case studies of Armenia's and Georgia's migration management reforms. In the energy sector, it scrutinizes their attempts (not) to diversify energy suppliers and sources in line with demands formulated by the EU. The book also investigates whether the factors that account for the adoption and implementation of EU policies in these sectors until 2013 can explain why ENC chose to sign Association Agreements with the EU or to integrate into the Russian-led Eurasian integration regime instead. Based on these analyses, the book argues that EU policy transfer to the contested Eastern neighborhood is best understood as the result of the strategic interaction of semi-democratic incumbents with multiple incentives provided by both the EU and Russia – an argument that is outlined in greater detail in the next section.

Neighborhood Europeanization as a strategic choice under multiple constraints

This book hypothesizes that different degrees of EU policy transfer, defined as full, shallow and non-compliance with the ENP's bilateral reform program, the so-called Action Plans (AP), are a strategic choice of ENC governments that is made under multiple constraints and opportunities resulting from their relationship with both the EU and Russia. These choices are theoretically assumed to be shaped by the structural patterns of regional interdependence (Dimitrova and Dragneva 2009), the institutional contexts ENC are embedded in or the overall compatibility of their domestic structures (Lavenex and Schimmelfennig 2009) with those of the EU and Russia. In addition, they can be shaped by more agency-centered factors (see e.g. Börzel and Langbein 2014), such as the provision of various incentives and capacity by external actors. Based on the analysis of EU policy transfer to Georgia and Armenia in the area of JLS and energy policy, this book argues that full, shallow and non-compliance with EU policies in the contested neighborhood are a function of the interplay of two agency-related factors:

First, I show that preferential fit is a sufficient condition for full or shallow compliance with EU policies. I label the status in which an EU policy benefits the incumbent government in terms of welfare, security or power vis-à-vis other internal or external actors' 'preferential fit' (Ademmer and Börzel 2013), taking into consideration the costs and benefits that emerge from EU policy transfer on an incumbent's specific power base. I argue that the EU is unlikely to empower a larger variety of state and non-state actors in ENC given their overly powerful executives, but that EU-demanded policy change is also not always costly for domestic incumbents in semi-democratic environments: as the EU also strives to enhance the capacities of neighboring states or their effectiveness in regulatory matters, ENC incumbents can also use EU-demanded change for furthering their own political agenda (see also Ademmer and Börzel 2013; Börzel and Pamuk 2012; Börzel and Risse 2012b). In addition, I show that incumbent governments in semi-democratic ENC are able not only to choose to comply or not to comply, but also comply shallowly by formally adopting EU policies without implementing them in practice.

Second, I argue that whether an initial preferential (mis)fit translates into full, shallow or non-compliance depends on its interplay with policy conditionalities provided by both the EU and Russia. The EU, for instance, conditions the benefit of visa liberalization or greater market access on the fulfillment of domestic reforms by ENC. While Russia does not have a similarly formalized neighborhood policy, it often uses functional equivalents to policy conditionality by linking the withholding of sanctions or the provision of benefits to certain decisions or policy choices of ENC. In this vein, full compliance occurs under conditions of preferential fit and a lack of rivaling policy conditionality by Russia. Shallow compliance is the result either of a preferential misfit and policy conditionality by the EU or a preferential fit and rivaling policy conditionality by Russia. This suggests that policy conditionalities by the EU and Russia incentivize merely cosmetic, rather than profound domestic changes. Non-compliance occurs in cases of preferential misfit and a lack of policy conditionality to incentivize reforms. In cases in which both Russia and the EU attach conditionalities to different policy choices, the ENC governments choose the offer that best fits their agenda. I thus argue that under conditions of an increased external rivalry, they can pick and choose from the various offers what they find most beneficial for increasing their domestic power and welfare. The causal mechanism that dominates EU policy transfer to ENC is consequently a strategic form of lesson drawing, by which domestic governments use the EU policy to further their own domestic agenda. This book therefore concludes that Russia and the EU matter especially as foreign policy agents, rather than through the structural or institutional characteristics of their relationships to the ENC.

Third, the findings of the book provide the answers to the question about the conditions under which Russia impacts EU policy transfer in different ways: I find that Russia indeed has a countervailing impact on EU policy transfer, when Russia, and only Russia, uses policy conditionalities to incentivize non-compliance with an EU policy. In these cases, even an ENC in which there is a general preferential fit with the EU policy only complies shallowly to avert potential costs induced by Russia. Put in more technical terms, I find that the absence of such an exclusive form of rivaling Russian policy conditionality figures as a necessary condition for full compliance with EU policies. However, the cases in which Russia indeed reverts to such a form of rivaling policy conditionality have so far been relatively few in number. More often, Russia sanctions ENC without applying specific policy conditionality. These negative incentives that are not clearly linked to specific demands, however, often make third countries seek shelter in compliance with EU policies in order to be eligible for (geo)political and economic alternatives. They hence exert a supportive effect of EU policy transfer.

The book also tests whether these arguments can account for the choices of ENC (not) to sign the Association Agreement (AA) with the EU. Presenting evidence of developments in Georgia, Armenia, but also from Moldova and Ukraine, it shows that the same factors that make EU policies travel, can also largely account for these broader integration choices of ENC.

Contributions to the literature

By making these arguments, this book contributes to the literature on neighborhood Europeanization and external governance, as well as to the broader debates on EU and Russian foreign policy in the post-Soviet space.

This book adds to the literature on neighborhood Europeanization by systematically including Russia as a second external actor in the equation of neighborhood Europeanization. Since the beginning of the 1990s,

Europeanization research has dealt with the question of how EU politics, polities and policies impact on the nation-state and how this impact can be explained (Radaelli 2003). For a long time, this strand of research mainly focused on the impact of hierarchical steering by the EU on its member states (Börzel and Risse 2000; Knill and Lenschow 1998). Processes of Europeanization beyond the EU moved to the center of attention as students looked closer at transformation processes that occurred in CEEC after the fall of the Berlin Wall. The rapid and thorough democratic transformation, including the takeover of EU rules in these post-Soviet or former communist countries, was largely explained by the EU's incentive of membership (Schimmelfennig and Sedelmeier 2005a). The latter was made conditional upon the takeover of the entire acquis communautaire and compliance with the EU's political, institutional and economic conditions defined in the Copenhagen Criteria, which empowered liberal over illiberal domestic actors in the CEEC (Börzel and Risse 2000; Börzel and van Hüllen 2011; Vachudova 2005). Domestic reform-friendly agents were perceived as having been targeted by the active conditionality of the EU, but also used its passive leverage in order to push through reforms against the veto of domestic political opponents (Vachudova 2005; see also Brusis 2005). In this vein, compliance was largely considered the result of cost-benefit analyses of domestic actors in the CEEC underscoring the dominance of the rationalist logic of consequentialism, as opposed to the social-constructivist logic of appropriateness that has been linked to socialization processes (March and Olsen 1998; Schimmelfennig 2007). While this literature has not been fully blind to the presence of other external actors, their theoretical and empirical relevance in the post-communist accession states has largely been disregarded. The USA and international institutions such as the International Monetary Fund (IMF) or the World Bank, which also applied conditionality in the CEEC after the end of the Cold War, were largely perceived as adding to the EU's conditionality without challenging it (Schimmelfennig and Sedelmeier 2005a: 15). As opposed to this, the neglect of Russia in the study on accession Europeanization in the post-Soviet space has been justified by arguing that Russia would be unable to provide incentives that compete with the overarching incentive of EU membership (cf. Schimmelfennig and Sedelmeier 2004: 674).

Due to the fact that the EU lacks this prominent tool in its neighborhood policy, the scholarship on the ENP has tried to study neighborhood Europeanization from new perspectives, but only sporadically included 'competing governance providers' such as Russia into these concepts (Lavenex and Schimmelfennig 2009: 803). While the ENP copies the enlargement tools and logic (Emerson et al. 2005; Kelley 2006), its neglect to offer a membership perspective to the non- or semi-democratic ENC questioned the application of the accession-related 'external incentives' model. Instead, an 'external governance' approach has been brought forward, designed to explain both democracy promotion in the ENC as well as more policy-specific transfer processes via sectoral cooperation (Freyburg et al. 2009; Freyburg et al. 2011;

Lavenex and Wichmann 2009). This approach advocates a structure-focused, rule-based view of EU rule transfer to the neighborhood which respects the greater parity in the relationship of the EU and the ENC (Lavenex and Schimmelfennig 2009: 794; Stulberg and Lavenex 2007). In this model, the EU fosters rule adoption via functional cooperation with the ENC: governmental actors in the ENC get acquainted with and internalize EU policies and norms of democratic governance in transgovernmental networks and in areas where such policies are highly institutionalized (Freyburg 2012; Lavenex and Schimmelfennig 2009). Socialization has hence been deemed a dominant mechanism that triggers neighborhood Europeanization in the absence of a membership perspective (Schimmelfennig 2012: 22).

The external governance literature has also been the first to suggest a structural conceptualization of Russia's impact on rule adoption in the ENC (Lavenex and Schimmelfennig 2009). In a case study on Ukraine a highly asymmetric interdependence with Russia and the Commonwealth of Independent States (CIS) has been found to undermine the EU's efforts to induce policy change via the ENP (Dimitrova and Dragneva 2009). In this vein, Russia's influence on the region has often been considered a function of its asymmetric ties with ENC, in terms of trade or migration linkages, for instance (see also Cameron and Orenstein 2011; Delcour and Kostanyan 2014; Levitsky and Way 2006). These structural approaches have, however, faced criticism with a view to their blindness towards domestic actors and powerful elites in the target countries (Langbein and Wolczuk 2012; Tolstrup 2013). Consequently, students of the ENP have also started to discuss the effectiveness of the ENP from an agency-centered perspective in terms of external incentives and domestic empowerment, conceptualizing policy transfer again as the result of rationalist cost-benefit analyses (Ademmer et al. 2016; Ademmer and Börzel 2013; Börzel and Pamuk 2012; Casier 2011b). In this vein, scholars studied the effect of the liberalized access of goods and persons to the EU that is offered to the ENC in return for sector-specific reform progress (Ademmer and Börzel 2013; Gawrich et al. 2010; Langbein 2011; Langbein and Wolczuk 2012). This policy conditionality or 'conditionality-lite' (Sasse 2008) has been found to be an effective tool that can indeed bridge the absence of the membership perspective in the respective areas (Schimmelfennig 2012). The interplay of key domestic veto players with policy conditionality and capacity building by the EU has been found to account for diverse policy changes (Ademmer and Börzel 2013; Buzogány 2013; Dimitrova and Dragneva 2013).

There are a few studies that include Russia in the equation of neighborhood Europeanization, also from an agency-centered perspective (Ademmer et al. 2016; Langbein 2015). They mostly share a sectoral approach to studying Russia's impact on EU policy transfer, as patterns of interdependence or conditionalities can vary across policy sectors, and not only countries (Ademmer et al. 2016; Dimitrova and Dragneva 2009; Hagemann 2013; Langbein 2015; but see Schmidtke and Chira-Pascanut 2011). In addition, they suggest analyzing Russian influence 'through the prism of domestic actors' preferences' (Dimitrova and Dragneva 2013: 663; see also Hagemann 2013) that filter multiple external influences and drive EU policy change in the region (Ademmer et al. 2016).

However, comprehensive analyses that include Russia both as a structural force and a foreign policy actor in the region are still rare. Some conceive of Russia mostly as a source of interdependence (Dimitrova and Dragneva 2009), or as a provider of cross-conditionalities (Hagemann 2013). Others investigate Russia's impact on broader political or democratic developments and often find unintended and counterproductive effects of Russian pressure (Börzel 2015; Delcour and Wolczuk 2015a; Schmidtke and Chira-Pascanut 2011; Tolstrup 2009). A study on Ukraine that systematically analyzes patterns of interdependence, as well as cross-conditionality and capacity provided by Russia, finds that Russia is indeed not only a countervailing force for EU-demanded regulatory policy change in Ukraine (Langbein 2015). Langbein's study focuses on changes in market rules, in which also private actors qualify as important change agents, and shows that Russian business actors are not necessarily obstructive to the further alignment of ENC with EU rules, but also lobby for domestic change if it suits their business interests. Russia has also been found to support and undermine EU policy change in other policy areas and neighboring countries (see, for instance, Buzogány 2016; Delcour 2016; Hagemann 2013; Wolczuk 2016).

This book contributes to this emerging literature in multiple ways. First, it investigates how and under what conditions Russia and the EU shape domestic policy-making in two policy areas that lie at the heart of a state's sovereignty: JLS and energy policy. It offers a systematic inclusion of Russia as a structural, institutional and more agency-centered force in the neighborhood, while acknowledging the centrality of ENCs' domestic actors in this process. It does so by studying EU policy transfer as a rational, strategic choice of ENC under multiple constraints that emerge from their interdependent relationships with the EU and Russia, the institutional context in which they are embedded, and the various incentives and assistance that they receive from both the EU and Russia. The book thereby assesses the relative explanatory power of structural, institutional and more agency-related approaches, and identifies clear conditions for successful EU rule transfer to the contested neighborhood. It also adds to the debate about causal mechanisms that drive EU-induced change beyond EU borders, arguing that the causal mechanism that dominates neighborhood Europeanization is a strategic form of lesson drawing, by which domestic governments use the EU policy to further their own domestic agenda. Socialization in transgovernmental networks may shape attitudes of individuals in ENC administrations, but cannot explain the detected compliance patterns for the cases at hand.

Second, this book deviates from the assumption that the EU and Russia generally compete over policy changes in the region. Analyses that study Russia's impact on EU-promoted polity or policy change in the ENC usually conceptualize Russia only as a counterforce to the EU (Babayan 2015; Delcour and Wolczuk 2015a; Hagemann 2013; Langbein 2015; Melnykovska et al. 2012; Tolstrup 2014). This assumption and the consequent lack of variation in external rivalry, however, make it difficult to detect the impact of the EU's and Russia's competition on EU policy transfer in the first place. This book sides with research showing that the EU and Russia – including Russian-dominated regional organizations such as the CIS – provide for a much more diverse pattern of conflicting, compatible or complementary policies in their neighborhood (Casier 2012: 49; Dragneva and Dimitrova 2007). By systematically varying policy areas with regard to whether the EU and Russia diverge or converge in the policies they promote or at least represent in the neighborhood, it allows for an assessment of the impact of the external rivalry on policy-specific change in ENC. It shows that the competition of the EU and Russia over policy content does not automatically hamper EU policy transfer, even in policy areas where ENC are more dependent on Russia.

The focus on policy-specific change additionally adds content to the relatively woolly debate about 'spheres of influence', and addresses the critique that the study of broader democratic norms often lacks specificity, thus making it hard to trace the influence of the EU or Russia, instead of other non-EU, international or domestic forces (Schimmelfennig 2012). It thereby also contributes a more nuanced perspective to the widespread view that Russia seeks to bolster its own and reduce 'Western' influence in the post-Soviet space (Babayan 2015; Bugajski 2010; Kubicek 1999; Leonard and Popescu 2007).

Third, this book contributes to the debate about the (unintended) effects of competing external actors on domestic change. Research on neighborhood Europeanization shows that the EU managed to transfer some of its policies to the Eastern neighborhood (Börzel and Langbein 2014; Casier 2011a), but while they have been formally adopted, their implementation has frequently failed to follow suit (Freyburg et al. 2009; Freyburg et al. 2011). As a result, 'enclaves of Europeanization' instead of profound domestic change have been found to permeate the neighborhood countries (Solonenko 2008: 32).

Likewise, Russia's foreign policy in the region has rarely been effective in living up to its goal of keeping the countries in Russia's sphere of influence and maintaining pro-Russian-oriented regimes in the neighborhood (Hedenskog and Larsson 2007; Oliker et al. 2009; Trenin 2005). Particularly its sanctioning policy has been considered ineffective, if not counterproductive (Schulze 2008; Stent 2008; Trenin 2009). As shown above, Russia has also been found to exert both supportive and countervailing effects on specific EU policy transfer, which echoes a debate that has emerged about unintended effects of external actors on polity changes, where liberal external actors have been found to empower illiberal domestic actors and vice versa (Börzel 2015).

This book suggests some explanations for these unintended effects and rather 'unsuccessful' foreign policies of both the EU and Russia from a policy-specific perspective. On the one hand, it argues that a differentiation of incentives that Russia provides to neighboring countries can help explain countervailing and mutually reinforcing effects on policy change in the neighborhood. While Russia's rivaling policy conditionality frequently constrains EU policy transfer, negative incentives that fail to specify the policy they target rather foster EU-demanded change, as ENC seek to gain greater autonomy vis-à-vis Russia by complying with EU demands. On the other hand, the book shows that a key reason for the overall limited effectiveness of the EU's and Russia's foreign policy lies within the domestic distribution of power within ENC that is strongly biased in favor of executive or executive-related groups that act as 'gatekeepers' (Tolstrup 2013) in the reform process, and filter external influences. Given that governments and their power bases in the ENC under scrutiny here are relatively unconstrained by other political actors and institutional checks and balances, they can also decouple formal policy adoption from de facto behavioral changes (Börzel and Pamuk 2012). The book argues that shallow compliance with EU policies is likely to occur when executive actors in the ENC are faced with costly reform demands by the EU that are tied to attractive incentives, or when incumbents initially have a preference for EU-demanded policy change, but face rivaling policy conditionalities by Russia that are not countered with an attractive offer by the EU. In a context of geopolitical rivalry, however, domestic incumbents can often pick and choose from various external offers or even play off Russia and the EU against each other. Unlike the image of the post-Soviet space as a region that is bullied by two powerful regional actors, this book rather shows a region that is characterized by relatively sovereign incumbents that frequently use the external rivalry about influence for their own political survival. I thus add a policy-specific and multidimensional perspective to the literature on the ENP that finds a stabilizing or even perverted effect of EU democracy and good governance promotion on authoritarian regimes in its neighborhood (Börzel and Pamuk 2012; Börzel and van Hüllen 2011; Van Hüllen 2015).

Fourth, this book also provides some preliminary insight into whether this argument can travel to more recent developments in the region. With the rise of the CU and Eurasian Economic Union (EEU) as more legalized and substantial Eurasian integration projects (Dragneva and Wolczuk 2012), Russia provides for a formal alternative to the EU's integration offers in the region. These latest developments may put to a substantial test the argument of powerful domestic agents that frequently use external resources, because of the incompatibility and increased legalization of competing integration regimes. I suggest that decisions of ENC (not) to sign AA with the EU can still be well understood by studying the interplay of executive preferences and multiple external policy conditionalities. This book does not strive to offer broader explanations for the conflicts that erupted in the region or provide answers to the question of whether and how policies associated with each integration regime will be adopted and implemented in the ENC. Rather, it seeks to provide some insight into the drivers of decisions that determine whether ENC commit to an even larger EU policy transfer in the first place.

10 *Introduction*

Finally, the book's findings entail some practical conclusions on how to transfer policies into an increasingly contested neighborhood. I argue that powerful executives and executive-related elites constrain Russia's and the EU's effectiveness in fostering profound domestic changes. Against the background of the ongoing review process of the ENP, I draw a relatively bleak picture of the EU's functional cooperation with ENC governments and recommend putting a greater emphasis on creating a level playing field for various actors in ENC in order to facilitate the empowerment of reform coalitions. In addition, the findings of the book suggest that greater attention on the 'neighbors of the neighbors' (European Commission 2015a) needs to go hand in hand with a greater focus on domestic developments and actor constellations in the region to prevent the increasing external rivalry from accelerating the process of usage of external opportunities by semi-democratic executives in ENC.

Plan of the book

The book consists of seven chapters. Chapter 2 develops the theoretical framework to account for neighborhood Europeanization in environments characterized by multiple external actors and semi-democratic regimes. It defines neighborhood Europeanization as compliance with policies covered in the ENP Action Plan – the bilateral EU-ENC reform program. The chapter conceives of EU policy transfer as a strategic choice by incumbent governments in neighborhood countries. Instead of focusing on top-down promoted EU policies, the theoretical framework considers policy transfer to the Eastern neighborhood as the result of a bottom-up process, in which domestic actors make strategic choices for or against EU policy transfer in a context of different structural, institutional or agency-based opportunities and constraints that emerge from their relationships to both Russia and the EU. The chapter also outlines the methodological approach of the book, which combines different qualitative methods to conduct structured and focused macro- and micro-level comparisons of compliance processes in Armenia and Georgia from 1999 to 2013 in the areas of JLS and energy policy. The chapter presents the choice of methods, data sources and cases in detail.

Chapter 3 tests if EU policies travel at all once the ENC are more dependent on Russia than on the EU in policy areas in which the externally promoted policies diverge. The chapter presents similarly hard cases for EU policy transfer and comes up with a puzzling finding: EU policies do travel to ENC under these conditions and they do so differently across countries and sectors. The chapter then continues to investigate whether other explanatory factors can account better for the variation in compliance of Armenia and Georgia in the areas of JLS and energy policy. While Chapter 3 finds some explanatory power for institutional and structural factors to account for variation in compliance across sectors, these factors cannot explain the differences in compliance between the two countries. The factors that vary between

Georgia and Armenia are agency based in kind – namely, preferential fit, external incentives and external capacity building.

Based on this finding, Chapter 4 then presents in-depth case studies of compliance with EU migration management policies in Georgia and Armenia. The case studies trace in detail how preferential fit, external incentives and capacity building shape the process of complying with specific EU policies in the area of migration management – namely, the conclusion of readmission agreements, the enhancement of document security, the adoption of national action plans on migration, and data protection. The chapter argues that the interplay of preferential fit and policy conditionalities by the EU can best account for full, shallow or non-compliance with EU migration management demands. While Russia does not invoke any rivaling policy conditionalities in this area, other negative incentives such as the distribution of Russian passports in Georgia's breakaway regions or the encouragement of Armenian emigration via the Compatriots Program catalyze, rather than undermine, compliance with EU requirements.

The chapter shows that full compliance with EU policies occurs when ENP migration management requirements can be used by domestic incumbents to further their own political goals. The reduction of emigration, the return of migrants and a more restrictive approach towards migration management corresponded with the agenda of both the Kocharyan and the Sargsyan administrations in Armenia. By contrast, in Georgia under Saakashvili's incumbency, the proposed policies proved at odds with the liberal governmental agenda, despite a comparable misfit with a view to the policy, polity or politics status quo. When policy conditionality was invoked by the EU, Georgia at the time frequently complied shallowly with the EU's migration management demands. In this policy area, capacity building by the EU, however, largely fails to explain compliance: in cases of preferential fit, governments also find other sources of financing reforms if they lack EU support. In case of preferential misfit, attempts of bureaucratic actors working on reform proposals with the help of EU capacity frequently get sacked. The chapter suggests that the manipulation of utility costs and lesson drawing instead of socialization processes make EU policies travel in the cases at hand.

Chapter 5 traces the process of energy diversification in Georgia and Armenia. It studies the evolution and neglect of policies to develop domestic hydropower and other renewable energies, as well as to achieve a greater regional diversification of energy supplies. In this vein, I also discuss the issue of the closure of the Medzamor nuclear power plant in Armenia. The case studies on energy diversification suggest that preferential fit is a sufficient condition for domestic change, which may, however, remain shallow if rivaling policy conditionality by Russia is invoked. The importance of (changes in) preferential fit is especially vividly illustrated in the case of Georgia. Here, the change of government after the Rose Revolution enabled EU-compatible reform processes that had previously been blocked by vested interests in the energy sector associated with the Shevardnadze-administration. While rivaling policy conditionality by Russia is found to undermine EU demands for policy change, the empirical evidence suggests that unconditional incentives and non-negotiable policies, such as the withholding of former energy subsidies or insecurities related to energy imports, accelerate reform dynamics in Georgia and Armenia. They indirectly encourage the countries to further seek autonomy and independence vis-à-vis Russia and support the EU-prescribed diversification agenda.

The chapter also discusses the explanatory power of multiple sources of capacity building, frequently channeled into the work of local non-governmental organizations (NGOs). Yet, capacity building is found to be largely contingent on preferential fit and with little explanatory value of its own. The chapter also problematizes the impact of actors other than the EU and Russia on domestic change, especially the US engagement with energy diversification in Georgia. Its findings again suggest that it is the manipulation of utility costs and lesson drawing instead of socialization processes that make EU policies travel in the case of energy diversification: capacity building, even if delivered via transgovernmental networks, fails to trigger policy change if this is at odds with the ENC's governmental agenda.

Chapter 6 asks to what extent the individual ingredients of neighborhood Europeanization as identified above – namely, multiple external incentives and preferential fit – help to explain the decisions of different incumbents in the ENC (not) to sign the AA with the EU. It argues that these choices can be well understood as a form of policy transfer under multiple external constraints, as the AA entail detailed and binding policies that ENC need to implement in practice. In addition, Russia and the EU have applied a variety of incentives to shape the choices of ENC for the AA or CU/EEU. The chapter analyzes recent developments in Armenia, Moldova, Georgia and Ukraine, and argues that the same factors that made ENC pick individual policies in the area of energy diversification and migration management may explain the decisions to sign the AA with the EU. Russia's quid pro quo bargaining frequently made ENC turn down the EU association offer, even though the alternative, integration into the CU, also remained shallow at times, as was the case in Armenia. Russia's sanctions to punish ENC for their broader foreign policy strategy, however, speeded up their EU integration process, as seen in Georgia and Moldova, for instance. The case studies once again stress the importance of preferential fit of the incumbency and its connected elites with the respective integration template to explain whether ENC opt for integration with the EU or its Eurasian alternative.

Chapter 7 contains the conclusions of this book. It wraps up the main findings presented in the previous chapters and discusses their theoretical and empirical implications. It presents the potential and the limits of the arguments made in this book for the study of policy transfer to other contested regions, as well as further countries and policy sectors in the EU's neighborhood. Finally, it reflects on the findings of this book in light of the recent debate about the review of the ENP.

Notes

1 The ENP targets both the EU's Southern and Eastern neighbors. Beyond the Mediterranean neighborhood countries, Belarus, Ukraine, Moldova, Georgia, Armenia and Azerbaijan are included in the European Neighborhood Policy in its Eastern dimension, which this book addresses.
2 Russia had formally institutionalized the cooperation with its so-called 'near abroad' after the breakup of the Soviet Union. Institutions included the CIS, the Collective Security Treaty Organization (CSTO) and the Eurasian Economic Community (EurAsEc), to name but a few organizations that preceded its most recent integration project of the Eurasian Economic Union (see Dragneva and Wolczuk 2013 for an overview).

2 Theorizing Russia's impact on neighborhood Europeanization

Many analyses have conceived of domestic actors in the EU's Eastern neighborhood merely as cue balls in the EU's and Russia's geopolitical rivalry over the region. This chapter argues, on the contrary, that it is of explanatory value to consider compliance with prescriptions of the ENP Action Plans as the result of the strategic interaction of ENC with multiple external actors. Toward this end, the chapter presents the theoretical framework of the book that draws on the rationalist-institutionalist tradition of Europeanization research, insights of the policy transfer and diffusion literature, and sides with recent agency-centered accounts of neighborhood Europeanization, which are adjusted to the multi-actor environment of the ENC. It provides for a number of hypotheses that link compliance with EU policies to different sources of costs and benefits that may impact the strategic choices of ENC in the contested neighborhood. In this regard, patterns of interdependence, variations in the institutionalization of their bilateral relationships, and the compatibility of their domestic administrative and economic systems with those of Russia and the EU, respectively, are presented as structural and institutional constraints to EU rule transfer. The chapter then theorizes that different degrees of compliance with the EU policies in the contested neighborhood may also be the result of the interplay of two agency-related factors: the initial compatibility or fit of preferences of ENC incumbent governments with an EU policy, and policy conditionalities provided by both the EU and Russia.

The chapter starts by outlining why this book builds on the tradition of rationalist institutionalism to study EU policy transfer to a contested neighborhood. It then specifies compliance with policies codified in the ENP Action Plans as the dependent variable that is chosen to assess different degrees of EU policy transfer. Subsequently, the explanatory factors are elaborated upon that account for compliance as the result of a strategic choice of the ENC in the contested neighborhood. The chapter then presents the selection of cases investigated and methods employed in the subsequent chapters.

Rationalist institutionalism and domestic change

In order to explain different degrees of EU-demanded policy change in the ENC, this book builds on the rationalist-institutionalist tradition of studying Europeanization in EU member and accession states, which is adjusted to the context of semi-democratic or hybrid regimes and of multiple external actors in the ENC.

The theoretical approach is chosen, as it considers domestic actors key for turning an initial difference between domestic and European structures, processes and policies into pressure of adaptation (Börzel 2000). This is valuable to study domestic change in the non-accession context, as the takeover of EU policies is no longer without alternatives given the absence of an – at least formal – EU membership perspective for ENC. The partial or complete refusal to adopt certain EU policies does not threaten countries that they will be put on hold in the accession process. As the large incentive structure of accession conditionality recedes, the freedom of domestic decision makers to choose or reject policy change hence increases. Consequently, a key explanation for compliance is likely to lie with the factors that impact the strategic choices of domestic actors in favor of or against EU-prescribed policy. As I argue in greater detail below, in the context of semi- or outright authoritarian ENC, it is especially domestic incumbents whose strategic choices of whether or not to adopt EU policies are likely to matter. In addition, as the EU is not the only available source of policies, opportunities and constraints in the Eastern neighborhood, the increase in competition of external actors about the region may constrain choices of ENC, but may also 'enhance the outside options of target countries' (Schimmelfennig and Sedelmeier 2005a: 15). Domestic actors are likely to engage in strategic decisions that are informed by these multiple external constraints and opportunities.

In line with the underlying ontological and epistemological understandings of rationalist institutionalism, the choices of adopting and implementing EU policies are hence assumed to be 'both individual and collective (social) outcomes in terms of *individual goal-seeking under constraints*' (Snidal 2002: 74, emphasis in original). Siding with the methodological individualism inherent in rational choice approaches, I assume the basic preferences of relevant political actors in the ENC as fixed and exogenously given (Pollack 2006: 32). Political actors can generally be assumed to seek to defend or maximize their political power, security and welfare, which Jeffrey Frieden labels preferences over outcomes (Frieden 1999: 44). In a similar vein, Fritz Scharpf defines 'the maintenance or survival interests in ensuring adequate organizational resources [and] defending organizational autonomy' as key preferences of political actors (Scharpf 2000: 771). Theoretically, these preferences over outcomes are formed prior to the interaction with external actors and lead to the strategies that actors employ in a given strategic setting (Frieden 1999; Van Hüllen 2015).

However, can compliance with EU policies indeed be a strategy of the ENC to fulfill their preferences over outcomes? Particularly the assumed intrinsic interest of political actors to stay in power has inspired the early pessimistic assessments of the ENP, arguing that domestic change in the ENC was highly unlikely, as the semi- or outright authoritarian regimes in the EU's neighborhood had no interest in democratization attempts likely to erode their power base (Schimmelfennig 2012, see also Kelley 2006). Yet, research on authoritarianism shows that non-democratic regimes may engage in domestic change as a strategy to fulfill their preference to stay in power, to generate welfare or security. Ruling elites in these countries engage in regular adaptation and modernization processes to respond to demands and integrate usually highly exclusive societal groups that support their hold on power (Albrecht and Frankenberger 2010: 53ff.). Likewise, any political system, including non-democratic ones, requires a minimum degree of legitimacy and resources to prevail: the takeover of external policies and the cooperation with external actors may provide target states with both capacities to govern, as well as with legitimacy resulting from improvements in their international reputation (Blank 2012; Van Hüllen 2012). When considering the policy specificity and stability paradigm prevailing in the ENP (Börzel et al. 2008; Gawrich et al. 2009), domestic agents may hence indeed find their preferences over outcomes realizable via compliance with EU policies, in terms of enhancing the stability of their rule, increasing welfare or promoting security via cooperation with the EU.

In the pursuit of their preferences over outcome, domestic actors are then assumed to engage in strategic interactions based on instrumental rationality, and weigh the costs and benefits of different strategic options under the constraint of the behavior of other actors (Börzel and Risse 2000: 6). While this approach usually assumes agency to be ontologically prior to structure (Aspinwall and Schneider 2000: 24), actors still face constraints or opportunities to realize their preferred outcomes by the institutional and structural context they are embedded in, and adjust their strategies accordingly (Scharpf 2000). Yet, unlike in constructivist perspectives, the structure in which agents are embedded is considered less determinate, in that the setting of strategic interaction may affect actors' preferences over strategies without uniquely shaping their initial preferences over outcomes (Katznelson and Weingast 2005: 3).

This perspective is well suited to grasp systematically the many structural, institutional and more agency-centered ways in which both the EU and Russia can impact strategic choices of ENC: first, Russia's and the EU's interdependent relationships with the ENC may enable or constrain the choices of EU rule transfer (Dimitrova and Dragneva 2009). Costs and benefits may also emerge from the various institutional contexts in which domestic agents are embedded when choosing their strategies (Lavenex and Schimmelfennig 2009). Finally, the EU and Russia figure as external actors[1] that grant benefits or enact sanctions toward their neighborhood (Langbein 2015). By conceiving of EU rule transfer as a strategic interaction of ENC with multiple external actors, I can thus empirically assess the relative importance of structural or institutional versus agency-centered explanations and their potential interaction rather than treating them as outright competing explanations. This also encourages an investigation of explanatory factors on different macro-, meso- and micro-levels, which the policy transfer literature considers key to deepening our understanding of rule transfer and its scope conditions (Marsh and Sharman 2009: 273). As a result, this approach is likely to provide answers to the questions of whether, how and under what conditions Russia impacts the effectiveness of EU policy transfer in the increasingly contested neighborhood.

While true preferences cannot be observed but have to be assumed, different sources of costs and benefits that domestic actors factor in when choosing their strategies can be assessed. The next section elaborates on the different sources of costs and benefits as factors that may explain why and under what conditions ENC choose (not) to comply with EU policies. Before doing so, however, it specifies in greater detail why different degrees of compliance with the ENP Action Plans are studied as the dependent variable in this book.

Compliance with the ENP Action Plans

The impact of the ENP on target states has been discussed in different conceptual terms, ranging from compliance and convergence to policy transfer. This book defines compliance with policies codified in the ENP Action Plans as the dependent variable, despite the fact that compliance studies have predominantly focused on the takeover of international law or internationally negotiated agreements within EU member or accession states (Börzel 2000; Checkel 2001; Noutcheva 2009; Schimmelfennig et al. 2003; Schimmelfennig 2007; Tallberg 2002). While the ENP constitutes a non-accession policy, presenting an alternative to enlargement (European Commission 2003a), it largely mimics the setup and the tools of the accession process that shall support the implementation of the ENP Action Plans (Kelley 2006; Khasson et al. 2008). As the specific policies incorporated in the Action Plans are internationally negotiated yet not legally binding agreements that target the unilateral takeover of policies by the ENC, they qualify as an object of compliance studies.

In addition, studying the takeover of policies codified in the Action Plans as a form of compliance allows for a qualitative assessment of the degree of rule-bound behavior. Different degrees or dimensions of compliance are usually distinguished (Börzel and Risse 2002; Lavenex and Schimmelfennig 2009): the formal adoption of a policy in the domestic legislation is referred to as the output dimension. The outcome dimension measures to what extent the formally adopted rules have been applied in administrative and political practice. This differentiation enables me to assess whether domestic agents decouple the formal adoption of a policy from its practical application and thus hollow its intended effect.

As opposed to this, 'convergence' constitutes a frequently used concept for the study of neighborhood Europeanization. It is at times used interchangeably with the above outlined conceptualization of compliance (Barbé et al. 2009; Langbein and Wolczuk 2012). More narrowly defined though, convergence describes a 'tendency [...] to grow more alike, in the form of increasing similarities in structures, processes and performances' (Drezner 2001: 53). Yet, convergence is not the automatic result of compliance, as policies can be fully decoupled from their normative contents when transferred into another context (Börzel and Pamuk 2012: 80). In addition, some policies codified in the ENP Action Plans do not apply to EU member states themselves, while they are formulated as a prescribed reform agenda for neighborhood countries. Their takeover would hence figure as a form of compliance with the ENP Action Plans without necessarily leading to convergence with EU member states. Thus, in order to allow for decoupling effects and respect bilaterally codified rules as the benchmark against which the takeover of EU policies is measured, the utilization of the concept of 'compliance' with policies codified in the ENP Action Plans is considered more appropriate to measure the extent to which ENC engage in rule-bound behavior. Furthermore, compliance and convergence as dependent variables have to be analytically separated from policy transfer or diffusion. While compliance and convergence relate to the outcome in terms of the takeover of precisely codified rules, policy transfer and diffusion predominantly investigate the processes by which rules may travel between states in less direct and intentional ways (Evans 2004b; Holzinger et al. 2007). This is particularly important for the study of Russia as a second external actor in the post-Soviet space. Prior to the initiation of the more rule-bound EEU, Russia has fallen short of negotiating a formal reform agenda with its post-Soviet neighbors that may result in an *outcome* qualifying as a distinct form of Russian-prescribed compliance. Yet, as Russia's informal neighborhood policy has been considered to challenge the EU's both in content and scope (Wilson and Popescu 2009), Russia may shape the *process* of policy transfer and diffusion of norms in its neighborhood without necessarily prescribing a distinct competing or complementary set of norms to comply with.

What exactly do neighborhood countries have to comply with? While the Europeanization literature has usually focused on the acquis communautaire as a form of secondary international law, compliance studies have predominantly investigated how international conventions and regulations travel. Softer and non-legal forms of policies and their transfer have been examined by students of public policy and comparative politics. Yet this literature incoherently distinguishes between policies and programs (Marsh and Sharman 2009; Rose 1991), goals, contents and instruments (Bennett 1991b), and at times even uses these terms interchangeably (Holzinger and Knill 2007). Given that the ENP Action Plans comprise highly different norms, ranging from acquis rules, to international conventions and bilaterally agreed reform prescriptions, this book sides with Evans's definition that captures a 'policy' 'as a course of action or plan that has been conceived to deal with a particular political problem' (Evans 2004a: 6). In order to grasp the ENP requirements for compliance, the term 'policy' is thus used, while 'programs' defined as 'an action oriented activity which [...] will, at least in theory, lead to the implementation of the policy' (Evans 2004a: 6) already corresponds to the first step in the compliance process itself, namely formal policy adoption. Some of the policies that feature in the ENP Action Plans have already been codified in the Partnership and Cooperation Agreements (PCA) of Georgia and Armenia that entered into force in 1999, which is respected in the analysis (see 'Policies and time frame', below). The PCA have formed the contractual basis of the cooperation between the EU and both countries. Georgia's PCA was replaced by an AA in 2014, but Armenia's is still valid at the time of writing.

Compliance as the dependent variable of this study is thus defined as rule-bound behavior and measured both in its output and outcome dimension defined as rule adoption and rule application in reference to Lavenex and Schimmelfennig (2009). Compliance is analyzed both on a policy-specific level and on an aggregate, sectoral level. In the micro-qualitative case studies of Chapters 4 and 5, output compliance is measured in terms of the formal adoption of a specific policy by the relevant state authorities, be it through governmental or presidential degrees, laws passed by parliament or inter-ministerial decisions. Outcome compliance is measured in the practical application of the policy in administrative and political practice, be it via the implementation of projects or the *de facto* distribution of resources or knowledge. The label 'full compliance' is assigned if the formal adoption of a policy is followed by its practical application. 'Non-compliance' implies that neither formal nor practical adoption takes place. A compliance outcome is called 'shallow' if a formal decision is not followed by any implementation or if only parts of a policy are selectively adopted and implemented, while others are not.

The macro-qualitative case study in Chapter 3 requires aggregate data on sectoral compliance patterns. Hence, I conducted a content analysis of the progress reports that the European Commission issues on a yearly basis. Within these reports, statements were coded with the term 'compliance' once the progress report mentions the formal or legal adoption of a policy in domestic law or regulations. 'Emerging compliance' was assigned in cases where the progress report hints at non-legal or preparatory measures that were undertaken to adopt a policy, which imply statements such as 'X made progress towards', 'further work continued' or 'institution XY was set up for'. Statements were coded as 'shallow compliance' once a policy has been adopted, but its implementation is explicitly mentioned as lacking or encountering problems. In cases of conventions, the code 'shallow compliance' was assigned if a convention is not ratified two years after the signature. 'Non-compliance' is used as a code to mark statements that imply a lack of rule adoption and implementation or which receive the Commission's comment that 'further progress is needed'.[2] In addition, the Commission's data are triangulated with alternative reports and interview data gathered during field research trips in September and October 2010 and 2011 (see Appendix I).

Explaining compliance in a contested neighborhood

In line with rationalist institutionalist approaches, explanations for compliance are likely to lie with the factors that alter the cost-benefit analysis of domestic actors in favor of or against EU-prescribed policy change. While there are various structural and institutional patterns that may inform strategic decisions of ENC, I hypothesize that it is especially the interaction of agency-centered factors that can explain compliance with policies codified in the ENP Action Plans in an increasingly contested neighborhood. This section first introduces interdependence, domestic resonance and institutional ties as prominent structural-institutionalist explanations for different degrees of compliance in the contested neighborhood. I then present an agency-centered model of neighborhood Europeanization that stresses the peculiarities of differential empowerment in ENC and introduces the concept of preferential fit. It suggests that compliance with the ENP in the contested and semi-democratic neighborhood may be understood as a function of preferential fit and policy conditionalities provided by both the EU and Russia. It also discusses capacity building as an additional agency-related explanatory factor.

Structural and institutional approaches

EU rule transfer to the neighborhood has often been studied as a form of external governance by which the EU externalizes its internal system of rules and policies beyond its borders (Lavenex 2004; Lavenex and Schimmelfennig 2009). In order to account for the effectiveness of EU policy transfer in this way, structural and institutional explanations have figured prominently in the literature, but have rarely been systematically applied to the trilateral relationship of Russia, the EU and the ENC.

Interdependence and policy divergence

The central starting point of any study of policy transfer is the concept of interdependence. Interdependence is defined as mutual, though not necessarily symmetrical dependence (Baldwin 1980; Keohane and Nye 1987), and signifies a major structural feature of the international system that ties international actors together, shapes their environment of interaction and – in cases of asymmetric interdependence favoring one actor – equips it with the necessary leverage to anchor its policy solutions in third countries (Braun and Gilardi 2006; Freyburg et al. 2009; Lavenex 2004; Lavenex 2008). A growing political and economic interdependence between sovereign states is hence considered the main reason why practices, policies and structures of one state travel to another, as interdependent units may not only be affected by foreign policy decisions of states, but also by internal policy decisions (Holzinger et al. 2007). An often-cited example stems from economic policy-making: the adoption of more liberal economic policies in one country may result in increased capital flows into its constituency. In seeking to avoid the costs associated with the potential loss of capital, governmental agents in other countries are likely to follow the liberal policy example in order to attract back the potentially 'lost' investments (Elkins and Simmons 2005:

42). In short, even in the absence of the intention of an external actor to impact third countries, its internal policy changes may thus inflict costs on a third country under conditions of interdependence via the mechanism of competition (Marsh and Sharman 2009). In addition, high and potentially asymmetric interdependence of the ENC, Russia and the EU are likely to be correlated with other factors that may also directly impact the transfer of rules between states. Asymmetric interdependence favoring the EU is a means to secure the EU's superior bargaining power and its potential to apply its conditionality coherently and consistently in accession countries (Schimmelfennig and Sedelmeier 2004: 673). Interdependence is also one of the few factors that have been systematically discussed with a view to Russia and EU policy transfer. The frequently high interdependence of the ENC with Russia and the countries of the CIS is conceived of as a structural constraint to EU rule transfer, as it may equip Russia with comparatively greater leverage and bargaining power vis-à-vis the ENC than the EU (Dimitrova and Dragneva 2009; Lavenex and Schimmelfennig 2009). Interdependence hence figures not only as a structural condition for indirect rule transfer, but also as a measurement of the potential of external actors to inflict costs and benefits directly on third states.

Interdependence in the neighborhood has mostly been measured in terms of trade and investment linkages or historical legacies that bind ENC, Russia and the EU (Dimitrova and Dragneva 2009; Langbein 2015). In this vein, the concept is closer to Levitsky and Way's (2006: 383) notion of linkage that measures the density of cross-border flows and ties between two states, than to Keohane and Nye's (1977: 9) understanding of interdependence as a situation in which there are not only potential but *de facto* 'reciprocal (although not necessarily symmetrical) costly effects of transactions'. While Keohane and Nye's approach has been applied elsewhere to rule transfer in the neighborhood (see Ademmer 2015), this book sides with the former approach.

In order to assess the degree of interdependence, the relative dependence of the ENC to the EU and Russia in the sectors under scrutiny in this study is measured. Where mutual dependence is either equally high or low, symmetry prevails, while asymmetry can be either favoring or disfavoring the external actor. Inspired by a recent study on authoritarianism and cooperation with the EU on democracy promotion (Van Hüllen 2015), interdependence is measured with a view to both resources and socio-economic, sectoral interconnectedness in Chapter 3: power and potential leverage over third countries are first assessed in terms of resources, comparing the size, population, economy and military capacities of countries (Baldwin 2002), and measured by the gross domestic product (GDP), territorial size, population and military power of the ENC, the EU and Russia, respectively, using data from the World Bank and the Stockholm International Peace Research Institute (SIPRI). Socio-economic and sectoral interdependence is determined by measuring the asymmetry of flows (e.g. energy supplies) that may shift differences in pure power resources between countries (Baldwin 1980; Keohane and Nye 1977).

This is also in line with the approach of the external governance literature that considers issue-specific interdependence in terms of associated enforcement or distribution problems as pivotal for EU rule transfer (Lavenex 2008: 939f.).

In the case of energy policy, policy interdependence is thus operationalized as the mutual dependence on energy imports of the ENC and the external actors. Symmetry is defined as a situation in which the bilateral export–import ratio of energy supply is either balanced or highly diversified among different actors; asymmetry as a situation in which one actor qualifies as an importer only, lacks alternative suppliers, and hence depends on the exporting country. The data to determine these energy flows are provided by the World Trade Organization (WTO), Eurostat, the World Bank and secondary literature.

Unlike in the case of energy, where a country depends on cooperation with an external actor to secure energy supplies, cooperation in the JLS area targets the disruption of flows of 'threats'. Symmetry again prevails if the ENC and the external actor are both importers and exporters of 'threats', while asymmetry prevails if one actor is only importing (disfavorable asymmetry) or exporting (favorable asymmetry) 'threats'. As it is difficult to operationalize 'threat' as an intersubjectively understandable category, I measure the direction of uncontested, internationally codified categories of 'threats' that qualify as transborder crimes – i.e. illegal migration, money laundering, human trafficking, organized crime and trafficking of narcotics. The data on routes of organized crime are provided by Europol, and data on directions and flows of human and narcotics trafficking are derived from US State Department databases. Moneyval (the Council of Europe's Committee of Experts on the Evaluation of Anti-Money Laundering Measures and the Financing of Terrorism) provides information on routes of money laundering. The World Bank's migration database, Frontex annual reports and secondary literature provide data and estimates on legal and illegal migration flows and their directions. In the case of illegal and legal migration, which signifies a broad subsection of JLS policies, the relationship may be less asymmetrical in cases where the socio-economic impact of remittances of migrants is high. I hence measure remittance flows to control for potential alterations in dependence patterns. Data on remittance flows are provided by the World Bank.

In order for the EU and Russia to make a difference to policy change via interdependence, a divergence of EU and Russian policies towards the ENC is central. Policy divergence matters to assess whether multiple interdependencies alter the cost-benefit analysis of domestic actors in similar or opposing directions. This divergence has usually been simply assumed in the case of Russia and the EU. Yet, there are some studies that show variations in this regard between different policy sectors (Casier 2007, 2012; Dragneva and Dimitrova 2007), calling for an empirical test instead of normative assumptions. One of the difficulties in comparing EU and Russian policies in the neighborhood lies in the fact that Russia has not formulated a catalogue of policies comparable to the ENP Action Plans. The few studies pinpointing that policy divergence or convergence of the EU and Russia indeed varies significantly, focus on policies that have been stipulated in institutional frameworks, which are largely considered to be Russian-dominated (see Dragneva and Wolczuk 2013 for an overview). Likewise, Russia has formalized foreign policy concepts toward the Eastern neighborhood and shows distinct patterns of cooperation or defection with the EU in all policy areas that the EU promotes in the neighborhood as well. Russia can hence be considered indirectly to stand for, or at times directly encourage, a set of policies in its neighborhood despite this lack of formalization. Whenever the remainder of this book thus mentions the promotion of policies by Russia, it is this convergence or divergence of its policies with the EU script that is referred to.

I hence define policy convergence as the congruence of policies promoted by both the EU and Russia. Due to its lack of a codified and programmatic approach to the ENC, I consider in Chapter 3 as a proxy for policy convergence or divergence whether Russia has codified any policies that conflict or converge with EU rules in its foreign policy strategies or in the framework of the Russian-led regional organizations of which the countries under scrutiny here are currently or have previously been part. Armenia and Georgia are or have been members of the CIS that they joined in the early 1990s. Armenia has also been part of the Russia-led military alliance, the Collective Security Treaty Organization (CSTO), and decided to join the EEU in 2015. The development of certain binding policies in the framework of the EEU, however, is too recent to be systematically considered in this book, which consequently concentrates on the CIS and the CSTO for measuring policy divergence or convergence. In addition, I take the relationship between the EU and Russia on sectoral policy issues as a second indicator in this regard. I analyze whether there are formal or informal (dis)agreements between both actors on the policy level.

Based on these thoughts, the first hypothesis of this book hence states that if the EU's and Russia's policies diverge, compliance with EU policies is the more likely, the more the interdependence of the ENC and external actors favors the EU and disfavors Russia.

Institutional setting

The strategies that domestic actors choose with a view to compliance or non-compliance may be further affected by the institutional context, in which external policies are promoted. In a rationalist-institutionalist perspective, institutions present the strategic setting, in which domestic actors follow their preferences over outcome. This overall institutionalist assumption has been key to any study on Europeanization (Börzel and Risse 2000; Knill and Lenschow 1998; Sedelmeier 2011). In general, it is hypothesized that rules travel better the more legalized and legitimate they are (Lavenex and Schimmelfennig 2009: 802). In this regard, the codification, institutionalization and internationalization of EU rules are likely to matter (Freyburg et al. 2009).

Rationally, states are expected to be more likely to comply with external policies, the more specific, mandatory and enforceable rules are, given the increased possibility of monitoring and sanctioning (Lavenex and Schimmelfennig 2009: 802). As a result, a higher codification of policies that have been formulated by the EU toward third countries would lead to the expectation of increased patterns of compliance. This assumption can also be applied to the ENC and Russia, and the codification of rules in the framework of the CIS or the newly created EEU. As the EEU and its rules, however, have only been operational since 2015 in one of two countries under scrutiny here, they are not discussed in greater detail in the following. Adjusting the operationalization of Freyburg et al. (2009) for bilateral EU rule transfer to the multiple external actor environment of the ENC, the codification of rules is thus measured by the extent to which they are defined in the national, regional (EU or CIS) or international context: codification is considered weak in cases where rules are adapted to the third country only, i.e. are defined in the ENP Action Plans or the PCA only. Codification is defined as medium where either references to regional or international law are made, and strong where both contexts are alluded to. If both the EU and Russia have hence codified competing policies, the relative degree of codification is likely to affect the compliance process.

In addition, the existence of institutionalized transgovernmental networks has been identified as enhancing compliance with EU rules beyond its borders (Freyburg et al. 2009: 918). The assumption is that the more policy-makers of third countries are exposed to external rules, i.e. the EU acquis communautaire, the more likely they are to internalize these rules into their own national behavior. Socialization of mid-level officials in these networks is hence considered the key mechanism for rule transfer to the ENC in this regard (Freyburg 2012). The argument made in the literature of external governance is thus a sociological one, based on the logic of appropriateness. Yet the same institutionalization hypothesis figures prominently in rationalist-institutionalist accounts of the impact of formal institutions on compliance, too. Formal institutions are perceived to provide actors with information and material resources to seize potential opportunities and thus promote the adoption of policies by changing their logic of consequentialism (Börzel and Risse 2000). Again, also the CIS provides for institutionalized networks of mid-level officials who gather in regular meetings. Institutionalization is hence measured in the extent to which national, regional or international institutions promote the respective external rules (Freyburg et al. 2009): it is considered weak in cases in which they are only promoted in third countries' forums; medium when only bilateral forums deal with the rules under scrutiny; and strong if bilateral and EU or Russian/CIS-controlled regional forums promote them. If both the EU and Russia have hence institutionalized divergent policies, the relative degree of institutionalization is likely to affect the compliance process.

Closely related to this is the process of an internationalization of external rules, which may equip external actors with a higher capacity for rules to be anchored in third countries (Freyburg et al. 2009; Schimmelfennig and Sedelmeier 2004: 676). In close connection to rule codification and institutionalization, this hypothesis builds upon the theoretical expectation that compliance increases if additional monitoring, capacity building and legitimacy are provided. The more the externally promoted policies are ideationally and financially supported by other international actors, the less a third country can elude the external requests without losing international support. Adjusting the operationalization of Freyburg et al. (2009) again to the environment of multiple external actors in the ENC, a strong internationalization is considered to prevail in cases in which both the EU or Russia and other international actors, such as the USA, promote the same policies. It is considered weak if only international and not regional actors promote the policies, and medium if only the EU or Russia (CIS) do so. Again, in case of diverging policies promoted by the EU and Russia in the CIS, the relative degree of internationalization is likely to matter.

Jointly, these thoughts motivate the overall institutional setting hypothesis of this book, which considers compliance with EU policies to be more likely, the denser the institutional setting of EU-promoted policies and the less dense the institutional setting of CIS-promoted policies.

Domestic resonance

In addition to the structure of the international system, the various characteristics of the ENC domestic structures have been considered to matter in order to determine the costs and benefits of compliance for a state. Going back to the classical goodness of fit argument in the literature of member state Europeanization (Knill and Lenschow 1998), and the similarity hypothesis in diffusion research (Holzinger et al. 2007: 30), the resonance or compatibility of domestic rules and practices has been considered to matter for EU policies to travel (cf. Schimmelfennig and Sedelmeier 2004: 676). For EU member states, this factor is usually captured by the extent to which requirements of EU law have already been codified in the domestic constituencies of member states in order to assess the degree of costly adaptation requirements. In diffusion research, the similarity between different external and internal structures is also expected to matter more indirectly, as decision makers in one country may look for effective policies in seemingly similar countries to guarantee the compatibility of the imported policy with the domestic institutional and structural arrangements (Holzinger et al. 2007: 30).

Likewise, many studies also investigated the impact of Soviet legacies on compliance with EU norms and transformation processes in the CEEC (Jahn and Müller-Rommel 2010; Schimmelfennig and Scholtz 2010). Given their shared administrative past and at times similar pathways of transformation, the Eastern ENC may potentially display a greater resonance of domestic structures with Russia than with the EU, which may challenge EU policy transfer processes by rendering the adoption of policies particularly costly or by making the ENC look for policy solutions not in the EU, but in Russia. The domestic resonance hypothesis hence generally expects compliance with EU policies to be the more likely, the more the ENC's domestic structure fits the EU's and the less it fits Russia's.

As this book looks at policy-specific compliance with EU rules, however, a plethora of domestic structures on various levels may affect the compliance decisions of ENC: first, the regime type of the ENC has been considered to affect the costs it may face from policy adoption (Börzel and Risse 2012b). The more the regime type of an ENC corresponds to the EU, the more EU policies have usually been deemed to fit the incumbent's preferences and its assessment of how costly a chosen policy is. Compliance with EU policies is thus the more likely, the more the ENC regime type corresponds to that of the EU and the less it corresponds to that of Russia. Likewise, this logic is likely to apply to the sectoral compliance processes. As Lavenex and Schimmelfennig state, 'economic and administrative autonomy and openness should facilitate the selection and adoption of EU rules and, together with high state capacity, should promote rule application as well' (Lavenex and Schimmelfennig 2009: 805). If the ENC's economic system corresponds to that of the EU, but the administrative system is still at odds with it, adjustments to EU market policies are more likely to be made than requirements for genuine reforms addressing the state administration. The compatibility of economic and administrative domestic structures with those of external actors is thus likely to matter, also with a view to Russia.

Furthermore, non-compliance may emerge as an involuntary result if the state lacks the necessary capacity to adopt or implement a policy (Tallberg 2002). The Europeanization literature that stems from research on democratic, consolidated EU member states usually simply considered the necessary administrative capacities of governments to adopt and implement decisions as a given (see for a discussion, Börzel and Risse 2012b). This is likely to be different in the case of the ENC, as their degree of state capacity may be lower than the EU's. However, very high degrees of state capacity are not necessarily more favorable to compliance, as authoritarian regimes may possess even more capacity to govern than the average EU member state. What is likely to matter is a medium degree of state capacity (Van Hüllen 2015), which I capture as the relative comparability of the ENC to EU member states. Finally, the compatibility logic is also likely to apply to microprocesses of adaptation, in terms of the specific 'misfit' between the EU policy and its compatibility with the domestic status quo (Börzel and Risse 2000). As Russia does not provide for a specific policy script with which the ENC are supposed to comply, the compatibility of the ENC and the EU policy is considered to matter unilaterally.

The various (in)compatibilities between the ENC and the EU or Russia are measured in the following way:[3] the compatibility of regime types is measured with the help of aggregated data on political rights and civil liberties by Freedom House, and informs the case selection of this book, as outlined below. Chapter 3 shows the compatibility of economic systems with the help of the Heritage Foundation's Economic Freedom Index which assigns scores for the openness of markets in different aspects of the economy.[4] It also assesses the degree of market transformation with the help of the Bertelsmann Transformation Index's (BTI) status index which ranks the degree of transformation toward market-based democracies over time on a scale from 1 (failed or blocked transformation) to 10 (consolidated or advanced transformation). The BTI, however, ranks transition countries only and not the entire EU. The Czech Republic hence serves as a conservative proxy to the overall EU value. I also use data on the rule of law as presented by the World Bank Governance Indicators in Chapter 3 to check for the overall fit of administrative systems. The Governance Indicators measure the rule of law prevalence in countries on a range from approximately −2.5 (no rule of law) to +2.5 (consolidated rule of law). Likewise, state capacity is measured with the help of the World Bank Governance Indicators, which provide for comparable information on regulatory quality, government effectiveness and the control of corruption over time. Finally, the policy-specific misfit is measured by comparing the domestic, policy-specific status quo in the ENC with the requirement of the PCA and the ENP Action Plans at their time of initiation prior to the in-depth case studies of Chapters 4 and 5. This is done with a view to content (policies), processes (politics) and structures (polities) (Börzel and Risse 2000).

Toward an agency-centered framework for neighborhood Europeanization

While structural and institutional factors crucially shape the context of EU policy transfer to the contested neighborhood, the next section sides with more recent agency-centered accounts of domestic change in the region (Börzel 2015; Delcour and Wolczuk 2015b; Langbein 2015). It portrays EU policy transfer as a result of the interplay of preferential fit with multiple external incentives.

Preferential fit

Costs and benefits for domestic actors stem from the international environment or the structural and institutional settings in which ENC are embedded, but they especially emerge from within the target countries themselves. Compliance with EU policies often triggers redistributive effects, inflicting costs on some domestic actors while granting benefits to others, irrespective of other externally provided constraints or opportunities. Early Europeanization research coined the term 'misfit' as outlined above to capture incompatibilities between EU policies, polities or politics and the status quo in EU member states. Misfit figured as a necessary condition for EU-induced domestic change in EU member states, as domestic policies, institutions or processes that perfectly fit the EU requirement were supposed to render any domestic change obsolete in the first place (Börzel and Risse 2000). In this context, it has been suggested that a substantial misfit with EU policies, polities or politics would ultimately entail costs for domestic governments as change would have been enacted without EU pressure otherwise – an argument that was also transferred to the context of enlargement Europeanization without any major changes (Schimmelfennig and Sedelmeier 2005a: 16). As a result, different degrees of adaptation costs for domestic governments and other domestic veto players have been identified as crucial to explain success or failure of domestic, EU-prescribed change (Schimmelfennig and Sedelmeier 2005a: 16; Tsebelis 1995). The empowerment of domestic actors has then figured as the sufficient condition to turn misfit into domestic change: once the costly change and its redistribution effects empower reform-minded actors over reform-unwilling ones, these newly empowered actors promote compliance (Börzel and Risse 2000; Vachudova 2005). Rationalist-institutionalist explanations for Europeanization in EU member or accession states hence scrutinized a plethora of different domestic actors to be empowered or constrained by EU institutions. Liberal intergovernmentalists found national executives to have benefited most from processes of integration, while functionalists argued that societal and sub-national actors were able to circumvent the national level to lobby for change in Brussels (Börzel and Risse 2000). In the case of accession countries, liberal parties have been identified as having gained most from Europeanization processes (Schimmelfennig 2007; Vachudova 2005).

For the ENC, however, most of these considerations are likely to be flawed. First, the empowerment of various governmental and non-governmental actors via the EU operates on the assumption of a democratic level playing field, in which all actors within a given constituency have a roughly equal possibility to be empowered and lobby for change. For neighborhood countries, however, the range of actors to seize or to be constrained by external opportunities is likely to be much smaller. Unlike in the consolidated or new democracies in the EU's old and new member states, most ENC qualify as semi-authoritarian or semi-democratic regimes. Considering scholarship on hybrid regimes in Eurasia, these forms of government are usually characterized by overly powerful executives and 'single pyramid' arrangements of power, in which a chief patron and his related networks marginalize other groups (Hale 2015). The separation of power is blurred favoring the incumbent executive and a relatively small core elite that seeks influence via informal and highly exclusive channels of societal participation (Albrecht and Frankenberger 2010). The core source of authority (*Herrschaft*) is thus nested within these smaller, executive or executive-related groups.

Likewise, the ENC harbor weak civil societies (Astourian 2000; Börzel 2011: 405; Hale 2006; Langbein 2015: 10; Tudoroiu 2007), which are additionally unlikely to be empowered, as the ENP predominantly targets state actors (Börzel et al. 2008). The focus on state actors also did not change substantially with the initiation of the Eastern Partnership in 2009, the regional complement to the bilateral ENP (Börzel and Lebanidze 2015). The emphasis on state actors is especially pronounced for the countries and policy areas under scrutiny here, as JLS and energy policy lie in the heart of a state's sovereignty. The scarcity of non-governmental veto players increases the importance of governmental actors and their cost-benefit analyses with a view to compliance or non-compliance (Schimmelfennig and Sedelmeier 2005a: 17). Instead of scrutinizing multiple societal and political veto players and formal institutions (Evans 2004b: 37), the study of costs and benefits that the adoption of EU policies poses for governmental decision makers and their related elite fractions in the ENC is thus likely to shed light upon processes of compliance and neglect.

Second, while the rationalist models of Europeanization in CEEC conceived of rule adoption as a generally costly process, as it would have otherwise occurred in the absence of EU membership conditionality (Schimmelfennig and Sedelmeier 2005a: 16), research on neighborhood Europeanization shows that despite the lack of a membership perspective, ENC incumbents can also hold positive preferences for EU-prescribed policy change and emerge as change agents (Ademmer and Börzel 2013; Börzel and Pamuk 2012; Börzel and Risse 2012b). In these cases, an external policy may be perceived by ENC to effectively solve a domestic policy problem, trigger 'lesson drawing' (Rose 1991), or it may legitimate and justify decisions that have already been taken (Woll and Jacquot 2010). The incumbent government may also use resources that external actors provide for compliance in order to pursue a previously held agenda (Bennett 1991a: 33). Domestic actors may refer to the externally available policies for 'tactical reasons' (Evans 2004b: 34). Adaptation benefits in terms of security, welfare or power are thus likely to result in forms of 'utilization' (Bennett 1991a: 33) or 'instrumental use' (Brusis 2005) of EU policies that help the ENC executives to pursue their preferences over outcomes.

Instead of focusing on internal adaptation costs and external benefits only, it is hence important to scrutinize positive preferences of domestic governmental actors towards the EU policy requirement. In order to do so, I capture positive governmental preferences by the notion of preferential fit. Preferential fit is defined as the compatibility of the EU policy with the incumbent's preferences over outcomes, in terms of power, welfare and security (see also Ademmer and Börzel 2013). Unlike preferences over strategies, these preferences are exogenous to the state's interaction with external actors in the first place (Frieden 1999). Preferential fit hence denotes domestic benefits of adaptation for the incumbent regime, while preferential misfit denotes domestic costs. If no other external incentives are attached, the more the adoption of an EU policy hence helps to increase the incumbent's power, security or welfare vis-à-vis other domestic or external actors, the more likely is compliance with the respective EU policy.

In order to determine the preferential fit or misfit that prevails in an ENC, I follow a two-step approach. First, I deductively derive domestic preferences in accordance to Frieden (1999: 54) by assessing the costs and benefits of domestic change in terms of the veto power potential stemming from within the ENC government and its closely connected elites. As Armenia and Georgia figure as hybrid regimes, the power and stability of their governments depend on their ability to exert control over other political, security and economic elites (Stefes 2010). Opponents to or supporters of reforms are likely to stem from the executives and co-opted elite fractions themselves, as they define the nations' properties (Frieden 1999: 54), and constitute the relevant domestic informal institutions defining national interest (Rogowski 1999). As a result, the political costs or benefits that incumbents face when implementing EU policies are equally likely to be linked to constraints imposed by different elite fractions, than from losses of public support of a government.

I present the different bases of power that the dominant ruling fraction relies on with regard to security, political and economic elites in Chapter 3. I also outline the dominant discursive notions that connect different groups within an ENC and may qualify as discursive power resources that incumbent elites can draw upon (cf. Lambach and Göbel 2010: 84ff.). I then assess to what extent this power base may host reform-hostile actors in each sector. The data for this assessment are taken from secondary sources which are cross-checked and complemented by media outlets and regular country assessments provided by think tanks such as the Economist Intelligence Unit (EIU), Freedom House or the Bertelsmann Foundation.

Second, I operationalize preferential fit by sticking to Frieden's recommendation to 'specify a nation's preferences by looking at those who constitute them' (Frieden 1999: 56). While tracing the individual compliance processes in Chapters 4 and 5 in greater detail, I inductively assess the costs and benefits that the ruling elite incur from compliance with EU policies, considering statements and actions by policy-makers and independent observers (Frieden 1999: 58). I triangulate the sources for this assessment, whenever possible combining data collected in interviews with decision makers, representatives from international organizations (IOs) and NGOs, as well as secondary sources and media outlets to safeguard my analysis from taking strategic statements of policy-makers as expressions of intrinsic preferences.

Multiple external incentives

External actors may also impact domestic change in third states beyond the structural and institutional settings of the respective bilateral relationships. This has been amply demonstrated by the literature on diffusion, policy transfer and enlargement Europeanization (Börzel and Risse 2009; Evans 2004b; Marsh and Sharman 2009; Schimmelfennig and Sedelmeier 2005a). Particularly, the provision of benefits or sanctions of external actors to third states figures as a well-researched tool either to enhance the benefits for compliance or inflict costs for non-compliance (Evans 2004b; Vachudova 2001). Students of Europeanization have focused predominantly on the size of EU-granted benefits to third states and argued with a view to accession conditionality that the larger the rewards of the EU, the more likely is compliance with its rules. For the specific case of the ENP, the size of EU rewards is equally low, as it has been declared a non-membership policy. Instead, the EU has reverted to a form of policy conditionality or 'conditionality-lite' (Sasse 2008) in order to bridge the lack of the membership perspective. The EU offers a greater stake in the EU's internal market and visa facilitation for sector-specific reform progress (Gawrich et al. 2010). This offer was upgraded with the Eastern Partnership (EaP) to the prospect of visa liberalization and a greater political and economic integration via AA that included a Deep and Comprehensive Free Trade Area (DCFTA) (Council of the European Union 2009b). The positive effect of these forms of policy conditionality on compliance with the ENP has been well established in the literature on neighborhood Europeanization (Ademmer and Börzel 2013; Gawrich et al. 2010; Langbein 2011; Langbein and Wolczuk 2012).

However, the EU is no longer the only game in town, when it comes to the provision of incentives to the ENC. Unlike the EU, Russia does not formally specify concrete ex ante criteria that enable ENC to reap benefits or thwart sanctions. Yet Russia has been found to employ sectoral incentives or levers in post-Soviet states, too (Bilgin 2011; Hedenskog and Larsson 2007; Perovic 2005: 78). The application of incentives may be more ad hoc and at times decoupled from directly targeted and specific policy change. Yet Russia's incentives may still increase or decrease benefits and costs of specific policy choices. In this way, Russia may also – on purpose or unintentionally – affect the assessments of costs and benefits of domestic policy-makers in the compliance process.

Russia's informal provision of incentives at times also mimics the EU's policy conditionality approach, whenever Russia engages in bargaining with the ENC and offers a similar quid pro quo approach as the EU. Consequently, Russia has been assumed to constrain the adoption and implementation of EU policies whenever it ties policy-specific incentives for 'key domestic veto players' to maintaining the status quo (Langbein 2015: 23). Any cost-benefit calculation, however, hinges less on the size of externally granted rewards. As Schimmelfennig and Sedelmeier argue, 'EU conditionality would not be effective if the target government had other sources offering comparable benefits at lower adjustment costs' (Schimmelfennig and Sedelmeier 2004: 674). The initial costs or benefits of adaptation for 'key domestic veto-players' who are – as argued above – likely to be incumbent elites in the policy areas under scrutiny here – hence matter decisively to assess the impact of different forms of incentives on governmental strategic choices (cf. Spendzharova and Vachudova 2012). In cases of multiple policy conditionalities, domestic governments can decide about which incentives to pick and choose. In cases of preferential fit of an EU policy, they can strategically comply and reap the incentive structure for 'tactical reasons' (Evans 2004b: 34) by using it as further political support to foster their own domestic agenda (Jacquot and Woll 2003; Woll and Jacquot 2010). On the contrary, they are likely to pick available alternatives if the policy is at odds with their preferences over outcomes.

The interplay of multiple policy conditionalities and preferential fit in the contested neighborhood may determine the compliance outcome in a fourfold way: if domestic ruling elites initially welcome the EU-recommended policy as a means to realize their preferences over outcomes, concerted policy conditionality by both the EU and Russia (that incentivizes the same policy choice) is likely to further enhance the benefits and facilitate *full compliance*. If confronted with rivaling conditionality, the domestic decision makers can pick and choose what best fits their preferences and thus either fully comply or keep the status quo and reap the alternative incentive, which would result in *non-compliance*.

In cases of preferential misfit and concerted policy conditionality favoring change, non-compliance is punished by increased costs or the sensitive loss of future benefits. In this case, however, a *shallow compliance* outcome is likely to prevail. If external actors incentivize policy choices, domestic governments may have to induce domestic change in order to deter sanctions or secure rewards. Formal policy change, however, does not necessarily need to be followed by *de facto* policy application in this context. Non-democratic or hybrid regimes are characterized by the co-existence of formal institutions and informal mechanisms that help to prevent constraints to the behavior of executives and their connected elites. Likewise, strong executives and a lack of enforceable legal remedies or strong civil societies allow domestic governments not to abide by or circumvent rules once they are legally adopted. Governments may thus revert to what the literature calls 'intense chameleonism' (Albrecht and Frankenberger 2010: 53f.) – namely, to mimic reforms or introduce modernization without implementing a *de facto* behavioral change. As policy processes generally leave 'some room for maneuver' (Woll and Jacquot 2010), governments are thus likely to adopt shallow compliance strategies to pretend formal compliance (output) and reap external rewards or deter external sanctions, while subverting a *de facto* loss of political power, welfare gains or domestic legitimacy towards its power base (outcome). Table 2.1 summarizes the hypothesized outcomes of the interplay of domestic preferences and multiple policy conditionalities.

Yet, quid pro quo-based forms of policy conditionality are not the only type of incentive that Russia has provided to ENC in the past. One peculiarity of Russia's foreign policy is that some of its actions towards ENC lack the bargaining element that is key to policy conditionalities. At times Russia increases gas prices or conducts large-scale deportations of ENC labor migrants without tying them to requests for or against specific policy change. While some of these incentives are widely interpreted as punishing ENC for an overall pro-Western foreign policy course, others also simply emerge as externalities from Russia's domestic economic or political decisions, such as deporting migrants or increasing gas prices without negotiations. These negative externalities or unconditional incentives, however, can still affect the cost-benefit analysis of governments:[5] they are likely to function as incentives

Table 2.1 Interaction effect of preferential fit and multiple policy conditionalities

Domestic preferences	External policy conditionality	
	Concerted policy conditionality	Rivaling policy conditionality
Preferential fit with EU policy	Full compliance	Full compliance
Preferential misfit with EU policy	Shallow compliance	Non-compliance

for change, as they render the domestic status quo more costly and encourage incumbents to seek greater autonomy and independence from Russia to prevent these costs from arising in the future. In this way they may also indirectly support EU-demanded policy change, as they further increase the attractiveness of EU offers, such as the prospect to access the EU internal market after a Russian trade embargo. I hypothesize that they provide incumbents with further incentives for EU-demanded policy change, but amplify rather than change the dynamics associated with preferential fit and (EU) policy conditionalities. After all, ENC may still comply shallowly with policies that contradict their preferences over outcome, but which are required to strategically reap the EU's benefits and alleviate Russian-induced costs.

Russia's approach to the neighborhood has also been discussed as a form of coercion (Delcour and Wolczuk 2015a). Coercion is an established causal mechanism in diffusion research, usually defined as a form of legal force or physical imposition (Börzel and Risse 2012a). In the neighborhood, however, Russia and the EU have so far not exerted any form of legal force comparable to hierarchical steering in nation-states or the EU – a dynamic that is likely to change for ENC that chose to integrate into the EEU from 2015 onwards. So far, physical force has been employed by Russia during the war with Georgia in 2008 and in the recent 'hybrid war' in Ukraine. Yet Russia did not impose any policy choices on Georgia's or Ukraine's central governments and thus did not invoke a form of physical coercion in the traditional sense. Likewise, the 'economic occupation' (Oliker et al. 2009) of the post-Soviet space by Russian companies is often considered a form of quasi-coercive influence seeking. Yet economic activities of foreign-based companies do not occur without the prior direct or indirect consent of target states, but are frequently characterized by elements of (at times highly asymmetrical) negotiations with domestic actors in ENC. While boundaries are certainly fluid, these forms of influence seeking are theoretically considered to be more accurately subsumed under the heading of incentives and/or policy conditionality.

External incentives are hence operationalized as the provision of benefits or sanctions by external actors in the compliance process. While they can be ex ante and formally specified in foreign policy strategies of external actors, I particularly consider their *de facto* application, as well as their perception by domestic actors in the individual compliance processes. In Chapter 3, I thus compare the provision of sector-specific policy conditionalities and other incentives by both the EU and Russia to the ENC, which enables me to assess the amount and type of incentives provided per external actor, ENC and policy sector. I trace the effect of policy conditionalities and other incentives in the policy-specific compliance processes in Chapters 4 and 5.

Multiple capacity building

Capacity building is defined as the provision of financial and technical assistance 'geared towards building institutions and capacities that are necessary to facilitate reform' (Börzel and Pamuk 2012: 81). As Börzel and Pamuk (2012) argue in reference to Jacoby (2006), capacity building may function as an incentive for compliance as it alleviates potential social or economic consequences of domestic change. Yet, the mechanism that links this form of 'reinforcement by support' to compliance differs from the provision of benefits or sanctions as forms of 'reinforcement by reward or punishment' (Schimmelfennig et al. 2003), as it is provided under conditions of non-compliance as opposed to benefits or sanctions, which are tied to having established compliance in the first place (Langbein 2015: 16). Capacity building thus targets the ability of governments to strategically opt for policy change instead of intentionally manipulating its utility costs (Chayes and Chayes 1993). Increases in externally provided capacity may thus lead to increased patterns of compliance. Capacity building is usually directed at the ENC bureaucracies and affects 'the leverage of participating departments within the executive bureaucracy and increase[s] their leeway to pursue a specific policy agenda' (Andonova 2008: 485). As Langbein (2015) shows with regard to transnational market rules in Ukraine, capacity building also creates or diversifies broader demands for domestic policy change, also among non-state actors. From a rational choice perspective, she argues that capacity building increases the costs of sticking to the status quo for the remaining domestic actors, as sectoral capacity building helps reform-minded actors to better make their claims. An alternative, non-rational pathway to compliance via capacity building has been brought forward by the external governance approach to EU rule transfer. Here it is hypothesized that capacity building triggers socialization processes with individuals in the target countries. As bureaucratic actors receive capacity building via technical assistance and interact in transgovernmental networks (such as TAIEX (Technical Assistance and Information Exchange Instrument) and Twinning), they internalize externally promoted norms (Freyburg 2012). Thus, capacity building may also change the initial preferences of bureaucrats toward policy change, challenging the rational 'usage' and 'strategic capacity' arguments.

Unlike in the realm of transnational market rules, however, in sovereignty-laden policy areas, such as JLS or energy policy, there are fewer non-state actors to empower in the first place. In addition, translating the socialization of or a diversified demand among lower-level state actors into EU policy change is likely to be dependent on a general preferential fit prevailing in the ENC. Lower-level bureaucrats are by definition subordinate to ministers and the central government. Even if they receive external training and technical or financial resources, they are unlikely to reside over the power resources to lobby successfully against preferences of a ruling elite that commands the core sources of state authority (see Dimitrova and Dragneva 2013 for a related argument). The effect of capacity building on domestic policy change is hence likely to be contingent on an incumbent's initial preferential fit with an EU policy to ensure that lower-level initiatives are not blocked by more powerful actors who risk losing from the respective policy change.

This is especially the case if domestic actors are faced with multiple sources of externally provided capacity from which they can pick and choose what best fits their needs. Various offers of assistance may provide for a greater choice of externally provided financial resources to implement previously held domestic agendas, and hence facilitate their 'strategic usage' (Jacquot and Woll 2003). While Russia does not have a similarly formal approach to capacity building in place as the EU, ad hoc cooperation and support as well as economic subsidies by Russian state-owned companies may *de facto* figure as functional equivalents of assistance to third states. Capacity building by Russia has thus been considered to potentially counter EU capacity-building efforts (see e.g. Langbein 2015 for a discussion of Russia's 'cross-capacity building'). Again, the extent to which capacity building by Russia counters EU-demanded policy change is likely to depend on whether the respective EU policy helps incumbents to fulfill their preferences over outcomes. In this vein, four different outcomes of the interplay of multiple sources of capacity building and the initial preferences of domestic governments are conceivable (Table 2.2). First, full compliance with an EU policy is expected in cases of preferential fit with an EU rule, as actors are likely to use EU capacity and neglect Russia's capacity, if the latter does not support the EU policy that fits the incumbent (rivaling capacity building). Incumbent governments are likely to profit from both the EU's and Russia's capacity if they help to implement its previously held agenda (concerted capacity building). Non-compliance, however, is expected in cases of preferential misfit, as the domestic actors are free to neglect the external assistance or take it without actually implementing policy change.

Table 2.2 Interaction effect of preferential fit and multiple external capacity building

Domestic preferences	Capacity building	
	Concerted capacity building	*Rivaling capacity building*
Preferential fit with EU policy	Full compliance	Full compliance
Preferential misfit with EU policy	Non-compliance	Non-compliance

Capacity building of external actors is operationalized as the provision of financial or technical assistance. This usually comprises 'financial transfers, training and assistance for institution building and reporting' (Andonova 2008: 485). In order to assess the relative effect of capacity provided by the EU, I compare the financial budgets assigned to support the specific sectors in both countries in a macro-qualitative analysis in Chapter 3. The budget for capacity building provided by the EU is defined in the annual Action Plans of the Technical Assistance to the Commonwealth of Independent States (TACIS) and the European Neighborhood and Partnership Instrument (ENPI), which list the yearly country-specific budgets available, as well as the thematic and regional assistance assigned. I compare the amount of assistance assigned per sector and country. Russia's functional equivalents to capacity building are provided via cooperation with ENC in the framework of bilateral or CIS agreements or ad hoc cooperation that equips the ENC with additional material, financial or human resources, or expertise in a given policy field. In order to assess the amount of *de facto* capacity provided by Russia as outlined above, I thus cannot rely on formal budgeting procedures, but assess the amount of assistance in specific policy fields on the grounds of interviews with stakeholders in the target countries, as well as secondary literature and reports of IOs. I define as capacity building not only state-to-state cooperation via which the Russian Ministry of Foreign Affairs or the presidential apparatus provide the ENC with financial or technical assistance, but also capacity building through Russian state-owned companies, as political and commercial activities in the energy sector have been recentralized under the state authority since the rise to power of Vladimir Putin and blurred the political and commercial spheres (Stent 2008: 1090). In the in-depth case studies of Chapters 4 and 5, I hence trace whether the EU and Russia financially or technically support the adoption and implementation of specific policies in the ENC.

Comparison and methodology

In order to investigate the empirical soundness of this rationalist-institutionalist approach to neighborhood Europeanization, I develop a structured, focused comparative research design (George and Bennett 2005: 67) that aims at detecting the conditions and the underlying causal mechanism that shape the transfer of EU policies to its Eastern neighborhood, and the impact that Russia may exert on this process. Methodologically, the book combines macro- and micro-qualitative analyses in order to investigate the relative importance of structural, institutional and more agency-centered explanations (Marsh and Sharman 2009).

The book follows a two-pronged methodological approach. Chapter 3 first presents a macro-level analysis. As I am not only interested in whether, but also in how Russia influences EU-prescribed policy change in the ENC, I first construct a most-likely case for Russia to impact EU policy transfer as predicted by the structuralist approach to neighborhood Europeanization. In a most-similar systems design (cf. George and Bennett 2005: Chapter 8), I compare countries and sectors that are highly dependent on Russia, while the policies chosen vary with regard to policy divergence between the EU and Russia. This allows me to investigate whether there is indeed a systematic structural impact of Russia on the ENP compliance process.

The second part of that chapter then turns toward a more inductive approach, inspired by the puzzling finding that EU rules travel despite higher interdependence of the ENC with Russia and divergent policies promoted by the external actors. The chapter thereby aims to assess the relative explanatory importance of further structural and institutional, as well as agency-based factors for compliance, and correlates the sectoral compliance patterns with the plethora of explanatory factors that have been discussed in the theoretical framework of the book. It constitutes a macro-qualitative analysis that is time indifferent and correlates cross-country as well as cross-sectoral factors with the detected compliance output. Chapter 3 reveals preferential fit, external incentives and external capacity building as factors that vary between the countries and policy sectors and are hence likely to explain differences in compliance behavior, while the number of cases is too low to draw final conclusions.

Chapters 4 and 5 then increase the number of observations and shed more light upon the underlying causal mechanisms. In order to trace empirically the theorized interplay of preferential fit, external incentives and capacity building, both chapters provide for micro-comparisons of specific processes of policy adoption and implementation in two countries and two policy sectors. The comparisons additionally control for potential differences in the initial policy-specific misfit of the ENC and the EU promoted policies. I also conduct within-case studies in the course of the comparative study to testify the assumed causality between the explanatory variables and the (non-)compliance of the target state (George and Bennett 2005: 205f.). In order to check the rationalist-institutionalist argument against prominent, sociological-constructivist alternative explanations, the case studies contrast the findings against the hypothesis of socialization in transgovernmental networks which considers compliance to be the result of specific institutionalized forms of capacity building.

This research builds on a combination of data sources respecting the different needs of macro- and micro-qualitative frameworks of analysis. The macro-qualitative studies are predominantly informed by data provided by governmental and international organizations, such as the World Bank, the IMF, as well as Eurostat. Country reports of renowned international think tanks like Transparency International, the EIU or Freedom House help to further assess the characteristics of different explanatory factors.

In order to construct the in-depth case studies in Chapters 4 and 5, I predominantly revert to the method of elite, expert or specialized interviewing that is frequently employed in the absence of written primary or secondary literature on a subject (Bogner and Menz 2009; Dexter 2006; Martens and Brüggemann 2006). Given the shortage of readily available information on specific policy transfer processes in neighborhood countries, I conducted semi-structured interviews[6] with decision makers, and NGO and IO representatives in the framework of research trips to Georgia and Armenia in 2010 and 2011, in order to reconstruct compliance processes and identify relevant factors that led to or hampered the adoption of EU policies in the national contexts. The method of interviewing hence pursues the goal of systematizing knowledge of involved decision makers and informed experts (Bogner and Menz 2009).[7] The sampling of interview partners followed the principle of snowballing after intense pre-departure research on organizations and individuals involved in the decision-making process or related sectoral policies. The quality of interviews strongly depended on the knowledge, involvement and governmental insight that the interviewees had, which varied substantially from interviewee to interviewee. Despite its valuable contribution to knowledge generation, elite interviewing hence bears the risk of being overly biased toward certain highly informed interview partners and their 'story' of how and why a policy was (not) passed, tending to ignore valuable alternative readings of a compliance process (Berry 2002). Being aware of this risk and the approaches toward its minimization, I tried to diversify the range of interview partners and their organizational backgrounds, checked given information for its plausibility, and compared information across time and interview partners (Dean and Whyte 2006: 104ff.). I triangulated the data from single sources with statements of alternative interview partners, media outlets or data from international reports or secondary literature whenever possible. I also contrasted 'my' narrated story against alternative explanations in order to make as scientifically accurate statements as possible. The details of the interviews in terms of dates, locations and institutional affiliation of the interviewees are listed in Appendix I.

Chapter 6 is constructed to provide for tentative insights into whether the findings of the book may travel beyond highly specific policy changes under scrutiny here. It defines the ENC choices for or against signing AA, including the DCFTA with the EU, as its dependent variable and investigates whether they are also shaped by the ingredients for neighborhood Europeanization that were identified in the previous chapters. Rather than rigorously controlling for other explanatory factors, this chapter is exploratory in kind and draws on official documents, country reports and secondary literature, to assess the costs and benefits that emerge from either integration choice for the ruling elite and its connected elite fractions. The chapter analyzes the interaction of this preferential (mis)fit with conditionalities and other incentives provided by both the EU and Russia to investigate whether the resulting patterns match the findings of the previous chapters. Chapter 6 also includes Moldova and Ukraine in addition to Georgia and Armenia in the analysis of the decisions (not) to sign the AA with the EU in order to provide for a comprehensive picture of the decisions of all four countries that initially started to negotiate Association Agreements with the EU. The next section discusses the case selection for the analyses of compliance processes in Chapters 3 to 5 in greater detail.

Case selection

This study mainly focuses on Georgia and Armenia as two out of six countries that are targeted by the European Neighborhood Policy in its Eastern dimension. They are selected due to their characteristics with respect to some of the independent variables that I intend to control for in the macro-level analysis. Compliance with the ENP is studied in the policy fields of JLS and energy policy. As outlined in greater detail below, the countries represent most-likely cases for Russia to impact EU policy transfer and similarly hard cases for neighborhood Europeanization, while the chosen policy sectors vary with a view to the divergence and convergence of externally promoted policies in order to prevent a selection bias (King et al. 1994: 128ff.).

Countries

Georgia and Armenia are chosen for the case studies of this book as they present most-likely cases for Russia to impact EU policy transfer and similarly hard cases for EU policies to travel. The country selection focuses on some of the most crucial explanatory variables, including regime type and size of EU rewards. In addition, Georgia and Armenia are located in the same geographical zone – a factor that is not of explanatory power in itself, but usually correlates highly with other conditions for external policy transfer (Ambrosio 2010).

First, Armenia and Georgia represent regime types that do not resonate well with the types of regime prevailing in EU member states. They feature semi-presidential political systems with strong executive powers. Georgia's semi-presidential system only turned into a parliamentary one in November 2013 after the presidential elections. They constitute typical cases of the third wave of democratization, in which the democratic transformation process has remained in limbo between democracy and autocracy (Beichelt 2007: 207). Armenia's and Georgia's regimes have mostly been labeled hybrid or semi-authoritarian (Fischer 2006: 8f.; Kekic 2006; Papava 2006: 666; Wheatley and Zürcher 2008: 5). Both qualify as 'partly free' in the Freedom House Index and have predominantly not been defined as electoral democracies since their independence after the breakup of the Soviet Union (Freedom House 2011a, 2011b). The Freedom House Index aggregates scores for individual countries, evaluating the guarantee of political and civil liberties ranging from 7 (maximally unfree) to 1 (maximally free). Countries are evaluated as 'partly free' if their aggregated scores amount to at least 3.0 and to fewer than 5.5 points.[8]

The Freedom House data (Figure 2.1) suggest that Armenia and Georgia are closer to Russia than to EU member states. Qualifying as robust democracies, the EU member states on average receive the grade of 1 ('free'). In contrast to this, Russia has been ranked predominantly as 'not free' since 1999, owing to increasingly authoritarian tendencies (Ekiert et al. 2007: 11). Both ENC are not only sandwiched in between EU member states and Russia, but largely display a stronger similarity with Russia's scores.

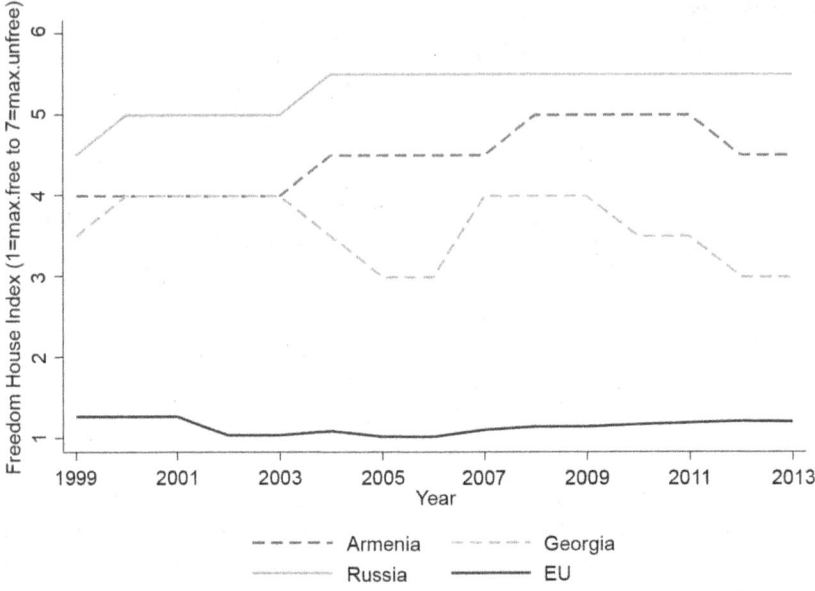

Figure 2.1 Aggregated Freedom House Index scores, 1999–2013
Note: The EU average has been calculated by aggregating the data of individual EU member states, accounting for variation in membership patterns over time.
Source: author's illustration, based on Freedom House 2015c, Freedom in the World Country Ratings.

Armenia's record, however, has been slightly worse than Georgia's, with differences of up to 1.5 points. While Georgia improved from 2003 onwards, Armenia displayed the opposite tendency of aggravating authoritarian tendencies. The presidential election of 2003, in which the incumbent Robert Kocharyan was confirmed in office, was accompanied by the violent dispersion of opposition supporters and allegedly widespread ballot box stuffing (Freire and Simão 2007). Similar irregularities occurred during the 2007 parliamentary elections in which the governmental parties kept their absolute majority: opposition parties were significantly disadvantaged in media coverage and administrative resources were abused for pro-government election campaigns (Freedom House 2011a). Finally, Armenia's brutal crackdown on protesters which resulted in ten people being killed in the aftermath of the 2008 presidential election left significant doubts about Armenia's transition process towards democracy. In the parliamentary elections of 2012, the Armenian National Congress, previously an extra-parliamentary opposition coalition, won several seats in the Armenian National Assembly. Despite some irregularities and the fact that the ruling Republican Party kept its majority, the elections were considered more competitive and peaceful than previous ones (Freedom House 2013). The presidential election in 2013, however, was labeled 'least competitive' (BTI 2014a) and was marred by irregularities, eventually confirming Serzh Sargsyan in office. The opposition refused to accept the election results, leaving the political climate increasingly polarized.

Georgia improved in the index after the Rose Revolution of 2003, which brought a young, Western-oriented government into power. However, the hopes of a quick transition to democracy were disappointed in November 2007 by the post-revolutionary government's violent crackdown on the opposition's street protests which were directed against President Saakashvili's increasingly authoritarian style of governing Georgia (International Crisis Group 2007). International observers also noted several irregularities during the early presidential elections that were initiated as a result of the street protests, as well as during local elections in May 2010 (Freedom House 2011b; Wheatley 2010). Georgia has thus been considered increasingly 'sliding towards authoritarianism' since 2007 (International Crisis Group 2007; see also Hale 2006: 306). Georgia witnessed its first peaceful change of power via elections in 2012, when the wealthy businessman Bidzina Ivanishvili and his Georgian Dream (GD) coalition won the majority of parliamentary seats. Until the presidential election in 2013, won by Giorgi Margevlashvili (GD), the political landscape of Georgia was marked by the uneasy 'cohabitation' of Saakashvili as president with a GD-controlled government under Prime Minister Ivanishvili. While the political control of state institutions seemingly decreased after 2012, reports of what some called 'witch hunts' against United National Movement (UNM) members (Freedom House 2015a) also cast doubts on the democratic commitment of the new government.

Despite the fact that the countries display some differences in their individual democracy scores over time, a change of power by election has occurred only once in Armenia, namely in the parliamentary elections in May 1990, and twice in Georgia, namely in October 1990 and in the parliamentary and presidential elections of 2012/13. Yet both countries have mostly qualified as 'partly free' and can be considered rather stuck in their transition to democracy (Kucera 2011; Wheatley and Zürcher 2008: 2). As a result, both countries represent similarly hard cases for EU policy transfer and qualify as likely cases for Russia to impact policy transfer given their comparably greater resonance with Russia's regime type.

Second, Armenia and Georgia are subject to the same size of rewards granted by the EU for enacting domestic reforms in line with the ENP Action Plans. Both South Caucasian countries have been included relatively late in the ENP by a decision of the Council of the EU in June 2004 (Council of the European Union 2004). Like all ENC, they lack a membership perspective, but are subject to the 'reduced membership perspective' that Romano Prodi once labeled 'everything but institutions' (Beichelt 2007: 209). As outlined above, they initially received the prospect of increased access to the EU market and visa facilitation, which were enhanced with the EaP to include greater political and economic integration via AA, the DCFTA and full visa liberalization. Even though Armenia decided not to initial the AA with the

EU in September 2013, but to join the CU instead, it had been vividly engaged in the negotiations about the AA until then (Delcour 2014). For the period under scrutiny here, the size of rewards on offer is hence comparable for both countries and remains below the prospect of membership. As these smaller rewards have frequently been assumed not to pay off the large transformation costs, the prospect of EU policy transfer is rather bleak in both ENC.

Third, Armenia and Georgia share a similar geographic location in between the EU and Russia. Having been part of the Soviet Union, the region emerged relatively late as a point of interest to the EU (Jawad 2007). Neither country shares a direct land border with the EU, but they border Turkey, Azerbaijan, Russia or Iran, none of which figures as a consolidated democracy. While geographic proximity is not a cause of policy transfer itself, it is often correlated with the degree of institutional ties or interdependence that may exert a supportive effect (Ambrosio 2010: 384f.). This renders the South Caucasian countries once more unlikely cases for EU policies to travel and more likely cases for Russia to impact this process.

Policies and time frame

The policies chosen also follow the logic of most-similar systems designs and again represent most likely cases for Russia to impact EU policy transfer, while they vary with a view to policy convergence or divergence between the external actors.

First, for the set-up of the macro-qualitative study I chose the policy field of JLS, as well as the energy sector, due to their characteristics with a view to the relative interdependence of the ENC with the EU and Russia. Both ENC have been more dependent on Russia than on the EU in these issue areas – a fact for which more detailed evidence is provided in Chapter 3. Due to this lack of asymmetric interdependence favoring the EU, EU conditionality is usually deemed unlikely to be effective (Lavenex and Wichmann 2009: 97), while Russia may be more capable of dictating its terms and conditions due to its relatively higher bargaining power.

The policy sectors, however, vary with a view to the policy content that is promoted by both the EU and Russia (see Chapter 3 for details). Hence, this study seeks to investigate first whether the process of policy transfer is hampered in cases in which Russia enjoys a theoretically greater structural leverage over both countries in terms of interdependence, but offers different policies to the ENC than the EU.

While the macro-qualitative study focuses on sectors as a unit of analysis and aggregates compliance patterns accordingly, the micro-qualitative, in-depth case studies focus on specific policies within these sectors, which are presented in the introduction to Chapter 3 and 4. The policies are chosen due to their comparability across the two countries, as they have roughly the same wording in the ENP Action Plans and thus the same degree of specificity. In addition, I control for the policy-specific misfits in terms of content, structures and processes related to the passage of an EU policy that both countries are faced with at the beginning of the PCA or ENP initiation, as outlined in the case studies.

The time frame of the empirical analyses covered in Chapters 3, 4 and 5 mostly ranges from the entry into force of the ENP Action Plans in 2006 until the end of 2013. However, as the reform recipes codified in the ENP Action Plans at times originate in the PCA that entered into force in Armenia and Georgia in 1999, the empirical analysis starts in 1999 whenever appropriate. This is additionally motivated by the fact that Russia's foreign policy towards the South Caucasian countries has been considered assertive since the beginning of Vladimir Putin's first presidential term in 2000. The analysis mostly stops at the end of 2013, when the new AA that will replace the PCA and the ENP Action Plans was initialed with Georgia, and Armenia decided not to sign the AA but to integrate into the Russian-led CU. As Chapter 6 elaborates on the events that led to the decision of ENC (not) to sign the AA with the EU, it covers a more recent time frame which is chosen in accordance with the point in time when the decision to join either integration scheme was made in the respective ENC.

Notes

1 The first chapter referred to 'Russia' and the 'EU' without specifying different actors in Russia or the EU, which seemingly implies that both are unitary foreign policy actors. In line with Orttung and Overland (2011), I choose to do so for reasons of simplicity and the fact that Russia is indeed a state with a distinct foreign policy. In addition, the Russian state is the main foreign policy actor in the policy sectors under closer scrutiny in this book, as JLS policies lie at the core of a state's sovereignty, and the two main energy-exporting companies are government controlled. Likewise, the European Commission has been mandated with the realization of the ENP and as a result mostly represents the EU institutions in this regard. Whenever other Russian governmental or non-governmental actors, individual institutions like the European Parliament, the Council of the EU, or individual member states are crucially active with a view to the ENP in the cases at hand, this is made explicit.
2 The number of statements coded per sector is subsequently divided by the entire number of statements made for the country's sector, and percentages are drawn providing for a weighted account of statements for each sector. This is done to convey a broader impression of the overall assessment of the sector and bridge two major methodological shortcomings. First, the amount of statements made in the progress reports for each sector can vary over time and countries, which is respected in the weighted compliance coding. Second, the progress reports are usually highly politicized. In order not to get trapped into coding the Commission's political statements beyond *de facto* compliance or lack thereof, the coding allows for assigning compliance only for the mention of legal or formal measures and distinguishes compliance from emerging compliance. In addition, the coding follows a rigorous approach of assigning shallow compliance. Hence, whenever the smallest implementation problems are recorded, this is coded as shallow compliance.
3 As EU policies are on average more likely to travel, the more the domestic structure of the ENC corresponds to the EU, the measurement of that ENC's values is

undertaken in reference to the scores of external actors and no fixed value categories are assigned. However, if specified in the indices, the resonance is considered high if the ENC and the EU are ranked in the same category of countries, while it is considered low if they are not. The index data are supplemented by secondary resources and qualitative reports.
4 The Economic Freedom Index assigns different scores for business freedom, trade freedom, fiscal freedom, government spending, monetary freedom, investment freedom, financial freedom, property rights, freedom from corruption, and labor freedom.
5 This argument has been developed in greater detail with regard to its relation to Keohane and Nye's (1977) concepts of vulnerability and sensitivity, in Ademmer (2015).
6 Nigel King labels this a 'structured open-response' interview, in which interviewers construct an interview schedule with blocks of questions, which are open to deviation and adjustable to the interview situation (King 1994: 16).
7 I refer to Bogner and Menz (2009: 65) to define an expert as any individual who functions 'as a source of information with a view to the reconstruction of processes and social situations' (my own translation). For a discussion of the different approaches to the term, its strengths and weaknesses, see Bogner and Menz (2009: 67ff.).
8 Freedom House changed this measurement slightly in 2003, when countries with an aggregated score of 5.5 were already considered as not free.

3 Constraining EU policy transfer?
A bird's-eye view

As shown in Chapter 2, neighborhood Europeanization has been considered to be determined by a number of institutional, structural and agency-related factors in the literature. I suggested that it is especially the interplay of agency-related factors that drives compliance in the contested post-Soviet neighborhood. This chapter examines the relative explanatory power of these diverse factors in a macro-level analysis of compliance with EU demands in the area of JLS and energy policy in Georgia and Armenia. It specifically tests if and why EU policies travel at all to ENC that are more dependent on Russia than on the EU in policy areas in which the policies diverge that the two external actors represent. Towards this end, the chapter first correlates patterns of sectoral interdependence and policy convergence and divergence with sectoral compliance. The analysis suggests that EU policies travel to countries and sectors in spite of policy divergence and a higher dependence of the ENC on Russia. It then continues to enquire whether other institutional, structural or more agency-centered factors can better account for this puzzling compliance pattern.

Divergence and convergence of external policy transfer

To what extent do the EU and Russia promote diverging policies in their shared, Caucasian neighborhood? Are they indeed sources of rivaling neighborhood policies in their attempt to prevail over one another in competing 'spheres of influence' (Schulze 2008; Simão and Freire 2008: 229)? In order to assess the *de facto* policy divergence or convergence for JLS and energy policies, the next section discusses whether Russia has codified any policies in the framework of the CIS or the CSTO that correspond to or challenge the prescriptions of the ENP Actions Plans and the bilateral PCA which form the contractual basis of the EU-ENC cooperation for the period under investigation here (European Commission 2006b, 2006c; European Communities 1999a, 1999b).[1] In addition, I analyze the relationship of Russia and the EU in the relevant policy area to further determine policy convergence or divergence.

Justice, Liberty and Security (JLS)

JLS policies have been stipulated in the bilateral and regional frameworks of the ENC, Russia and the EU since the very beginning of bilateral and multilateral cooperation. At odds with the narrative about the EU–Russian rivalry, however, their policies in the JLS area show a large degree of overlap. JLS policies in the ENP Action Plans (AP) and the PCA cover issues of money laundering, border management, migration issues, trafficking and organized crime, drug trafficking, and police and judicial cooperation,[2] which are also addressed by the CIS and the CSTO, as well as Russia's strategic foreign policy documents.

In the area of money laundering, the PCA and ENP AP foresee the adoption and implementation of the 2005 Council of Europe (CoE) Convention on laundering, search, seizure and confiscation of the proceeds from crime and on the financing of terrorism, and call for greater international cooperation toward this end with international institutions such as Moneyval. Money laundering has been an issue of concern for CIS countries, too, which led to the establishment of the Eurasian group against money laundering and terrorism financing. The EU directly encourages the ENC in the ENP AP to further strengthen their cooperation with the Eurasian group (European Commission 2006b, 2006c).

The EU also asks the ENC to intensify transborder cooperation with EU member states and neighboring countries and to implement a type of technical assistance that resembles the Border Management Program for Central Asia (BOMCA). In line with this, a CIS action plan on a coordinated border policy was passed in 2010 and aims to strengthen cooperation with FRONTEX (the European Agency for the Management of Operational Cooperation at the External Borders of the Member States of the European Union), EU-UNDP (United Nations Development Programme), and BOMCA (CIS Council of Heads of States 2010: 2.1.3).

The adoption of national action plans of migration and asylum, the conclusion of readmission agreements, the introduction of enhanced document security standards and biometric passports form part of the migration and asylum section of the PCA and the ENP AP. In addition, the countries are asked to ratify and implement the principles of the 1951 Geneva Convention and the 1967 Protocol, and adjust their domestic legislation on asylum and refugees to European standards in the field. They shall establish electronic databases for the control of migration flows, implement measures to foster the protection of internally displaced persons (IDPs) and refugees, and implement reintegration programs for returnees within the ENC. Migration has also figured prominently on the CIS, CSTO and Russian foreign policy agenda.[3] Article seven of the CIS Charter refers to joint activities in the field of migration policies (Sakwa and Webber 1999), as the Bishkek Agreement of 1992 established visa free travel between the CIS member countries. Although the agreement was followed by diverse bilateral and multilateral agreements that no longer adhered to a unified CIS approach (ICMPD 2005: 27), the CIS used its competence to develop migration-related regulations and to fight illegal migration (Molodikova 2010: 15), broadly in line with EU policies. In 2004 an amended cooperation agreement to fight illegal migration recommended concluding readmission agreements. Likewise, in 2007, a Council of Heads of Migration Bodies was established and a Declaration on the Coordination of CIS Migration Policies was passed followed by several action plans and programs. The program on fighting illegal migration for 2009–11 codified the directions that CIS migration services had agreed upon in 2006 (Molodikova 2010: 25). It foresaw the introduction of biometric passports and recommended the conclusion of readmission agreements. Legal and illegal migration were also recognized as problems in Russia's foreign policy strategies (Medvedev 2008; Putin 2000a; Putin 2000b), and CSTO members have shown interest in increasing the organization's scope to fight against illegal migration (Marat and Murzakulova 2007).

The PCA and ENP AP sections on the fight against human and drug trafficking and organized crime largely draw on international conventions to be implemented in the ENC contexts, comprising the 1988 United Nations (UN) Convention against Illicit Traffic in Narcotic Drugs and Psychotropic Substances, the UN Convention on Transnational Organized Crime and the Protocol against the Illicit Manufacturing of and Trafficking in Firearms, their Parts and Components and Ammunition. Armenia and Georgia are also asked to implement actions recommended by the Organization for Security and Co-operation in Europe's (OSCE) action plans on organized crime, to develop a national anti-drug strategy and implement their already adopted national action plans for the prevention of trafficking in persons. In addition, the EU wants them to strengthen their law enforcement bodies and engage in regional cooperation to efficiently fight these threats. Relatedly, in the area of judicial or police cooperation, Armenia and Georgia agreed to accede to and implement the CoE Convention for the Protection of Individuals with regard to the Automatic Processing of Personal Data, the Second Protocol to the European Convention on Mutual Assistance in Criminal Matters, as well as to the 1980 Hague Convention on Civil Aspects of International Child Abduction. The ENP AP also foresee enhanced cooperation with Europol and in the Black and the Caspian Sea region.

Likewise, CIS members signed an agreement on combating organized crime, which includes provisions to fight trafficking in narcotics and nuclear material in 1995. A number of conventions were passed, with the Convention on Legal Assistance and Legal Relations in Civil, Criminal and Family Matters being the most prominent. By 2004, the CIS had already passed 18 treaties in the area of migration, the fight against terrorism and drug trafficking (Willerton and Beznosov 2007: 52). The CIS Secretariat stresses the international connectedness of CIS policies in this area to the CoE and other international conventions (CIS Executive Committee 2011a). The fight against drug trafficking and organized crime also figures prominently in the foreign policy and national security concepts of Russia (Medvedev 2008; Putin 2000a;

Putin 2000b). Likewise, the CSTO declared combating 'international terrorism and extremism, the illicit traffic in narcotic drugs, psychotropic substances and arms, organized transnational crime, illegal migration' a central organizational task, which was supposed to be fulfilled under the auspices of the UN and in cooperation with other intergovernmental organizations (CSTO 2002: Art. 8). The comparison of JLS-related EU demands and policies codified in Russia's regional frameworks of cooperation hence suggest policy convergence rather than divergence. However, does this convergence also prevail within the bilateral EU-Russia cooperation?

Formally and in practice, cooperation between Russia and the EU on JLS issues has made significant progress and indeed displays a large convergence of interest and mutual agreement about the substance of cooperation in this area. Formally, the EU and Russia agreed to cooperate in the JLS sphere within their PCA of 1997 and at the Petersburg summit in 2003, where the 'Common Spaces' of the EU and Russia were invented as a new framework of cooperation. The latter approach allowed for a deviation of the 'one-size-fits-all' ENP (Börzel et al. 2008), and satisfied Russia's demand for a special neighborhood status. Yet, the PCA as well as the Road Map for the Common Space on Freedom, Security and Justice that was developed together with the Action Plans for the other common spaces in 2005 formally mirror the actions stipulated in the ENP framework. Its implementation provides evidence of rule convergence between Russia and the EU in the JLS sphere.

Formally, the PCA and the Roadmap foresee cooperation in the fight against money laundering, organized crime, illegal migration and human as well as drug trafficking. At odds with the action plans of the Caucasian neighborhood countries (CNC) is a special section on the fight against corruption in both documents, which is lacking in the JLS part of the ENC AP. Within the PCA, the fight against illegal migration forms part of the areas of cooperation, explicitly mentioning practices of readmission (European Communities 1997: Art. 84). Likewise, the EU and Russia agreed to work toward the facilitation of the movement of persons in the 'Roadmap' framework, while at the same time they cooperate on readmission agreements and border issues with the potential establishment of joint training programs (European Commission 2005c). In 2005, both sides agreed to jointly assess the scale of illegal migration by exchanging information of migratory flows, cooperating on statistics and developing legislative frameworks. The Roadmap also foresees that Russia and the EU will 'cooperate as appropriate in this field in relation to third countries'. Russia and the EU launched a migration dialogue in May 2011.

Money laundering is supposed to be combated in the relevant international frameworks of the Egmont group and the Financial Action Task Force (FATF). In addition, the Roadmap's security section touches upon cooperation on travel document security and mentions the introduction of biometric identifiers as well as Interpol cooperation. The fight against drug trafficking and the trafficking in human beings has been added to the cooperation agenda. The police and judicial cooperation codified in the Roadmap foresee particularly close ties between Russia, Europol and Eurojust.

The *de facto* cooperation in the JLS area has been characterized as being of mutual strategic interest for Russia and the EU (Emerson 2005; Potemkina 2010). This is supported by evidence of the implementation of the Roadmap (European Commission 2011h, 2011k). As regards the fight against organized crime, Russia and Europol signed a strategic agreement in 2003 to cooperate and issue threat assessments. In addition, the European Police College and Russia have agreed to enhance common training activities for law enforcement personnel. Cooperation on the fight against drug trafficking resulted in a Memorandum of Understanding between the European Monitoring Center for Drugs and Drug Addiction (EMCDDA) and the Federal Service for Drugs Control in October 2007, which facilitates the exchange of information between the two agencies. Broadly speaking, the most remarkable progress occurred with regard to migration issues, which has been identified as being at odds with the usual negative rhetoric surrounding EU-Russian cooperation (Korneev 2011).

With regard to border management, Russia and FRONTEX signed a working agreement in 2006 to enable operational cooperation on the common border. Statements of experts in the field suggest that the cooperation has been running smoothly, particularly as regards the Kaliningrad border, where the cooperation has indeed improved border control.[4] In addition, Russia and the EU progressed with regard to visa facilitation and readmission agreements. Both were agreed and signed at the EU-Russian summit in Sochi in May 2006, and they entered into force in June the following year. The EU-Russian readmission and visa facilitation agreement is usually considered a model agreement for the EU's mobility policy toward other ENC. In the course of the negotiations on the readmission agreement, the 'package approach' was invented, linking readmission to visa facilitation in order to make the deal more attractive to Russia (Hernandez i Sagrera 2010).

All in all, the sectoral progress of EU-Russian cooperation hence suggests that both share a common interest in the JLS area (Korneev 2008, 2011; Potemkina 2010). It can thus be assumed that the policies promoted by the EU and Russia with regard to JLS converge, if we take as measurement the CIS and CSTO cooperation framework, the strategic Russian foreign policy documents, and the formal and *de facto* cooperation between Russian and the EU. To what extent do we see similar patterns of policy convergence in the case of energy policy?

Energy

Unlike in the area of JLS, Russia and the EU clearly diverge with regard to energy policy. The neighborhood policies promoted by the EU with regard to energy policy can be broadly classified into three issue areas which predominantly target the electricity and gas sectors of the ENC. Those comprise regulatory convergence, renewable energy and energy efficiency, as well as regional diversification and security of supplies. Again, all three issue areas are mostly identical in both Armenia's and Georgia's AP and PCA, with the exception of the European demand to close the outdated Soviet-style nuclear power plant in the Armenian city of Medzamor. Energy policy has also traditionally occupied a prominent place in the foreign policy concepts and strategies of the Russian Federation, given its large dependence on resource-related economic growth and overreliance on energy exports. The CIS can also look back on a long history of regional cooperation in the energy sector. Given the EU's focus on electricity and gas, Russia's and the CIS policies are analyzed in these two sectors.

Concerning regulatory convergence, the ENC are asked to 'establish a list of measures for gradual legal and regulatory convergence towards the principles of the EU internal electricity and gas markets, accompanied by time schedules and a financing plan' (European Commission 2006b, 2006c). In addition, the regulatory authorities of the energy sectors in Armenia and Georgia are supposed to be further developed in order to comply with the EU Electricity and Gas Directives 2003/54 and 2003/55. The focus on regulatory convergence has already been established with the passage of the PCA. Within the PCA, cooperation of the EU with Armenia and Georgia is envisaged within the principles of the European Energy Charter Treaty and the Protocol on Energy Efficiency (European Communities 1999a, 1999b). The Energy Charter Treaty of 1994 was developed on the basis of the 1991 Energy Charter, a process initiated by the European Community at the time to foster international energy cooperation. The 1994 Charter Treaty is a legally binding instrument and establishes principles and rules for energy cooperation, including the protection of foreign investment, non-discriminatory conditions for trade of energy products and clauses to safeguard cross-border transit of energy flows. In addition, it stipulates dispute mechanisms and the promotion of energy efficiency.

As regards regulatory convergence of the CIS energy markets, no clear formal regulations have so far been stipulated, but the *de facto* convergence of regulatory frameworks by Russia and the EU is doubtable. Few rules have been regionally anchored with regard to gas market regulation. A CIS agreement of 1997 formalized cooperation between CIS countries on the cooperation in the exploration and usage of natural resources and considered the convergence of CIS countries in this area as a goal, but left specific frameworks for cooperation to be dealt with by bilateral treaties. In the early 1990s CIS countries already agreed to create institutional structures to coordinate their policies on electric energy. In 1992 the CIS Electric Power Council (EPC) was established, which had been chaired by Anatoly Chubais from 2000 onwards, the CEO of Unified Energy System (UES), and Russia's electricity monopolist at the time (RIA Novosti 2007). EPC-initiated integration attempts followed in 1998, and succeeded in introducing the parallel operation of CIS electricity networks (Vinokurov 2008). The technical standards for the network operation of the CIS are not compatible with the technical parameters of EU-wide networks. In May 2005 the EPC passed a strategy to determine the main directions of cooperation in the CIS electricity sector, which was followed by the Concept of the Formation of a Common CIS Power Market in November the same year. The CIS countries agreed on the formation of the CIS integrated electricity market in 2007 (CIS Council of Heads of Governments 2007), and passed a roadmap to its realization in 2010 (CIS Council of Heads of Governments 2010). While the broader formal principles of the concept have been identified as compatible with European market rules, its *de facto* reconcilability hinges on the entire liberalization of the sector by the signatory states, particularly by Russia (Vinokurov 2008: 14). As a result, Ukraine refused to sign the agreement in 2007 on the grounds of a lack of free and fair competition with Russia (Government of Ukraine 2007). Since then, Russia has made some progress toward the gradual liberalization of its electricity market, but the remainder of powerful state-owned companies and the interventionist approach of state authorities in the area of electricity and gas challenge the *de facto* liberalization process (Ketting 2008; Milov et al. 2006). The concept also envisages the harmonization of national rules within the CIS, which was found to be incompatible with EU structures in a report by the EPC and Eurelectric, an EU-based industrial group, in 2005 (CIS Electric Power Council and Eurelectric 2005). In addition, the CIS documents do not refer to the principles of the Energy Charter Treaty and its Protocols, which form the underlying basis of the EU energy approach to the South Caucasian states.

In the area of renewable energy and energy efficiency the ENC are asked by the EU to develop the use of renewable energy resources, to reinforce institutions that deal with energy efficiency and renewable energy, and to develop financial, legislative and economic measures to this end (European Commission 2006b, 2006c). The PCA of both Armenia and Georgia demand the development of hydropower and other renewable energy sources, the promotion of energy efficiency and the implementation of the Energy Charter Protocol on Energy Efficiency and Related Environmental Aspects (PEEREA). The PEEREA entered into force with the Energy Charter Treaty and requires the signatories to establish regulatory frameworks, energy policies and strategies to promote efficient energy usage and reduce the environmental impact in the energy sector (Energy Charter Secretariat 2004: 2).

Energy efficiency is also addressed in the CIS framework and foreign policy documents of Russia, and formally corresponds to EU rules in this area. In October 2002 a first initiative toward increased energy efficiency was launched, when an agreement on cooperation among CIS members to secure energy efficiency and energy saving was passed (UN Economic and Social Council 2011: 6). The agreement stipulates increased information exchange on energy efficiency, technological and economic cooperation, and refers to a harmonization of the national legislation of the CIS without specifying, however, the content of potentially harmonized legislative frameworks.

Article 5 also alludes to cooperation with the EU for the implementation of energy efficiency projects. Three years later a decision of the CIS Economic Council introduced further energy efficiency and energy saving measures (CIS Economic Council 2005). The document touches upon regulatory, financial, economic and technical means to foster energy efficiency, and added a detailed plan of national energy efficiency projects to be implemented. Additionally, it recommended critically studying advanced foreign experience in the field (CIS Economic Council 2005: 11.4). This was in line with Russia's domestic energy strategy, which aimed to increase the energy efficiency of its economy, as Russia wasted more than three times more energy than the EU in 2003 (Government of the Russian Federation 2003). Yet, Russia's domestic energy efficiency policies failed to be implemented (Milov et al. 2006: 290). The development of renewable energy has been subject to very few projects (CIS Economic Council 2005: 11.10). Beyond the CIS framework, Russia's foreign policy strategies only mention cooperation on environmental aspects as part of its international cooperation efforts and domestic reform attempts, but they are rather related to the worldwide fight against climate change than to the promotion of concrete regional or bilateral rules (Medvedev 2008; Putin 2000a).

There is a clear divergence of interests with regard to the diversification of energy routes and sources. In the ENP AP and PCA, the diversification of supplies and energy security provisions are directed toward enhanced cooperation with the Caspian and Black Sea littoral states and focus on progress on energy networks especially with regard to electricity and natural gas, trade and transit. Armenia and Georgia are encouraged to develop a diversified infrastructure that is supposed to facilitate transit of energy toward the EU. The improvement of energy supply and its security is also expressed as a goal in the PCA, where the exchange of information on infrastructural developments and investments is stipulated. Toward this end, Georgia and Armenia have been asked in the AP to develop a long-term strategic policy for the energy sector. In the case of Georgia, the AP states that this policy targets convergence with the 'EU energy policy objectives including security of supply' (European Commission 2006b). In the case of Armenia, this is closely tied to the closure of the Medzamor nuclear power plant. The strategy is supposed to 'address a reasonable level of security of the energy sector including diversification of energy sources by routes and types and the development of own resources, including hydropower, energy efficiency and the use of renewable energy sources' (European Commission 2006c). Concerning the nuclear power plant, the Armenian authorities are asked to implement a decommissioning strategy and a cost evaluation plan to close the plant.

While little regional effort has been undertaken within the CIS framework to institutionalize cooperation in the area of energy diversification, the triangulation of Russia's foreign policy and energy strategy as well as secondary literature lend support to the rivalry assumption. The Foreign Policy Concept of 2000 codifies Russia's energy policy toward the Caucasus, the Black and the Caspian Sea region as aiming at 'help(ing) advance Russian economic interests, including in the matter of choice of routes for important energy flows' (Putin 2000a). This implies the participation of Russian joint stock companies in the operation of international energy transport projects of 'strategic interest' (Government of the Russian Federation 2003). A former Russian minister is quoted as saying, 'if the Caspian oil goes via Georgia and Turkey, there will be a new geopolitical situation in the South Caucasus and a diminished influence of Russia. The financial loss will be higher than the one caused by the war in Chechnya' (Freitag-Wirminghaus 1999: 263, my translation). Hence, the European attempts to build diversified pipeline infrastructures that also aim at circumventing Russian territory and Russian businesses can thus be considered at odds with the Russian strategy to promote its own interconnection of the Caspian region, Southeast Europe and Turkey. The diversification of supply hence signifies an issue of strategic policy divergence between Russia and the EU, as Russia intends to maintain and intensify its energy cooperation and routes with CIS countries, while the EU wants these countries to engage in the alteration of its energy supplies beyond Russia to enhance further the EU's energy security via diversified transit routes (Freitag-Wirminghaus 1999: 275; Trenin 1999: 296). Hence, the analysis of foreign policy strategies and the CIS framework suggests a policy divergence as regards energy diversification and regulatory convergence, which is further supported by a lack of incorporation of the principles of the European Energy Charter Treaty and its related Protocols. Formal policy convergence only prevails in the sphere of energy efficiency.

In line with these findings, the cooperation between Russia and the EU also mostly displays elements of policy divergence. Although formal cooperation has been advanced within the PCA and the Common Economic Space, the legal basis for cooperation is still disputed. Repeated disagreement in EU-Russian energy relations additionally suggests profound policy divergence except for the area of energy efficiency. Formally, the PCA touches upon the need for fostering the principles of a market economy, the improvement of security of supply, energy saving and energy efficiency, as well as the modernization of energy infrastructure (European Communities 1997: 65). While it refers to most of the issue areas that are also tackled within the Caucasian PCA, it lacks references to the binding Energy Charter Treaty and the Energy Efficiency Protocol, and only alludes to the non-binding Energy Charter in its preamble. Russia indeed signed the Energy Charter Treaty and the related Protocol in 1994, but never ratified it (Westphal 2006). While Russia announced that it would provisionally apply both the Treaty and the Protocol, it declared in 2009 that it did not intend ever to become a full member and suspended its provisional application. The EU-Russian energy relations thus lack a sound legal footing.

In order to cooperate further on these issue areas the EU-Russian Summit in October 2000 gave birth to the Energy Dialogue which aimed to deepen the EU-Russian energy partnership (European Commission 2011d). It was followed by the creation of thematic working sub-groups to address separately the different issues such as supply security and energy efficiency (Monaghan 2006). The EU and Russia have also cooperated on energy issues in the framework of the Common Economic Space since the passage of the relevant Roadmap in 2005 (European Commission 2005c). Instead of anchoring the Energy Charter Treaty as such, the Roadmap refers to the 'principles guiding' the Treaty in the cooperation on fair trade in transit of energy products. Both parties agreed to cooperate on the convergence of energy strategies, including those related to energy efficiency. In addition to technological cooperation and energy transport safety, the Common Space foresees a gradual integration of both electricity markets to level the playing field for market access, basic rules, infrastructure openness and environmental protection. However, the Roadmap fails to outline clearly who converges towards whom, leaving the clauses on regulatory convergence without substance (Emerson 2005: 2).

With a view to potential interest divergence in the area of energy diversification, Russia and the EU agreed to cooperate on energy infrastructure of 'common interest' and to assess mechanisms to avoid non-commercial dangers of energy projects. The Roadmap also codifies the promotion in the area of energy-efficient technologies and renewable energy, and to launch business dialogue between EU-Russian energy companies. In addition, cooperation on nuclear energy issues has been incorporated into the document. Another formal institution of the bilateral energy relationship was established with a Memorandum of Understanding that created an early warning mechanism on 16 November 2009, establishing contact points on both sides to prevent supply interruptions and facilitate early communication of potential fallout (European Commission 2009c).

The *de facto* cooperation of both the EU and Russia is constrained by the lack of legal clarity due to the hesitation of Russia to ratify and apply the Energy Charter Treaty and the Energy Efficiency Protocol. Concerning regulatory convergence, the Energy Charter Treaty stipulates the rules for investment, trade and transport and comprises dispute settlement mechanisms. In addition, the treaty provides for a transit protocol, which is supposed to guarantee non-discriminatory access to oil and gas transit. This protocol figures as the most contentious issue in the bilateral relations as Russia anticipates encountering competitive disadvantages on the European markets (Goldthau and Geden 2007: 66). As a result, European companies have reportedly experienced legal difficulties on the Russian energy market. BP and Shell, for example, were obliged to sell key assets of their companies to Gazprom in order to be eligible for further operation in Russia (EurActiv 2011a). Furthermore, regulatory disagreement was also on the rise when the EU passed its third energy package in 2009, which foresees reforms in the energy and gas market including greater competition via unbundling. Unbundling, the separation of generation and supply from transmission works, is at odds with the vertically integrated Russian companies on the EU market, particularly the state-owned Gazprom (EurActiv 2011b; RIA Novosti 2011). The unbundling of the energy sectors in the ENC has also been described as diminishing Russia's leverage of energy for political goals (Leonard and Popescu 2007: 60). The Russian authorities openly declared that regulatory convergence with the EU acquis represents a 'no go' for Russia (Konoplyanik 2009: 269). As a result, EU-Russian relations in terms of regulatory convergence are marked by disagreement rather than agreement.

Concerning cooperation on diversification and energy supply security, the EU and Russia are bound to each other by strong mutual dependencies, as Russia depends on the EU as an important export market, and the EU on Russia to satisfy 30 to 40 percent of its required gas imports (Eurostat 2015; Henderson and Mitrova 2015). The diversification of the sources of imports, which the EU aims at with its neighborhood policy, or the diversification of the destination of Russian exports hence threatens to shift the dependence in favor of one or the other actor, creating potential for conflict. Yet, the economic balance of interdependence, which used to result in an overall reliance on Russia as an energy supplier (Westphal 2006: 45), has already been destabilized by several political disputes between Russia, the EU and third countries.

First, long before the crisis in 2014, the gas conflicts of Russia and Ukraine in January 2006 and 2009 about gas prices left Ukraine without gas supply, lowered the pressure in gas pipelines leading to Hungary and Western Europe, and accelerated the loss of confidence in Russian energy supplies. The re-emerging conflict in 2009 occurred despite the EU-Russian agreement on the principles of an early warning mechanism at the Summit in Samara in 2007.

Second, the announcement by Gazprom's chief Alexej Miller in mid-April 2006 that Russia intended to diversify its exports market (Altmann 2007), and the war between Russia and Georgia in August 2008, immediately triggered voices within the EU institutions to further diversify Europe's energy supplies in return and reduce dependence on Russia (Council of the European Union 2008). EU-Russian relations in terms of energy diversification and supply security are hence marked by disagreement rather than consent, despite the mutual dependence on import and export markets. Their relations with regard to energy efficiency and renewable energy also lack the legal basis of the Energy Charter Treaty Protocol; however, the *de facto* cooperation displays patterns of agreement. Despite the fact that some reports underline a general divergence in terms of overall approaches to environmental protection (Monaghan 2006: 3), many projects have been implemented with regard to energy efficiency measures in Russia with EU support (European Commission 2011e), which corresponds to the focus of the CIS cooperation on these issues.

In a nutshell, the policies promoted by the EU and Russia with regard to energy policies predominantly differ, taking as measurement the CIS and CSTO cooperation framework, as well as the strategic Russian foreign policy documents and the formal and *de facto* cooperation between Russia and the EU. What is formally at odds with this overall policy divergence is the area of energy efficiency, which is indeed embraced by both Russia and the EU.

All in all, the patterns of policy convergence and divergence show a general overlap in the JLS area and energy efficiency, while other energy policy areas figure as competitive policies in the neighborhood. Is Russia or the EU better equipped to anchor these policies in the neighborhood? The next section assesses their relative power potential in terms of interdependence.

Multiple interdependencies

Interdependence with the EU or Russia and resulting power asymmetries have been considered a prominent driver of external policy transfer (see e.g. Dimitrova and Dragneva 2009). If measured in terms of size, economic potential and military capacity, both Russia and the EU are more powerful than Armenia and Georgia which qualify as small states. While Russia is larger in terms of territorial size, the EU dominates in terms of population, economic power and aggregated military capacity.[5] A more relational perspective on interdependence, however, modifies the clear dominance of the EU in terms of military and economic leverage. Unlike the EU, Russia is militarily involved in Georgia's and Armenia's internal and international conflicts and operates military bases on their territories. The civil wars that erupted between Georgia and its region of South Ossetia in 1991 and in Abkhazia 1992 have been frozen since the negotiation of a ceasefire agreement in 1992 and 1994, respectively. Russia mediated the agreement that foresaw the establishment of a tripartite peace-keeping force in South Ossetia consisting of Georgian, Ossetian and Russian troops led by the latter. Likewise, Russia facilitated negotiations of the ceasefire agreement with Abkhazia in May 1994. CIS peacekeeping forces and a UN observer mission (UNOMIG) were stationed in Abkhazia, while the UN mission was withdrawn after the Russian–Georgian military conflict in South Ossetia in August 2008. Russia also operated four military bases in Georgia proper until 2007 (Nichol 2011: 8; Wilson and Popescu 2009: 322). Apart from military capacity via peace-keeping forces and military bases, Russia provided significant budgetary support and legitimacy to the *de facto* republics South Ossetia and Abkhazia,[6] while their authorities delegated border control to Russian military personnel and border guards (Kipiani 2011).

The EU lacks a similar dense involvement in the conflicts. The French EU presidency negotiated the ceasefire agreement after the August war with Russia and the EU provided an EU Monitoring Mission (EUMM) to Georgia. The monitoring mission, however, has not been allowed to monitor developments in South Ossetia and Abkhazia proper, but operates from the territory that is controlled by the Georgian central government. The EU acts as a mediator in the negotiations about the 'Geneva process' together with the UN and the OSCE. Armenia is in a frozen conflict with Azerbaijan about the Azeri enclave Nagorno-Karabakh, which is populated with ethnic Armenians and strives for autonomy from Azerbaijan. An outright war lasted from 1992 to 1994, in which Armenia occupied the region of Nagorno-Karabakh as well as a buffer zone, which constitutes approximately 7 percent of Azerbaijan's territory. During the war Russia supplied Armenia with arms and an overall 'security umbrella' (Iskandaryan 2011a: 54f.). In addition, Russian military forces operate two bases on Armenian territory whose presence has been regularly extended and is expected to last at least until 2044, as agreed by Armenian and Russian authorities in August 2010 (Nichol 2011: 8; see also Wilson and Popescu 2009: 322). Russia also mediates between Azerbaijan and Armenia in the conflict about Nagorno-Karabakh within the OSCE Minsk group which is co-chaired by France and the USA.

In terms of security provision, both Armenia and Georgia hence display asymmetries in their interdependence with Russia: despite the greater military capacity of the EU, Russia possesses greater leverage on internal conflict dynamics. Russia is needed in both countries to solve the internal conflicts (Georgia) or provide a sufficient degree of security vis-à-vis the opponent (Armenia). While Russia is hence directly or indirectly militarily involved in the ENC, the EU rather fulfills the role of a mediator and critical observer.

In terms of economic interdependence, the dominance of the aggregated economic potential of EU member states is significant. The imports from and exports to the EU member states outdo bilateral trade flows with Russia, despite the fact that Russia had been an important trading partner for both countries, when the ENP was initiated.[7] Georgia's economic interdependence with Russia was further reduced after Russia enacted trade embargos against Georgia in 2006 that were only lifted with the rise to power of the new GD government (see Chapter 6). In addition to trade flows, Armenia and Georgia profit from large amounts of development assistance. In total, official development assistance including the contributions by the EU has accounted for around 6 percent of Armenia's and Georgia's gross national income (GNI) in 2004 and even more in the late 1990s (World Bank 2015). Russia is not engaged in the provision of development assistance. However, Russian gas subsidies to CIS countries are estimated to have amounted to US$75 billion from 1992 to 2008, which outdoes the amount of 'Western' aid provided to the CIS countries at the same time (Sasse 2013: 5).

On a macro-level, interdependence of Georgia and Armenia in security and economic terms varies between the EU and Russia. Interdependence is highly asymmetric in favor of Russia in security terms, while it is more favorable to the EU in economic matters, which leaves the measurement somewhat unclear. A more policy-specific approach to interdependence is thus presented in the next sections.

Justice, Liberty and Security

With regard to the fight against illegal migration, organized crime, money laundering or border control, Armenia and Georgia have been traditionally more dependent on Russia than on the EU.

Interdependence of the EU and the ENC in JLS issues in general and migration matters in particular is rather asymmetric favoring the ENC. First, the Caucasian countries figure as migrant-sending countries to the EU. This has resulted in large diasporas of Armenians in France and smaller ones of Georgians in Germany and Greece (Jgamadze and Markarashvili 2009: 9; Manaseryan 2004: 3). The estimated number of migrants from Armenia and Georgia to the EU, as compared to their numbers in Russia, however, is comparatively low, as World Bank estimates (Figure 3.1) and secondary sources indicate (Popescu and Wilson 2009: 34) – a pattern that has only slightly changed over time.

While there are no precise data on illegal migration available due to its very nature, reports suggest the CNC to be sources of illegal migration to the EU via the 'Eastern border route' (European Commission 2007b: 33; Frontex 2011). Given the direction of migration flows, the EU hence depends more on the Caucasian countries to fight irregular migration than vice versa. This dependence is not alleviated by high remittances that stem from migrants in Europe. Remittances indeed provided for a substantial portion of the ENC's GDP in the early 2000s (Tishkov et al. 2005: 28), but most of these remittances originate in Russia – a pattern that has been relatively stable over time. When calculating the relative share of remittances with the help of World Bank data on estimated flows (World Bank 2010b), remittances from Russia show to provide for around 57 percent (Armenia) and 62 percent (Georgia) of all

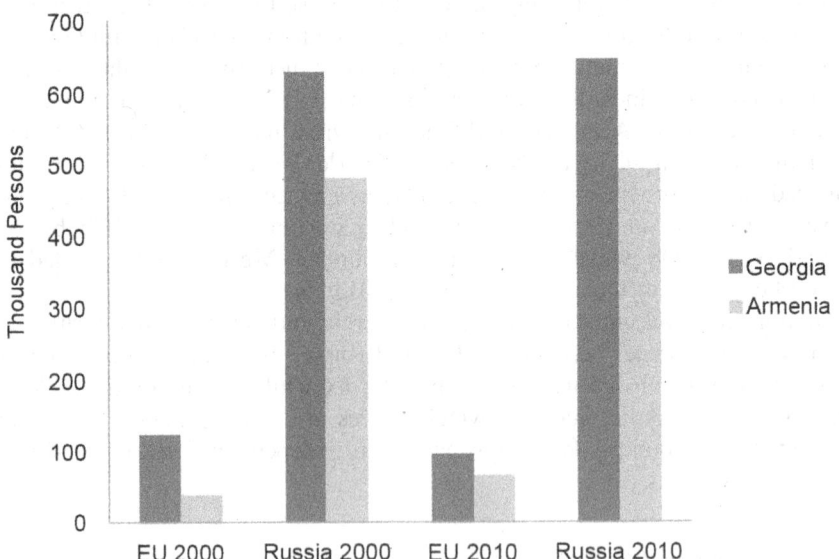

Figure 3.1 Estimated number of migrants from Georgia and Armenia in Russia and the EU
Source: author's illustrations, based on World Bank 2010a, 2011.

remittances received by these countries in 2010, while remittances from EU member states only account for 9 percent (Armenia) and 10 percent (Georgia).

In terms of border control and management, the ENC share no (Armenia) or only a maritime border with the EU since the 2007 EU enlargement (Georgia). Interdependence in terms of human trafficking is also asymmetrical between the EU, Armenia and Georgia, disfavoring the EU. The US State Department reports on human trafficking consider Armenia and Georgia source and transit countries for human trafficking to the EU, particularly to Greece and Germany (US Department of State 2002, 2003, 2004b).

Money laundering is not a substantial threat emanating from Armenia and Georgia, despite the fact that high unemployment, corruption and the shadow economy make both countries vulnerable to this form of crime. Yet, they have figured constantly as 'other countries' in the US State Department's threat analysis, meaning that they are neither ranked as being of primary nor of medium concern (US Bureau for International Narcotics and Law Enforcement Affairs 2005; US Department of State 2006, 2008, 2010).

Drug trafficking routes, however, are an additional indicator of asymmetric interdependence disfavoring the EU. Both, Armenia and Georgia are countries of origin, transit and, to a lesser extent, destination for narcotics trafficking (Michaletos 2009). The same is true for organized crime. Europol finds that EU countries are targeted by crime groups from Armenia and Georgia (Europol 2004: 9), which are also occasionally interconnected with governmental or economic elites within the countries (Michaletos 2009).

To summarize, then, in the realm of JLS the EU is predominantly the target and not the source of threats emanating particularly from illegal migration, drug trafficking and organized crime originating from Georgia and Armenia. With regard to illegal migration, this asymmetric dependence of the EU on the CNC to reduce these threats is not or is to a very limited degree leveled by remittance payments from EU-located migrants.

Armenia and Georgia are more symmetrically bound to Russia with regard to JLS issues in general, and legal and illegal migration flows in particular. Since the 1990s, the migration of Armenian and Georgian citizens to Russia has flourished, given the prevailing societal and linguistic ties stemming from Soviet times and increasingly porous borders after the breakup of the Soviet Union, which resulted in large diasporas of Armenians and Georgians in Russia (ILO 2008: 15).[8] The CIS visa-free regime with Russia applies to Armenia, whereas Russia unilaterally introduced visa requirements for Georgia in 2001 due to political tensions between the countries. Despite this difference and the impossibility of illegality due to the visa-free travel with Armenia, the number of irregular work migrants from both countries was significant in the early 2000s. Reportedly, 650,000 Armenian and 200,000 Georgian migrants qualified as irregular work migrants at the time (Ivakhnyuk 2009: 33).

Despite the fact that Russia is targeted by legal and illegal migration flows from Georgia and Armenia to a greater extent than the EU, its dependence on Armenia and Georgia to solve problems of illegal migration is rather limited. First, the increase of illegal migration despite tougher Russian migration laws and reduced labor quotas can be attributed to domestic problems in Russia, such as corruption, a large shadow economy and the porous border with Belarus, through which most Georgians enter Russia (Genov and Savvidis 2011).[9] Second, Russia has to cope with the paradox of a dire need of migrant workers to solve its unfavorable demographic situation (Trenin 2005: 8) and widespread xenophobic attitudes within its society. Given their small populations, the increased 'Caucasophobia' within Russia and Central Asian states as alternative sources for migrants, Russia does not necessarily depend on Armenia and Georgia to satisfy its migrant worker need. While the Caucasian states might hence contribute to less illegal migration via introducing some forms of migration management, the solution to the problem predominantly lies within Russia. In addition, the asymmetry is further shifted to favor Russia, as migration flows from the Caucasian ENC to Russia created strong financial dependencies via remittances (Alturki et al. 2009). The CNC hence rely on Russia's openness and its informal labor market to generate a substantial amount of income.

In addition, unlike with EU countries, Georgia shares a direct land border with Russia, while Russian border troops in Armenia safeguard the external CIS borders with Iran and Turkey. Interdependence in terms of human and drug trafficking is also more symmetrical between Russia, Armenia and Georgia, slightly favoring Russia as a country of origin, however. The relevant US State Department reports identify Georgia as a transit country for victims from Russia, while Armenia figures as both a transit and sending country of victims to and from Russia (US Department of State 2006, 2010).

Georgia also constitutes a source and transit country for drug trafficking from Central Asia to Europe, while many drugs are assumed to be smuggled from Russia via its secessionist territories (US Department of State 2009). In the case of Armenia, drug trafficking is less pronounced due to it being landlocked, but here, too, Russia figures as one of the main countries of origin of drugs to Armenia, especially for opiates and heroin in the early 2000s (US Department of State 2000, 2004a). The same is true for organized crime. Europol finds that crime groups from Armenia and Georgia are often interconnected with Russian crime groups (Europol 2004: 9). Hence, Georgia and Armenia rely on cooperation with Russia as regards the fight against organized crime, and human and drug trafficking.

To sum up, Georgia's and Armenia's interdependence with Russia is overall more asymmetric in the realm of JLS, disfavoring the countries. Threats that the EU intends to fight also emanate from Russia or are closely linked to it, particularly with regard to human and drug trafficking and organized crime. Russia's dependence on the ENC with regard to the fight against illegal migration is low and further reduced by the high dependence of the ENC on remittance payments from migrants in Russia. As a result, Russia possesses generally larger potential to inflict costs on its post-Soviet neighbors than the EU in this policy area.

Energy

The dependence on energy imports differs between the EU, Russia and the ENC. While Georgia and Armenia, as well as the EU, figure as net importers to satisfy their overall energy consumption, Russia exports more energy than it actually needs for its own consumption (Figure 3.2).

The EU depends particularly on energy supplies from Russia, while its interconnectedness with Georgia and Armenia is marginal. Georgia and Armenia do not (Armenia) or hardly (Georgia) export energy into the EU, and energy imports from EU countries have only provided for 0.2 to 0.4 percent of total trade in the case of Georgia from 2001 to 2010, and even less in Armenia (Eurostat 2011). Consequently, the dependence of Georgia and Armenia on the EU in the realm of energy policies is small.

The EU's attempts to reduce its own energy dependence on Russia via cooperation with Armenia and particularly Georgia, however, indicate a shift of asymmetry favoring the ENC. In the early 2000s the European Commission hinted at the importance of the South Caucasian states for Europe's energy security, given their geostrategic location as potential transit countries for transporting alternative resources from the Caspian Basin (European Commission 2000). It re-emphasized the importance of developing the so-called southern gas corridor for the supply with Caspian and Middle Eastern gas in its strategic energy review of 2008 (European Commission 2008f).

While the EU politically backed projects in the region that would circumvent Russia as an energy provider and allow the EU potentially to diversify its energy sources, the financial commitment was left to private companies, and the external energy dimension to the competences of the individual member states (Tchirakadze 2007). The Lisbon Treaty codified a stronger communautairization of external energy policy (Prange-Gstöhl 2009). As a result, the European Commission was mandated to negotiate a treaty with Caspian littoral states to build a Trans-Caspian Pipeline System in September

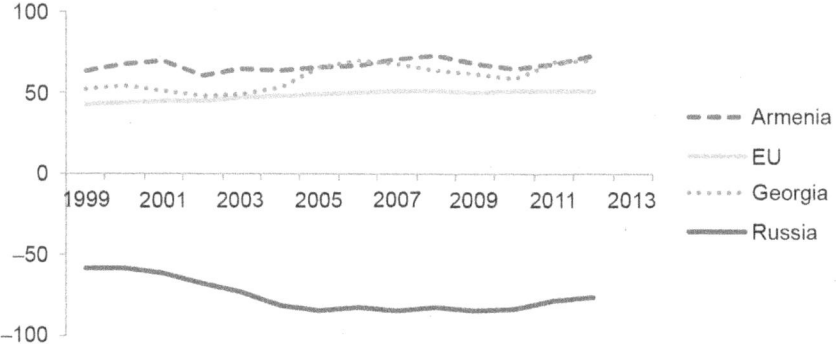

Figure 3.2 Net energy imports, in percent of energy use
Source: author's illustration, based on World Bank 2015.

2011 for the first time (Nichol 2011: 45; RAPID 2011). Seeking closer ties with the South Caucasus as transit countries in this regard, the EU can be considered more dependent on the ENC in terms of enhancing its supply security then the ENC are on the EU.

On the contrary, both Armenia and Georgia have been or are strongly dependent on Russian energy supplies, particularly on gas and oil, which cannot be generated domestically (European Commission 2005a, 2005b). In 1999, when the PCA entered into force, gas had been provided exclusively by Russia, given the absence of alternative pipeline routes that would have connected Georgia and Armenia to diversified suppliers at the time (European Commission 2005a, 2005b). In addition to infrastructural dependence, Russian gas had initially been supplied at prices well below the market level (Reisner and Kvatchadze 2005: 27). This pattern only changed in the mid-2000s (see Chapter 5), and should hence have equipped Russia with a large power potential in this sector at the time of the initiation of the PCA and the ENP.

Apart from gas, the electricity supply of both countries also depends on cooperation with and imports from Russia. Armenia's electricity need is to a large extent satisfied by electricity generated from its nuclear power plant in Medzamor, while Georgia depends on the hydropower plant on the Enguri river to generate a substantial amount of electricity (INOGATE 2011b). The fuel for the operation of the Armenian nuclear power plant is exclusively supplied by Russia and needs to be regularly imported by Armenia. In Georgia, the hydropower plant is located in the conflict zone in Abkhazia. While the dam is on Georgian territory proper, the turbines and generators are situated in Abkhazia (WTO 2010: 67). In order to use the full potential of the power plant, Georgia hence depends on the functioning of the technical means on Abkhaz territory and the supply of electricity across the *de facto* border, which is controlled by Russia.

Furthermore, the functioning of domestic energy markets has been highly dependent on capital imports from Russia, which is particularly remarkable in the case of Georgia, in which foreign direct investment (FDI) from Russia has also flourished at times of political tension (Doggart 2009). In the early 2000s, Russian state-owned companies were expanding into the region, acquiring large, strategic assets in Armenia and Georgia. By 2004, Russia's UES had acquired 75 percent of the shares of the formerly American Georgian energy distribution company AES, owned two generation units in Tbilisi and held 50 percent of the shares of AES Transenergy, which delivers electricity to Turkey (Closson 2009: 765; Secrieru 2006: 301). As one observer noted at the time, 'the Russian monopolist has control over all private and industrial users in Tbilisi, to whom it may now dictate the terms' (Secrieru 2006).

Likewise, the Armenian energy sector has largely been penetrated by Russian state-owned firms. In 2005, the company Interenergo announced that it had bought Armenia's energy distribution company that was formerly held by the British Midland Resources Holding (EIU 2005a: 19). In addition, FDI to both Armenia's and Georgia's energy sectors has mainly stemmed from Russian state-led and private businesses, while many European investors have been reluctant (cf. Soghomonyan 2007: 45).

In a nutshell, Armenia and Georgia have thus been marked by a highly asymmetric interdependence favoring Russia in the energy sector, especially when the PCA and ENP AP were developed. As opposed to this, the EU, Georgia and Armenia are less interconnected in their energy supplies, and plans by the EU to change this shift the patterns of interdependence to disfavor the EU even further. As a result, Russia's leverage potential has been higher in the energy sector than that of the EU.

Compliance patterns

The analysis of patterns of policy divergence and convergence resulted in a straightforward finding of convergence between externally promoted Russian and European rules in the area of JLS. In terms of externally promoted energy policy divergence prevails both with regard to diversification as well as to regulatory convergence. Energy efficiency figures as the exception to the rule in the energy sector and displays overlaps between Russian and EU foreign policy. Given high levels of asymmetric interdependence in both policy areas favoring Russia, policy divergence in the energy sector and policy convergence in the area of JLS, we would expect to see high levels of compliance with EU policies in the JLS sector and lower compliance levels in the energy sector.

The results of the content analysis of ENP progress reports, however, show substantial variation in compliance across countries and policy sectors. Table 3.1 shows the average percentages of progress report codings for non-, shallow, emerging and full compliance in the Commission's bilateral progress reports of 2008–14, which cover the reporting period of 2007–13. At odds with the expected findings, the coding results suggest that compliance of both countries is better in the policy field of energy than in the sphere of JLS.

Table 3.1 Compliance coding across sectors and countries, in percent

	JLS		Energy	
	Georgia	*Armenia*	*Georgia*	*Armenia*
Non-compliance	25.7	17.5	11.7	19.0
Shallow compliance	17.0	12.6	1.3	0.0
Total	42.7	30.1	13.0	19.0
Emerging compliance	18.7	23.8	41.6	37.0
Compliance	38.6	46.2	45.5	44.0
Total	57.3	69.9	87.0	81.0

Justice, Liberty and Security

The content analysis of the JLS sections of the progress reports results in a diverse picture ranging from full to non-compliance. At odds with the assumption of the interdependence hypothesis, the compliance with JLS policies in both countries is less pronounced than expected, despite the fact that both Russia and the EU can be assumed to promote similar policies in their neighborhood.

Figure 3.3 shows JLS compliance patterns over time in both countries. Both Georgia and Armenia display substantial levels of non-compliance and shallow compliance, but there are also remarkable differences between Georgia and Armenia. On average, Armenia performs better than Georgia, whereas Georgia's compliance pattern substantially varies over time: until 2010, the sector is rather characterized by non-compliance or emerging compliance. In the reports of 2010 to 2012 positive assessments slightly outdo the rather negative ones, but a much clearer break is noticeable in the 2013 and 2014 reports covering the period 2012–13. During this period, Georgia's and Armenia's compliance ratings converge, with Georgia even receiving slightly better assessments than Armenia.

When looking more closely at the developments behind these numeric data, the negative assessments of compliance by both Armenia and Georgia partly stem from the failure to sign or implement international conventions in the area of the fight against organized crime or law enforcement cooperation, respectively, such as the third Protocol against the Illicit Manufacturing of and Trafficking in Firearms, their Parts and Components and Ammunition, supplementing the UN Convention against Transnational Organized Crime (European Commission 2009b, 2011f). While Georgia additionally lacks

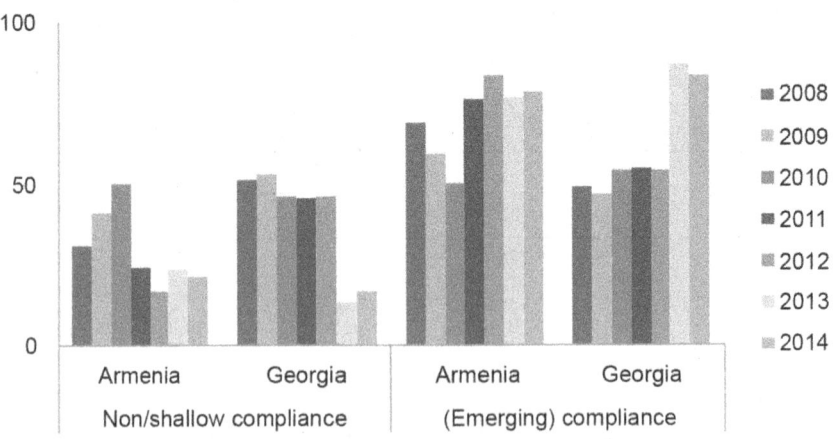

Figure 3.3 Overview of JLS compliance patterns in Georgia and Armenia

some progress on border demarcation, Armenia advanced slowly with regard to border management in 2010.[10]

The dominant difference, which supposedly causes the more positive coding of Armenia's JLS performance – especially until 2012 – however, occurs in the sphere of migration management. With regard to the development of migration management strategies, the enhancement of document security, the conclusion of readmission agreements and the upgrading of migration institutions, Armenia has been the forerunner, while Georgia managed to catch up slightly in late 2009[11] and then substantially improved its performance in 2012 and 2013 (see Chapter 4).

Energy

The content analysis of the energy sections of the Commission's progress reports displays overall positive assessments of both Armenia and Georgia. This contradicts the original expectation of the interdependence-divergence hypothesis: although the ENC are highly dependent on Russia and policy divergence prevails in the EU-Russian relationships, the overall compliance patterns of both countries are predominantly coded as instances of 'emerging compliance' or 'compliance' (Figure 3.4). There are few negative assessments of 'non-compliance' or 'shallow compliance' reported. Despite this general positive finding across countries, Georgia performs better than Armenia with regard to the overall compliance pattern, and mostly displays only minor occurrences of non- or shallow compliance.

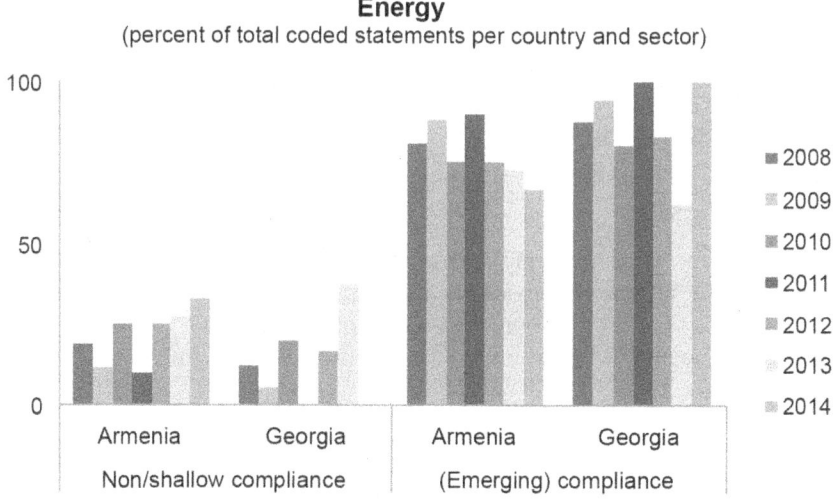

Figure 3.4 Overview of energy compliance patterns in Georgia and Armenia

66 Constraining EU policy transfer?

Both countries are generally evaluated in a positive manner, with regard to diversification processes, regulatory convergence and the development of renewable energy and energy efficiency. When taking a closer look at the compliance patterns in both countries, however, divergence in their (non-)compliance patterns still stands out (see Chapter 5): Georgia displays non-compliance with regard to the establishment of regulatory measures to comply with EU rules, especially in the area of renewable energy and energy efficiency (European Commission 2009b, 2011g).[12] Armenia, on the contrary, progresses very well with these regulatory measures, but is evaluated with more non-compliance codings than Georgia in the area of energy diversification. Even though Armenia operates a newly inaugurated gas pipeline with Iran, delays in supplies were reported until 2009 (European Commission 2008a, 2010). In addition, Armenia fails to meet the demand of substituting the outdated Medzamor nuclear power plant with alternative energy supplies (PanArmenian.net 2007; RFE/RL 2011a).

Overall, the generally positive compliance assessment in the energy sector of both countries and the more negative assessment of the JLS sphere are at odds with the policy divergence and convergence divide within these sectors, which are both characterized by a strong and asymmetric interdependence with Russia. How can this finding be explained?

Explaining variation in compliance patterns

As Chapter 2 has outlined, the institutional settings in which policies are promoted and the structural resonance of the ENC with external actors constitute additional factors that may shape the strategic decisions of domestic governments to adopt EU policies or discard them. Likewise, preferential fit, the amount of capacity building and the application of incentives by external actors in the countries and policy sectors have been theoretically assumed to affect the cost-benefit analysis of domestic governments to favor or reject EU policies. The next section discusses the explanatory power of each of these factors.

Institutional setting

Institutions form the strategic setting in which actors can pursue their preferences. They represent constraints and opportunities, equipping actors with information or material resources to seize opportunities, or depriving them of room to manoeuver via the institutionalization of rules and the potential of monitoring (cf. Börzel and Risse 2000).

Rule codification

In this vein, states are assumed to be more likely to comply with external rules, the more specific and binding rules are (Lavenex and Schimmelfennig 2009). As a result, a stronger codification of EU policies would lead to the expectation of increased patterns of compliance. The codification hypothesis should also apply to policies that are promoted by Russia. Prior to the institutionalization of the EEU, this happened predominantly in the framework of the CIS. Unlike the EEU (Dragneva and Wolczuk 2012), however, the CIS has produced an immense amount of paperwork and common decisions, but lacks any mechanism or authority to enforce decisions and exert direct effects in its member states (Donaldson and Nogee 2009): all decisions require unanimity of those voting, while any CIS country is free not to vote. Even those countries that formally back a decision at CIS meetings are not bound to comply with it. Unlike EU member states, the CIS countries thus do not engage in a transfer of sovereignty to the regional level, and 'as a matter of practice, most of the decisions reached have not been put into effect' (Donaldson and Nogee 2009: 165). The weakest form of rule codification requires at least the commitment to the adoption of policies in the states that are parties to an agreement. As the CIS lacks this feature and Russia does not have a formal neighborhood policy corresponding to the ENP Action Plans (Krastev and Leonard 2010: 40; Wilson and Popescu 2009: 318), a similar compliance-enhancing mechanism resulting from codification is unlikely to emerge for Russian or CIS rules. The next section elaborates on the codification of EU policies in the sectors of JLS and energy only, and investigates their explanatory power for the cases at hand, while the codification of CIS rules can be considered weak at best.

In the sector of JLS, a mélange of bilateral, EU codified and international conventions are referred to by the ENP Action Plans and the PCA (European Commission 2006b, 2006c; European Communities 1999a, 1999b), resulting in overall medium degrees of rule codification. In the area of money laundering, the ENP AP refer to the 2005 CoE Convention on Laundering, Search, Seizure and Confiscation of the Proceeds from Crime and on the Financing of Terrorism, and endeavors of the third countries that need to be implemented. No reference to the EU acquis is made, resulting in medium degrees of codification in this sub-category. Border management fully relies on the implementation of policies that are codified in the domestic context only, such as establishing cooperation mechanisms between the relevant national law enforcement agencies. Georgia's AP provides for more detailed descriptions of actions to be undertaken with a view to border management, but these remain limited to the national context and fail to make any references to EU or international law. Thus, they do not increase the rule codification in the case of Georgia. Strong degrees of codification are noticeable in the area of migration and asylum. The ENP AP of both countries refer to the 1951 Geneva Convention and the 1967 Protocol and ask the ENC to bring their national legislation on asylum and refugees in line with EU and international standards. This relates to the procedures concerning the treatment of asylum applications, in particular.

In the area of trafficking in human beings and drugs the ENP AP refer to the 1988 UN Convention on Illicit Traffic in Narcotic Drugs and Psychotropic

Substances, the UN Convention against Transnational Organized Crime and its protocols, and the OSCE action plan to combat trafficking in human beings. As no reference to EU rules is made, the borrowing of rules from international organizations hence leaves this area with a medium degree of codification, too. Lastly, this degree of legalization also shapes the clauses on police and judicial cooperation, which refer to the Second Protocol to the European Convention on Mutual Assistance in Criminal Matters and the 1980 Hague Convention on Civil Aspects of International Child Abduction. The ENC are also asked to implement the 1981 CoE Convention for the Protection of Individuals with regard to Automatic Processing of Personal Data, but the AP fail to make any reference to the EU acquis in this sub-category. The area of JLS is thus marked predominantly by medium degrees of rule codification for both Armenia and Georgia.

In the energy sector, the EU promotes the adoption of the acquis communautaire and bilateral rules, resulting once more in medium degrees of codification. First and foremost, the EU promotes regulatory convergence toward the EU acquis with a view to the electricity and gas markets and the regulation of independent, national energy regulatory commissions. In addition, it wants both Armenia and Georgia gradually to converge with EU policy objectives in the energy sector. Apart from references to the acquis in the area of regulatory convergence, no references are made to international law, leaving these policies with a medium level of codification. The diversification of energy supplies points to initiatives that should be taken by the ENC only, such as the development of action plans or energy infrastructure, and falls short of making any reference to either international or EU law. The issue area of diversification hence remains subject to a weak degree of rule codification. In the area of energy efficiency, the PCA refer to the Energy Charter Treaty Protocol on Energy Efficiency, which can be considered a piece of international law; however, no reference to any EU acquis is made. This results again in a medium degree of codification for this sub-category. Overall, the energy sector is thus marked by a predominantly medium codification of rules for both Armenia and Georgia.

In a nutshell, both the energy and the JLS sector are marked by medium degrees of codification in both countries, while the degree of codification of CIS rules can be considered comparatively weak. As a result, these findings suggest that the differences in compliance patterns between the countries and sectors under scrutiny do not go back to variation in the codification of rules, while they may indeed contribute to the general transfer of EU policies to the ENC despite a high dependence on Russia.

Institutionalization

As Chapter 2 has shown, different forms of national, regional or international institutionalization of EU policies have been identified to facilitate policy transfer (Lavenex and Schimmelfennig 2009), either due to increased interaction and socialization of mid-level officials in transgovernmental networks, or – in a more rationalist setting – due to the opportunities to gain access to information and material resources.

In the area of JLS, the institutionalization of EU policies is strong. Many bilateral and EU-dominated regional organizations promote the policies that have been stipulated in the ENP AP and PCA. *Bilaterally*, the Cooperation Council has been established with the PCA as an intergovernmental forum to discuss JLS issues among others. In addition, in the framework of the ENP, the EU established so-called JLS sub-committees. These are designed for bilateral dialogue on JLS issues only and were set up in 2008 in Georgia and in 2010 in Armenia.

Regionally, the EU has a substantial number of organizations in place that cover all aspects of JLS issues ranging from money laundering, border and migration management, to instances of trafficking and police and judicial cooperation. First, the CoE provides for institutionalized cooperation in the fight against money laundering, organized crime, drug trafficking and migration issues. While its founding members were EU member states only, Russia, Armenia and Georgia have become members to the CoE in 1996, 2001 and 1999, too. Moneyval is a sub-organization of the CoE, of which Georgia, Armenia and Russia are members. It monitors the implementation of anti-money-laundering legislation.

In addition, the issue area of border management has been prominently included in the EU's regional Eastern Partnership Initiative and figures as one of its flagship initiatives. Migration and asylum issues have been additionally covered by three EU-led dialogues: the Söderköping, Budapest and Prague processes.

The Söderköping process (UNHCR et al. 2012), which Armenia and Georgia joined in April 2011, is a platform for new Eastern EU member states and their neighbors, focusing on issues of migration, asylum and border management. It is clearly an EU-led initiative, receives its funding from EU member states, and promotes the takeover of migration-related acquis provisions to non-EU member states (UNHCR et al. 2012). Russia is not participating in this process. In addition, the Budapest process is an intergovernmental dialogue which aims to spread best practices in the areas of migration and asylum, visas, border management, trafficking and readmission procedures (ICMPD 2012). It was initiated by Germany in 1991, and Armenia and Georgia, as well as Russia and Eurasian organizations, are members of it. Russia, Armenia and Georgia are also part of the Prague process, which came into being in 2009 to promote migration partnerships between the EU members and Schengen countries, and Southeast and Eastern Europe, Central Asia and Turkey. Finally, a Panel on Migration and Asylum has been established in the framework of the Eastern Partnership promoting cooperation and information exchange in migration matters on a regional level (European Commission 2012e).

Again, there are few institutionalized Russian-dominated frameworks for cooperation on JLS-related matters with Georgia and Armenia, while Russia does participate in European ones, as shown above. *Bilaterally*, no institutions have been created with Georgia and Armenia. The Russian Federal Migration Service operates in Armenia, but it does not engage in institutionalized political dialogues, but rather implements specific projects on a case-by-case basis. *Regionally*, all JLS-related issues have been integrated into the CIS framework. Border management, drug trafficking, organized crime, human trafficking and migration are discussed in the respective CIS councils and forums, such as the Council of Heads of Migration Bodies of the CIS. Armenia is slightly more included in Russian-dominated regional forums in the area of JLS. First, Georgia quit the CIS in 2009 due to the war with Russia in August 2008. In addition, only Armenia is part of the CSTO which has also addressed JLS issues; however, it does not affect the overall pattern of medium institutionalization in this area.

In the area of energy, EU policies are also strongly institutionalized. *Bilaterally*, the Cooperation Council that was established with the partner countries serves as a forum in the framework of the PCA. After the initiation of the ENP, the EU also institutionalized sub-committees on nuclear safety, transport, the environment, and energy, which specifically address energy policy cooperation of the EU and the ENC. Those sub-committees convened for the first time with Georgia and Armenia in October 2010. *Regionally*, EU-controlled institutions work toward the adoption of EU rules in this policy area, too. The INOGATE Program that started operation in the mid-1990s addresses the three issue areas of the ENP AP. INOGATE stands for 'Interstate Oil and Gas Transport to Europe', and was less concerned with renewable energy and market convergence at the beginning, but rather with energy security in the oil and gas sectors. Regulatory convergence towards EU rules, renewable energy development and the diversification of supplies were first introduced into the INOGATE roadmap developed in 2006. This reflected the results of an interministerial conference in Baku of EU, Caspian, Black Sea and littoral states in 2004 which gave birth to the Baku Initiative, a form of political dialogue between these states and their neighbors. Both Armenia and Georgia are members of the initiative which promotes regulatory convergence toward EU rules, renewable energy development, and the security of energy production, transportation and supplies. Russia holds only observer status to the initiative. In the aftermath of the conference in Baku in 2004 that led to the Baku Declaration and the establishment of the Baku Initiative as such, the Russian representatives 'express[ed] reservation of their attitude towards the Conclusions and attached Concept Paper' (European Commission 2004b).

Another institution that promotes the EU's market rules, diversification of supply and the development of renewable energy is the Energy Community. It was established in July 2006 and formulates as one of its goals to extend 'the EU internal energy market to South East Europe and beyond on the ground of legally binding framework' (Energy Community 2012). Contracting parties, which can be non-EU member states, have to take over the EU acquis in the area of energy efficiency, renewable energy, electricity and gas markets and the environment. They also commit to the implementation of specific security of supply legislation and a dispute settlement mechanism to enforce the Community legislation. The Energy Community is hence a clearly EU-dominated regional framework, which intends to spread the EU acquis beyond its borders. Both Georgia and Armenia have been observers to the Energy Community. Georgia has held this status since December 2007 and applied for full membership in January 2013, while Armenia has been an observer since October 2011. Russia does not participate in this initiative.

In addition to the regionally organized Energy Community, the EU established the Black Sea Synergy Initiative in 2008, as a complementary institutionalized form of regional cooperation to the primarily bilaterally organized ENP. The Black Sea Synergy is a multi-issue framework of cooperation, and deals with energy matters among others. It encourages membership in the Energy Community and the takeover of the acquis in this area, but also fosters regional cooperation on infrastructural projects. Armenia and Georgia, as well as Russia, have been included in this initiative. Russia, however, has again been reluctant to join statements of the initiative, preferring agreements between the EU and less EU-dominated organizations, such as the Organization of the Black Sea Economic Cooperation (BSEC) (European Commission 2008d). Finally, the Eastern Partnership Platform on Energy Security provides for a regionally institutionalized dialogue (Council of the European Union 2009a).

The institutionalization of Russian-dominated forums is again limited to the CIS, which provides for regular meetings of the CIS-Electric Council, the Economic Council and the Intergovernmental Committee for Oil and Gas that address energy issues. Beyond the CIS framework, Russia largely falls short of providing alternative regional or bilateral frameworks to institutionalize energy cooperation with either Georgia or Armenia.

Yet, in the realm of energy, both Armenia and Georgia have also participated in forums dominated by neither Russian nor the EU – one of which is the above-mentioned BSEC. BSEC was initiated in 1992 and deals with trade, economic and energy cooperation between the Black Sea and littoral states, including Armenia, Georgia and Russia, but also EU members such as Greece, Romania and Bulgaria (BSEC Permanent International Secretariat 2010).

Another forum of third countries that includes Georgia only is the GUAM, which is an international organization established by Georgia, Ukraine, Azerbaijan and Moldova. Founded in 1997, it was revived in 2005 after the colored revolutions in Ukraine and Georgia. Its charter envisages cooperation on energy diversification among other issues. Despite the fact that GUAM has been considered to lack structure, resources and activism particularly after the war in 2008 (cf. Sakwa 2010: 209ff.; Schulze 2008: 176), Georgia might be subject to additional learning and socialization processes via this forum. I hence also find a strong pattern of institutionalization of energy policies for the EU and its externally promoted rules, while the institutional framework provided by Russia is less dense.

In summary, both policy sectors display a strong degree of institutionalization of EU policies in both countries, and medium degrees of institutionalization with regard to Russian/CIS policies. The fact that Russia participates frequently in EU-dominated forums in the JLS sphere, while it refuses to do so with a view to energy policy, hints once more at an underlying policy convergence between the EU and Russia in the former issue area. The strong institutionalization of EU policies is likely to contribute to the fact that EU policies indeed travel to the Eastern neighborhood. However, as there is no variation between the patterns of EU institutionalization between the ENC and across sectors, it cannot account for the variation in compliance patterns of the cases at hand.

Internationalization

The internationalization of policies is considered to enhance the monitoring efforts of individual external actors, their capacity-building activities and the legitimacy of the policies they promote, all of which are likely to facilitate EU policy transfer.

Just as dense as the institutionalization in both issue areas is the internationalization of the EU policies which are promoted by a plethora of international actors that are engaged in the Caucasian region. For the issue area of JLS, the EU promotes its policies with the backing of the other international organizations, national development agencies and private humanitarian organizations. In the area of border management, the EU efforts have been supported internationally by single EU member states in Georgia (European Commission 2011c) and international organizations, such as the International Organization for Migration (IOM) and the OSCE in Armenia. Issues of migration and readmission have been tackled internationally as well. Finland, France, Germany, Slovenia and Poland provide assistance to Georgia, while Finland and IOM are engaged in Armenia (European Commission 2011b, 2011c). The Swiss Federal Office for Migration is also providing assistance for the reintegration of readmitted people to both countries.[13] Refugee issues are dealt with by France, Norway and IOM in Armenia, and Germany, Poland, Norway and Sweden in Georgia (European Commission 2011b, 2011c). With regard to migration and refugees also (non-)governmental organizations are involved in both countries, especially the Danish Refugee Council and the UN High Commissioner for Refugees (UNHCR) (European Commission 2003b, 2007b; Gevorgyan 2008).

Organized crime and police and judicial cooperation are subject to cooperation by both Armenia and Georgia with EU member states, non-EU member states and international organizations. Norway and Italy cooperate on these issue areas in the case of Armenia, and the USA in the case of Georgia (European Commission 2011b, 2011c). Additionally, the OSCE has been engaged in anti-trafficking policies in the region (European Commission 2007b). Russia, however, is not engaged in development assistance or any further provision of JLS policies beyond the framework of the CIS. It closely cooperates with IOM and OSCE in JLS issues, but does not have any specific international organizations beyond the above-mentioned that would additionally back the policies promoted in the CIS framework.

The international backing for EU policy promotion is substantial in the sphere of energy policies. First and foremost, the World Bank and the IMF have been active in the region since the mid-1990s (European Commission 2007b, 2007d: 36). They have been engaged in restructuring the energy sector in Georgia and Armenia, promoting regulatory reforms such as the establishment of independent regulatory bodies, and have made this a conditional for the provision of further financial assistance (Sargsyan et al. 2006: 40). Another international organization that supports the development of renewable energies is the International Renewable Energy Agency (IRENA), to which Armenia and Georgia are signatories. The International Energy Agency (IEA) is also providing information on renewable energy and energy efficiency while its *raison d'être* used to be work on energy security.

In addition to international organizations, EU member states and non-members promote ENP-related reform in the energy sector. In Armenia, France, Greece and Germany have been active in this regard, the latter being active in Georgia as well (European Commission 2011b, 2011c). The German federal government has also been engaged in the reform of the energy sector (European Commission 2007b, 2007d). As non-EU member states, Norway and the USA have shown increasing interest in the region. Particularly, the US government promotes renewable energy, energy efficiency and energy security as well as market reforms in the Southern Caucasus under its bilateral assistance schemes and the Millennium Challenge Corporation (European Commission 2007d: 37). In addition to states and international organizations, development banks have lent financial support to reform processes in both countries. The European Bank for Reconstruction and Development (EBRD) and the German Development Bank (KfW) are cases in point. Russia's policy in both countries is backed by Russian companies, which at times also operate internationally and expand in the region. Yet no other forms of other classical international organizations are involved.

Hence, EU policies enjoy the support of other EU- and non-EU players on the international level and can thus be considered strongly internationalized in both issue areas. As opposed to EU policies, there is no international organization promoting CIS policies beyond the organization itself. Patterns of internationalization may thus account for the overall transfer of EU rules despite the fact that high degrees of dependence of the ENC on Russia prevail in both sectors, but it cannot explain why rules travel differently across sectors and countries.

To conclude, the institutional features of externally promoted policies are much more developed in the case of the EU than of Russia. Medium degrees of codification and high degrees of institutionalization and internationalization of EU policies are challenged by little to no codification and internationalization on the side of Russia, while the institutionalization of Russian-dominated forums remains medium. These findings back the hypothesis that institutionalist factors support processes of external policy transfer in general and may account for the fact that EU policies indeed travel to ENC despite their strong dependence on Russia in the respective policy sectors. Yet, as there is no variation in patterns of institutionalization, codification and internationalization between the ENC and across the considered policy sectors, they fail to explain the cross-country and cross-sectoral variation for the cases at hand. Hence, the next section investigates to what extent this might be accomplished by scrutinizing the compatibility of domestic structures of the ENC, the EU and Russia.

Domestic resonance

As Chapter 2 has shown, EU policies are the more likely to travel to the neighborhood, the better they resonate with the domestic structure that prevails in the target country (Lavenex and Schimmelfennig 2009). Domestic governments may either look for policy solutions in seemingly similar countries, or are confronted with fewer adaptation costs due to the compatibility of their domestic structures with the context from which the policy is imported. So how do Armenia's and Georgia's political-administrative systems and their market economies fit those of the EU or Russia?

The rule of law

Democracy and the rule of law not only figure in the Copenhagen Criteria for accession countries to the EU, but are also likely to increase the effectiveness of policy transfer to the neighborhood (Lavenex and Schimmelfennig 2009: 804). This is particularly true for the JLS sector, which also entails notions of good governance and the rule of law. Yet, as data from the World Bank's governance indicators suggest, there is a significant incompatibility between the ENC and the EU in this regard (Figure 3.5).

As Figure 3.5 shows, Russia and the EU define the two poles of the rule of law score. Apart from 1999 to 2003, when Georgia at times scores worse than Russia, the latter is demarcating the bottom line of the rule of law measurement, while the average of EU countries is ranging at the top end of the scale. The minor downgrading of the EU average strongly correlates with the enlargement rounds of 2004 and 2007. Comparing the scores of Georgia and Armenia, a relatively low but stable performance is identifiable in the case of Armenia, while Georgia, starting from a lower position, improved more drastically over time. Both Armenia and Georgia have figured roughly at the same value since 2005, with reports continuously citing numerous incidents of government interference in the judiciary, arbitrary police arrests and abuse of governmental authority (Freedom House 2011a, 2011b). Hence, both display a significant lack of resonance in terms of rule of law measurement vis-à-vis EU countries. In addition, despite improvements in their ratings over time, in

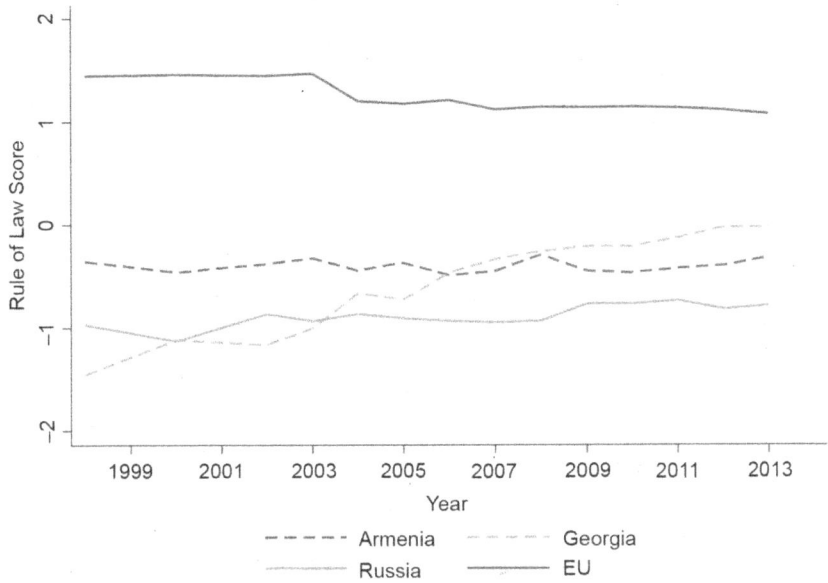

Figure 3.5 Governance Indicators, Rule of Law score
Note: For this and the following figures, the EU average has been calculated by aggregating the data of individual EU member states, accounting for variation in membership patterns over time.
Source: author's illustration, based on World Bank 2014.

Georgia particularly due to its lower starting point, they are still both closer to Russia's rule of law scores that to those of the EU.

Economic freedom and transition to a market economy

Economic openness has been considered another important precondition for EU policies to travel, which may be of particular importance for policy transfer processes in the field of energy policies, the economic sector under scrutiny in this book. Armenia and Georgia qualified as growing economies prior to the financial crisis in 2009, on a double-digit level at times (EIU 2003c; European Commission 2009a: 6). Armenia in particular proved one of the strongest reformers in the region, going back to the implementation of macro-economic reforms, privatization programs and a rather transparent legal market framework in the early 1990s (BTI 2003). In Georgia, the process of *de facto* market reform implementation started later, especially with the takeover of power of Mikheil Saakashvili, who formed a government of liberal economic reformers (BTI 2006; European Stability Initiative 2010a). The Heritage Foundation's data suggest a high compatibility of the economic openness in both the EU and the ENC (Figure 3.6). This conclusion is also

76 *Constraining EU policy transfer?*

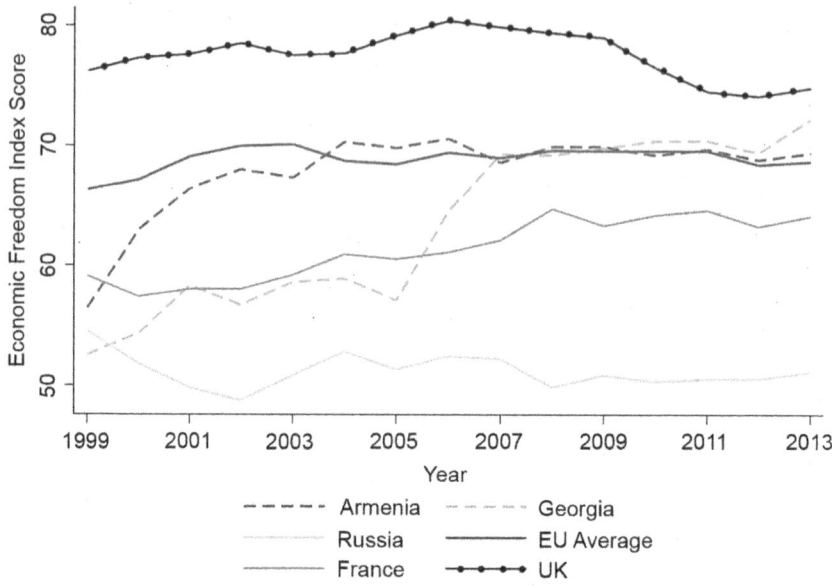

Figure 3.6 Comparative Economic Freedom Index score, 1999–2013
Note: The Economic Freedom Index scores for EU members have been aggregated respecting changes in membership patterns over time.
Source: author's illustration, based on The Heritage Foundation 2015.

supposed to be valid over time, taking into consideration the large differences between individual member states, as shown in the example of France and the UK. According to the Heritage Foundation's index, the economic freedom prevailing in the ENC can hence be considered compatible with the EU's economic freedom on average, particularly from 2006 onwards.

The index, however, falls short of providing information on the general transition of the countries to market economies beyond the openness for trade and businesses.[14] Both economies are still struggling with high degrees of unemployment, poverty and the limited access of a broader population to the economy, which has been *de facto* controlled by a small elite in Georgia and the so-called oligarchs in Armenia (BTI 2003, 2006). In addition, the prevailing elite corruption in Georgia and widespread bribery in Armenia hamper or subvert the application of legal frameworks.

As the BTI data (Table 3.2) show, both countries still do much worse with regard to sustainable socio-economic development than the EU proxy, the Czech Republic, and are fairly close to Russia's scores, which again figure at the opposite side of the scale that ranges from 1 (worst) to 10 (best).

Russia, Armenia and Georgia can hence be considered to approximately rank in the same group of countries on the borderline of the BTI label 'countries with deficiencies in market-based democracy' and 'good prospects for market-based consolidation' (Bertelsmann Foundation 2006). While Georgia

Table 3.2 BTI Status Index scores, Transformation to Market Economy

	Armenia	Georgia	Russia	Czech Republic
2003	6.29	3.71	6.00	9.14
2006	6.43	5.36	6.57	9.00
2008	6.82	6.36	6.54	9.57
2010	6.50	6.00	6.14	9.50
2012	5.93	5.61	6.11	9.57
2014	6.07	5.82	6.07	9.43

Data source: Bertelsmann Foundation 2015.

and Armenia thus display a significant lack of resonance with the overall economic structures of EU markets, the data suggest that they share similar degrees of economic freedom.

State capacity

A relatively high degree of state capacity is one of the features that EU member states have in common and which supposedly facilitates the effectiveness of EU policy transfer in the neighborhood (Lavenex and Schimmelfennig 2009). The ENC have usually been characterized as weak states (Börzel 2010), displaying significantly less capacity to govern than their Western and Central European counterparts. This is confirmed by the World Bank data on regulatory quality, government effectiveness and the control of corruption (Figures 3.7, 3.8 and 3.9). The indicators show similar patterns for the ENC in all three issue areas. First, the performances of Armenia and Georgia are on average closer to that of Russia than the EU. Second, Armenia and Georgia increased their state capacities over time, while they share a similarly low starting point in 1999. Armenia, however, shows overall better and rather stable scores in the early 2000s in all three indicators and thus qualifies as stronger in regulatory terms than Georgia during the Shevardnadze period (Way and Levitsky 2006). With Saakashvili coming to power, Georgia managed to strengthen its state capacities by rooting out day-to-day corruption, integrating the formerly uncontrolled region of Adjaria, and by building a modern army and infrastructure (Cheterian 2009: 158). Since 2004, it has started to outdo Armenia in its regulatory quality, government effectiveness and control of corruption, even though elite corruption and a 'deep-rooted culture of distrust and clientelism' could not be rooted out (BTI 2008).

Both countries hence have the capacity to govern outwardly, which lies in their overall dominance of domestic executives, a functioning, loyal military apparatus and a weak opposition (Cheterian 2009; Way and Levitsky 2006). Despite the differences over time, their overall weakness in comparison to the EU, their semi-authoritarian outward state capacity mixed with internal

78 *Constraining EU policy transfer?*

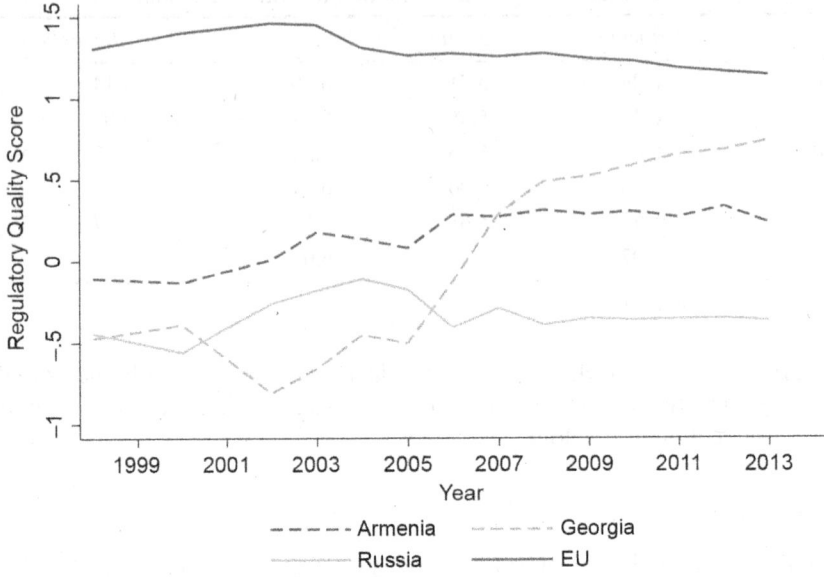

Figure 3.7 Governance Indicators, Regulatory Quality score
Source: author's illustration, based on World Bank 2014.

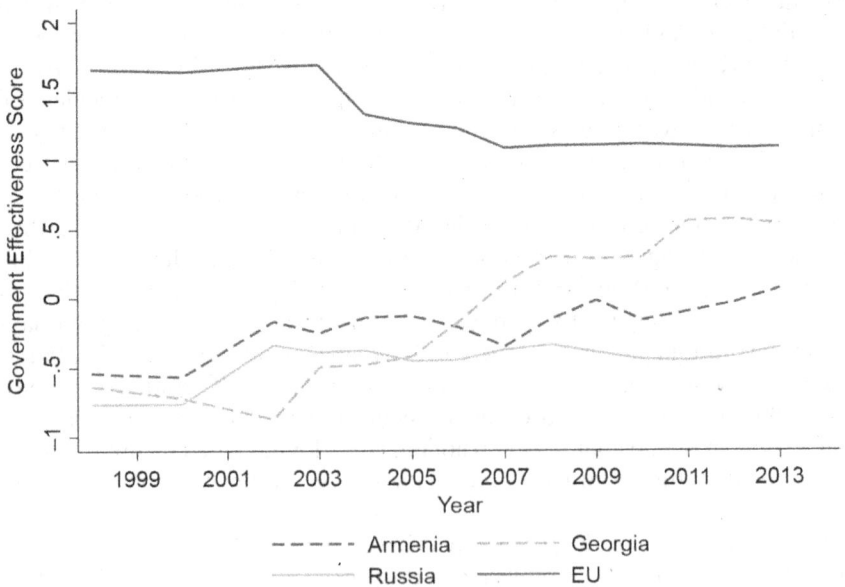

Figure 3.8 Governance Indicators, Government Effectiveness score
Source: author's illustration, based on World Bank 2014.

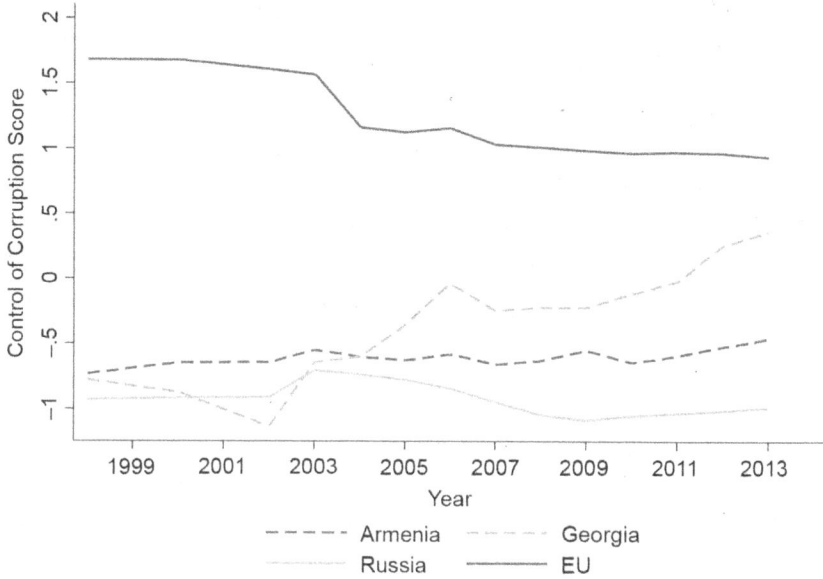

Figure 3.9 Governance Indicators, Control of Corruption score
Source: author's illustration, based on World Bank 2014.

weaknesses, and their mostly greater similarity with Russia still render the two countries largely comparable with regard to their structural differences in state capacity in comparison to the EU average.

Taken together, this section has shown that Armenia's and Georgia's domestic structures figure in between the two poles of Russia and the EU, with a tendency to resonate better with their Russian than their European counterparts. Concerning the degree of rule of law, both countries continuously display poor levels of rule-of-law scores as measured by the World Bank governance indicators. This may generally account for an unsatisfactory performance in the area of JLS which is more closely related to provision of democratic governance than the economy-related energy sector. Insights of the Heritage Foundation Index support this suggestion, as they show a high degree of convergence of the ENC and the EU with regard to economic freedom which correlates with a good compliance record in the energy sector.

State capacity and the degree of transition to a market economy are similarly low in both countries, with some variations between the ENC over time. All in all, the domestic resonance may thus account for the overall variation of compliance across sectors, but it cannot capture the cross-country variation between Georgia and Armenia. This is particularly true if we compare the differences between Armenia's and Georgia's rule of law, transition to a market economy and state capacity. Since 2006, Armenia has mostly scored slightly worse with a view to the rule of law and its state capacity, but still receives better JLS compliance ratings. In contrast to this, Georgia has long lagged behind with regard to economic freedom and has been similarly ranked to Armenia since 2006, while Armenia outdoes Georgia with a view to the transition to a market economy. Yet, Georgia displays better compliance patterns in the energy sector.

External incentives and domestic agents

Can this variation be better explained by more agency-related variables? In order to answer this question, the next section maps the provision of capacity and external incentives by the EU and Russia, and assesses the preferential fit or misfit that prevails in Georgia and Armenia.

Capacity building

Capacity building by the EU is considered to affect positively the choices of domestic governments toward compliance with the ENP by empowering reform-minded actors or allowing domestic actors to act strategically in the first place (Andonova 2008; Chayes and Chayes 1993). If provided via transgovernmental networks, it may also facilitate socialization processes (Freyburg 2012), but also Russia may provide alternative or additional capacity to the ENC.

Since the breakup of the Soviet Union and until 2007, the majority of EU assistance to its Eastern neighborhood had been provided under the umbrella of the Technical Assistance to the Commonwealth of Independent States (TACIS). In 2007, TACIS was replaced by the European Neighborhood and Partnership Instrument (ENPI). From 2014 onward, funding has been provided via the European Neighborhood Instrument (ENI). Bilateral assistance has been delivered via different programs, such as the Food Security Program, the European Community Humanitarian Office, the European Initiative for Democracy and Human Rights, and Rehabilitation and Macro-financial Assistance. The national contributions of the European Community to Armenia amounted to roughly €630 million from 1991 to 2013 (European Commission 2007b, 2007c, 2011b). For Georgia, this amount has been significantly higher, exceeding €800 million for the period 1992 to 2013 (European Commission 2007d, 2007e, 2011c). The higher levels of assistance to Georgia were predominantly a result of the Rose Revolution in 2003 and the August war with Russia in 2008. A donor's conference in 2004 made the European Community pledge of €125 million, which signified a doubling of its total assistance to Georgia for the period 2004 to 2006 in comparison to the previous period (European Commission 2007d). After the 2008 war with Russia, the EU allocated up to €500 million as support to the Georgian government (Delegation of the EU to Georgia 2012b). Despite these obvious differences in overall national allocations, much of the financial assistance within the two sectors under scrutiny has been distributed primarily through regional ENPI programs or via the Development Cooperation Instrument (DCI) and its thematic programs, which is compared in greater detail below.

As opposed to the EU, Russia only started its rebirth from a primarily assistance-receiving to an assistance-granting country in 2004, mainly as a reaction to its commitments made under the G8. Since then, its development assistance has been channeled through bilateral and multilateral channels and focused on health and food security, but also on energy and education issues (Provost 2012; Wierzbowska-Miazga and Kaczmarski 2011; World Bank 2013). However, systematic information on specific sectoral assistance by Russia is scarce (Larionova et al. 2014: 24). Programmatic capacity-building efforts of the EU in Georgia and Armenia are hence compared with and complemented by information from different sources on specific sectoral capacity building of the Russian state or state-led companies wherever applicable.

Under the heading of JLS, Georgia and Armenia have profited from financial and technical assistance provided through a diverse set of EU instruments.[15] First, national and regional TACIS and later ENPI allocations have targeted JLS-related issues. The thematic program of migration and asylum, formerly AENEAS, provided for additional migration-related capacity building.

Both Armenia and Georgia were assisted in the setup of integrated border management systems in 2007, and in 2011 when integrated border management was declared one of the flagship initiatives in the Eastern Partnership. In addition, regional programs addressed drug trafficking in the Southern Caucasus Anti-Drug Program, as well as the fight against organized crime and trafficking in persons. Migration management and the prevention of illegal migration were especially targeted by DCI thematic programs. They supported legal migration through capacity building, the Prague process and overall migration management initiatives in both Armenia and Georgia. Yet, until 2011 Georgia was awarded with more funding under these thematic budget lines due to its early visa facilitation and readmission agreements with the EU, and also received some individual assistance for reintegration purposes. Armenia profited from additional support for governance of labor management in cooperation with Russia and for migration policy development in 2005.

Nationally, Twinning and TAIEX facilities were set up for the implementation of ENP Action Plan provisions entailing legal approximation and policy development in the area of JLS in Georgia and Armenia, with only small differences in the amount of funding. A difference between Georgia and Armenia in national allocations has mostly shown under the TACIS and ENPI umbrella due to allocations to Georgia that addressed the aggravated situation of IDPs as a cause of its internal conflicts and the August war with Russia in 2008. Since 2011 Armenia and Georgia have received support to facilitate the implementation of the new bilateral agreements with the EU, especially in the framework of the EU's Comprehensive Institution Building Program – also in the area of JLS (European Commission 2012a, 2012b, 2013b, 2013c). While the EU's support with regard to the implementation of the DCFTA was withdrawn after Armenia's decision to join the Eurasian Customs Union in 2013, support for the implementation of visa facilitation and readmission agreements was kept in place (European Commission 2013a).

Unlike Georgia, Armenia has been rewarded with some capacity building by Russia. Russian border guards operate at the outer CIS border of Armenia with Turkey and Iran, providing operational capacity to their Armenian colleagues (Nygren 2008: 115; RFE/RL 2012a). They also operated in Georgia in the past, but left the country in 1999 (Nygren 2008: 266). Additionally, the Police of the Republic of Armenia implemented awareness-raising campaigns in 2005 and 2006 jointly with the embassy of the Russian Federation in Armenia and the Russian Federal Service for Migration. It aimed at informing Armenian citizens about the migration situation in Russia (Gevorgyan 2008: 28f.). Similarly, Russia started to operate its so-called Compatriots Program in 2009 which provided legal work opportunities for Armenians wishing to migrate permanently to Russia (Grigoryan 2011b).

In the policy area of energy, both Georgia and Armenia have been subject to diverse sources of capacity building. First, national allocations under the TACIS and later the ENPI annual action plans have addressed energy as an issue area. Second, energy was on the agenda of regional TACIS and ENPI funding, predominantly via the INOGATE program. Third, both Armenia and Georgia have been subject to financial and technical assistance under the umbrella of the DCI thematic program, 'Environment and sustainable management of natural resources including energy'. In addition, the Nuclear Safety Cooperation Instrument that used to be called TACIS Nuclear Safety provides for capacity building in the energy sector (European Commission 2012f). Finally, the Neighborhood Investment Facility (NIF) is a financial mechanism to support capital-intense infrastructural projects in the neighborhood by bringing together grants from the European Commission, EU member states and European or international financial institutions, such as the EBRD, the European Investment Bank (EIB) or the KfW (European Commission 2012g; European Investment Bank 2011a). Thus, the sheer access to sources of funding, as in the JLS area, has been the same for Armenia and Georgia.

When comparing the *de facto* provision of financial and technical assistance in the countries under scrutiny, variation prevails in some of the issue areas that are targeted by funding in the energy sector. Georgia has been subject to intense funding in the area of infrastructure projects via the NIF, national and regional ENP and TACIS allocations. While the NIF was used in Armenia, amongst others, to facilitate the Yerevan metro construction and a water municipality project, it particularly addressed energy infrastructure in Georgia (European Commission 2012g, 2013e). In total, national support to Georgia in the area of energy via the NIF amounted to €21 million from 2008 to 2013, while there has been no specific national support to Armenia in this area (European Commission 2013e: 31). For instance, the NIF contributed to the rehabilitation of the Enguri hydropower cascade located at the Georgian border to Abkhazia. Earlier stages of the project had been financed with TACIS and ENPI national allocations in 2004, 2007, 2008 and 2011, and were running under the heading of confidence-building measures in the Abkhaz–Georgian border region. In addition, Georgia only had been subject to a pre-investment project in 2008 under the ENPI regional programs that dealt with the Trans-Caspian Gas Corridor. A second area of variation is nuclear safety, in which Armenia has received significantly more funding than Georgia. The assistance especially consisted of capacity building for the national regulator as well as on-site assistance to enable a safe operation and an early decommissioning of the Soviet-style Medzamor nuclear power plant.

Apart from these differences, though, the assistance provided under national, regional and thematic programs targeting energy diversification, regulatory convergence and renewable energy, and energy efficiency development displays little variation between the countries. Nationally, Twinning and TAIEX facilities were set up for the implementation of ENP Action Plan provisions entailing regulatory convergence and legal approximation in the energy sectors of Georgia and Armenia, with only a little difference in the amount of funding. In addition, energy diversification and security as well as energy efficiency and renewable energy development were supported by the INOGATE regional funds and the DCI energy program, which comprised assistance provision to both Georgia and Armenia.

Russia, as opposed to the EU, does not have instruments at its disposal to engage in external capacity building of a non-commercial and unconditional nature in the energy sector. Yet, the energy sectors of both countries largely profit from significant degrees of FDI from Russian companies (Soghomonyan 2007: 45). While these do not qualify as forms of unconditional assistance, they may still exert a capacity-enhancing effect on the energy sector and constitute functional equivalents.

Georgia has profited from slightly more EU capacity building than Armenia in both areas, with the exception of assistance provision for Armenia's nuclear safety. Russia, in contrast, has not provided any form of overall assistance to the ENC apart from smaller projects that it undertook in Armenia in the realm of JLS policies and commercial operations in the energy sector. The greater provision of assistance by Russia to Armenia correlates with its better compliance outcome in the area of JLS. Yet, in spite of higher amounts of EU capacity building in the area of JLS in Georgia, especially until 2011, it has scored worse with a view to compliance in this policy field during this time and only managed to catch up later on. Similarly, Armenia performs particularly poorly in areas in which it has received most of its funding, i.e. in the decommissioning of the nuclear power plant. Hence, while the provision of capacity by external actors indeed varies among countries and policy sectors, it seemingly does not provide a consistent explanation in itself as to why EU policies travel better to some countries and issue areas than to others.

External incentives

Chapter 2 has argued that both the EU and Russia may render the adoption and implementation of the ENP more costly or beneficial by linking specific positive or negative incentives to the respective (non-)compliance outcomes. The EU complements threats to suspend bilateral agreements, to freeze assistance payments or impose visa bans with policy-specific, positive conditionalities linked to the opening of the Single Market for ENCs' products or a simplification of visa regimes (Börzel and Pamuk 2012: 83). Russia's incentives do not necessarily stem from programmatic or transparently communicated foreign policy commitments. They find expression in ad hoc foreign policy decisions. The next section thus discusses to what extent the EU and Russia have indeed applied policy conditionality and other incentives in Armenia's and Georgia's JLS and energy sector.

The EU applies policy conditionality in the JLS sector in order to exert its leverage in the ENC (Cassarino 2011). With the initiation of the ENP it offers an increase in mobility to the ENC, if they fulfill certain conditions in return. The first carrot attached to JLS reforms consists of visa facilitation, including a cheaper and simplified visa procedure for ENC citizens, who have been subject to strict and at times humiliating visa application procedures of EU member states. The reward of visa facilitation dates back to a Commission Communication on Strengthening the ENP in 2006. It defines visa facilitation as a reward granted to the ENC under conditions of progress in the JLS area, such as 'well-managed mobility and migration, addressing readmission, cooperation in fighting illegal immigration, and effective and efficient border management' (European Commission 2006a). This respects the Common Approach on Visa Facilitation of the Council of the EU, which in 2005 had already specified the conditions under which negotiations on visa facilitation should be considered (Council of the European Union 2005: 3). In the framework of the ENP, the substance of the respective visa facilitation agreement is also made conditional upon progress on JLS issues. The Council of the EU stated that it would consider ENC visa policies and the introduction of biometric passports to determine the scope of the visa facilitation agreement (Council of the European Union 2005: 3). In practice, particularly readmission agreements figure as a condition in the visa facilitation process.[16]

In addition to visa facilitation, the EU offers mobility partnerships to third countries that agree to cooperate on migration management and readmission. Mobility partnerships established an overall framework for managing migration movements, i.e. providing for increased study and work opportunities within the EU (European Commission 2007a). However, visa facilitation and mobility partnerships are only considered a first step toward increased mobility. Visa-free travel is the second one. In the framework of the EaP the EU extended its visa carrot also to comprise the prospect of potential full visa liberalization (European Commission 2008e). This has again been linked to specific policy conditions. Unlike the overall policy conditionality of visa facilitation, visa liberalization is linked to a precise set of reforms. A country-specific roadmap for reforms in the areas of 'document security; the fight against irregular migration, including readmission; public order issues, and external relation issues, including human rights of migrants and other vulnerable groups' has to be implemented by the ENC in order to be eligible for visa liberalization with the EU (European Commission 2008e: 6).

The opening of both visa facilitation and visa liberalization negotiations, however, depends on decisions of the Council of the EU taking into account also foreign policy prioritizations and security concerns. The Council needs to award the Commission with a negotiation mandate to start negotiations. Hence, while the policy conditionality is clearly formulated, the start of this progress is not only bound to domestic reform efforts.

Unlike the EU, Russia does not have a formal set of policy conditionalities in place. However, it has used its leverage on JLS issues resulting from legacies of CIS cooperation in the past and awarded Georgia and Armenia with positive and negative incentives, which, however, often remain decoupled from policy-specific demands. Russia and the CIS installed a visa-free regime within the CIS in 1992, which allowed all members to travel freely in CIS countries. In 2001, however, Russia unilaterally introduced visa requirements for Georgia, due to political tensions between the countries. The move was justified on the grounds of Georgia's failure to control its borders adequately, particularly in the Pankisi Gorge, in which Chechen terrorists were reportedly seeking shelter (EIU 2000b). The introduction of visa requirements was followed by several military actions by Russia in the area which supposedly targeted potential Chechen terrorists (EIU 2001b). The negative incentive structure was hence seemingly designed to sanction Georgia's poor border management and control.

In addition to the conditional provision of sanctions, Russia has also reverted to policy incentives in the JLS area, which lack a clear communication of related policy goals. Russia has used its possibilities to deport Georgian and even a larger population of Armenian migrant workers (Savvidis 2011). At the peak of the so-called Georgian-Russian spy crisis in 2006, in which Georgia arrested Russian officials on the grounds of espionage, Russia deported up to 2,000 Georgians from Russia (Hedenskog and Larsson 2007: 41; Khutsidze 2007). Russia also imposed an economic blockade and a visa ban on Georgia, and threatened to cut the cash flows of the Georgian migrants in Russia to their home countries (Schulze 2008: 189). The Russian foreign minister justified these steps on the grounds of Georgia's investment into military armament against its secessionist republics (Myers 2006). In addition, Russia started to distribute passports in Georgia's secessionist republics – a gesture that was presented as a humanitarian move to enable Abkhaz and South Ossetian citizens to travel internationally (Abushov 2009: 199). The international community evaluated this as open support for the secessionist regimes in the area (Schulze 2008). Thus, Russia sanctioned Georgia's stance towards its territorial integrity via policy sanctions in the JLS area, but these were not made conditional on clear policy changes, especially not in the area of JLS. In comparison to the application of policy conditionality by the EU in this area, Russia's provision or withholding of incentives is linked to few policy-specific provisions in Georgia, leaving Armenia largely untouched.

In the energy sector, the EU does not apply policy conditionalities, with few exceptions to the rule. The ENC are invited to join the EU's Energy Community, which is conditional upon the implementation of certain EU directives in the energy field. However, both Armenia and Georgia have only figured as observers to the Community for the period under investigation in this book, which leaves the potential conditionality without leverage. In addition, Armenia's nuclear plant – located in a seismic zone – has triggered concerns within the EU since the 1990s and the EU has asked for it to be closed (European Commission 2001). The EU linked the provision of €100 million for the development of alternative energies to the announcement of a binding early decommissioning date by the Armenian authorities (European Commission 2005a). Despite the fact that the EU falls short of announcing clear conditionalities in the sector, apart from the Medzamor issue, other international actors, i.e. the World Bank and the IMF, have provided for policy conditionalities since the mid-1990s in EU-promoted areas, such as the establishment of independent regulators, unbundling and the privatization of energy markets for both Armenia and Georgia.

Russia, however, has indeed used conditional benefits and sanctions to anchor its economic objectives in Armenia's and Georgia's energy sector. It has made use of its leverage with regard to subsidies on gas deliveries and high debts (Schulze 2008: 163) to penetrate the energy sectors of both countries. In 2001, for instance, Armenia was highly indebted to Russia due to its payments for and high dependence on Russian energy supplies. As Armenia was unable to cover its debt, periodic gas supply interruptions were the result. In June 2001 Armenia successfully negotiated an agreement that foresaw the debt beginning to be repaid by the end of 2001. Some of it, however, was transformed into joint venture investments in, among other things, the power sector and the Hrazdan thermal power plant of Armenia, which was taken over by Russia's state-led UES (EIU 2002, 2003a). A similar debt for equity swap occurred in 2003, at a time when Armenia had accumulated debts for nuclear fuel supplies from Russia amounting to $40 million. In mid-2003, the Medzamor nuclear power plant had to be stopped for a short period of time, and was only made operational again when the Armenians transferred the financial management of the power plant to Russia's UES (EIU 2003a). Likewise, in 2006 Russia increased its gas prices for deliveries to Armenia. In order partially to pay for this and prevent further price hikes, Armenia again transferred various energy assets to Russian companies and the state-led Gazprom took over control of the management of the Iranian–Armenian gas pipeline (Woehrel 2009). Over the years, Russian state-owned companies have thus made the release of debt or the waiving of gas price increases conditional on the provision of stakes in the gas and electricity markets, the majority share in large energy diversification projects and the financial control of Armenia's nuclear power plant.

In Georgia, Russia used similar conditionalities and unconditional negative incentives. In 1998, as in Armenia, Russia only resumed previously stopped gas supplies to Georgia after debt rescheduling agreements had been signed (Vertlib 1999: 158). In addition, energy infrastructure was severely affected by bombings of Russian military forces in Georgia's mountainous regions bordering Russia in 2002, which left the Enguri power plant and the Khadori hydropower plant damaged. In late 2005, Gazprom additionally announced a gas price increase. Shortly afterward, bombings of the pipelines by unknown saboteurs stopped the entire supply of Russian gas to Georgia. In November 2006, Russia threatened to cut supplies to Georgia fully, unless Georgia either agreed to sell its main gas pipeline to Russia or to accept a 100 percent increase in gas prices (Woehrel 2009). A second increase in gas prices in December 2006 marked an end of the subsidies that Russia had provided to the independent republics of the former Soviet Union in preferable tariffs after independence (Transparency International Georgia 2008b).

Georgia has thus been frequently subject to sanctions applied by Russia that targeted the ownership and functioning of infrastructure in gas and hydropower sectors and impacted on the structure of the Georgian energy market. Comparing the provision or withholding of conditional rewards and sanctions in this area, Russia clearly outdoes the EU. While the EU does not apply any policy conditionality toward the countries in the energy sphere except for Armenia's nuclear power plant, Armenia and Georgia are targeted by a variety of external incentives by Russia, which are frequently also linked to specific policy demands.

To sum up, the *de facto* application of policy conditionalities and other incentives to Georgia and Armenia by both the EU and Russia indeed varies considerably. Individually, however, it does not explain the compliance patterns at hand: in the case of energy policies, Russian policy conditionality is widespread, while EU conditionality partially targets Armenia, which displays worse compliance patterns than Georgia. Visa-free travel to the EU is clearly linked to conditions in the JLS area, which yet qualifies as a sector of overall poor compliance if compared to the energy sector.

Preferential fit

As theorized in Chapter 2, preferential fit is likely to matter in the process of compliance with EU policies. This is particularly true for Armenia and Georgia which lack institutionalized veto powers to constrain a highly powerful executive (Wheatley and Zürcher 2008), fall short of strongly developed political parties whose members rally behind party programs rather than charismatic leaders (Chiaberashvili and Tevzadze 2005: 189), and do not feature vivid civil societies.[17] In order to determine the preferential fit or misfit of EU policies by assessing the potential of intra-elite veto players in Armenia and Georgia, the following section is dedicated to scrutinizing the government-associated elite constellations in both countries. I present the actors who form the power base of Georgia's and Armenia's hybrid regimes, by reverting to Christoph Stefes's differentiation between the necessary co-optation of security forces, political and economic elites for stable hybridity (Stefes 2010: 32f.), while it also includes the dominant framings of incumbent regimes and their politics as a basis of discursive power.

ARMENIA

Ever since its independence in 1991 Armenia's hybridity has been stabilized by the incumbent's continuous stronghold on security and political forces, economic elites and the national unification project that has emerged around the 'Karabakh idea' (Stefes 2010: 33). An elite rupture occurred in 1998 with the rise to power of Robert Kocharyan, who succeeded Armenia's first post-independence president, Levon Ter-Petrosyan. Since then, the Armenian government has relied on political coalition partners representing the financially and politically influential Armenian diaspora, powerful oligarchs and parts of the traditional security forces in Armenia. With the rise to power of Kocharyan's hand-picked successor Serzh Sargsyan in 2008 this did not substantially change.

Levon Ter-Petrosyan, Robert Kocharyan and Serzh Sargsyan have enjoyed a substantial backing of the security and military forces of Armenia. The Nagorno-Karabakh war that started in 1988 between Armenia and Azerbaijan led to the formation of a security apparatus that is founded on the organizers of the (armed) Karabakh movement, warlords and veterans' organizations. In particular, the veterans' organization Yerkrapah (the guards of the country), created in 1993 by Vazgen Sargsyan, the defense minister at the time, was strongly supported by the Armenian military forces and known for its impact on domestic politics (Khachatrian 2002; Wheatley and Zürcher 2008). Ter-Petrosyan had Yerkrapah's backing in his successful re-election in 1996. In 1997 though, Yerkrapah withdrew from the political alliance with Ter-Petrosyan's Armenian National Movement and soon openly supported Robert Kocharyan, who had himself been a leading figure of Karabakh's armed resistance and a former president of the enclave (Manutscharjan 1999: 54). Yerkrapah's head, Defense Minister Vazgen Sargsyan, and Serzh Sargsyan, the powerful minister of the interior at the time, backed the ouster of Ter-Petrosyan in favor of Robert Kocharyan.

In 1998 the military Yerkrapah organization merged with the political Republican Party of Armenia, a highly nationalist, but small political force in the Armenian party landscape, which soon emerged as Armenia's major ruling party under Robert Kocharyan (Jamestown Foundation 1998). Kocharyan's rise to power in 1998 thus also symbolized the empowerment of the war veterans (Iskandaryan 2008: 526). In general, the tight linkage between the governmental elite, veterans' organizations and the security forces has equipped the governing elite with a substantial degree of power.

The support of the security forces for Kocharyan was amply demonstrated in spring 2004, when the police violently dispersed public uprisings that addressed the failure of the authorities to deal with the allegedly rigged presidential election of 2003 (Freedom House 2011a). Serzh Sargsyan could similarly rely on the loyalty of his security forces. In the course of the massive protests that erupted in March 2008 against the flawed presidential elections, Armenian army units were ordered into central Yerevan. The clashes of security forces and protestors left ten people dead and more than 200 others injured, but Sargsyan's position as president remained largely untouched.

After having come to power, both Robert Kocharyan and Serzh Sargsyan successfully managed to co-opt and largely control the main political and economic elites. Robert Kocharyan's hyper-presidentialism was still constrained immediately after his election and the following parliamentary election in 1999, due to the lack of a genuine political party to support his presidency (EIU 2002). The parliamentary vote of 1999 brought to power a coalition of the Republican Party – which had merged with the Yerkrapah parliamentary fraction before – and the People's Party of Armenia, the Unity Bloc, which significantly weakened Kocharyan's grip on power for a short period. The alliance consisted of a fraction of hardliners and veterans of the Nagorno-Karabakh conflict, led by Prime Minister Vazgen Sargsyan and then Parliamentary Speaker and former first secretary of the Communist Party Karen Demirchyan, who opposed parts of Kocharyan's policy agenda, particularly in terms of his economic and foreign policy (EIU 1999).

Yet constraints to Kocharyan's presidential power were short lived. In October 1999, a group of armed individuals stormed the Armenian National Assembly and shot both Vazgen Sargsyan and Karen Demirchyan – an incident which provoked rumors about Kocharyan potentially masterminding the shootings (Stefes 2006: 50). The assassinations temporarily caused a deadlock in the Armenian political scene, when deputies of the Unity Bloc left the National Assembly to protest against Kocharyan. However, he soon managed to co-opt the Republican Party, when he appointed its representative, Andranik Markarian, as prime minister in May 2000 (EIU 2000a). With their backing and the support of his powerful defense minister, Serzh Sargsyan, Robert Kocharyan also successfully ran in the 2003 presidential election, while the Republican Party dominated the parallel parliamentary election and won most seats as a single party.

The subsequently formed government coalitions allowed Robert Kocharyan to control important economic and political forces, such as the diaspora-connected Armenian parties. The most powerful one was the socialist Armenian Revolutionary Federation-Dashnaktsutyun (ARF) party that Ter-Petrosyan considered a 'foreign organization controlled from abroad' and banned in 1994 (Panossian 2005: 234). The Dashnaks had incorporated a highly nationalist program as its *raison d'être*, which was hence in line with the overall ideological orientation of the ruling Republican Party. Its members also considered the close ties to Russia as the central element of Armenia's security (Manutscharjan 1999: 25). Kocharyan rehabilitated the Dashnaks and his ruling Republican Party formed a coalition government with the ARF and the Rule of Law Party (Orinats Yerkir) after the parliamentary election in May 2003.

In addition, the economic elite has been closely interwoven with the ruling forces since the very beginning of the Armenian state-building process. The post-Soviet privatization process in Armenia resulted in the establishment of a dense oligarchic structure, which also originated in a relatively low degree of foreign investment. State assets were channeled back into the hands of elites and the Armenian diaspora, which internationalized some of the investments (Vertlib 1999: 176). This led to the establishment of a domestic 'bourgeoisie' (Soghomonyan 2007: 50). Certain segments of the economy were soon controlled by very few business people, who acquired immense wealth and were usually connected to the political elites at the highest levels. Reportedly, the oligarchs were particularly close to the Kocharyan and Sargsyan duo, financed presidential election campaigns and helped to disperse the 2004 protests by involving their bodyguards (Danielyan 2006). During the parliamentary election of 2003, the oligarchs subsequently secured formal political power, when almost half of the seats in parliament were given to business actors, seven of which had run on a Republican Party ticket (Soghomonyan 2007: 47ff.).

The parliamentary election in May 2007 and the subsequent presidential election of 2008 did not alter this coalition of power. The Republican Party emerged as the winner of the 2007 election. On its ticket, about two dozen businessmen had again been elected into parliament in 2007 (Bedevian 2012). The Republicans sought a coalition with the newly established Prosperous Armenia Party, founded by the wealthy business tycoon Gagik Tsarukyan and the ARF-Dashnaks, while the latter only agreed to an informal coalition in order to come up with their own presidential candidate (EIU 2007a). Orinats Yerkir, one of the main opposition parties contesting the election (Wheatley and Zürcher 2008), also joined the governmental forces, leaving only the Armenian Heritage Party in opposition. While the diaspora-connected ARF formally refrained from acceding to the coalition, it still held ministerial posts in the Republican-dominated government. It only left the coalition in 2009 due to the reconciliatory stance of Serzh Sargsyan toward Turkey, but even then the opposition only counted 23 parliamentary seats in total (Iskandaryan 2011b: 71).

Yet, Serzh Sargsyan was challenged in the close presidential election race of 2008 by several opposition candidates – most prominently by former President Levon Ter-Petrosyan, who accused the authorities of not having tackled corruption or solved Armenia's conflicts (EIU 2007a). Serzh Sargsyan won the election, which was widely considered to be rigged and drove masses of Armenians onto the streets, who were violently dispersed by the Sargsyan-loyal security forces. In the aftermath of the election, Ter-Petrosyan managed to organize a diverse coalition of opposition forces under the broad roof of his Armenian National Congress. After a dialogue with the government that had started in 2011, the Armenian National Congress participated in the parliamentary election of 2012 and won seven seats in the National Assembly (Iskandaryan 2013; OSCE and ODIHR 2012). In addition, the previously reported tensions between the Republican and the Prosperous Armenia Parties became apparent in the run-up to the 2012 parliamentary election, when the Prosperous Armenia Party left the ruling coalition (Iskandaryan 2011b: 71; Iskandaryan 2013). Yet, despite these developments and reports about irregularities during the presidential election in 2013, both elections confirmed the ruling Republican Party and its incumbent President Serzh Sargsyan in office (BTI 2014a) – arguably owing to the even greater weakness of the opposition (Iskandaryan 2014).

Throughout the South Caucasus, the frozen conflicts have become the most salient part of political identities (Iskandaryan 2008: 558) and dominate the political discourse of incumbents and the opposition alike. In Armenia, the victory in the Karabakh war constitutes an integral part of Armenia's nationalism, which is linked to the notions of hay dat, Araratism and Miazum (see Hofmann 2009: 268f.): Hay dat (Armenian court) aims at the condemnation of Turkey by an international court to gain justice for the 1915–17 genocide of Armenians in the Ottoman Empire. Araratism symbolizes the importance of the return of the worldwide diaspora, while Miazum implies the unification of Armenia with regions that were largely perceived as historically Armenian, among them Nagorno-Karabakh (Hofmann 2009).

This nationalist program and the historic experiences of mass expulsion and genocide (see Savvidis 2011) form part of the national consensus in Armenia, as they enjoy the support of large parts of the population and political forces, which the ouster of Levon Ter-Petrosyan in 1998 amply demonstrated (Manutscharjan 1999; Soghomonyan 2007: 63). Levon Ter-Petrosyan, who had led the 'Karabakh movement' as a national revolution against the Soviet regime, had lobbied for a more reconciliatory approach towards Turkey and Azerbaijan in order to overcome Armenia's isolation and economic blockade. While the opposition was split about market reforms and foreign policy orientations at the time, Ter-Petrosyan's approach towards the Karabakh question united the opposition and internal opponents alike, who claimed that Ter-Petrosyan was about to break with the traditional nationalist program (Manutscharjan 1999). In 1997, many Armenian National Movement parliamentarians joined the ultra-nationalist Yerkrapah Union of Vazgen Sargsyan, who turned against Ter-Petrosyan (Manutscharjan 1999: 54). As a result, he resigned from office in 1998 and Robert Kocharyan successfully won the election against the communist Karen Demirchyan with the support of large parts of the Armenian diaspora and nationalist Armenian parties (Hofmann 2009).

GEORGIA

Georgia's political regimes have been considered hybrid despite a significant rupture in its governing elite after the Rose Revolution in late 2003. While Georgia's second post-independence president, Eduard Shevardnadze, failed to fully consolidate his power over the political, security and economic forces within the Georgian mainland, this was even more the case for the breakaway regions of South Ossetia, Abkhazia and Adjaria. After the Rose Revolution and his rise to power in 2004, Mikheil Saakashvili consolidated his power base more successfully, by extending the presidential powers, reforming the security and co-opting political forces behind an ultra-liberal reform consensus. However, Saakashvili and his United National Movement (UNM) eventually lost their power to the opposition coalition Georgian Dream in the parliamentary election of 2012 and the subsequent presidential election of 2013 – the first peaceful transfer of power via elections in Georgian history.

Eduard Shevardnadze inherited a failed Georgian state from Zviad Gamsakhurdia, the ultra-nationalist and authoritarian first president of post-independence Georgia, who was ousted in 1991 by a coalition of paramilitary groups, former communists and pro-Western intellectuals. Shevardnadze was appointed president of the State Council in 1992, the 'pseudo-parliament' at the time (Stefes 2006: 42), and confirmed as the head of Georgia's government after the election in 1993. His time in office was marked by an increasingly consolidated, but still weak statehood, little scope for his monopoly of force, and a weak cohesion of the ruling elite (Way and Levitsky 2006). Shevardnadze was confronted with a highly fragmented security apparatus that consisted of diverse paramilitary and criminal groups and warlords that had initially put him into power, among them Gamsakhurdia's former National Guard and a paramilitary group called Mkhedrioni (horsemen or knights) (BTI 2010: 3; Reisner 2009: 254f.). They shared the control of Georgia's mainland, while supporters of the ousted President Zviad Gamsakhurdia had established a stronghold in the western part of the country (Stefes 2006: 42).

By 1993 Shevardnadze had regained control over the security apparatus with the help of Russian troops that lent their support to the Georgian army in exchange for Georgia's entry into the CIS and the establishment of Russian military presence in the country – a rotten compromise particularly for the radical nationalists in the country (Reisner 2009: 256). Joint Russian-Georgian troops had soon defeated the Zviadists in western Georgia, which was further consolidated by the fact that Gamsakhurdia had passed away in dubious circumstances. In 1995 Shevardnadze finally disbanded the Mkhedrioni and the National Guard and arrested their leaders (Stefes 2006: 43). As a result, he managed to clear his police to some extent of paramilitary elements and to establish a certain degree of monopoly of force with his security forces, despite the fact that he failed to fully reintegrate the secessionist provinces into Georgia's core. However, the police forces under Shevardnadze were badly paid, often involved in organized crime and lacked loyalty to the incumbent regime (cf. Stefes 2010). This was most obviously demonstrated in the course of the Rose Revolution in 2003. Prior to and during the protests that led to Shevardnadze's ouster, the police and security forces frequently switched sides to support the opposition and failed to stop the protestors from breaking into the parliamentary building, the incident after which Shevardnadze immediately stepped down (Stefes 2010: 35).

When Mikheil Saakashvili was elected president with more than 96 percent of the vote in January 2004, after the successful Rose Revolution, he immediately reformed the security forces by a rigid restructuring and fight against corruption. The new government fired the heads of the law enforcement agencies and the entire, highly corrupt traffic police (World Bank 2012). Vacant posts were awarded to those loyal to Saakashvili, many of whom used to work with him in the Liberty Institute prior to the Rose Revolution, such as the Minister of the Interior and then Prime Minister Vano Merabishvili. In a short time, Saakashvili thus managed to establish a tight control over the power and security ministries (EIU 2005b). The loyalty of the security forces was demonstrated when they violently dispersed protests against the incumbent regime in November 2007 and May 2011. Yet, when the joint opposition forces led by the billionaire-turned-politician Bidzina Ivanishvili won the parliamentary election in 2012, the new GD government again immediately dismantled the security structures aligned with the previous regime: high-ranking military and security personnel, amongst others from the Ministry of Interior, were arrested and charged with the abuse of power (Fairbanks and Gugushvili 2013).

Unlike in Armenia, Shevardnadze, Saakashvili and also the new administration since 2012 failed to fully re-establish the monopoly of force over the entire territory within Georgia's international borders. Under Shevardnadze, Russia had brokered a ceasefire agreement with Abkhazia, while the president failed to extend his monopoly of force to the secessionist territories. With the help of Russian mediation, Saakashvili managed quickly to re-establish the monopoly of force in Adjaria, where the clan of the *de facto* President Aslan Abashidze was dissolved in the course of the fight against corruption (Soghomonyan 2007: 68). Saakashvili also tightened his stance towards South Ossetia and Abkhazia. He was, however, constrained by his fellow revolutionists, post-revolutionary Prime Minister Zurab Zhvania, and Speaker of Parliament Nino Burjanadze, who campaigned for a moderate center-right policy (EIU 2004c). When Zhvania died in February 2005, Saakashvili was left largely unconstrained in his more radical policies toward the breakaway regions (EIU 2005b), but he failed to reintegrate the secessionist territories, and lost the outright war with Russia over South Ossetia in 2008. When Russia recognized the independence of the territories, their secessionist status was further cemented. The new GD administration – despite a less confrontational stance toward Russia – has so far failed to change this situation (Gordadze 2014).

Politically, Shevardnadze consolidated his political power by co-opting the fragmented political forces that prevailed in Georgia. He appointed former high-ranking communist leaders to government positions and made sure to install those loyal to him as heads of regional administrations (Wheatley and Zürcher 2008). In addition, Shevardnadze created the Citizen's Union of Georgia (CUG) as his political party, which dominated the Georgian parliament from 1995 onward. However, his party was a basin for diverse political forces, ranging from the old communist nomenclature to liberal, Western-educated reformers (Stefes 2006).

Shevardnadze co-opted parts of the economic elite by weaving a dense network of clans that was mostly directly or indirectly connected to his family.

The Jokhtaberidze and Akhvlediani clans and associates related to his nephew, Nugzar Shevardnadze, were awarded with influential positions in politics and big business (Chiaberashvili and Tevzadze 2005). Apart from Shevardnadze's family ties, oligarchs did not exert great leverage on political decision makers. Billionaires such as Kakha Bendukidze or Badri Patarkatishvili were renowned for the riches they had acquired in the early 1990s in Russia, but unlike in Armenia, the Georgian economic elite could not be co-opted by selling parliamentary seats to the most influential businessmen (Soghomonyan 2007: 49). This was due to the fact that Georgia relied on a large presence of foreign, predominantly Russian, British and American capital in its privatized larger businesses (Reisner and Kvatchadze 2005; Soghomonyan 2007: 50). In addition, the changing empowerment and disempowerment of different economic and political elites during Georgia's independence period hampered the development of a strong and stable oligarchy. As Hanf and Nodia (2000) note, when the Mkhedrioni militia was destroyed by Shevardnadze, it also fully lost the economic gains of economic and military power, while many other influential business figures of the 1990s went bankrupt. Thus, there was little talk within Georgia about a politically influential group of oligarchs until the early 2000s, when people started to complain about the economic control of the 'Shevardnadze clan' (Hanf and Nodia 2000: 57).

Shevardnadze's power structure thus rested on three, rather fragile and fragmented pillars (Wheatley and Zürcher 2008): first, an economic elite that held close ties to the president's family and controlled the largest banks and businesses; second, the old communist nomenclature stemming from his Soviet networks that controlled the regions politically; and third, a distinct, pro-Western elite within the CUG that held close ties to the NGO sector and soon dominated the CUG's parliamentary fraction.

Starting from 2000, however, this fragile power base soon began to erode. Politically, the reform-oriented fraction of the CUG provoked internal dissent. Criticism of Shevardnadze was related to the high levels of corruption that penetrated Georgia's political and economic spheres. In 2001 Shevardnadze's CUG lost its parliamentary majority due to the defection of several CUG deputies who criticized Shevardnadze for widespread corruption. In an attempt to subvert the criticism, Shevardnadze unsuccessfully tabled a proposal to create the post of a prime minister, envisaged to be filled by Zurab Zhvania, the CUG speaker of parliament and a prominent representative of the reformist CUG wing (EIU 2001a). The then Minister of Justice Mikheil Saakashvili left the ruling party and founded a new opposition party, the UNM, in 2001 and another highly popular CUG figure left the party and joined the opposition in 2003: Nino Burjanadze, the speaker of parliament (Tudoroiu 2007).

The UNM, led by Saakashvili, and the Labor Party emerged as the main opposition parties and gained a majority in the city councils after local elections in 2002. Still, Shevardnadze's governors remained in power in the regions (EIU 2003b). Yet, Shevardnadze's control of the economic elite began to fade away, when a pro-business wing left the ruling party and some of the few Georgian oligarchs, such as Badri Patarkatishvili, openly supported Saakashvili's UNM (Escobales et al. 2008; Kuntz 2011). In addition, Zurab Zhvania and the liberal intelligentsia in Georgia soon joined Saakashvili and Burjanadze (EIU 2002; EIU 2003b).

The parliamentary election in November 2003 was widely perceived as being rigged. The anti-Shevardnadze forces had participated in two distinct blocs: Zurab Zhvania and Nino Burjanadze campaigned on a joint platform, the Burjanadze-Democrats, while Mikheil Saakashvili and his UNM, as well as the New Rights Party and the Labor Party, ran on their own behalf (Kuntz 2011: 206). The official results showed Shevardnadze's 'For A New Georgia' coalition to have won the election with 21.3 percent, while Saakashvili's UNM achieved 18.1 percent – results that international observers considered significantly flawed (OSCE and ODIHR 2004). Mass demonstrations were sparked in Tbilisi and the regions immediately after the election. On 22 November, the first session of the newly elected parliament was scheduled, when Saakashvili and his supporters gathered in front of and eventually broke into the parliament building to interrupt the session (Stefes 2006: 54). Following what became known as the Rose Revolution, Shevardnadze stepped down as president on 23 November. Nino Burjanadze, the speaker of parliament, became the interim president, and parliamentary and presidential elections were announced for 2004.

As a result of the elections, the post-revolutionary government established a stronghold of power in government and parliament. On 4 January, Mikheil Saakashvili was elected president with 96 percent of the popular vote. The partially renewed parliamentary election in March 2004 resulted in a landslide victory of the united bloc comprising Saakashvili's UNM and the Burjanadze-Democrats with 66 percent of the vote. Those loyal to Shevardnadze in the 'For A New Georgia' platform did not run in the renewed election for seats under the proportional system, but kept their previously won seats via direct mandates. The New Rights Party, hosting market-oriented members and liberals, entered parliament, while Aslan Abashidze, the leader of Adjaria, and his Union of Democratic Revival failed to succeed in the March election.

The revolutionary triumvirate of Saakashvili, Zvhania and Burjanadze was in command of the central political institutions in Georgia: Mikheil Saakashvili as president, Zurab Zhvania as prime minister and Burjanadze as the speaker of parliament. While Saakashvili controlled the power and security ministries and determined the foreign policy of the country, Zurab Zhvania and his team steered the macro-economic policy of post-revolutionary Georgia (EIU 2005b, 2007b). Despite the fact that Saakashvili had been considered a populist, leftist presidential candidate prior to the Rose Revolution, his government soon united behind an ultra-liberal reform consensus (European Stability Initiative 2010b).

One of the highly influential, pro-market reformers was Kakha Bendukidze, who became part of the government in 2004 after a joint request by

President Saakashvili and Prime Minister Zhvania (The Economis 2004). Bendukidze had made his fortune in Russia, where he figured as one of the influential oligarchic tycoons. His businesses had blossomed in the 1990s, but were negatively affected by Putin's increased political grip on the economy. Having returned to Georgia, he masterminded the deregulatory liberal economic reforms that rewarded Georgia with the World Bank label of the best reformer in 2006 and promoted a maximum reduction of state interference in domestic concerns (European Stability Initiative 2010b; Lynch 2006: 28).

The highly liberal economic reform agenda also took the wind out of the sails of one of the newly established opposition parties, the New Rights Party (EIU 2007b), which itself campaigned for less state interference in the economy. Even after Zhvania's death in 2005 and Bendukidze's resignation from his post within the government in late 2008, the ultra-liberal reform consensus was not renegotiated. Bendukidze was considered to continue to operate behind the scenes via his ultra-liberal think tank, while Nika Gilauri, the new prime minister in 2009, had previously figured as a close associate to Zhvania and Bedukhidze. Internally, the post-revolutionary government has been marked by frequent reshuffles and little continuity, which some judged as 'proof of the unwillingness of Saakashvili to tolerate anybody with some authentic authority beside him' (BTI 2010: 24). Saakashvili sacked internal critics, such as his minister for conflict resolution for defying the arrest of two Russian diplomats traveling through South Ossetia (EIU 2006).

Saakashvili was hence left largely unchallenged within his government and also by the Georgian opposition, despite the fact that the increasingly authoritarian tendencies and remaining high levels of poverty soon mobilized protestors to fill Tbilisi's streets. Mass protests took place in November 2007, which were violently dispersed by the Georgian police. As a result, Saakashvili agreed to schedule early parliamentary and presidential elections in 2008. However, the elections failed to significantly constrain the power of the ruling elite, despite the fact that Nino Burjanadze, the former parliamentary speaker of the ruling majority, had also switched sides in 2008 and openly supported the opposition. The united opposition received 18 percent of the vote and 17 seats in the parliamentary elections, still leaving the ruling party with a robust majority. Levan Gachechiladze the leader of the nine-bloc opposition party, came only second in the controversial early presidential elections of January 2008. The opposition failed to effectively challenge the de facto 'hegemony' and 'unrivalled power' of the government (BTI 2010: 8ff.; Wetzinger 2011: 75f.), mostly due to its internal lack of unity and the co-optation tactics of the ruling government. Shifting alliances emerged around a handful of popular figures who had often been connected to the incumbent government before, such as Nino Burjanadze, the former Prime Minister Zurab Nogaideli, Irakli Alasania, Georgia's former ambassador to the UN, or Irakli Okurashvili, Saakashvili's former defense minister (Kuntz 2011: 133). In addition, the ruling party frequently successfully co-opted the moderate opposition. It also tried to delegitimize the opposition by a fierce anti-Russian rhetoric after the 2008 elections and ad hoc demonstrations in 2009 and 2011 (EIU 2008b, 2009, 2011).

This changed with the appearance of Bidzina Ivanishvili on the political scene in late 2011. Ivanishvili managed to unite a diverse set of conservative, liberal, but also nationalist opposition parties in the opposition GD coalition in early 2012 (BTI 2014b). The movement's common denominator was again merely 'not [...] policy positions or constituencies but [...] disgust with the government' (Fairbanks and Gugushvili 2013: 119). Due to a lack of ties to the previous government and the immense wealth that Ivanishvili also channeled into representative (re)construction projects, he increasingly gained trust among the population in the course of 2012 (BTI 2014b). After a highly polarized pre-election period and various attempts by the ruling party to undermine the GD's campaigning, the GD eventually won the parliamentary majority in October 2012 (Fairbanks and Gugushvili 2013). While it subsequently gained control of most government posts, Saakashvili remained president – initiating the period of so-called cohabitation (BTI 2014b). Cohabitation ended with the presidential election in October 2013, which was won by GD's candidate Giorgi Margvelashvili. Bidzina Ivanishvili soon voluntarily resigned as prime minister and Irakli Garibashvili was confirmed as his first hand-picked successor in November 2013.

The new government also started investigating potential abuses of the previous administration, arresting and investigating high-ranking UNM representatives – a practice that sparked criticism both from the UNM and from international observers, which called on the GD not to engage in selective justice (Freedom House 2015a). Taken together, the electoral successes and arrests and investigations against high-level UNM figures allowed the GD to consolidate its political power in less than two years after its foundation.

As opposed to Armenia, a full capture of the business elite was not established under the rule of Mikheil Saakashvili. Next to Kakha Bendukidze, who was indeed included in the government until 2008, the second most influential economic figure in Georgia, Badri Patarkatsishvili, soon emerged as a supporter of the opposition. His TV and radio stations belonging to the Imedi group increasingly covered opposition activities, and Patarkatsishvili was considered as having supported the opposition protests in late 2007 (*The Telegraph* 2008). Shortly after the anti-government protests, the Georgian state charged him with plotting a coup attempt and his TV station was temporarily closed (Cutler 2008). After having unsuccessfully tried to challenge Saakashvili in the presidential elections in early 2008, he fled to London, where he died reportedly of a heart attack in February the same year.

The UNM government was also confronted with allegations of violating property rights and of making political ties a precondition for economic success (BTI 2014b). Attempts to influence politically active businessmen also showed in the case of Bidzina Ivanishvili, but while he faced government action against his business assets and had to dispute his citizenship with the authorities prior to the elections (EIU 2011), Ivanishvili yet became prime minister. The frequent rise of influential business figures as opposition politicians and the latest victory by Ivanishvili hence demonstrate the lack of a tight control of economic elites within Georgia.

Since its independence, the domestic and foreign policy of Georgia has been dominated by the struggle for territorial integrity (Donaldson and Nogee 2009: 182). Similar to Armenia, the political power discourse in Georgia centers on the unresolved conflicts of Georgia's territory. However, Georgia's nationalism is also deeply embedded in a strong anti-Russian national movement (Iskandaryan 2008: 536) due to the fact that its struggle for independence against Soviet rule has been strongly connected to its territorial integrity and independence from Russia in the pre- and post-independence years (Reisner 2009: 252). As Hanf and Nodia (2000: 53) argue, the political party landscape in Georgia after its independence from the Soviet Union has been less defined by the economic or social agenda than by the position toward Georgia's independence from Russia. Given Russia's involvement in the problems of secessionism in Georgia and the resulting lack of national unity, an anti-Russian and pro-integrationist stance toward the breakaway territories was largely shared among the population and the opposition parties alike (EIU 2006, 2008b). This has resulted in a specific discursive political power in Georgia to which the Shevardnadze and Saakashvili administrations reverted. Both frequently challenged their opponents with a view to their positions toward Russia, appealing to what seemed to be consensual within large parts of Georgia's population. During the 1999 parliamentary election, in which the opposition indeed formed a united bloc built around Adjaria's *de facto* leader Aslan Abashidze, Shevardnadze dismissed Abashidze as a pro-Russian candidate unacceptable to the West. Also, Saakashvili's administration reverted to an anti-Russian rhetoric to dismiss the opposition and anti-government protestors. The opposition Labor Party, which advocated greater state interference in the economy, at odds with the governmental agenda, for instance, was delegitimized by its supposedly 'softer' stance on Russia (EIU 2007b; Wetzinger 2011: 75f.). Saakashvili also blamed larger demonstrations as being steered by Russia (Kramer 2011). Unlike its predecessor, the new GD administration has put forward a more reconciliatory rhetoric toward Russia, while sticking to its European foreign policy orientation (Gordadze 2014).

MAPPING THE PREFERENTIAL FIT IN GEORGIA AND ARMENIA

Comparing Armenia's and Georgia's domestic power distribution reveals that their internal power composition varies significantly. Armenia's government both under Robert Kocharyan and Serzh Sargsyan has relied on a power base that is closely connected to the armed forces and organizations of the Karabakh war. It also builds on the co-optation of socialist and diaspora-connected parties, while the control of economic forces has been stabilized via the incorporation of Armenian oligarchs in the ruling Republican Party, and from 2007 onward in the coalition built with the Prosperous Armenia Party, which only started to show cracks in 2012. At the same time, the discursive legitimacy of both the Kocharyan and the Sargsyan regimes relied on the nationalist program of hay dat, Miazum and Araratism.

The power base of the Georgian government shifted significantly with the rise to power of Mikheil Saakashvili and then again with the GD coalition in 2012. While Eduard Shevardnadze's fragile grip on power was based on disloyal and highly corrupt security forces and business elites, and a weak party umbrella to diverse political parties, Mikheil Saakashvili managed to re-establish control over the majority of political forces within the country by breaking up Shevardnadze's clan networks within the security and political structures of Georgia. Politically, Saakashvili's government rallied behind an ultra-liberal reform consensus, while opposition parties were co-opted for certain policy initiatives or silenced with anti-Russian rhetoric. The new GD government instead relies on a more conservative power base which has shown especially in a less confrontational stance toward Russia (Gordadze 2014) and a greater emphasis on the role of the state in providing for social welfare (Matusiak 2014).

The costs that domestic executives face in cases of compliance processes are thus likely to be different in both countries. They might exert different effects on EU policy transfer, both with regard to socio-political reforms, as in the case of JLS-related issues, and with a view to economic reforms, as in the case of energy policy. While the Georgian government under Saakashvili did not rely on coalition partners until the elections of 2012, Armenia's ruling party needed to co-opt significantly more forces for change, both in the political and the economic realms. For most of the period under investigation here, the number of intra-elite veto players is hence likely to be higher in Armenia than in Georgia.

This may account for Armenia's poorer performance with a view to energy policy compliance. A further diversification and internationalization of the countries' energy sectors may receive the support of the ultra-liberal fraction in Georgia more easily than in an oligarchy-connected Armenian ruling fraction. In addition, Georgia's reliance on anti-Russian discursive power may make its surrender to negative Russian incentives politically more costly, which might account for its better compliance record with energy policies, despite negative incentives from Russia.

However, this difference cannot account for all detected compliance patterns. While the preferential fit of governments in Armenia and Georgia for or against EU policies can thus be safely assumed to vary within the policy sectors under scrutiny here, its impact on compliance processes cannot be fully captured by focusing on the number and not necessarily on the *de facto* preferences of intra-elite veto players in the specific compliance processes. The next chapter thus provides for this in-depth and policy-specific analysis.

Summary

This chapter provided a macro-level perspective on whether and why EU policies travel to the neighborhood under conditions of high asymmetric interdependence favoring Russia and policy divergence between both external actors. It showed that energy policy figures as an instance of policy divergence between the EU and Russia, whereas both external actors converge with regard to the policies they promote in the area of JLS. Even though Armenia and Georgia are more dependent on Russia than on the EU in both policy sectors, the chapter revealed high degrees of compliance with EU policies in the energy sector, and lower degrees in the realm of JLS. Compliance also varies across countries, despite similar patterns of interdependence with both Russia and the EU. The results challenge the prominent hypothesis that patterns of interdependence drive EU policy transfer, even in cases of policy divergence between Russia and the EU. Hence, the sheer potential of external actors to inflict costs and benefits on third countries cannot account for the compliance patterns of Armenia and Georgia with a view to energy and JLS policies.

The chapter then investigated whether other institutional, structural or more agency-related explanatory factors are able to account for this puzzling compliance pattern. I showed that institutional factors explain why EU policies travel at all under conditions of multiple interdependencies as the institutional setup of EU policies is far more developed than Russia's, which supposedly facilitates EU policy transfer. Yet, they do not shed light on cross-sectoral and cross-country variation.

I also compared the compatibility of the EU, Russian and ENC degrees of rule of law, economic freedom and state capacity, and found that these structural features are able to provide an explanation why EU policies generally travel better in the realm of energy policy. Yet, structural (in)compatibilities did not explain the differences between the two countries.

The third part of this chapter shed light on more agency-based factors, namely the provision of assistance, the application of incentives by external actors and the preferential fit in terms of intra-elite veto player potential in the ENC. While all three factors exert some explanatory power for compliance in the cases under scrutiny here, they fail to account individually for all instances of cross-sectoral and cross-country compliance. Unlike institutional or structural factors, agency-related explanatory variables vary between the countries and the policy sectors at hand. Given the low number of cases, this chapter hence pointed at sources of variation, but failed to provide satisfactory conclusions. In order to study the effect and the potential interplay of preferential fit, multiple external incentives and capacity building in greater detail, the next chapters climb down the ladder of abstraction and increase the number of cases by tracing policy-specific compliance processes in Georgia and Armenia with a view to two subfields of the area of JLS and energy policy: migration management and energy diversification.

Notes

1 The newly adopted AA with Georgia has only been provisionally applied since September 2014, while Armenia's refusal to sign the negotiated AA with the EU prolonged the validity of the PCA and ENP Action Plans.
2 The PCA and ENP for both Armenia and Georgia are almost identical in this regard, with minor differences regarding border management due to the internal dimension of Georgia's secessionist conflicts.
3 If no other references are indicated, this information is derived from CIS Executive Committee (2011b).
4 Phone interview with an expert on JLS in EU external relations, European University Institute, Florence, 10.11.2011.
5 According to the World Bank's *World Development Indicators* (2015), the EU's GDP per capita in 2013, for instance, was close to ten times higher than Georgia's and Armenia's, and more than twice as high as Russia's. Data from SIPRI (2015) also show that the EU's joint military spending in 2013 (US$279.1 billion) exceeded Georgia's and Armenia's (both $0.4 billion) and Russia's ($87.8 billion) by far. While the absolute size of these differences has changed over time, the general pattern has not.
6 Russia recognized South Ossetia and Abkhazia as independent states after the August war with Georgia in 2008.
7 As an example, Armenian (Georgian) exports to the EU amounted to $454 (217) million in 2005, exports to Russia to $119 (154) million. Imports varied accordingly: Armenia imported products of a value of $609 (784) million from the EU and products of $243 (384) million from Russia (IMF 2012).
8 For an overview of the migration processes of Armenians and Georgians to Russia, see Genov and Savvidis (2011).
9 Interview with local migration experts, Danish Refugee Council (DRC) Georgia, Tbilisi, 03.10.2011.
10 Interview with a local expert, IOM Armenia, Yerevan, 11.10.2011.
11 Interview with a staff member, Targeted Initiative Georgia (TIG), Tbilisi, 29.09.2011, and a local expert, IOM Georgia, Tbilisi, 30.09.2011.
12 Interviews with a local expert, Energy Efficiency Center of Georgia, Tbilisi, 05.10.2010 and 27.09.2011, and with an energy expert, Kreditanstalt für Wiederaufbau (KfW), Tbilisi, 12.10.2010.
13 Follow-up interview with an official of the State Migration Service (SMS) of Armenia, Ministry of Territorial Administration, Yerevan, 13.10.2011.
14 The Economic Freedom Index broadly measures the liberalization of business and trade activities, labor freedom and freedom from corruption, while the Transformation Index provides for information on the socio-economic level of development, sustainability of the economy, currency and price stability, and the overall regulatory framework of the economy.
15 The following discussion of detailed sectoral funding schemes is based on a systematic assessment of the European Commission's annual action programs from 2002 to 2011 (European Commission 2012c, 2012d). For all details and sources other than those especially mentioned in the text, see Ademmer (2013: Tables 24–30).
16 For an overview see Trauner and Kruse 2008b.
17 While the development of civil society was considered slightly stronger in Georgia before the Rose Revolution when Eduard Shevardnadze allowed its relatively free development, post-revolutionary Georgia saw a co-optation of civil society forces by the new government, which had held close connections with highly influential domestic NGOs, such as the Liberty Institute (Stewart 2009: 808).

4 Migration management[1]

Cooperation with migrants' countries of origin is an important tool for the EU to control its external borders and to fight illegal and irregular migration into the EU. In this vein, cooperation on migration management with third states has become a cornerstone of the external dimension of the EU's Justice, Liberty and Security (JLS) policies (Lavenex 2004). The Eastern neighborhood in general, and Georgia and Armenia in particular, are no exception in this regard. The EU has *inter alia* sought to make them readmit and integrate migrants that the EU seeks to return, control their national borders more effectively and issue travel documents that are better protected against fraud. As shown in the previous chapter, migration in the post-Soviet space and its management have yet been much more linked to Russia – the region's 'migration magnet' – than to the EU, due to visa-free regimes, language skills or other institutional arrangements that facilitate migration (Brunarska et al. 2014: 135f.). Even though the EU and Russia do not diverge, but converge with regard to the policies they promote in the overarching area of JLS, Chapter 3 showed that compliance with EU demands was relatively weak, varied over time, as well as between Georgia and Armenia, especially with regard to migration management. While Georgia remained a laggard in this area until late 2009, Armenia had already been busily engaged *inter alia* in concluding bilateral readmission agreements with EU members. Georgia then started very slowly to catch up and eventually progressed with greater pace on migration management reform from 2012 onward.

This chapter explains why the EU has been so unevenly successful in making Georgia and Armenia reform their migration management systems under these conditions. In order to do so, it draws on the findings of Chapter 3 and studies the interplay of agency-related factors, namely preferential fit, multiple capacity building, and multiple external incentives in the process of adopting and implementing migration management policies in Georgia and Armenia.

The chapter begins by describing the initial differences between specific EU demands and the migration management in both countries. It outlines the incompatibilities or the misfit between EU demands and the countries' initial status quo of policies, polities and politics, to show that differences in compliance patterns are not simply the result of varying adaptation needs. The chapter then goes on to trace the process of adoption and implementation of specific EU demands in this area, namely the conclusion of readmission agreements, the enhancement of document security, the passage of national action plans on migration and asylum, and the adoption of data protection legislation.

Mapping the status quo in 1999 and 2006

The EU has confronted Georgia and Armenia with comparable and highly specific demands to reform their migration management systems, all of which caused substantial policy, polity or politics misfits in both countries. This is particularly true for the conclusion of readmission agreements, as well as the reform of document security standards, migration and asylum policies and data protection laws, as requested in the PCA in 1999 or the ENP AP in 2006.

Readmission agreements have come to figure as a key EU foreign policy tool to fight illegal migration (Roig 2007; Trauner and Kruse 2008a). Georgia and Armenia agreed to readmit their own nationals who illegally reside in the territory of an EU member state and vice versa, in the PCA of 1999 (European Communities 1999a, 1999b). The PCA also commits the Georgian and Armenian authorities to conclude bilateral agreements with EU member states to regulate the readmission of third country nationals to Georgia or Armenia, who transit through the Caucasian countries to the EU (European Communities 1999a, 1999b). The ENP AP reiterate the importance of readmission agreements with a view to third country nationals and outline the conclusion of EU-wide readmission agreements as a potential result of an enhanced dialogue on mobility issues (European Commission 2006b, 2006c).

These readmission clauses caused policy and politics misfits when they entered into force in both countries, despite the fact that at first sight, readmission seems to be a natural principle of international law. Corresponding to article 13 of the UN Universal Declaration of Human Rights, every citizen has the right to return to his or her own country. In principle, readmission agreements do not change or establish this obligation, but they facilitate the process of readmission (Roig 2007: 364). The inclusion of third country nationals and stateless persons into the readmission agreements, however, requires a profound policy change compared to the Human Rights Declaration and the established policy in Georgia and Armenia in 1999 (*policy misfit*). Until then neither country had agreed to readmitting third country nationals and stateless persons with any other country. Georgia had negotiated one bilateral readmission agreement with Italy in 1997, but this was not implemented due to the failure of establishing the necessary intra-state procedures (Government of Georgia 2010b). The readmitting country is also obliged to reply and process readmission requests in a precisely determined timeframe that is negotiated within the readmission agreements. Due to a lack of these procedures for readmission before 1999 in Georgia and Armenia, the processing of readmission requests required a procedural deviation from the status quo (*politics misfit*). In addition, readmission agreements are likely 'to overstretch the capacities of third-country governments to respond, of their labor markets to absorb and of their societies to tolerate' the return of readmitted migrants (Roig 2007: 380). This is particularly true for Georgia and Armenia, which can be considered emigration countries, meaning that more people leave than enter the country, a trend that was particularly obvious in both countries in the late 1990s. Finding employment for returnees in countries that both chronically suffer from unemployment is a challenging task, and integrating long-term migrants who have been detached from their home societies for a long period of time causes additional social stress to returnees and the home society. Furthermore, rapid urbanization due to rural migrants resettling in urban areas and re-migration can be the result of readmission processes (Trauner and Kruse 2008a). The conclusion of readmission agreements is hence also likely to necessitate institutional change in terms of designing or appointing authorities that institutionalize the reintegration of returning migrants to subvert or alleviate these effects (*polity misfit*). In terms of policy, polity and politics, the implementation of readmission agreements hence displays similar incompatibilities in both countries.

Additionally, the ENP AP require the countries to enhance their document and visa security in conformity with international standards and introduce biometric identifiers into travel documents (European Commission 2006b, 2006c). This picks up a clause of the PCA, which foresees rather vaguely that the countries need to introduce 'appropriate travel documents for readmission' (European Communities 1999a, 1999b). Yet Georgia and Armenia lacked the required policies and structures in 1999, when the PCA entered into force. Looking back on a shared Soviet past, a large amount of Georgia's and Armenia's populations still held Soviet passports in 1999, which only became invalid in the early 2000s (ICMPD 2005). Neither country issued travel documents that fulfilled international standards at the time, and concerns about fraud and multiple passport holders were widespread.[2] Introducing higher security standards in the domestic systems required policy change, as well as technical equipment and financial capacities for the set-up of registry systems that could process biometric data, as opposed to the paper-based registration that was still in operation in the countries at the time. They hence triggered both a *policy* and *politics* misfit in 1999.

The EU further asked the countries to adopt and implement 'a comprehensive, coherent and balanced national action plan on migration and asylum issues', and to strengthen the institutional capacities of the Migration Agency of the Ministry of Territorial Administration in Armenia and the Ministry of Refugees and Accommodation, the Department for IDPs in Georgia (European Commission 2006b, 2006c). This causes a *policy misfit* and exerts pressure for domestic adaptation in both countries, given the absence of a similar document prior to the initiation of the ENP. Likewise, the development of a national action plan on migration requires the appointment of a coordinating policy institution. Both Armenia and Georgia have been part of the Geneva process – an international initiative that particularly targeted migration management with a special focus on displaced persons and refugees in CIS countries in the late 1990s (IOM et al. 2000). It led to the creation of the Ministry of Refugees and Accommodation (MRA) in Georgia and the Department for Refugees and Migration in Armenia (IOM et al. 2000). Despite their creation, both countries suffered from a lack of coordination and cooperation with a view to migration matters prior to the ENP initiation. As the commission country report notices for Georgia: 'The capacity of the government to manage migration has remained low [...] Insufficient coordination and cooperation among concerned Ministries remained a problem' (European Commission 2005b). The same is true for Armenia at the time of initiation of the ENP. Armenia lacked a precisely defined authority to oversee migration management issues and overlapping mandates between different administrative bodies led to bureaucratic tensions and ineffectiveness (Kabeleova et al. 2007: 17). Both countries hence needed to define precisely an institution to deal with the development of a national action plan (*polity misfit*), and to establish coordinating procedures (*politics misfit*) enabling the institution to address migration as a horizontal issue area in exchange with other involved ministries.

The countries are additionally requested to accede to or implement the 1981 Convention on Protection of Individuals Regarding Automatic Processing of Personal Data, and the additional protocol on supervisory authorities and transborder data flows, which is required for closer cooperation between law enforcement agencies. This requirement has only been formulated in the ENP AP and not in the PCA. The ENP provisions on data protection constitute a major prerequisite for international cooperation on migration in issue areas such as visa policies and illegal migration for the EU (Kabeleova et al. 2007: 50). Europol and Eurojust, for example, need to be sure that data exchanged with Georgia and Armenia are purposefully processed and not misapplied or inappropriately shared.[3] The Convention on the Automatic Processing of Personal Data (Council of Europe 1981) and the additional protocol (Council of Europe 2001) aim at reconciling the principle of free flow of information with an effective ban on practices aiming at eluding data protection legislation in one country by storing and processing data in countries with weaker data protection standards. The convention thus requires its parties to establish a national data protection law that ensures that any personal data are progressed in a fair and lawful way. The additional protocol on supervisory authorities and transborder flows requires the establishment of one or more supervisory authorities to ensure the implementation of the domestic law that gives effect to the convention (Art.8).

The stipulations of the convention and the additional protocol constitute a major *policy, politics* and *polity* misfit. Neither Georgia nor Armenia had ratified the convention and the protocol at the time of the start of the ENP. Georgia, unlike Armenia, had acceded to the convention in 2001, but had not ratified it in 2006. This, however, did not necessarily trigger a different status quo. Both countries showed a general formal adherence to the convention by having domestic laws in place that were largely compatible with the convention's substance: the 'Administrative Code' of Georgia and the 'Law on Personal Data' of Armenia (Banisar 2006). Both countries, however, fell short of establishing independent supervisory authorities to ensure their proper implementation (European Commission 2011g; Hardabkhadze and Kvernadze 2006; Sandukhchyan 2006: 8f.). Compliance with this ENP provision hence requires both countries to formally adopt a new law on data protection that includes a supervisory authority (*policy misfit*), to establish this new institution (*polity misfit*), and to change administrative practices to incorporate its functions (*politics misfit*). Hence, the domestic status quo in both countries at the entry into force of the PCA and the ENP AP, respectively, caused comparably high degrees of policy, polity and politics misfit in both Georgia and Armenia.

Migration management reform in Georgia

Georgia has been a laggard with regard to reforms in the area of JLS, including migration management, for a long time; it slightly improved its compliance record from 2010 onwards and greatly accelerated its pace of reforms in 2012 and 2013. Can Georgia's compliance with individual EU demands in this area be explained by the interplay of preferential fit, multiple external incentives and capacity building?

Readmission agreements

The Georgian President Eduard Shevardnadze negotiated the PCA with the EU in 1996, which foresaw the conclusion of bilateral readmission agreements with EU member states, but failed to make significant progress toward the *de facto* adoption or implementation of these agreements. The only readmission agreement that his administration signed, with Italy in 1997, was never implemented because it lacked the necessary intra-state procedures (Government of Georgia 2010b). In 2003, a second agreement with Bulgaria entered into force. At the time, however, Bulgaria had not yet been admitted as an EU member state.

After Mikheil Saakashvili's rise to power in 2004, the newly elected president rallied an economically highly liberal government behind his agenda of fighting corruption and reintegrating Georgia's breakaway regions. With a view to stimulating and facilitating doing business in Georgia, one of Saakashvili's first actions in office was to amend the 'Law on temporary entry, stay and exit of foreigners' in 2004. In line with the economic policy of his Prime Minister Zurab Zhvania and then Minister of Economy Kakha Bendukidze, he created a liberal visa regime with the aim to attract and facilitate the inflow of investors and tourists (World Bank 2005: 24). Facilitated migration for both foreigners and Georgians alike was declared key to the 'Singapore model' of economic growth as promoted by Saakashvili (Saakashvili 2010). The establishment of the liberal visa regime in Georgia, however, increased the costs of concluding readmission agreements for the Georgian authorities. As entering Georgia was perceived to be an easy exercise, Georgia became more attractive as a transit country for potential illegal migrants on their way to Europe. Related political and administrative costs of potentially more and more readmitted third country nationals risked challenging the administrative and political resources of the country. As an expert of IOM remembers, there was some cooperation and discussion on readmission, but this lacked organizational capacity and the government did not see the benefits.[4] Until 2009, only two further readmission agreements were concluded with Schengen members, namely with Germany in 2008 and with Switzerland in 2005 (IOM 2008: 12).

Russian and EU incentives trigger first steps toward reform

Evidence suggests, however, that this cost-benefit analysis was soon to be significantly changed due to policy conditionality invoked by the EU side, and negative, unconditional incentives from Russia, which enhanced the leverage of EU conditionality. Russia had started systematically to distribute its passport in Georgia's breakaway territories, particularly from 2006 onward (Goble 2008), which seemingly undermined Saakashvili's reintegration agenda. Aggravating this trend was the conclusion of a visa facilitation agreement between the EU and Russia which entered into force in June 2007 and facilitated the travel of selected groups of Russian citizens to the EU. As a result, the citizens of the secessionist republics of Georgia were eligible for facilitated travel to the EU under the condition that they accepted the Russian passport, while general or passportization-unwilling Georgian citizens were unable to profit from this enhanced mobility with EU countries. The move threatened to undermine Georgian citizenship (Boniface et al. 2008: 22), particularly because the procedure of handling these Russian passports was treated differently from member state to member state.[5] The Georgian authorities considered this an unintentional encouragement of separatism and urged the EU also to reward Georgia with the visa facilitation carrot. They fiercely criticized the EU's visa policy as 'endanger[ing] Georgia['s] peace effort' and setting a 'terrible and dangerous precedent' (Samadashvili 2007). However, the frequent calls by the Georgian authorities in 2007 were not matched by concrete migration-related domestic reform outputs at the time, nor did they trigger any offer to start negotiations about visa facilitation from the EU.

This changed with the outright war between Georgia and Russia over South Ossetia. After Russian troops had invaded Georgia in August 2008, the French EU presidency negotiated a ceasefire agreement and established the EU Monitoring Mission, which, in the words of an EU official was 'almost becoming a security guarantee for Georgia'.[6] The war also provided Georgia with the urgently wanted prospect to open negotiations on visa facilitation. After the war, as one Commission official remembers, the EU 'needed to show some political sign to Russia that [the EU was] supporting Georgia [and was] willing to improve [its] cooperation and integration with Georgia'.[7] Subsequently, the Commission recommended providing the formal mandate for negotiating visa facilitation agreements with Georgia in order to establish 'facilitations for Georgian citizens equivalent to those granted to Russian citizens' in reference to decisions taken at the Extraordinary Council of the EU after the war (RAPID 2008). The mandate was given on 28 November 2008 (Council of the European Union 2011a).

Despite the war, the visa facilitation agreement came with strings attached. The EU clearly linked visa facilitation to the signing of the readmission agreement with the EU in 2008, as had been the case in all visa facilitation negotiations before. After the clear announcement of this policy conditionality, the Georgian government indeed increasingly engaged in the respective reform processes.[8] During 2009, the Georgian government started negotiations on readmission agreements with several EU member states. In addition, the negotiations of an overall EU readmission agreement started (Delegation of the EU to Georgia 2012a).

During the first round of negotiations, the EU delegation introduced the Georgian negotiators to the overall text of the agreement. Little resistance was encountered with a view to the general readmission of Georgian citizens, to which the authorities had committed themselves in the PCA.[9] The EU readmission proposal, however, also foresaw that third country nationals had to be readmitted back to Georgia, if their documents showed that they had been in Georgia before. This proposal raised severe criticism from the Georgian side, also because it was not compatible with the open-door policy of the incumbent government.[10] The clause threatened to lead to potentially more and more readmitted migrants who had easily entered Georgian territory at some point before illegally migrating to the EU.[11] After multiple rounds of negotiations, the provision was watered down by the Georgian negotiators so that the final document only listed to be readmitted those third country nationals who had either migrated into the EU directly from Georgia or who held a valid or shortly outdated visa from Georgia (European Union 2011: Art. 3).[12]

The negotiations on both agreements were successfully finished on 17 June 2010, when the EU and Georgia concluded the visa facilitation agreement (RAPID 2010). The readmission agreement was signed in November 2010, while both agreements were passed by the European Parliament in December 2010 and entered into force in March 2011 (Council of the European Union 2011a). Hence, output compliance was indeed achieved after policy conditionality was invoked. Observers to the process declared the EU pressure as the main driving force behind the relatively quick negotiation process.[13] In this reading, the Georgian government signed the readmission agreement to get visa facilitation. As one NGO representative closely working with the government on migration issues put it, 'if you could have one without the other they [the Georgian government] would have wanted it.'[14]

Anticipated incentives guide the implementation process

The implementation of the readmission agreements proved to run smoothly. Being aware of the fact that the correct and thorough implementation of readmission agreements was one of the conditions for further progress toward visa liberalization (Pataraia 2011),[15] the Georgian authorities engaged in a quick implementation of the agreement. Yet, the EU had not yet conducted the fact-finding mission preceding the visa liberalization dialogue, nor had it drawn up the precise Visa Liberalization Action Plan (VLAP) for Georgia toward this end. Even before being rewarded with the start of this formal progress in June 2012, however, the Georgian government anticipated future policy conditionality. The officials in the Ministry of Foreign Affairs (MFA) reportedly studied the VLAPs of Ukraine and Moldova in order to find out about the conditions they needed to fulfill to qualify for visa-free travel, one of which was the implementation of the readmission agreement.[16] Consequently, the Ministry of Internal Affairs (MIA) was put in charge of dealing with procedural and organizational readmission matters, in close cooperation with the MFA, the Ministry of Justice and the MRA (IOM 2012). As the alternative progress assessment of the Open Society Foundation Georgia reports:

> According to the MIA, Georgia received 449 readmission requests from the EU member states as of 17 November, 2011. 405 applications (over 90 per cent of requests) have been approved [... E]ven incomplete applications are being considered as long as a person subjected to readmission fulfils the requirements under the Readmission Agreement.
> (Open Society Georgia Foundation 2011: 15)

This corresponds to evidence provided by the MFA and the MIA showing a total of 92 percent of readmission requests that had been processed, while the unprocessed requests were mainly due to shortcomings in the information provided by EU member states and had to be submitted again.[17] More updated numbers in an IOM report in February 2012 verify this number (IOM 2012: 3). By early 2012, Georgia had hence fully implemented the agreement, even before Georgia and the EU launched their visa liberalization dialogue in June 2012 (Civil Georgia 2012).

Apart from the administrative processing of readmission demands from EU member states, the Georgian government also needed to reintegrate readmitted migrants. As the returnees were frequently poor or in bad health, their reintegration into Georgian society proved a difficult and costly exercise. In order to coordinate the reintegration process, newly created institutions were charged with the implementation of the readmission agreement. In February 2011 a working group on reintegration issues was set up under the roof of the State Migration Commission which had itself only been established in October 2010.[18] The high costs of readmission were shouldered by an EU-funded project that started in December 2010 before the readmission agreements entered into force in 2011. Targeted Initiative Georgia (TIG), a flagship project headed by the Czech Republic under the umbrella of the EU and Georgian mobility partnership established in 2009, provided capacity to the MRA.

110 *Migration management*

One of its components implied the formation of a Mobility Center to provide financial and advisory support to the returned migrants, which was given to approximately 200 migrants by October 2011.[19] In addition, the Danish Refugee Council (DRC) was involved in supplying assistance to the returned, providing training for small and medium-size enterprise set-ups in how to write business plans. They established a returnee database to follow the development of the returned migrants. All these projects were funded by the EU.[20] As one IOM expert notes, the reintegration process was hence 'relatively painless' to the Georgian authorities for the simple reason that their budget did not have to cover it.[21]

Change as the result of multiple external incentives

The above evidence suggests that the general lack of positive preferences for readmission gave rise to non-compliance in Georgia until late 2008. The situation changed when Georgia was rewarded with the concrete prospect of visa facilitation with the EU, which was needed to divert negative effects of Russia's passportization in the breakaway regions. The expected shallow compliance outcome, however, did not occur. The application of conditionality that was linked to the implementation of the agreement and intense capacity building in the implementation stage lowered the costs of reintegration to a minimum and triggered profound domestic change from late 2009 onwards. Capacity building hence indeed reduced the costs of implementation. The TIG also constituted a transgovernmental network that may have accelerated the internalization of the readmission norm by the Georgian partners. Yet, unlike the negative incentives provided by Russia coupled with policy conditionality by the EU, it does not explain why Georgia consented to negotiating the readmission agreement in 2009 in the first place, while capacity building in these newly established networks only started in 2010.

Document security

In the case of Georgia, the enhancement of document security was closely intertwined with ongoing reforms within the Ministry of Justice's Civil Registry Agency (CRA)[22]. From 2005 onward, the US Agency for International Development (USAID), the UNDP and the OSCE had started to significantly fund the CRA to update the Civil Register of Georgia. The modernization aimed at reducing bureaucracy and rendering public services for Georgian citizens more effective, among other things, by issuing electronic ID cards for online services (USAID et al. 2007). This goal was very much in line with the ideological underpinnings of the libertarian Georgian government at the time, while the international donors targeted particularly the CRA database that fed the voter lists for elections. The assistance to the CRA proved further necessitated after the local elections of November 2006, during which inaccurate voter lists had been found to impede the election environment in Georgia (OSCE and ODIHR 2006: 1). Being assigned additionally the administration of passports, the CRA modernized the old generation of Georgian passports in 2006 and increased their security compliant with international standards (Civil Registry Agency Georgia 2007). As a result, their falsification proved more difficult than the duplication of the old Soviet passport, but they still lacked the highest international standards that the EU promoted – namely, biometric features.

Yet, while the CRA worked toward the introduction of biometric databases in the Civil Registry System, the Georgian government was not particularly receptive to the idea of introducing biometric passports in 2007. At the early compliance stage, their introduction proved a costly process, especially in administrative and financial terms. It required the passage of legislation, technical know-how and costly equipment. The decision-making process, in particular, was considered a rather long-term endeavor (Holtved 2011: 7). As the strategy of the CRA outlined, 'funding constraints' figured as a major impediment to the passport's introduction in 2007 (Civil Registry Agency Georgia 2007: PO3.3). As one official in the MFA remembers, by late 2008, when the prospect of visa facilitation was granted after the war with Russia, the Georgian government hoped that visa facilitation would be awarded in return for the conclusion of readmission agreements only, as had been the case in Moldova and Ukraine.[23]

EU policy conditionality kicks in

The hopes of circumventing these costs before being rewarded with visa facilitation vanished when Franco Frattini, EU commissioner for justice, freedom and security, called for the introduction of biometric passports by 2009 if Georgia hoped to profit from visa facilitation (IOM 2008). In addition to the readmission clause, the introduction of biometric passports was hence included in the negotiations as a non-negotiable part for facilitating visa requirements.[24] While Russia was not providing direct incentives to the introduction of biometric passports, it added additional leverage to the EU demand due to the illegal passportization which further encouraged the Georgian authorities to strive for visa facilitation.

After the passport condition had been communicated by the EU, the revised CRA strategy intended to create the legal basis for the introduction of biometric passports by mid-2009 (Civil Registry Agency Georgia 2007). In 2009, however, the Georgian government delayed the introduction of biometric passports for several months, reportedly due to shortages in funding in post-war Georgia (Government of Georgia 2010b). This was soon bridged by intense financial assistance from the EU in the framework of the Supplies for the Production of e-Passports in Georgia' project, implemented by the CRA of Georgia under the ENPI umbrella (Civil Registry Agency Georgia 2010; EaP Community 2012; Kirtzkhalia 2010). In addition, the EU financed the launch of the first tender for the production of the biometric passports.[25]

112 Migration management

Following statements by the CRA, the costs of the introduction of biometric passports amounted to roughly €7 million, which was mostly financed by the EU (Civil Registry Agency Georgia 2010). On 15 April, the first biometric passport was issued and 'sold' to the public as a tool to facilitate travel to the EU (Civil Registry Agency Georgia 2010). Output compliance was thus established in the realm of document security after the EU had made it conditional on visa facilitation agreements, while the costly administrative process was facilitated by financial assistance from the EU.

A politically costly implementation process

The implementation process for biometric passports, however, triggered unanticipated political costs. In October 2010, an alliance of eight opposition parties discovered the biometric passport issue for its own purposes. Corresponding to the original intention of external donors to support the reform of the CRA with a view to improve voter lists, the newly united opposition presented proposals to use biometric passports for voter registrations on election day and make the reformed CRA responsible for the verification of voter lists (Civil Georgia 2011a; RFE/RL 2011c).[26] In this way, the opposition parties aimed to prevent rigged voter lists and multiple voting in the 2012 parliamentary election (RFE/RL 2011c). The advantage of biometric passports and their identification means was that voter lists based on biometric identifiers could not be duplicated or faked, and thus safeguarded that each Georgian could only vote once. The proposal of the opposition was found to be 'complex and extremely well thought through' by US experts, who still recommended not using biometric passports but instead biometric IDs for election purposes (Holtved 2011: 11). In October 2010, however, Georgia had not yet introduced biometric IDs, but had put a lot of effort into the production of biometric passports to profit from visa facilitation. The rather technical issue of the introduction of biometric passports hence turned out to be a politically costly exercise for the incumbent government.

In March 2011, the ruling party, the UNM, answered the opposition's request by presenting an alternative proposal for the reform of the election code. It rejected the nationwide distribution of biometric passports on the grounds of high administrative costs, but agreed to their distribution in Tbilisi. The authorities calculated that the distribution of biometric passports to every Georgian citizen would cost at least $110 million (Civil Georgia 2011a; RFE/RL 2012b). The opposition calculated differently, referring to Bolivia as an example: a country five times the size and double the population of Georgia had managed to introduce biometric passports within three months and for €75 million only (Bendeliani 2012; RFE/RL 2011b). Insisting on the introduction of biometrics for the election to continue talks on the reform of the electoral code, the opposition's talks with the government soon faced a dead end (*The Messenger* 2011). In order to save them, the EU ambassador to Georgia, Philip Dimitrov, issued a statement in April 2011 in which he appealed to the parties in the conflict to foster the reform of the electoral code to enhance Georgia's integration process into the EU (RFE/RL 2011b).

There was little hope of compromise, however. The ruling UNM started separate talks with the National Democratic Party and the Christian Democratic Movement, and again presented revised proposals on 24 June 2011. Among other things, the new proposals foresaw the allocation of roughly $600,000 to any party that would score at least 5 percent in the 2012 parliamentary election and would endorse the proposal of electoral reform (without the nationwide introduction of biometrics) of the ruling party by 27 June (Civil Georgia 2011b). An observer to the process was quoted rejecting the UNM's provision as 'insulting' and 'a blatant attempt to bribe unprincipled political forces' (RFE/RL 2011c). Yet, this proposal proved partially successful. Four parties – the National Democratic Party, Industry will Save Georgia, the Christian Democrats and the New Rights Party – formally agreed to the UNM's proposal, while two – the Christian Democrats and the New Rights Party – simultaneously left the opposition alliance (Civil Georgia 2011b; RFE/RL 2011c). The remaining opposition forces rejected the June amendments, particularly the ultimatum to endorse the UNM proposal to be eligible for state funding after the parliamentary election (RFE/RL 2011c). They also continued to lobby for the nationwide introduction of biometric passports and presented the outcome of a consultancy by experienced European companies claiming that the use of biometric data for election purposes would indeed be feasible (Chelea 2011).[27] Likewise, Bidzina Ivanishvili, the billionaire-turned-opposition politician who entered the political scene in October 2011, offered to finance the nationwide introduction of biometric passports in Georgia to improve the election environment prior to the 2012 elections (*Weekly Georgian Journal* 2011).[28] The majority of UNM parliamentarians rejected Ivanishvili's offer immediately (GHN News Agency 2011), while the opposition continued to criticize the lack of political will in the ruling party (Bendeliani 2012).

By 27 December, the Georgian parliament – thanks to the UNM's large majority – passed the new electoral code on the grounds of the final UNM proposals and with only minor amendments in the last reading. The new electoral code, including its procedure to verify voter lists, triggered international and national criticism. Watchdog groups such as Transparency International Georgia and the Georgian Young Lawyers' Association (GYLA) criticized the code for aggravating the election environment and for again establishing an Electoral Commission to verify voter lists instead of involving the reformed CRA (RFE/RL 2012b). The OSCE and the Council of Europe's Venice Commission termed the involvement of civil society and multiple political parties in a commission verifying the voter lists 'a welcome step', but cautiously reminded: 'the impact of this commission in practice will have to be assessed more precisely and, in particular, in the context of the next elections due to be held in 2012' (Venice Commission and OSCE/ODIHR 2011b: 15).

By November 2011, roughly 300,000 biometric passports had been issued, which made around 10 percent of the Georgian population biometric passport holders (Open Society Georgia Foundation 2011). Some opposition leaders campaigned to encourage more people to register voluntarily to de-duplicate the public register of the CRA prior to the election (Bendeliani 2012). Yet, as the data to compile the voter lists were not provided by the CRA only (OSCE and ODIHR 2008: 9), this procedure was likely to be limited in effect. Likewise, the attractiveness of biometric passports for normal citizens was constrained by its high price of 100 lari (approx. \$45)[29] and hence unlikely to support the voluntary registration process (The Georgia Times 2010). The scope of the distribution of biometric passports was thus limited and failed to positively impact the election environment as a side effect of its implementation.

However, this did not constitute an instance of non-compliance with the EU requirement of the introduction of biometric passports at the time. The Georgian authorities indeed complied with the provisions of enhanced document security by distributing passports on a voluntary and individual basis only. It also paved the way for a relatively smooth compliance process with EU requirements once the new GD administration had received the VLAP from the EU in February 2013. The new administration quickly responded to the EU's request to phase out non-biometric passports and to roll out biometric passports in Georgia's consulates which enabled Georgia to achieve the document security benchmark relatively quickly that was needed for progressing with visa liberalization (European Commission 2013d, 2015b).

Preferential misfit meets policy conditionality

The above-presented evidence suggests that the initial preferential misfit of the Georgian government to introduce biometric passports due to high administrative costs was overcome by the EU's application of policy conditionality and the subsequent provision of financial capacity from 2009 onwards. Capacity building in this case indeed helped to bridge governmental resistance to this issue, which was grounded in the fear of an increased burden on the Georgian budget. As capacity building was only provided in the form of financial assistance, the EU did not provide for any transgovernmental networks to facilitate the work on biometric identifiers. Additionally, the EU's policy conditionality gained leverage by Russia's negative incentive which further increased the anticipated benefits of visa facilitation for Georgia. The political costs that a nationwide distribution of biometric passports might have triggered domestically via improved national voter lists were successfully avoided by the Saakashvili regime, without violating the ENP requirement of enhanced document security. In addition, the new GD administration quickly implemented the necessary document security requirements as outlined in the VLAP. All in all, compliance with the EU's document security requirements proved successful in both output and outcome dimensions, but it did not trigger democratic change, which was originally intended by international donors when modernizing the CRA.

National action plan on migration and asylum

In 2006 the MRA showed interest in the issue of developing a national action plan on migration and asylum, as had been stipulated in the ENP AP. The ministry, however, did not enjoy any particular renown within the Georgian government and was considered rather powerless.[30] It reportedly understood an increase in international activities as a way to enhance its political weight within the government.[31] In 2006, the MRA applied for an AENEAS-funded project, Towards Durable Reintegration Mechanisms in Georgia, and received €600,000 from the EU for its implementation, jointly with the DRC. The project partners interpreted the project guidelines broadly to allow for the development of a migration management strategy and created a working group of relevant stakeholders under the roof of the state minister for Euro-Atlantic integration (IOM 2008).[32] The working group consisted of representatives from the MIA, the MFA, the Ministry of Justice and the MRA, the latter figuring as its head and coordinating body that was supposed to draft a migration policy and action plan (IOM 2008). The ministry subsequently created a draft version of a potential national action plan in 2008 with the help of the DRC (UNHCR and IOM 2007). In addition, external EU expertise was provided via a TAIEX project, in which officials from the ministry became acquainted with the EU policy on labor migration (European Commission 2011j).

The draft was circulated on a medium governmental level in the ministries, revised and re-circulated, but reportedly encountered resistance at the highest level. As one state official from the State Office of Euro-Atlantic Affairs reports, Vladimir Gurgenidze, the prime minister at the time, opposed the draft and asked his government not to limit the freedom of movement via managing migration.[33] IOM additionally reported that high officials within the ministries shared the opinion that migration policy had to primarily reflect the goal of investment and labor force attraction (IOM 2008). This corresponds with the perception of non-governmental observers claiming that the government never wanted a strong migration management due to its highly liberal visa policy and the general beneficial nature of outward migration due to remittance payments.[34] Contextualizing the overall governmental situation at the time, remittances seemingly figured as one of the few social stabilizers, as Saakashvili's liberal economic policy was increasingly under pressure from the population and the large-scale protests erupting in 2007. The capacity building provided by the EU was seemingly unable to empower the ministry vis-à-vis high-level government resistance. The ministry was portrayed as unable to convey any urgency on this issue.[35] Giorgi Kheviashvili, one of the heads of the MRA at the time, seemingly failed to occupy a renowned and powerful position within the government and was openly criticized by Saakashvili for the misuse of public funds (Tsotniashvili 2007). The draft law ended on ministerial shelves without having been considered by the cabinet in late 2008.[36]

This evidence suggests that the overall migration management approach of the EU was at odds with the ideological and economic disposition of the Georgian government at the time and created a substantial preferential misfit. In the absence of tangible incentives, the MRA's attempt to profit from the EU's financial assistance, and its inclusion in the EU-provided TAIEX networks, did not trigger output, or outcome compliance, as it lacked the support of the overall government.

External incentives on the rise

The non-compliance prevailing with a view to the establishment of a National Migration Action Plan changed in 2010, however, supposedly following decisive alterations in the EU incentive structure throughout 2009. The initiation of the Eastern Partnership Summit in May 2009 provided the prospect of potential visa-free travel to the ENC. By June 2010, the negotiations of the visa facilitation agreement were finalized, and as one Commission official remembers, the Georgian government was striving for a 'quick acknowledgement and quick assessments of progress just to be able to take next steps'.[37] Moldova and Ukraine had advanced toward further visa liberalization by mid-2010, when the Commission negotiated VLAPs that outlined specific reform needs to advance in the direction of visa-free travel, among them the need to designate an institution responsible for migration management and the creation of the national action plan for migration (Sushko 2012: 4). In order to be eligible for visa liberalization, too, the Georgian government reportedly consulted the VLAP of its fellow EaP countries (Open Society Georgia Foundation 2011: 14f.). When asked about the conditions of visa liberalization with the EU, a government official replied: 'We can guess them from the Ukrainian and Moldovan roadmaps [...] We are doing our homework, before the EU asks us.'[38]

On 13 October 2010 a Governmental Decree 'on Creating [a] State Commission on Migration and Approving its Provision' was passed which transferred the responsibilities for coordinating migration policy development to the CRA of the Ministry of Justice in October 2010 (Government of Georgia 2010c: Art. 5). The commission's purpose was to develop a single migration policy and draft proposals based on the migration requirements stipulated in the ENP AP (Government of Georgia 2010c). Under the auspices of the CRA, the first meeting of the commission took place in December with the task of working on migration policies (Ministry of Justice of Georgia 2010). The CRA and the Ministry of Justice were considered to possess the relevant financial, technical and political capabilities to successfully launch this project, which some considered to have led to 'absolutely different conditions' for the work on migration issues in Georgia.[39]

Evidence suggests that this process was further stimulated by developments on the EU-Russian agenda. In April 2011, the EU and Russia had announced 'groundbreaking' developments in the progress of Russia and the EU toward visa liberalization, when the EU provided Russia with a 'list of joint steps' as conditions to pave the way toward a full waiver of visa requirements (Potts 2011). The Georgian minister of foreign affairs, following a trip to Brussels a few days later, reacted to these developments, urging the EU to provide the same incentive to Georgia:

> [W]e are warning our friends that it would be very unwise to give Russia visa liberalization before us – not because we are against it in principle, but because of Russia's illegal passportization. It would be very damaging for EU's policies in support of Georgia's territorial integrity and sovereignty.
> (Baramidze, quoted in Pop 2011)

Likewise, an EU official reasoned that 'they [the Georgian authorities] are very concerned also about parallelism, not with Armenia, but with Russia'.[40] The mélange of anticipated policy conditionality from the EU and the remaining unconditional negative externalities of Russia's passportization hence supposedly accelerated the work on migration management reforms in Georgia. This is supported by statements of NGO representatives in Georgia, arguing that the entire process of migration management reform was 'driven from the outside, rather than from the inside', because Georgia does not have any interest in migration management.[41] Indeed, shortly after the announcement by the EU and Russia in April 2011 about deepening their cooperation on visa liberalization issues, the State Commission on Migration decided to establish a working group charged with the task of developing a national action plan on migration and asylum in May 2011 (Ministry of Justice of Georgia 2011; Open Society Georgia Foundation 2011).

With the financial and technical assistance of the TIG, a first meeting of the migration strategy working group was held in July 2011, to which also EU experts were invited.[42] It focused on the elaboration of the main pillars that a Georgian migration policy should cover and set a timeframe for the creation of a draft, which the Georgian representatives in the commission foresaw as the end of the year.[43]

One of the most critical issues with which the EU confronted Georgia in terms of its migration policy was its highly liberal visa regulations, which opened the door for unregulated labor migration – a concern for the European Commission (2008b). As opposed to previous years, in which the government had predominantly focused on fostering legal migration, one official of the CRA noted that the first meeting also broadly identified the prevention of illegal migration and reintegration of returning migrants to be tackled by the strategy.[44] A mission of international experts was conducted in September 2011, during which all the major ministries involved in the drafting of the document were defined.[45] Subsequent sessions of the State Commission in November 2011 and April 2012 did not result in the formal adoption of a concrete policy, but the work on the strategy was reportedly ongoing and, according to the CRA, a draft was anticipated to be passed by the State Commission in Spring 2012.[46]

Compliance remains shallow

Yet, despite the creation of formal institutions, evidence suggests that little change of substance occurred with a view to Georgia's highly liberal and unregulated migration policy until the end of 2012. While the CRA was pushing the migration strategy development, the progress on its *de facto* creation still proved to be a 'critical issue' for the overall government (Ministry of Justice of Georgia 2011). Jointly with representatives of IOM, state officials expressed that any thorough compromise of the Georgian authorities on the liberal visa policy was highly unlikely to be achieved.[47] As noted by the CRA official in October 2011 with a view to Georgia's liberal visa policy:

> I can guarantee there is not even a preliminary decision, but this is one main issue about which we are criticized by European states [...] We are working on some research. We are going to offer them some alternatives. One alternative is the status quo to stay on this stage and there will be another two options, but I do not think that there will be fundamental changes to this.[48]

In line with the research objective, the Georgian side insisted on initiating a multi-stakeholder process prior to submitting the draft strategy for discussion in the overall government.[49] The process was to be launched including different international organizations and national interest groups. The EU partners generally welcomed this idea,[50] although it seemed to significantly delay the adoption of a strategy. This was aggravated by the fact that the broader strategic document needed to be developed further into a precisely timed roadmap to make it an ENP-required action plan. Thus, despite the fact that the CRA was appointed as the relevant coordinating institution and formal measures had been taken to work toward compliance, a substantial and timely change in the unregulated migration policy of Georgia was not achieved, resulting in shallow compliance only.

An alternative explanation for the above-presented 'preferential misfit' argument might be a lack of capacity to account for the 'death' of the 2008 strategy. In this vein, the failure to establish a national action plan was considered a result of large new inflows of IDPs into Georgia proper, due to the military confrontation. The responsibility for arranging housing, reintegration and basic assistance to the IDPs lay with the MRA and the tense IDP situation supposedly distracted the MRA and the government from further pursuing work on the Action Plan in the aftermath of the war.[51] In this line of reasoning, the Russian military intervention indirectly contributed to non-compliance with ENP requirements by triggering negative externalities that absorbed the ministry's capacities. Yet a lack of capacity would have led to the assumption of a delay in compliance to a point when the capacities of the ministry allowed for re-engagement with the subject matter, but two developments contradict this assumption: first, the MRA was fully stripped of its competences for drafting the migration policy and was hence limited in its functions to further pursue the work it had started with the DRC in 2007; second, the draft was not reactivated, as participants to the process confirm,[52] but ignored, even when the issue was taken up on the CRA's agenda again in mid-2011.

Likewise, the delay in post-2010 compliance has been attributed to a potential lack of capacity and resources of the government (Open Society Georgia Foundation 2011). However, the process suggests having been delayed due to the multi-stakeholder process that Georgia insisted on initiating, which was linked less to generating capacity than to making sure that domestic interest groups would consent to the developed strategy. In short, the capacity-building argument contradicts some of the empirical developments with a view to the reform process until 2012.

A new government faces strong incentives

Major reforms in this area, however, occurred after the parliamentary election of 2012 and under the new administration. In October 2012 a Secretariat for the State Commission on Migration was established with support from the EU in order to better coordinate activities of the commission and other stakeholders (Civil Development Agency 2015). Very shortly after the presentation of the VLAP to Georgia in February 2013 and its specific conditionalities linked to the reward of visa liberalization, a Migration Strategy for 2013 to 2015 was approved in March and a related action plan in June. The administration had received support from the TIG toward this end and the action plan respected the requirements of the VLAP, outlining concrete actions and implementing agencies (European Commission 2013d). In addition, the new administration also addressed the previously contested liberal visa policy of Georgia and approved a new and more restrictive Law on the Legal Status of Foreigners and Stateless Persons in October 2013 (European Commission 2013d). While the law received praise in the EU's progress reports (European Commission 2015b), it was fiercely criticized by a variety of stakeholders in the civil society, *inter alia* for constraining investment and study possibilities of foreigners in Georgia (Civil Development Agency 2015; Transparency International Georgia 2014). Apparently, it had also been drafted without the advice of Georgia's economic council (Transparency International Georgia 2014), showcasing the new administration's deviation from Saakashvili's strong pro-business approach and hinting at a change in preferential fit. While this suggests that Georgia had achieved full compliance by 2013 with the EU demands to adopt and implement a national action plan on migration and asylum, doubts remain on the sustainability of this development. In response to the fierce domestic criticism, the parliament has more recently again passed amendments that have re-liberalized the law on the legal status of foreigners (Ademmer and Delcour 2016), and it remains to be seen whether this change is at odds with EU requirements.

Concerted external incentives meet preferential misfit

The emergence of EU policy conditionality linked to the migration management strategy in 2010 and unconditional negative incentives by Russia only contributed to some formal, institutional changes in Georgia until 2012. A lack of capacity or capacity building fails to account for the differences in compliance outcomes. The MRA indeed sought capacity-building measures by the EU in order to advance its domestic political standing. It was also included in transgovernmental networks with the EU in the framework of a TAIEX project that may have facilitated the socialization of the participating Georgian officials into the EU norm. Yet, the MRA's initiatives were prevented by the central government. Likewise, the war deprived the ministry of some of its capacities, but instead of re-engaging its previous work into the new attempts to create an action plan, the ministry was stripped of its duties. The evidence presented above hence suggests that the interplay of concerted external incentives by both the EU and Russia and a preferential misfit on the side of the Georgian government can best explain the shallow compliance outcome until 2012. It was only with an increase in policy conditionality and a change of government in 2012 that a migration strategy, a respective action plan on migration and asylum, and a more restrictive visa policy were passed.

Data protection

The work on data protection legislation reform in Georgia started in early 2006 after Gia Kavtaradze had been appointed minister of justice and put the issue on the agenda of his new ministry.[53] Prior to this position, he had served as an executive secretary to the Council of Justice of Georgia, a time during which Georgia also signed the Council of Europe convention on data protection (Ministry of Justice of Georgia 2012a). His work toward data protection legislation reform was subsequently supported by a national TACIS project in 2006 that targeted the drafting of new legislation in this field. However, Kavtaradze's reform course was reportedly short lived. He left the ministry in August 2007 to continue private legal counseling, and by 2010 emerged as one of the critics of the government's legal reform attempts (Civil Georgia 2007b; Corso 2010). Under the newly appointed minister Eka Tkeshelashvili, the reform stalled. An official in the ministry notes:

> There was no interest in this issue, because we had some general view, recommendations and provisions, but for more development of this draft we needed the answers from the government, but they did not give them.[54]

The non-compliance with data protection legislation reform reportedly changed in November 2008, after the Russian–Georgian war, with the appointment of Zurab Adeishvili as minister of justice. Adeishvili was considered a close ally of President Saakashvili and had previously occupied posts as the head of his Presidential Administration and as prosecutor-general. In the latter position, he had been subject to fierce criticism by the opposition and the Georgian ombudsman, who claimed in parliament that he had evidence that Adeishvili, together with the powerful and then incumbent Minister of the Interior Vano Merabishvili, had ordered the police to use force against the protestors in November 2007 (*The Georgia Times* 2009). When Adeishvili took over the position on 2 November, the war with Russia had awarded Georgia an early visa facilitation perspective, which was formally given by the Council of the EU on 28 November.

The EU sets incentives

Again, the visa facilitation perspective came with strings attached. A representative of the EU delegation noted that in the meetings data protection legislation was treated as if it were a condition for visa facilitation.[55] Correlating with the newly offered incentive from the EU side, the CRA under the roof of the Ministry of Justice started re-working on data protection legislation in late 2008.[56] A working group was set up comprising members of the Analytical Department of the Ministry of Justice and its CRA to work toward this end, closely involving NGOs and the private sector into the work on the draft (Ministry of Justice of Georgia 2012b). Their efforts were supported under the ENPI heading of Criminal Justice Reform in Georgia starting from 2009 (Human Dynamics 2012).[57] During the stakeholder consultations in 2009 and 2010, the legislation met particularly pronounced resistance from business actors whom Saakashvili's liberal government had continuously tried to please since 2004. It threatened to increase the costs of their businesses by forcing them to introduce administrative and technical safeguards for the protection of clients' data, as the convention not only targeted the processing of personal data by the state, but also by private entities.[58] The GYLA was one of the most active NGOs involved in the process, and the only one that provided comments to the draft law circulated by the government in 2010.[59] The draft law foresaw that the supervisory authority, a data protection inspector, was to be appointed directly by the president for a five-year term (Government of Georgia 2010a: Art. 22). The GYLA opposed this provision, lobbied for an independent parliamentary supervisory authority and requested the specification of some provisions within the law to prevent abuses.[60] On 3 September 2010, a reworked legislative proposal was presented for a first reading in parliament. The new proposal had indeed considered the comments by the GYLA on the supervisory institution. The renewed draft no longer foresaw a presidential appointment, but the establishment of a commission of parliamentarians, the government and NGOs, which would recommend a set of candidates to the prime minister, who had to choose the candidate from the commission's pool. By 3 September, the GYLA had approved of the changes, given that the prime minister's power was still much more restricted than the president's.[61] The parliamentary debate reportedly lacked discussion and the members of parliament apparently were unable to follow the complexity of the law. As non-governmental observers suggest, the ruling party engaged in inter-party struggles about the law behind closed doors rather than in the parliamentary hearing.[62] After the first reading in September 2010, however, the law seemed to be blocked. No second hearing was scheduled, which used to be only a matter of weeks in normal legislative procedures. By October 2011, stakeholders in the process were unable to tell what had happened to the draft.[63]

Shortly after the first reading of the law in parliament, the negotiations on visa facilitation and readmission with the EU were fully concluded. While the visa facilitation agreement was already signed, the readmission part was finalized in November 2010 and the European Parliament confirmed its consent to the agreements in December 2010 (Council of the European Union 2011a). The apparent conditionality that had been communicated by the EU officials was hence not invoked for the case of data protection legislation. However, at the time the Eastern Partnership had already opened the possibility of visa liberalization for Georgia, and the respective EU-Ukrainian roadmap, passed in November 2010, showed that data protection legislation was a requirement for further progress in this direction (Council of the European Union 2010). In addition, the EU and Russia progressed in their visa liberalization talks in April 2011, all of which seemingly accelerated the process of drafting data protection legislation. In December 2011, the second and third hearings were conducted on the proposed legislation, which passed the Georgian parliament on 28 December 2011 and was signed by the president on the same day. The process was further accelerated after Georgia had been provided with a VLAP that – as had been expected – listed data protection as one of the conditions linked to visa liberalization. In May and July 2013, Georgia finally signed and then ratified the 2001 Additional Protocol to the Council of Europe Data Protection Convention (European Commission 2013d). Formally, output compliance with the ENP prescription was hence achieved.

Implementation remains shallow

The substance of the adopted legislation did not display significant changes to the law presented in the first reading in September 2010, but varied with a view to the entry into force of different stipulations. The overall law entered into force in May 2012 (President of Georgia 2011: Art. 56). Articles 43 to 55, which define liabilities and sanctions for the violation of rules, only entered into force in January 2013. The post of the data protection inspector, however, was only filled and equipped with further human and financial resources under the new government in June 2013 (EC and HR 2014b: 17). In addition,

Articles 34, 35 and 39, which define the function of the data protection inspector, only entered into force in 2016 for the private sector. In this way, the application of the law was delayed in terms of its enforcement and undermined with a view to the private sector, which did not face any constraints prior to 2016.

The *de facto* application of the law was yet more profoundly affected by the constitutional changes that had been passed in the meantime, which challenged the fragile independence of the supervisory authority. In mid-October 2010, a month after the first reading of the draft law in parliament, amendments to the constitution shifted the dominant executive power from the president to the prime minister after the presidential election in 2013. This move was largely interpreted as Saakashvili's – eventually unsuccessful – attempt to switch to the post of prime minister after his second (and by law, last) consecutive term in office (Marcus 2010). For the newly enacted data protection law, it also meant that the prime minister as the newly upgraded head of the executive would be the appointing authority for the independent inspectorate and responsible for the overall internal auditing, which the GYLA rejected on the grounds that this mechanism did not qualify as a remedy to protect individual rights.[64] This was particularly true as the law foresaw simply a renewed tabling of suggestions by the commission, for cases in which the prime minister refused to appoint any of the candidates recommended by the commission (Art. 28, 5). The appointed inspector hence had to be generally acceptable to the executive's head before having a chance of being appointed.

Shallow compliance as a result of preferential misfit and external incentives

In a nutshell, despite the fact that the parliament of Georgia ratified the relevant conventions and signed a law on data protection which included a supervisory authority, evidence suggests that the *de facto* protection of personal data in Georgia has remained shallow, due to the increase in the prime minister's power and the delay of entry into force of many critical legal provisions. Capacity building alone has trouble explaining the variation in this case over time, as TACIS funding was also dedicated to the Ministry of Justice in this area prior to 2008, while no transgovernmental networks were created that may account for the change from non- to shallow compliance with EU policy. The above-presented evidence hence suggests that the interplay of a substantial preferential misfit and external incentives by the EU indeed triggered domestic change, yet this remained shallow.

Migration management reform in Armenia

As outlined in Chapter 3, Armenia outdid Georgia with a view to compliance patterns in JLS issues in general and migration management specifically for a long time – a pattern that only changed after Georgia had been awarded with the clear prospect of visa liberalization. The next section traces to what extent

Armenia's overall positive compliance pattern can be explained by the interplay of preferential fit and external incentives or capacity building.

Readmission agreements

The Armenian government started to formalize the readmission of Armenian citizens and third country nationals in the early 2000s and declared the conclusion of international agreements to return and resettle Armenian citizens a political goal (Government of Armenia 2004). This approach largely mirrored a consensus that seemed to have emerged among Robert Kocharyan's coalition government, the influential Armenian diaspora and domestic society at the time. The incumbent President Robert Kocharyan had campaigned on migration issues in his run for the presidential election in 2003. His program promised to 'take consistent measures to reduce emigration and support the return of emigrants on the government level' (Kocharyan 2003). The smaller nationalistic ARF-Dashnak Party easily endorsed this anti-emigration approach, as it took up the nationalistic, anti-emigration policy they had already formulated under Ter-Petrosyan's presidency (Shain 2007: 148). In addition, the financially viable and politically influential Armenian diaspora, which had left Armenia long before its independence in 1991, strongly endorsed the policy to halt more recent emigration from Armenia. The newly arriving, often illegal migrants, were perceived to threaten the older diaspora's reputation in their societies of choice (Savvidis 2011).[65] Unlike in Georgia, where a liberal, Singapore-inspired approach to unregulated outmigration prevailed especially under the incumbency of Mikheil Saakashvili, halting emigration and returning the Armenian diaspora to its native country strongly corresponded to the Armenian tradition of hay dat and Araratism, which enjoyed large support within Armenian society (Hofmann 2009). The negative perception of emigration from Armenia was additionally shared by the larger population, most likely due to the historical experience of massive flight and forced expulsions in the course of the century-long struggle over the Armenian Highland (Savvidis 2011: 218).

Readmission as a means to organize reintegration

Against the background of this overall political and societal consensus, the authorities started to work on readmission agreements as a means to 'develop [...] projects to support the reintegration of citizens readmitted to Armenia and negotiate with foreign states and international organizations in order to acquire financial and technical support and counseling in this field' (Government of Armenia 2004: 4). The main driver of this process was reportedly Gagik Yeganyan, the head of the Department of Migration and Refugees (DMR) at the time. The DMR frequently suffered from a lack of budgeting and resources (Gevorgyan 2008: 32), for example for the implementation of reintegration and awareness-raising policies – a problem that readmission agreements promised to tackle to some extent. In 2002, prior to the signature of the first readmission agreement with Denmark in 2003, Yeganyan declared:

> when this phenomenon [illegal migration] manifests itself through identification of illegal migrants in the countries of destination, it is necessary to organize their return, and this can be done by signing readmission agreements. And finally, in order to exclude recurring migration of returnees to the countries of destination, readmission should be supplemented by reintegration programs.
>
> (Yeganyan 2003)

Again, in 2006, Yeganyan reiterated that 'cooperation in such delicate issues [readmission] creates good perspectives for establishing effective cooperation in the other aspects of combating illegal migration (such as preventive measures, reintegration assistance etc)' (Yeganyan 2006). Likewise, the State Migration Service re-emphasized in 2010 that the Armenian government wanted the EU particularly 'not to forget about reintegration assistance [...]' as this was Armenia's 'additional interest'.[66]

Furthermore, the conclusion of readmission agreements encountered less domestic resistance in terms of potential externalities stemming from a highly liberal visa policy, as had been the case in Georgia. Armenia had established a visa regime that obliged most foreigners coming to Armenia to apply for a visa, among them EU citizens. The reason for this more restrictive policy was reportedly not that the Armenians were less interested in the attraction of investors or tourists, but rather that they feared that a unilateral liberalization of visa regimes with the EU would trigger a demand of reciprocity by Iran, too. Iran, one of the few close partners of Armenia in the region, however, hosted a large number of ethnic Azeris in its north (Teurtrie 2010: 173), which seemingly made the Armenian authorities fear an inflow of Azeris once the visa regime was abolished.[67]

Against the background of an overall domestic consensus and the prospect of being rewarded with reintegration assistance, readmission agreements were subsequently signed with Denmark in 2003 and Switzerland in 2004. Switzerland provided assistance to the DMR for the implementation of reintegration projects from 2004 until the end of 2008. By 2010, Armenia had 13 readmission agreements with EU or Schengen countries in place, comprising Belgium, Denmark (2004), Lithuania (2004), Bulgaria (2007), the Czech Republic (2010), Germany (2006), Latvia (2002), Lithuania (2003), Luxembourg, Norway, Sweden, the Netherlands and Switzerland (Grigoryan 2011a: 5; Ministry of Foreign Affairs of the Republic of Armenia 2011). Alongside Switzerland, the countries of Denmark, France, Belgium and the Netherlands provided assistance in return for bilateral readmission agreements.[68] Likewise, the Armenian authorities continuously engaged in negotiations on readmission and mobility issues with France, Qatar, Sweden and Liechtenstein in 2011 (PanArmenian.

net 2011a). Georgia, in comparison, had only signed four bilateral agreements at the time. In 2010, the Armenian government also passed a governmental decree to formally regulate the internal readmission process, and establish the procedures and timeframes, which had formerly only been informally agreed.[69]

Overall, Armenia thus achieved output compliance with a view to the PCA requirement to negotiate bilateral readmission agreements, which, as the above evidence suggests, was predominantly due to the fact that the Armenian authorities were able to use the EU's request to satisfy its own political agenda vis-à-vis the broader Armenian society, the diaspora and its own nationalistic coalition partners.

In a similar vein, bilateral partners and the EU positively assessed the implementation of the bilateral readmission agreements. The Swiss Agency for Migration hailed the cooperation with the Armenian Migration Agency and the overall satisfactory implementation of the readmission agreement in its final report (Bundesamt für Migration der Schweizerischen Eidgenossenschaft 2010), which was echoed by both the EU Advisory Group[70] and the Armenian authorities.[71] In order to solve problems related to a lack of identity documents of irregular Armenian migrants abroad, the Armenian side sent Armenian officials to the requesting countries two or three times a year to interrogate potential illegal migrants in the country of destination.[72]

Apart from the *de facto* processing of readmission requests, the Armenian authorities also implemented different schemes to reintegrate returned migrants and prevent re-emigration. For the implementation of awareness-raising campaigns the agency cooperated closely with IOM and the DRC (Gevorgyan 2008: 25f.). The implementation of readmission agreements was also supported by the EU's thematic program on migration and asylum in 2009 with an European Community contribution of approximately €0.7 million, involving non-state actors in the implementation process (Armenian UN Association 2009). The EU also provided capacity building to the Ministry of Diaspora via a TAIEX project in 2010 to set up a law on repatriation in line with the EU migration acquis (European Commission 2011i). Together with an amended law on citizenship and a lump sum of €3,000 paid to every migrant returning voluntarily,[73] the naturalization of returned migrants was encouraged and legally facilitated. This was further supported by private projects of the Armenian diaspora to make compatriots return, particularly in order to increase Armenia's defense capacities against Azerbaijan, which frequently cited out-migration from Armenia as a demographic solution to the Nagorno-Karabakh conflict (Aghajanian 2011). With the support of AENEAS funding, IOM and the Italian government piloted a Migrant Resource Center in 2006, which was handed over to the Armenian government in 2010 (IOM 2010a) and provided legal counseling and assistance to potential migrants. By 2011, 51 of those centers had been opened and operated by the state, mostly by the State Employment Service Agency of Armenia.[74]

Russia supports awareness raising

The international cooperation for the implementation of programs was not limited to 'Western' organizations and states. The DMR, renamed the Migration Agency in 2005, together with the Armenian police also cooperated with the Russian Federation in order to implement awareness-raising campaigns. Starting from 2004, the Armenian police organized meetings with representatives of the Russian Federal Migration Service (FMS) to inform Armenian citizens about the migration situation in Russia (Gevorgyan 2008; ICMPD 2005). Furthermore, in 2010 the FMS jointly with ILO developed a brochure to inform potential migrants and provide assistance to encourage legal migration and limit the number of illegal migrants.[75] The FMS also provided capacity to the Migrant Resource Center by training the coaches conducting awareness-raising campaigns at the center.[76] In addition, representatives of the FMS attended roundtable meetings on migration issues, organized by IOM Armenia.[77] Hence, Russia, the EU and international organizations jointly supported the implementation of the policy of readmission and return in Armenia, which enjoyed a broad consensus among political and societal forces. Armenia hence achieved full compliance with a view to both its output and outcome dimensions.

Incentives remain intangible

An alternative explanation to the preferential fit argument might be increased external pressure triggering the internal reform process via incentives. This is supported by some public statements by Armenian officials following the conclusion of readmission agreements with EU or Schengen countries in Armenia. By early 2008 Armenia had frequently asked the EU to set up the JLS sub-committee and to start visa facilitation negotiations.[78] The request was reiterated by the Armenian authorities in meetings with EU and member state officials in subsequent years (Ministry of Foreign Affairs of the Republic of Armenia 2009b, 2010c). In February 2011, after the parliamentary ratification process of the readmission agreement with the Czech Republic, Gagik Yeganyan presented the agreement as 'an opportunity to expand cooperation in migration processes and contribute to [... a] further expansion of a dialogue between Armenia and the EU' (Armenian News 2011b). Likewise, an agreement with France on the abolition of visa requirements for holders of diplomatic passports was presented as a first step toward visa facilitation with the EU (Ministry of Foreign Affairs of the Republic of Armenia 2009a).

Surprisingly, however, Armenia at that time had not even received the concrete prospect of visa facilitation talks with the EU. Unlike Georgia, Armenia was unable to achieve the early opening of visa facilitation negotiations. This was reportedly due to a delay in the mandating procedure in the EU institutions. A JLS sub-committee was set up and held its first meeting in

July 2010 (PanArmenian.net 2010). The EU hinted at a potential start of negotiations on visa facilitation and EU readmission agreements by the end of 2010. This was greatly appreciated by Armenian's foreign minister, Edward Nalbandian (Ministry of Foreign Affairs of the Republic of Armenia 2010a, 2010b), who stated in December 2010:

> Already from the beginning of the next year the negotiations will start about the facilitation of the visa regime. It is a very important direction of negotiations with respect to people-to-people contacts; it will create more favorable conditions not only for humanitarian, but also for business ties. I think we will conduct the negotiations as soon as possible to speak in the next round about the visa liberalization regime. Of course, it is not a question for [the] near future. But that is our goal for the future.
> (Ministry of Foreign Affairs of the Republic of Armenia 2010d)

The start of the negotiations on visa facilitation, however, was delayed. The negotiation mandate of the Council was not awarded by the end of 2010 (Council of the European Union 2011b). Evidence suggests that this was due to the fact that the issue lacked priority on the Council's agenda[79] and – above all – that inter-institutional changes after the Lisbon Treaty enforcement kept the EU busy at the time (Martirosian 2011). The latter is confirmed by statements of officials of both the Armenian MFA and the European Commission. The former remember that the set-up of the External Action Service after the Lisbon Treaty hampered further progress in this direction.[80] Likewise, an EU official of the Directorate-General (DG) of Home Affairs stated that the reason for the delay in the Armenian case stemmed more from EU internal processes, while the opening of negotiations with Georgia was catalyzed by the war with Russia.[81]

In September 2011, three years after the Commission had recommended providing a mandate to negotiate visa facilitation with Georgia, Armenia was granted the same offer, together with Azerbaijan. The mandate was given by the Council on 19 December 2011 and negotiations started on 27 February 2012 (Danielyan 2012c; Delegation of the EU to Armenia 2012). The pace with which both the readmission and visa facilitation negotiations were concluded underlines the lack of domestic contestation of both agreements in Armenia: both agreements were already initialed in October 2012, had been signed and ratified by 2013, and entered into force in 2014 (EC and HR 2013b).

Preferential fit and the usage of multiple external capacities

The timing of the EU readmission negotiation process, which only commenced in 2012, and the initial timing of the Armenian authorities' conclusion of readmission agreements in 2003 hints at a weak explanatory power of external incentives in this case. Even if policy conditionality had been anticipated by the Armenian authorities prior to the *de facto* mandating procedure, this would have been the case either from 2008 onwards, when the Council had formulated its Common Approach to visa facilitation, or after the passage of the Eastern Partnership Declaration in May 2009, which introduced the long-term prospect of visa liberalization. Capacity building, provided in the form of financial assistance by both the EU and Russia, helped to reintegrate and inform potential migrants to reduce the number of illegally re-migrating Armenians. Yet, the timing of capacity building from 2005 onward and the conclusion of the first readmission agreement in 2003 suggest that this support figured as a convenient financial resource rather than as a stimulus to trigger reforms in the first place. Thus, the early compliance effort rather supports the preferential fit argument: readmission agreements served the domestic policy purposes of the Kocharyan and subsequent Sargsyan administrations at the time, rather than being triggered by the provision of external incentives or capacity building in the first place.

Document security

From 2007, the minister of economy, Nerses Yeritsyan, and the then head of the Central Bank and later prime minister, Tigran Sargsyan, had worked on a thorough e-governance agenda, which implied the issuance of e-IDs and biometric passports in order to improve the business environment of Armenia and facilitate the access of citizens to public services. Since the early 2000s this policy had been supported by multiple donor organizations, among them UNDP, USAID and the Swiss Development Agency, and gained momentum in 2007 with the newly elected government headed by Prime Minister Serzh Sargsyan (Probert 2009; Sandukhchyan and Misnikov 2004).[82] The initiation of the Armenian e-governance reform, including the introduction of biometric passports, was in line with the overall attempt of the new government to boost its international and domestic legitimacy particularly by economic reforms (cf. EIU 2007a: 9).[83] Then still incumbent President Kocharyan set up a working group to work toward the introduction of e-IDs and biometric passports, which was also presented as a means to facilitate the visa procedures with EU member states (Public Radio of Armenia 2008).[84] Related initiatives had, however, encountered criticism from members of the influential Apostolic Church and other religious groups in Armenia, who opposed the numbering of people on the grounds of religious dogma.[85] During consultations with multiple stakeholders, data protection concerns were additionally raised given the increase of information to be stored in biometric databases and e-ID cards with the police.[86]

As a result of the working group meetings a presidential decree was passed in March 2008. It foresaw the introduction of biometric passports and e-IDs from January 2010 onward (Kocharyan 2008). The decree justified the reform, referring to the UN and the European Parliament proposals to fight terrorism and the potential facilitation of visa procedures with the EU and the USA. In addition, its stated goals were to improve the public register with biometric data, reduce the possibility of identity fraud, 'simplify and automate identification processes' and identify 'unwanted persons' (Kocharyan 2008). The introduction of biometrics hence seemingly served the incumbent government. First, it would upgrade its public services via e-governance and enhance the capacity of the state by the gathering of biometric information. Second, the government considered the introduction of biometric identifiers a helpful means to fight terrorism and thus enhance its international standing. Third, the move potentially enabled more Armenians to travel and was thus additionally likely to provide the government with more domestic legitimacy. To subvert criticism, the decree also recommended avoiding any talk about identification numbers. Rather, it suggested using 'the term "Personal Public Service Number" (PPSN) instead [...] taken from a corresponding Irish legislative act' (Kocharyan 2008: 6).

International donors provide capacity

In 2007, the EU conducted a TAIEX mission in Armenia to help introduce biometric identifiers into its passports, as agreed in the ENP AP. The passport and visa department of the Armenian police, responsible for the issuance and preparation of new travel documents, had applied for a TAIEX project to exchange views with EU member states on their experience with biometric identifiers in 2007 (PAO Armenia 2007). While the TAIEX project provided some technical expertise to the police, the financial costs that had been feared by the Georgian government with regard to the introduction of biometric passports were balanced by international capacity building in Armenia. After the presidential decree was signed in 2008 and the newly elected President Serzh Sargsyan and his cabinet had taken office, the government approached OSCE and IOM for assistance to work toward the introduction of biometric passports.[87] The assistance was provided in the form of training, consultation and policy advice (IOM 2010b). IOM and OSCE jointly organized study tours to Switzerland and Portugal and invited international experts to assist the tendering procedure for the passport procurement.

Subsequently, in 2009 the Armenian government established an e-Governance Infrastructure Implementation Unit (EKENG) with the Ministry of Economy, a joint stock company that was supposed to plan and conduct the tendering procedure.[88] An action plan on a first tender was approved by the Armenian prime minister on 18 June 2009 (Hovhannisian 2011). However, the nomination of a company to provide the technical equipment and blank passports took some time. The first action plan foresaw a public-private partnership to implement the project – an approach that was recommended by experts of USAID and the Roland Berger consultancy in order to open the sector to foreign investors and privatize the overall endeavor (EKENG 2010).[89] The action plan triggered criticism of the incumbent government, reportedly due to the loss of full state control in a public-private partnership that implied the sharing of personal data of citizens with private companies.[90] IOM hence helped to revise the action plan again to follow a simple procurement approach to retain the issuance of passports under full state control. This renewed action plan was approved by the government in September 2010 and the tender was announced in October 2010 (Hovhannisian 2011). The Polish company Polish Security Printing Works won the tender in August 2011, after lengthy negotiations with a second, French bidder (Oberthur) that went to court over the decision of the Armenian government to prioritize the Polish company.[91]

The benefits of implementation and a lack of policy conditionality

By September 2011, the technical equipment had been made available and the new passport was considered compliant with the relevant international standards (Hovhannisian 2011). At the same time, the parliamentary discussions started with a view to pass the legal amendments necessary for the introduction of biometric passports (Khojoyan 2011). The new passport was critically discussed in parliament, particularly with a view to the reportedly high fee for the renewed travel documents, which centered around €60. Compared to the prior system of exit permits for €2 (Khojoyan 2011), the purpose of this expensive travel document without the tangible perspective of visa-free travel with the EU was questioned, as international observers note.[92] Despite the fact that the EU Commission had praised the introduction of biometric passports in the JLS sub-committee meeting since 2010, Armenia had still not been awarded a negotiation mandate for visa facilitation from the Council at the time, nor had this mandate been made conditional upon the introduction of biometrics. The introduction of biometric passports was hence not a clear-cut condition set by the EU for Armenia to profit from visa facilitation, nor was visa-free travel a tangible incentive in sight for the Armenian public. Still, as one government official described the prevailing mood in Armenia's National Assembly in October 2011:

> I think everyone understands that they must accept it anyway because it is really important to participate in the European Integration processes, otherwise you cannot; it is one of the prerequisites for starting this visa facilitation procedure.[93]

Indeed, the National Assembly – dominated by the ruling Republican Party and its coalition partners – passed the amendments to the laws in November 2011 to pave the way for the introduction of biometric passports in June 2012. By late 2011, Armenia had hence achieved output compliance with the ENP requirement to introduce biometric passports.

While in Georgia the opposition used the introduction of biometric passports to push for genuine democratic reforms by linking biometric technologies to the voting procedure, the Armenian government did not encounter similar political challenges. The passport and visa department of the police had already been in charge of compiling voter lists for elections since 2005, unlike its Georgian counterpart, the CRA (OSCE and ODIHR 2007: 7). While the CRA in Georgia had, however, emerged as one of the reform-oriented forces in Georgia, the passport and police department in Armenia was less open to external support for reforms (Brandstetter and Zakoyan 2012: ii). Instead, the Armenian opposition demanded the publication of voter lists immediately after the election to see who had voted and check whether it was indeed 'dead souls' that maintained the government's grip on power – a proposal that the ruling government rejected as incompatible with the Venice's Commission demands for a secret ballot (Hayrumyan 2011).

However, electoral reform indeed affected the scope of the implementation of biometric passports, as in Georgia. The amended electoral code of 2011 had been designed with a view to the old Armenian passport system, in which a single passport document was used as a domestic ID card and for foreign travel. As a result, the amended code foresaw that in order to prevent multiple voting, the electorate's passports should be stamped (Venice Commission 2011: Art. 66(4)). The amendment had been welcomed by international observers (Venice Commission and OSCE/ODIHR 2011a), but this stamping requirement ruled out that e-IDs could be used for voting purposes, mainly due to technical incompatibilities, as the magnetic cards could not be stamped (Gevorgyan 2012; Venice Commission 2011: Art. 64(3)). In order to ensure that all people could still vote without being forced to apply for an expensive biometric passport, the non-biometric, national passports needed to remain valid beyond a potential grace period (Gevorgyan 2012). Again, this constraint did not affect outcome compliance with the ENP requirement. The older, non-biometric passports still corresponded with International Civil Aviation Organization (ICAO) standards acceptable to the EU.[94] As the roadmap toward visa liberalization with Moldova shows, the ENC were only required to phase out non-ICAO standardized passports fully with a view to visa liberalization with the EU (Government of Moldova 2010). The Armenian government hence fully complied with the ENP prescription of introducing biometric passports, which supposedly corresponded with the incumbent's agenda to gain internal and international legitimacy, and at the same time extend the information capacities of the executive power.

An alternative explanation for Armenia's compliance with the biometric passport stipulation despite a lack of tangible incentives might be the additional exposure to learning or socialization processes in the CSTO framework. Armenia indeed participated in consultations about issues of passports and visa systems, and the new generation of biometrics in the framework of the CSTO Coordination Council for the Fight Against Illegal Migration (OSCE 2011). However, this institution was not set up before early 2008 (Marat and Murzakulova 2007; *Uzbekistan Daily* 2008), when Armenia had already taken steps toward the enhancement of document security.

Preferential fit and the usage of external opportunities

In short, the above evidence suggests that the full compliance of Armenia with the ENP prescription of enhancing document security was indeed triggered by an overall preferential fit of the incumbent government and the ENP requirement despite the fact that the EU did not provide any financial assistance for its implementation. The technical capacity building of the EU and further financial support by OSCE were seemingly used by the incumbent government to implement a previously held agenda. First, the Armenian government approached OSCE for support. In addition, the presidential decree includes references to European legislation in order supposedly to overcome societal resistance against the initiative, which hints at a form of ENC-driven lesson drawing, rather than an EU-driven process of domestic reform. Yet, as the set-up of Armenian-EU networks in the framework of the TAIEX project coincided with the start of work on the reform, an increased socialization of Armenian officials in this setting may indeed have supported the Armenian reform attempts in this case, too.

National action plan on migration and asylum

In Armenia, similar to Georgia, the work on the national action plan started in 2007. An AENEAS-funded project implemented by the British Council, the International Center for Human Development (ICHD) and the Migration Agency of Armenia had formulated the goal of developing a national migration policy (ICHD 2013). A multi-stakeholder process was initiated that brought together all decision makers of the governmental administration, IOs and local NGOs. The Migration Agency, representatives of the Ministry of Labor and Social Affairs, as well as representatives of ILO and the Armenian UN Association participated.[95] The multi-stakeholder process was complemented by TAIEX events, which particularly aimed at supporting the Migration Agency. Two TAIEX events in 2008 aimed at the preparation of a comprehensive national action plan on migration and asylum issues and on international refugee law. IOM delivered additional capacity building in 2008 via a report on the migration situation in Armenia, which was specifically conducted in light of the ENP and aimed at informing the Armenian national action plan on migration (Chindea et al. 2008).[96] Despite the fact that particularly the Migration Agency was financially supported and included in transgovernmental networks with the EU in the framework of TAIEX projects, the formal adoption of a national action plan on migration was a long time coming. Reportedly, intra-governmental veto players constrained the Migration Agency in its pursuit of adopting an action plan.

Intra-governmental veto players raise their voices

Observers of the stakeholder process noticed fierce competition between the Migration Agency and the Ministry of Labor and Social Affairs over migration policy issues.[97] The ministry, led by the smaller coalition party ARF-Dashnak, was reportedly of the opinion that the Armenian government should combat migration instead of managing it.[98] This was in line with the Dashnak approach of considering out-migration as a threat to the country (Shain 2007: 148).

The conflict between the two ministries was seemingly difficult to overcome, as the coordinating function and leading role for migration policy making was not clarified at the time.[99] The Migration Agency had been an autonomous body until 2005, when it was downgraded and incorporated into the 'Super Ministry' of Territorial Administration of Hovik Abrahamyan (Chobanyan 2012). Being loyal to Robert Kocharyan, the creation of the extended ministry and Abrahamyan's appointment at the time can be interpreted as Kocharyan's move to secure his power base in the government which became increasingly dominated by a reform-minded wing of the Republican Party under the auspices of Serzh Sargsyan (cf. Arakelyan 2011). In addition, the Migration Agency was further weakened after the election of Serzh Sargsyan as president. A Presidential Order (NK-53-A) issued on 15 March 2008 transferred all migration-related functions to the passport and visa department of the police (Kocharyan 2008). While this move was interpreted by some (also international) observers as a welcome centralization of migration issues,[100] ILO, UNHCR and the Migration Agency condemned it as a move to criminalize migrants, refugees and asylum seekers alike.[101] By late 2008, it hence seemed that the efforts of the Migration Agency and the AENEAS-funded project to adopt a migration policy had been put on hold by the March presidential decree and the internal opposition to the proposal. This is supported by statements of non-governmental and governmental participants to the working group process: ILO concluded that the output of the first working group was no more than a rough outline,[102] while the Migration Agency itself stated that the process of drafting the national action plan on migration did not start until the beginning of 2010.[103]

Governmental reshuffle facilitates reform

Evidence suggests that more governmental reshuffle and delicate incentives provided by Russia throughout 2009 gave greater support to the Migration Agency and its reform plans. Artur Baghdasaryan, outspokenly pro-Western and accused of high treason by Kocharyan due to a critical statement to a British diplomat prior to the 2008 presidential election, was appointed as the secretary of the National Security Council by Serzh Sargsyan in February 2008. The body was considered largely ceremonial under Kocharyan, but Sargsyan pledged that his post would gain significance (Saghabalian 2008). Consequently, Sargsyan shifted the overall coordination activities with the EU to the National Security Council. In April 2009 the coalition partner, the ARF-Dashnak Party, quit the ruling coalition due to the rapprochement of President Sargsyan with Turkey (Danielyan and Martirosian 2009). The role of minister of labor and social affairs was given to the second smaller coalition party, the Prosperous Armenia Party, in May 2009 (ILO 2009). Another government change had released Hovik Abrahamyan from the post of minister of territorial affairs (EIU 2008a). Armen Gevorgyan was appointed to fill his place on 21 April 2008. While he had been the one to sign the annex to the presidential decree of 15 March which empowered the police over the Migration Agency, his new position placed him at the top of the Migration Agency within the Ministry of Territorial Affairs, and reportedly exposed him to the lobbying efforts of its head, Gagik Yeganyan. As a staff member of the State Migration Service remembers:

> [Gagik Yeganyan] did not agree with that [the March 2008 decree] [...] Kocharyan signed the decree, but the annex was signed by Armen Gevorgyan [...] He was the head of staff of the President. After that, he had a new appointment as Minister of Territorial Administration and [...] vice-prime minister. Then [Yeganyan] had the chance to explain him in a very close situation. That was a very good option to explain him [...] He became aware that the transfer to the police is not the best solution [...] and he sent letters to the President and the Speaker of the National Assembly that we maybe have to change this.[104]

Change did indeed occur. A new interagency working group was set up on 16 April 2009 by Prime Minister Tigran Sargsyan which was chaired by Artur Baghdasaryan in order to work on Armenia's migration management reform. The working group recommended the upgrade of the former Migration Agency again to a State Migration Service and to charge it with policy-making authority, which was carried out by a presidential decree on 18 November 2009 (Chobanyan 2012). Being no longer blocked by intra-governmental opposition, the State Migration Service subsequently worked on a new draft of the policy document (OSCE 2010), which was reportedly developed from scratch[105] with OSCE/ILO-recruited experts and EU support from 2010 onward. The EU advisory group appointed a migration expert who worked closely with the State Migration Service to create the document. The draft version was circulated among the ministries, and while it received some comments on the distribution of competences, the overall concept was easily agreed.[106] On 30 December 2010 the government of Armenia adopted the 'Concept of the State Regulation of Migration in the Republic of Armenia' (N51) (Government of Armenia 2010), and on 10 November 2011, a national action plan on its implementation was finalized, which established output compliance with the ENP criteria. The concept paper and the action plan were explicitly framed to serve the implementation of a previously held governmental agenda as expressed in the National Security Strategy, the 2008 Governmental Program and the Sustainable Development Program (Government of Armenia 2010, 2011).

Negative incentives by Russia and the usage of the national action plan

Furthermore, the work on the national action plan coincided with the global financial crisis and the start of the 'Compatriots Program' of Russia's FMS in Armenia. The program invited Armenian-based Russian compatriots – a term that followed a political rather than an ethnic or civic notion – to settle permanently in remote Russian areas (Byford 2012: 3). In order to fight Russia's demographic decline, the program offered housing and work opportunities and facilitated naturalization to gain Russian citizenship. In Armenia, the initiative sparked fierce protests among non-parliamentary opposition groups and the ARF-Dashnaks alike, claiming that it undermined the Armenian-Russian relationship and Armenia's economic development by encouraging brain drain (Grigoryan 2011b). Likewise, the government was increasingly confronted with criticism by the Armenian diaspora and its connected parties on emigration matters (Armenian News 2011a; Garbis 2012). Members of the Armenian National Congress, led by Ter-Petrosyan, frequently referred to the rising degree of emigration as a threat to national security and development (Armenian National Congress 2010; Armenian News 2010), which culminated in the 2012 pre-election slogan, 'Whoever supports Serzh, supports emigration' (A1+ 2012). A 'migration meeting' at the president's office in July 2011 underlined the domestic urgency of the issue (Dilanyan 2011). When figures on emigration apparently peaked in 2011 and the opposition blamed the state for not tackling the problem of emigration, the EU-recommended national action plan on migration was presented as a 'migration control strategy' to counter the opposition's criticism (Armenian News 2011a; see also PanArmenian.net 2011b, 2011c).

Yet, despite the fact that the action plan was sold as a means to reduce emigration, evidence suggests that the Armenian authorities had still not endorsed the Dashnak approach of stopping emigration by all means. The EU's 'Global Approach to Migration', which was reflected in the action plan, rather foresaw limited, temporary and legal migration, while decreasing illegal migration flows (European Commission 2007f). As critical Armenian observers note, this was indeed very much in line with what the government hoped to achieve, bearing in mind the socio-economic effects of decreasing remittance payments and work opportunities abroad, let alone the human rights violation that a full stop of emigration from Armenia implied. Government critics accused the authorities of using Russia's Compatriots Program as a 'way to let off steam from [...] spreading discontent' (Grigoryan 2011b) in Armenia, a debate that was lighted by statements by Armenian Prime Minister Tigran Sargsyan. He reportedly replied to a journalist's question concerning the increased volume of emigrants from Armenia as follows:

> What can we do, we should do everything so these people won't flee, so that critical mass remains here and a revolution happens? What can we

do for people to stay in Armenia? We have to do it so that life in our country is better than [life] abroad.

(Sargsyan, quoted in Epress.am 2011)

External capacity building supports a smooth implementation process

Implementation of the national action plan progressed smoothly. In order to coordinate activities, implement and monitor the plan, as well as the Mobility Partnership that Armenia and the EU had signed in October 2011, Armenia set up an interagency committee (EC and HR 2013b). A first meeting of the committee was held in early 2012, which assigned the relevant institutions to prepare their implementation part of the plan. In addition, capacity to implement the plan was provided through the Twinning project 'Support to the State Migration Service for Strengthening of Migration Management in Armenia' (Delegation of the EU to Armenia 2011). The implementation of the migration action plan was further supported by the so called Targeted Initiative Armenia, a three-year project entitled 'Strengthening Armenia's migration management capacities, with special focus on reintegration activities in the framework of the EU-Armenia Mobility Partnership'. The project was launched under the umbrella of the Mobility Partnership in December 2012 with the participation of several EU member states and led by the French Office for Migration and Integration (EC and HR 2013b; Ghazanchyan 2013).

An alternative explanation for the preferential fit argument may be the rise of intense capacity building and external incentives that seemingly coincided with the developments towards the action plan development in Armenia. The EU Advisory Group was set up in 2009 as a pilot project to advise distinct ministries in their EU integration process. Yet it only started to operate formally in October 2009, when the interagency working group had already been set up (Delegation of the EU to Armenia 2009). While it helped to draft the strategy, it is thus unlikely that its support was causal to the initiation of the process. Likewise, the prospect of a Mobility Partnership may have functioned as an important trigger to put migration management reform on the agenda – an argument that is, however, at odds again with the timing of developments in Armenia. The general concept of Mobility Partnerships as an Extension of the Global Approach to Migration was already formulated in 2007, while the precise offer for Armenia was only made in 2011, when the concept paper and the national action plan were already on track. In addition, it is also unlikely that the plan was the result of anticipated visa liberalization conditionality. Armenia had not even been granted the Council's mandate for visa facilitation when the concept paper was passed. Visa liberalization, for which a national action plan was indeed needed, was only a very distant prospect.

A change in government triggers domestic change

Overall, if weighed against the presented alternatives, the evidence provided in this case study suggests that both output and outcome compliance were established in this case due to changed domestic conditions after the ARF-Dashnak Party left the ruling coalition in 2009. The change in the preferential fit of the Armenian government was hence caused by an internal governmental reshuffle, rather than by external stimulation. In addition, the policy change seemed to be rather ENC driven, as the passage of the national action plan served the Armenian government to implement governmental programs passed in 2007 and 2008, divert the increasingly loud protests of the opposition in migration matters and at the same time avoid the risk of increasing socio-economic tensions by fully reducing migration possibilities. Negative incentives by Russia did not drive the compliance process; rather, the passage of the national action plan was used by the authorities to divert criticism of the Armenian government caused by unconditional Russian incentives. The evidence hence suggests that external policies and the respective financial and technical assistance were used as financial and political resources to implement a preferred governmental agenda rather than changing preferences in the first place.

Data protection

The idea to reform data protection legislation in Armenia goes back to Robert Kocharyan's presidential decree of 2008, which aimed at the introduction of biometric passports (Kocharyan 2008).[107] Data protection was reportedly discussed as a point of concern in this process and different stakeholders expressed the fear that the collection of additional biometric data might be misused by state agencies.[108] Doing justice to widespread data protection concerns, Kocharyan's decree recommended:

> in order to make the subject of regulation of prospective laws consistent with the European legal regulation mechanisms, make justified suggestions on the functions and powers of an independent state inspectorate dealing with technologies ensuring security of personal data on the Internet and the Register, prevention, disruption, investigation of offences committed in the field of data protection [...].
>
> (Kocharyan 2008)

Subsequently, the police of the Republic of Armenia drafted a new data protection law with the help of IOM experts in 2009 (Hovhannisian 2011). From July 2010 onward, data protection was also constantly raised in the EU-Armenian JLS sub-committee.[109] While it figured as a condition for visa liberalization in negotiations with countries that had already established visa facilitation, it was not communicated as a condition to achieve visa facilitation with the EU in the first place.[110] Despite the lack of a clear-cut conditionality at the time, the EU provided capacity to the Armenian government as a means to facilitate domestic change. In November 2010, the Armenian-European Policy and Legal Advice Center (AEPLAC) conducted a two-day seminar with all relevant ministries and stakeholders of the Armenian government to brief them on data protection principles within the EU.[111] Cooperation with the Armenian authorities on this matter, however, reportedly proved difficult. EU officials unanimously reported a general misunderstanding of data protection principles by the Armenian state authorities. The police, when asked about data protection in Armenia, replied that they had 'secure lines'.[112] Likewise, an EU official of DG Justice confirmed that his request for information on data protection in Armenia resulted in a ten-minute presentation by an Armenian police official about data security and related software or hardware.[113] In light of the EU's understanding of data protection as a basic individual right, the Armenian focus on data security made the official conclude that 'sometimes one does talk at cross purposes'.[114] One of the members of the Advisory Group additionally remembers that the Armenian government was not very much in favor of having an independent supervisory authority.[115]

The Armenian government signed the Council of Europe Convention and the Additional Protocol on Supervisory Authorities in April 2011 and also drafted a law on data protection that was needed to fulfill its requirements (Hovhannisian 2011). In March 2012, the Standing Committee on Foreign Relations within the parliament was briefed by the deputy head of the police on the Council of Europe Convention and the Additional Protocol (National Assembly of Armenia 2012), which were ratified in May 2012 (EC and HR 2013b). Likewise, in the framework of the passage of biometric passport-related legislation, the head of EKENG underscored once more in October 2011 that the new passports would thoroughly protect the personal data that were gathered (National Assembly of Armenia 2011).

Russian incentives and non-compliance

However, the draft national law on data protection initially failed to incorporate the initial goals of the Council of Europe convention. It did not foresee an independent supervisory authority, but vaguely defined an 'Authorized State Body for the Protection of Personal Data [… that is] operating within the national executive body system' (Government of Armenia 2012: Art. 21). Even in the case of a passage of the draft law, the *de facto* protection of personal data by an executive state authority would have been rather unlikely. Evaluating Armenia's process in 2013, the European Commission hence stated that:

> Concerns persist on the draft data protection law; the designation in the draft of police and the security service as supervisory bodies is not in line with EU standards, notably with the independence requirement.
>
> (EC and HR 2014a)

In addition, some international observers to the process remarked that the close cooperation of the Armenian border police and its Russian counterpart may figure as a challenge to the implementation of a potential data protection reform. Russian border guards provide capacity to the Armenian border police at the Zvartnots airport and guard the outer CIS border with Iran and Turkey. Some feared that this cooperation might hollow out the provision of the data protection convention (Grigoryan 2011a). Yet, in opposition to this claim, a representative of IOM stressed that the Russian authorities operating in Armenia had to stick to Armenian law.[116] They would thus also be bound to this legislation when accessing or sharing data. Likewise, an EU official underscored that one has 'to be satisfied that these borders are properly managed with or without Russia'.[117] While the capacity was indeed provided to the Armenian authorities by Russia, its impact on compliance is hence difficult to evaluate, given the competing voices both within the EU and the ENC. None of the interviewed decision makers has so far raised this issue as a point of contention.

Preferential misfit and capacity building

In short, this evidence suggests that a substantial preferential misfit prevailed in Armenia with a view to data protection legislation reform, given the potential transfer of political power to an independent supervisory authority and the general misunderstanding of data protection as a security instead of a civil liberties issue. In the absence of any tangible policy conditionality invoked from the EU, the reluctance of the Armenian authorities to establish a politically costly supervisory authority remained unchanged and resulted in non-compliance. The capacity provided by Russia and the EU, also in the framework of transgovernmental exchanges with AEPLAC officials, appears to have had little or an as yet undetermined impact on this result.

Comparative analysis

The case study evidence for the policies of migration management (Table 4.1) suggests that preferential fit is a sufficient condition for domestic change. Full compliance has been achieved particularly with ENP migration management requirements, whenever adaptation costs were negative and domestic actors could use the reforms to further their own political goals. This was more frequently the case in Armenia, where the reduction of emigration, the return of migrants and a more restrictive approach toward migration management corresponded with the agenda of both the Kocharyan and the Sargsyan administrations. The introduction of biometric passports served the Armenian authorities to extend their executive power, while it increased the regime's domestic and international legitimacy after the flawed presidential election in 2008 at the same time. Readmission agreements were used to implement a nationalist agenda on reintegration and return, which

Table 4.1 Overview of cases: migration management

Case	Preferential fit	EU – policy conditionality	RUS – policy conditionality	RUS – uncond.	EU – capacity	RUS – capacity	Compliance
AM readmission	1	0	0	0	1	Concerted	Full
AM biometrics	1	0	0	0	1	0	Full
AM national action plan post-2009	1	0	0	1	1	0	Full
GEO biometrics post-2009	0	1	0	1	1	0	Full
GEO national action plan post-2012	1	1	0	1	1	0	(Full)
GEO biometrics pre-2009	0	0	0	1	0	0	None
GEO national action plan pre-2010	0	0	0	0	1	0	None
GEO readmission pre-2009	0	0	0	1	0	0	None
GEO data protection pre-2008	0	0	0	0	1	0	None
AM national action plan pre-2009	0	0	0	0	1	0	None
AM data protection	0	0	0	0	1	(Rivaling)	None
GEO national action plan 2010–11	0	1	0	1	1	0	Shallow
GEO data protection post-2008	0	1	0	1	1	0	Shallow
GEO readmission post-2009	0	1	0	1	1	0	Full

Note: AM – Armenia; GEO – Georgia; RUS – Russia. 0 stands for the absence, 1 the presence of a condition.

corresponded to the ideological basis of the coalition partners in the Armenian government. On the other hand, in the case of Georgia and Saakashvili's incumbency, the proposed policies proved politically more costly for the domestic government and at odds with their liberal agenda, despite a comparable adaptation pressure with a view to the policy, polity or politics status quo. When policy conditionality was not invoked by the EU, non-compliance largely prevailed in Georgia with a view to migration management.

The cases also show that the preferential fit of a policy and a governmental agenda might change over time. This, however, as in the case of Armenia and the national action plan of migration, has not been induced by external incentives, but by a change in domestic actor constellations. When the Dashnak-ARF Party, the alleged veto player in the action plan reform, left the Armenian government in 2009 and more internal governmental reshuffle empowered the reform-minded State Migration Service, the government indeed complied with the ENP provision to establish an action plan on migration, which additionally helped to silence the domestic opposition over emigration issues.

In addition, the cases at hand also mostly support the hypothesis on interaction effects of preferential misfit and policy conditionality. In cases of costly reforms linked to precise incentives from the EU, output compliance has indeed been noticeable, while outcome compliance remained shallow. When compliance with data protection legislation and the national action plan of migration were made conditions for further progress toward visa liberalization, the Georgian government anticipated EU conditionality from late 2010 onward. While formal output compliance was indeed established, the policy was either put in place only partially (the action plan) or hollowed out by provisions preventing the *de facto* loss of political power vis-à-vis a supervisory authority (data protection).

Yet the case of readmission agreements in Georgia is at odds with the assumed combined effect of preferential misfit and policy conditionality. Despite high costs of the *de facto* implementation of readmission agreements in Georgia, caused by a liberal visa regime that had political support at the highest level – at least until 2012 – readmission agreements were indeed implemented, with a high percentage of readmission requests processed and a large number of returnees reintegrated. Evidence suggests that this was largely due to the application of policy conditionality by the EU, which made the *de facto* and thorough implementation of the readmission agreement a condition to proceed further toward visa liberalization with the EU.

With regard to migration management reform, there has been no case of preferential fit of the ENC with an EU policy and rivaling policy conditionality by Russia. Russia catalyzes bilateral EU-ENC developments rather than incentivizing its own, potentially alternative, policy choices in this policy area. Negative, unconditional incentives by Russia supported the effect of EU policy conditionality in Georgia and further stimulated compliance processes in Armenia. The illegal distribution of Russian passports in Georgia's secessionist republics was one of the main drivers for Georgia to strive for and receive the prospect of visa facilitation with the EU. It added further leverage to continue the domestic reform process after visa facilitation was attained, as Russia was already moving forward with the EU on visa liberalization. The parallelism of Georgia and Russia, due to the negative externalities of Russia's policies in the secessionist republics, hence increased the attractiveness of further integration with the EU and altered the cost-benefit analysis of the Georgian authorities in favor of introducing (shallow) domestic change.

In Armenia, the launch of the 'Compatriots Program' by Russia's FMS was interpreted as a negative, though unconditional incentive, as it exposed the domestic government to intense public discontent, attacks from influential diaspora organizations and the (non-parliamentary) opposition. The work on the national action plan on migration hence further served the incumbent government to subvert this criticism, while at the same time upholding the possibility of increased legal migration to divert socio-economic tensions within the population. Negative incentives from Russia hence functioned as a complement to EU conditionality, but themselves did not trigger change in the first place. Georgia, for instance, faced the problem of illegal passportization prior to late 2008 and had also already pressured the EU on providing visa facilitation. Yet the Georgian government did not engage in potential reform efforts (i.e. the conclusion of bilateral readmission agreements) to this end before it had received the tangible incentive of visa facilitation. The reinforcement of the EU's incentive structure by Russian foreign policy actions proved to be rather indirect and is unlikely to be intended. Yet, in the case of JLS policies, it affected the sectoral compliance output in a positive way, both in Armenia and Georgia. This evidence indeed suggests that the diverse compliance patterns of Armenia and Georgia in the JLS sector can be explained by the interaction of preferential (mis)fit and external incentives provided by the EU and Russia.

For the policy-specific cases at hand, capacity building by the EU seems to be irrelevant to explain compliance in cases of preferential fit and in cases of preferential misfit without policy conditionality. As the case of biometric passports in Armenia shows, a financially costly but politically desired reform was implemented without a thorough provision of assistance by the EU. Instead, the Armenian government asked IOM and OSCE for financial and technical support. In cases where a reform attempt was opposed by powerful domestic agents, however, capacity building, also when provided in transgovernmental networks, fell short of inducing any change. The development of Georgia's data protection legislation prior to 2008 and the work on the national action plan before 2010 are cases in point. In both instances, reform-oriented forces within the government (the minister of justice and minister of refugees and accommodation in Georgia) indeed tried to use external financial and technical assistance either to boost their domestic standing within the government or implement individually pursued reform agendas. In both cases, however, the reform was prevented, delayed or both, due to resistance at the highest government level based on a lack of legitimacy of the norm (constraining the freedom of movement) or an incompatibility of political priorities (constraining business activities). This evidence suggests that compliance is indeed rather the result of the cost-benefit analysis of powerful government agents, rather than the outcome of a successful socialization of lower-level bureaucrats in transgovernmental networks.

Capacity building yet seems to support outcome compliance in the case of initial preferential misfit and policy conditionality, as shown in the case of biometric passports and readmission agreements in Georgia. In the former, the government opposed the reform on the grounds of its high administrative costs. When it became clear that these costs would be shouldered by the EU, the domestic point of contention was lost, as was the resistance against the reform. The political costs, which the Georgian government faced with a view to the opposition proposals to widen the scope of the biometric passports' distribution, could be derailed by the Georgian authorities without even triggering shallow compliance. In addition, readmission agreements were implemented with a large financial and technical support package that was delivered with the establishment of the TIG. This project took over the initial steps toward reintegration, organized legal counseling and services to the returned migrants. In short, the EU to a large part substituted the work of the Georgian authorities by implementing the agreement through its own project partners.

With a view to the effect of potential Russian assistance on the JLS reforms, the evidence suggests once more that capacity provided to Armenian authorities to support awareness raising against illegal migration helped the domestic reform in Armenia. The negative effect of alternative capacity building that Russia may have caused toward compliance proved less verifiable. The claim that the war with Russia had diminished the capacities devoted to the ENP compliance process in Georgia lacked plausibility, while the effect of Russia's support with a view to data protection in Armenia proved to be discussed ambiguously by both Armenian and EU officials and independent observers. As the comparative analysis shows, there is a lack of any migration management reform cases in which Russia clearly incentivizes non-compliance with EU policies. While this is an interesting finding in itself, as some might assume that Russia indeed tries generally to prevent the countries from further integration into the EU, it fails to surprise in light of a general policy convergence that has been found to prevail between both actors in this sector (see Chapter 3). The upcoming analysis of energy sector compliance hence provides this missing 'universe of cases'.

Notes

1 Parts of the material presented in this chapter draw on Ademmer and Börzel (2013) and on Ademmer and Delcour (2016).
2 Phone interview with an EU official, EC (DG Justice), Brussels, 30.08.2011.
3 Ibid.
4 Follow-up interview with a local migration expert, IOM Georgia, Tbilisi, 30.09.2011.
5 Phone interview with an EU official, EEAS, Brussels, 01.09.2011.
6 Ibid.
7 Phone interview with an EU official, EC (DG Home), 11.08.2011.

8 Follow-up interview with a local migration expert, IOM Georgia, Tbilisi, 30.09.2011.
9 Interview with an official of the State Office for Euro-Atlantic Integration (SOEAI), Tbilisi, 06.10.2010.
10 Interview with an official of the Consular Department, MFA Georgia, Tbilisi, 15.10.2010, and with an official of the SOEAI, Tbilisi, 06.10.2010.
11 Interview with an official of the SOEAI, Tbilisi, 06.10.2010.
12 Interview with an official of the Consular Department, MFA Georgia, Tbilisi, 15.10.2010.
13 Follow-up interview with a local migration expert, IOM Georgia, Tbilisi, 30.09.2011.
14 Interview with local migration experts, DRC Georgia, Tbilisi, 03.10.2011.
15 Phone interview with an EU official, EEAS, Brussels, 01.09.2011, and follow-up interview with an official of the SOEAI, Tbilisi, 04.10.2011.
16 Follow-up interview with an official of the Department for European Integration, MFA Georgia, Tbilisi, 28.09.2011.
17 Ibid.; interview with an official of the Ministry of the Interior, Georgia, Tbilisi, 04.10.2011.
18 Interview with a staff member, TIG, Tbilisi, 29.09.2011.
19 Ibid.
20 Interview with local migration experts, DRC Georgia, Tbilisi, 03.10.2011.
21 Follow-up interview with a local migration expert, IOM Georgia, Tbilisi, 30.09.2011.
22 In June 2012, the Public Service Development Agency was established on the basis of the CRA.
23 Follow-up interview with an official of the Department for European Integration, MFA Georgia, Tbilisi, 28.09.2011.
24 Phone interview with an EU official of the EU Delegation to Georgia, Tbilisi, 09.08.2011; interview with an official of the Department of European Integration, MFA Georgia, Tbilisi, 13.10.2010, and with an official of the CRA, Tbilisi, 08.10.2010.
25 Interview with a migration expert, Delegation of the EU to Georgia, Tbilisi, 08.10.2010.
26 The latter has been managed by a Central Election Commission, which was reportedly dominated and misused by the ruling UNM – a fact that triggered serious criticism by election observers after the parliamentary election in 2008 (OSCE and ODIHR 2008: 1f.).
27 News outlets reported that the introduction of biometric identifiers would cost approximately US$8 million, as opposed to Saakashvili's new mega-project to construct a new city on the Black Sea Coast, which was anticipated to cost $900 million (RFE/RL 2012b).
28 By this time, biometric ID cards had been introduced as well, a device that would have been less costly than the issue of biometric passports (Holtved 2011).
29 Follow-up interview with an official of the Department for European Integration, MFA Georgia, Tbilisi, 28.09.2011.
30 Interview with a migration expert, Delegation of the EU to Georgia, Tbilisi, 08.10.2010, with an official of the SOEAI, Tbilisi, 06.10.2010, and with a local migration expert, IOM Georgia, Tbilisi, 04.10.2010.
31 Follow-up interview with a migration expert, Delegation of the EU to Georgia, Tbilisi, 30.09.2011, and interview with local migration experts, DRC Georgia, Tbilisi, 03.10.2011.
32 Interview with local migration experts, DRC Georgia, Tbilisi, 03.10.2011.
33 Interview with an official of the SOEAI, Tbilisi, 06.10.2010.

34 Interview with local migration experts, DRC Georgia, Tbilisi, 03.10.2011, and with two local experts of the Caucasus Institute for Peace, Democracy and Development in Tbilisi, 11.10.2010.
35 Interview with an official of the SOEAI, Tbilisi, 06.10.2010.
36 Ibid.; and interview with a local migration expert, IOM Georgia, Tbilisi, 04.10.2010.
37 Phone interview with an EU official, EEAS, Brussels, 01.09.2011.
38 Follow-up interview with an official of the Department for European Integration, MFA Georgia, Tbilisi, 28.09.2011.
39 Interview with local migration experts, DRC Georgia, Tbilisi, 03.10.2011.
40 Phone interview with an EU official, EEAS, Brussels, 01.09.2011.
41 Interview with local migration experts, DRC Georgia, Tbilisi, 03.10.2011.
42 Interview with a staff member, TIG, Tbilisi, 29.09.2011.
43 Ibid.
44 Interview with an official of the CRA, Tbilisi, 05.10.2011.
45 Interview with a staff member, TIG, Tbilisi, 29.09.2011.
46 E-mail correspondence with a staff member of the CRA, 28.03.2012.
47 Interview with an official of the CRA, Tbilisi, 05.10.2011; follow-up interview with an official of the SOEAI, Tbilisi, 04.10.2011; follow-up interview with a local migration expert, IOM Georgia, Tbilisi, 30.09.2011.
48 Interview with an official of the CRA, Tbilisi, 05.10.2011.
49 E-mail correspondence with a staff member of the CRA, 28.03.2012
50 E-mail correspondence with a staff member of the TIG, 25.03.2012.
51 Interview with a migration expert, Delegation of the EU to Georgia, Tbilisi, 08.10.2010, and with an official of the Ministry of IDPs, Refugees and Accommodation, Tbilisi, 11.10.2010.
52 Interview with local migration experts, DRC Georgia, Tbilisi, 03.10.2011; follow-up interview with an official of the SOEAI, Tbilisi, 04.10.2011.
53 Interview with an official of the CRA, Tbilisi, 05.10.2011.
54 Ibid.
55 Follow-up interview with a migration expert, Delegation of the EU to Georgia, Tbilisi, 30.09.2011.
56 Interview with an official of the CRA, Tbilisi, 05.10.2011.
57 Follow-up interview with a migration expert, Delegation of the EU to Georgia, Tbilisi, 30.09.2011.
58 Interview with local migration experts, DRC Georgia, Tbilisi, 03.10.2011, and with an official of the CRA, Tbilisi, 05.10.2011.
59 Interview with an official of the CRA, Tbilisi, 05.10.2011; interview with Georgian lawyers, GYLA, Tbilisi, 03.10.2011. The draft of the 'Law on Personal Data Protection' as circulated by the government of Georgia was provided by a staff member of IOM Tbilisi to the author, Tbilisi, October 2011.
60 Interview with Georgian lawyers, GYLA, Tbilisi, 03.10.2011.
61 Ibid.
62 Ibid.
63 Interview with an official of the CRA, Tbilisi, 05.10.2011, and with Georgian lawyers, GYLA, Tbilisi, 03.10.2011.
64 Interview with Georgian lawyers, GYLA, Tbilisi, 03.10.2011.
65 Follow-up interview with a staff member, OSCE Mission to Armenia, Yerevan, 12.10.2011.
66 Interview with an official of the State Migration Service of Armenia (SMS), Ministry of Territorial Administration, Yerevan, 26.10.2010.
67 Interview with an official of the Delegation of the EU to Armenia, Yerevan, 11.10.2011, and with an official of the MFA Armenia, Yerevan, 14.10.2011.
68 Interview with an official of the SMS, Yerevan, 26.10.2010 and 13.10.2011.

Migration management 147

69 Follow-up interview with an official of the SMS, Yerevan, 13.10.2011.
70 Interview with a local migration expert, EU Advisory Group to Armenia (EUAG), Yerevan, 13.10.2011.
71 Follow-up interview with an official of the SMS, Yerevan, 13.10.2011.
72 Interview with an official of the Consular Department, MFA of Armenia, Yerevan, 12.10.2011, and follow-up interview with an official of the SMS, Yerevan, 13.10.2011.
73 Interview with an official of the Consular Department, MFA of Armenia, Yerevan, 12.10.2011, and with a local migration expert, EUAG, Yerevan, 13.10.2011.
74 Follow-up interview with two local migration experts, ILO Armenia, Yerevan, 18.10.2011.
75 Ibid.
76 Ibid.
77 Follow-up interview with a staff member, IOM Armenia, Yerevan, 19.10.2011.
78 Interview with an official of the European Department of the MFA Armenia, Yerevan, 25.10.2010.
79 Ibid.
80 Interview with an official of the European Department of the MFA, Armenia, Yerevan, 25.10.2010.
81 Phone interview with an EU official, EC (DG Home), 11.08.2011.
82 Follow-up interview with a staff member of EKENG, Yerevan, 18.10.2011.
83 Interview with an official of the Delegation of the EU to Armenia, Yerevan, 11.10.2011.
84 'Final Narrative Report (2007–2009)', provided to the author by ICHD staff, Yerevan, 2012.
85 Interview with a staff member of EKENG, Yerevan, 26.10.2010; follow-up interview with a staff member of EKENG, Yerevan, 18.10.2011; interview with an official of the SMS, Yerevan, 26.10.2010.
86 Interview with an official of the Consular Department of the MFA Armenia, Yerevan, 19.10.2010.
87 Interview with a local expert, IOM Armenia, Yerevan, 11.10.2011.
88 Interview with a staff member of EKENG, Yerevan, 26.10.2010.
89 Ibid.
90 Ibid.
91 Follow-up interview with a staff member of EKENG, Yerevan, 18.10.2011.
92 Interview with a local migration expert, EUAG, Yerevan, 13.10.2011.
93 Follow-up interview with a staff member of EKENG, Yerevan, 18.10.2011.
94 Phone interview with an EU official, EC (DG Home), 11.08.2011.
95 Follow-up interview with two local migration experts, ILO Armenia, Yerevan, 18.10.2011.
96 Interview with a staff member, IOM Armenia, Yerevan, 18.10.2010.
97 Follow-up interview with two local migration experts, ILO Armenia, Yerevan, 18.10.2011; interview with an EU official, Delegation of the EU to Armenia, Yerevan, 28.10.2010.
98 Follow-up interview with two local migration experts, ILO Armenia, Yerevan, 18.10.2011.
99 Follow-up interview with two local migration experts, ILO Armenia, Yerevan, 18.10.2011; interview with an EU official, Delegation of the EU to Armenia, Yerevan, 28.10.2010.
100 Interview with a local expert, IOM Armenia, Yerevan, 11.10.2011.
101 Interview with a local expert, IOM Armenia, Yerevan, 11.10.2011; interview with an official of the SMS, Yerevan, 26.10.2010.

102 Follow-up interview with two local migration experts, ILO Armenia, Yerevan, 18.10.2011.
103 Follow-up interview with an official of the SMS, Yerevan, 13.10.2011.
104 Ibid.
105 Follow-up interview with a staff member, IOM Armenia, Yerevan, 19.10.2011.
106 Follow-up interview with two local migration experts, ILO Armenia, Yerevan, 18.10.2011, and with a staff member, OSCE Mission to Armenia, Yerevan, 12.10.2011.
107 Interview with a local expert, IOM Armenia, Yerevan, 11.10.2011; follow-up interview with a staff member, IOM Armenia, Yerevan, 19.10.2011.
108 Follow-up interview with a staff member of EKENG, Yerevan, 18.10.2011; interview with an official of the Consular Department of the MFA Armenia, Yerevan, 19.10.2010.
109 Interview with an official of the Consular Department of the MFA Armenia, Yerevan, 19.10.2010, and with a local migration expert, EUAG, Yerevan, 13.10.2011.
110 Interview with a local migration expert, EUAG, Yerevan, 13.10.2011; follow-up interview with a staff member, IOM Armenia, Yerevan, 19.10.2011.
111 Presentation, 'Data Protection Principles in Armenia and EU', AEPLAC awareness-raising seminar, 19–21 November 2010, Tsaghkadzor, Armenia.
112 Interview with a local migration expert, EUAG, Yerevan, 13.10.2011.
113 Phone interview with an EU official, EC (DG Justice), Brussels, 30.08.2011.
114 Phone interview with an EU official, EC (DG Justice), Brussels, 30.08.2011, own translation.
115 Interview with a local migration expert, EUAG, Yerevan, 13.10.2011.
116 Follow-up interview with a staff member, IOM Armenia, Yerevan, 19.10.2011.
117 Phone interview with an EU official, EC (DG Home), 11.08.2011.

5 Energy diversification[1]

Energy policy symbolizes the contestation of the post-Soviet space like no other policy area. The EU has sought to anchor energy policy reforms in its neighboring countries by asking *inter alia* for a diversification of their energy sources, suppliers and routes by developing hydropower and other renewable energy sources and by enhancing cooperation with regional peers. At the same time, many of the neighboring countries, among them Armenia and Georgia, have been strongly bound to Russia and targeted by its foreign energy policy of gas price increases or strategic investments in infrastructure, to name but a few. Chapter 3 has shown that the EU and Russia diverge with regard to the energy policies they promote or represent in the region, but despite their greater interdependence with Russia, Armenia's and Georgia's compliance with EU policies in the energy sector has been better than in the area of JLS, in which the EU and Russia promote similar policies. Both Armenia and Georgia generally progressed well in diversifying sources and suppliers, but cross-country differences remain: Georgia generally shows higher levels of compliance, but lags behind in creating a regulatory framework for the development of renewable energy; Armenia falls short of complying equally well with regional diversification and shows non-compliance with regard to the closure of its nuclear power plant.

This chapter explains why Georgia and Armenia respond so differently to the EU's demands for diversifying their energy sources and suppliers. In order to do so, it draws again on Chapter 3 and investigates whether the interplay of preferential fit, multiple capacity building, and multiple external incentives can account for the adoption and implementation of energy diversification policies in Georgia and Armenia. The chapter starts by describing the differences between specific EU demands and the status quo of energy policies in both countries to assess their initial policies, polities and politics misfit. Subsequently, it traces the process of adoption and implementation of EU-demanded diversification policies with regard to hydropower and other renewable energy development, regional diversification via cooperation with regional peers and – in the case of Armenia – the closure of its nuclear power plant.

Mapping the status quo in 1999 and 2006

In the framework of the PCA and in the respective ENP Action Plans the EU asks Georgia and Armenia to diversify their energy sources and supplies. This entails a variety of legal, economic and financial measures that address both the domestic and foreign sources of energy supplies. All these requirements substantially challenged the status quo of policy, polities and politics in both countries when they entered into force.

The ENC are required to enhance their energy supply security via the diversification of their supply sources and – given their location in the EU's southern corridor – to develop 'a diversified infrastructure connected to the development of Caspian energy resources and facilitate transit' (European Commission 2006b, 2006c; see also European Communities 1999a, 1999b). Toward this end, the countries need to enhance their cooperation with regional peers and develop a long-term energy strategy converging with the EU's energy policy objectives addressing increased levels of security of supply (European Commission 2006b, 2006c). Furthermore, in the case of Armenia, one of the indicators of a successful diversification of sources and supplies is the decommissioning of the Medzamor nuclear power plant (NPP). Armenia had already promised in 1999 to close this plant by 2004 under the condition that sufficient alternative supplies were available. The EU asked the Armenian authorities for the early closure and precise planning of the plant's decommissioning (European Commission 2006c).

These demands significantly challenged the status quo in Armenia and Georgia. First, overall energy diversification and supply security was difficult to achieve given that both ENC were poor in energy resources, such as oil or natural gas. Second, the demand to develop a diversified infrastructure connected to the Caspian basin and to facilitate transit faced infrastructural as well as structural constraints within the countries. In Georgia 'the electricity and gas sectors suffer[ed] from severe financial difficulties due to non-payment, corruption and theft, which constrain[ed] new investments' (European Commission 2005b). In Armenia's country report of 2005, it says comparably: 'Armenia's energy sector is exposed to serious challenges including the bad state of infrastructure and networks suffering from losses including theft, inefficiencies, [...] underinvestment, non-payment of debts' (European Commission 2005a). The development of a diversified infrastructure hence presupposed costly rehabilitation efforts. Costs of changing the monopoly of gas supply by Russia were even higher in both countries, as Georgia and Armenia were still subject to Russia's subsidized gas provisions in 1999, which amounted to US $75 billion from 1992 to 2008 to all CIS countries (Sasse 2013: 5). Yet the potential for developing transit routes was given in both countries. Georgia held friendly relationships with Azerbaijan and Turkey, and while Armenia remained largely isolated within this regional triangle, it had the possibility to facilitate transit to the Caspian basin by cooperating with Iran. The strained relations between the West and Iran did not necessarily hamper these efforts, as the cooperation for energy diversification purposes was compatible with the international sanctions against Iran (Cheterian 2006). Still, negotiations about alternative gas supplies first constituted a *policy misfit* with the prevailing single, subsidized supplier model. In addition, the development of infrastructure required investments that were constrained by prevailing corruption in the countries, which prevented particularly Western foreign companies from investing. The need to change these structures constituted a significant *polity misfit*. In the case of Armenia, another significant *policy misfit* occurred with a view to the closure of the Medzamor NPP. The EU had asked Armenia to agree to a binding and early date to decommission the plant, to which the Armenian authorities did not consent at the time. The required decommissioning strategy was still lacking in 1999 as well as in 2006.

Georgia and Armenia are additionally encouraged to develop their own, domestic energy potential. This concerns first of all the development of their significant hydropower resources as agreed in the PCA and the ENP AP (European Commission 2006b, 2006c; European Communities 1999a, 1999b). In order to do so, the AP particularly request the ENC to work toward the financial viability of the electricity sector. The hydropower potential was largely untapped in Armenia and Georgia by the early 2000s, which also required policy and structural changes. Armenia used less than 50 percent of its overall economically feasible hydropower potential in 2002 which experts estimated to satisfy at least half of Armenia's overall electricity demand (UNESCAP 2002). Georgia, in the early 2000s only used roughly 10 percent of its hydropower potential, too, while its potential was considered to exceed even that of Armenia (EIU 2002). A problem in the development of hydropower was underinvestment and a lack of privatization of energy-related infrastructure, often due to the political-economic networks that had emerged in the energy sector in the post-Soviet period (see Closson 2009). The electricity sectors hence suffered from immense structural problems (*polity misfit*) that rendered them financially unviable. The Commission recorded in 2005 that non-payment and corruption in the Georgian electricity sector still constrained investment (European Commission 2005b) and also that Armenia's electricity sector was prone to underinvestment due to a tradition for the lack of payment of debts (European Commission 2005a).

The ENC had additionally agreed to develop an action plan on renewable energy[2] development and energy efficiency, and to establish legislative and economic mechanisms toward this end (European Commission 2006b, 2006c; European Communities 1999a, 1999b). They also consented to reinforce institutions dealing with energy efficiency and renewable energy in the ENP AP. By 1999, these issues lacked regulation in Armenia and Georgia (INOGATE 2011a, 2012). No energy laws specifically addressing renewable energies were in place and many renewable energies were commercially less viable than large hydropower stations or thermal generators. While privatization was a way to attract investments into the sector, it usually required feed-in tariffs to encourage investors to develop small hydro-, wind- or solar-power stations. This, combined with the lack of a strategic policy document laying out the financial, economic or legal mechanisms for change, constituted a serious *policy misfit* with the EU-prescribed policy. Also, the domestic processes on the energy market required change toward this end, causing a *politics misfit* for Armenia and Georgia. In order to regulate the energy sector appropriately for renewable energy, set prices and guarantee fair feed-in tariffs, an independent regulatory commission needed to function completely independently on the domestic energy markets. This corresponded to a cross-cutting prescription that the EU had formulated in its ENP AP for both countries.[3] The domestic status quo in both countries thus caused comparably high degrees of policy, polity and politics misfit in both Georgia and Armenia.

Energy diversification in Georgia

Georgia has achieved a positive evaluation for its energy sector reform with some shortcomings concerning legislative and regulatory policies. Can the interplay of preferential fit, externally provided incentives, and capacity building explain this outcome?

Hydropower development

Georgia's rich hydropower sources, among the largest in the world, remained largely untapped in the aftermath of Georgia's independence (EIU 2006). The reasons were manifold. Under President Shevardnadze, the energy sector emerged as one of the most corrupt economic spheres in Georgia, which linked political and economic elites in mutual dependence on one another and created opaque mergers between the central government in Tbilisi, regional governors and the owners of power companies (World Bank 2012). Despite the fact that Georgia was subject to a rigid World Bank program to reform its power sector, these structures, which secured Shevardnadze's power base, emerged as constraints to reform in the early 2000s (Lampietti et al. 2007b: 64f.). As a result, companies failed to operate cost-efficiently on the Georgian market, as the case of the American distribution company AES-Telasi had shown prominently in the early 2000s (see Closson 2009). Coupled with low electricity tariffs and a lack of discipline among the Georgian population actually to pay for electricity supply, the economic development of Georgia's power sector fell short of investments required to develop and rehabilitate generation capacities in the first place (Lampietti et al. 2007b: 65). Under Shevardnadze, compliance with the PCA prescription of hydropower development hence supposedly failed due to its destructive effect on his political power base which relied on the inefficient and corrupt energy sector.

The rise of a new government with new preferences

When Mikheil Saakashvili came to power in 2004, some observers feared his reform attempts to be undermined by the stronghold of Shevardnadze-loyal governors in the regions, who received a large portion of their income from the power sector (EIU 2004c; World Bank 2012). Yet the intense fight against corruption that Saakashvili declared after his rise to power, and which he reportedly used as a means to consolidate his power base (Börzel and Pamuk 2012), also targeted the Georgian energy sector. One of the first former government officials to be sued for abuse of office was Shevardnadze's former minister of energy and commissioner to Georgia's regulatory commission, Davit Mirtskhulava. In 2003 he was arrested on corruption charges and held as what he called a 'political prisoner' (Bzhalava 2008a, 2008b). The structural problems in the energy sector, however, prevailed after his arrest.

Blackouts in late 2004 and early 2005 sparked protests in two Georgian cities and put the issue of energy reforms and hydropower development on the agenda of the government (Corso 2005b). An energy commission was established in 2005 that was chaired by the prime minister and met twice a week (World Bank 2012). In February 2005 President Saakashvili announced the launch of an energy program. The program foresaw the acceleration of the governmental privatization agenda in order to finance investments in the energy sector, boost economic growth and develop Georgia's domestic power potential (Civil Georgia 2005; Saakashvili 2005). The privatization of the energy sector implied a breakup of former power structures that originated particularly from state-controlled assets of the Shevardnadze era (Closson 2009; World Bank 2012). The reform attempts, including the development of hydropower, hence seemingly provided the new government with a triple benefit: they pleased the people by enhancing the reliability of electricity supply, further consolidated the power base of the new president, and were likely to boost economic growth.

However, the reforms also implied financial and political costs, particularly due to the necessity to increase consumer tariffs in order to render private businesses cost efficient (EIU 2001a, 2003b). An increase in consumer tariffs, which was demanded by business actors in 2004, was dismissed on the grounds of its negative effect on the social situation of the country (Transparency International Georgia 2008d: 6). Evidence suggests, however, that negative incentives by Russia were soon to facilitate this reform.

Russia's negative incentives facilitate reform

After the explosions of two gas pipelines from Russia and the announcement of an increased price for Russian gas imports in late 2005 and 2006, the Georgian energy crisis was aggravated. In early 2006 Saakashvili initiated another energy commission meeting to discuss the future direction of the energy policy in Georgia once more, raising also the issue of increasing consumer tariffs. He stressed the importance of the development of hydropower sources via privatization and commercialization of the sector, which he justified additionally on the grounds of Russia's negative incentives. He said:

> It is quite clear that, together with the blow, we are also getting an incentive and an opportunity to make Georgia a country that is entirely self-sufficient in energy. The new prices also mean much more investment and that we will be able to get many more investors interested in the development of our hydroelectric energy sector.
>
> (Saakashvili 2006c)

Indeed, as then Prime Minister Zurab Nogaideli remembered, the reform was only conducted when the president saw that 'the political price of higher tariffs was less than the political cost of no electricity' (Nogaideli, quoted in World Bank 2012: 48). When the regulatory commission announced an increase in consumer tariffs in May 2006, the political opposition still tried to mobilize. The Labor and the Conservative Parties launched protests and activists went on hunger strike against the decision, calling for the government to step down. The incumbent government dismissed the opposition's protests and shifted the blame for tariff increases to Russia. Prime Minister Nogaideli told a Georgian TV channel on 11 May:

> The only reason why it became necessary to increase electricity tariff was Russia's politically motivated decision to increase gas price for Georgia and the people know this very well and that is why [people] react on this very adequately.
>
> (Civil Georgia 2006c)

Whether a result of anti-Russian rhetoric or not, public participation in the protests was low (Civil Georgia 2006c). Subsequently, with the tariff increased, the Georgian parliament also adopted a resolution in June 2006 on the 'Main Directions of State Policy in the Power Sector of Georgia', which stressed that Georgia was striving for energy independence (Parliament of Georgia 2006). The main goal of the resolution was Georgia's 'full and gradual satisfaction of the demand on electricity resources on the basis of its own hydro resources' (Parliament of Georgia 2006). The main means to achieve this was a rigid reduction of regulation and bureaucracy that mirrored other reforms masterminded by Kaka Bendukidze, the minister of economic reform. In addition, the government passed a 'State Program on Renewable Energy' in 2008 that targeted hydropower investments and established a purchase guarantee for investors, by which the government granted a realization of electricity produced in the winter months for ten years (Government of Georgia 2008b). Thus, the Georgian government had achieved overall output compliance with the ENP prescription of hydropower development in 2008 by passing strategies for hydropower development, increasing the tariffs and setting up a power purchase guarantee for newly constructed hydropower generation units.

Using external capacities for implementation

The *de facto* development of hydropower resources was thoroughly implemented especially with the help of Western donors, international development banks and Russian state companies. First, the EU directed much of its energy efforts in Georgia into the infrastructural development of the electricity sector in Abkhazia, particularly with a view to the rehabilitation of the Enguri hydropower plant. Enguri presents the largest hydropower cascade in Georgia, with generation facilities located in the separatist region of Abkhazia. The station was rehabilitated with TACIS and ENPI funding in 2004 and 2007, and with loans provided by the EIB, the EBRD and the Neighborhood Investment Facility in 2011 (European Investment Bank 2011b). In addition, USAID supported privatization and investment attraction by intense capacity building. Its 'Rural Energy Program' and 'Hydro Investment Promotion Program', launched in 2006 and 2010, respectively, supported the ministry in attracting investment and in identifying hydropower sites that could be developed by private investors.[4]

The privatization agenda indeed fueled the development of the sector. This was also due to the activity of Russian state-led companies in Georgia, which supported the implementation of Saakashvili's privatization strategy by investment. Russian companies had already penetrated the Georgian energy market and strategically purchased important energy infrastructure and plants under then-President Shevardnadze (Reisner and Kvatchadze 2005: 27).[5] To a large part this was due to the cautiousness of European and other investors who feared corruption and instable conditions on the ground (EU-Georgia Cooperation Council 2001). Even though Georgian-Russian relations worsened significantly from 2005 onward, Russian state-led companies were still involved in implementing the privatization strategy for the energy sector. Despite the participation of European companies in a tender for hydropower plants and other energy facilities in June 2006, the Russian UES company still bid for two of six tendered hydropower plants and reportedly acquired some facilities (Civil Georgia 2006b). Inter RAO UES also signed a Memorandum of Understanding with the Georgian government in late 2008 to jointly manage the Enguri hydropower plant more effectively (Doggart 2009).

The opposition severely criticized the governmental privatization strategy, fearing that the domination of Russian state-owned companies in the energy sector might expose Georgia to more political pressure from Russia (Civil Georgia 2006d; Nygren 2008). The government, however, defended its policy on the grounds of liberal market principles and stressed that privatization was not about 'a state owned something, [...] but] to have all the big companies privatized' (Bendukidze, quoted in Corso 2005a). Even after the pipeline explosions in 2006, Saakashvili drew a clear distinction between political 'blackmail' and 'sound commercial proposals' from Russia, adding that Georgia would always be open to the latter (Saakashvili 2006a).

Yet, the privatization process, which supposedly broke with Shevardnadze's corrupt power sector organization, did not necessarily result in fully transparent procedures for the transfer of state assets to private companies. The most telling example was the transfer of several hydroelectric power plants and two distribution companies to the Czech company Energo Pro in July 2007. The bidding procedure had been opaque and Energo Pro finally acquired the facilities, yet for half the price that was originally announced (EIU 2007b). The opacity of the deal particularly concerned the involvement of Georgia's independent regulatory agency in the negotiation of tariffs for Energo Pro. According to reports by Transparency International, the government circumvented the independent regulatory agency and its tariff-setting competences by negotiating side deals with interested investors in order to make the advertised assets even more attractive (Transparency International Georgia 2008d).

Despite instances of lack of transparency, the privatization process indeed helped to successfully develop Georgia's hydropower resources – a process that is still ongoing given the involvement of many new foreign and domestic investors in the Georgian market (European Bank for Reconstruction and Development 2012). According to data from the US Energy Information Administration, Georgia increased its hydroelectric net generation by 23 percent from 2000 to 2012 (US Energy Information Administration 2015a). This process was also continued after the change in power in 2012, even in cases of contested infrastructural projects, such as in the large-scale Khudoni hydropower project that had been promoted by the previous government. Citing national energy security concerns, the new government stuck to the planned construction of the plant which raised protests *inter alia* due to the need to resettle around 200 families (Civil Georgia 2014; EC and HR 2014b).

Hydropower development: benefiting a new government

With output and outcome compliance in place, the hydropower development of Georgia thus figures as a case of full compliance. The case study suggests that the policy change was initiated by the change in government in 2004, as it helped to consolidate Saakashvili's power base by drying up the channels of income generation of those formerly loyal to Shevardnadze. In addition, the privatization agenda matched the liberal consensus within the Georgian government. The post-revolutionary regime was hence able to fulfill its preferences over outcome via compliance with the ENP AP prescriptions. Likewise, incentives by Russia were seemingly used as a political resource by the authorities in Tbilisi to justify otherwise politically costly reforms, which were yet needed to implement a liberal reform course. The negative but unconditional incentive structure inflicted by Russia allowed the Georgian government to shift the blame for tariff increases on Russia and potentially helped to disperse public protests.

Energy diversification 157

To what extent might capacity building explain this outcome? Shevardnadze's government had been subject to intense international support. With a view to the necessary market structures, the World Bank and international financial institutions trained the Georgian authorities from the 1990s in tariff methodology and helped to craft the necessary institutions to create a functioning and attractive market (Lampietti et al. 2007b). This financial and technical assistance, however, exerted only a limited effect on the functioning of the power sector under Shevardnadze. Under Saakashvili no external capacity building was provided before 2005 that directly targeted output compliance in the hydro sector and may explain the set-up of the different strategies and programs at the time, such as the 2005 energy program. The marginal role of capacity building as a driver for change under this government is supported by high-ranking officials in the Ministry of Energy, who questioned the overall necessity of foreign support for this reform given that private companies indeed had 'the capacity to perform the same job'.[6] Indeed, the capacity to implement the reform was provided by development banks and private companies, side by side with Russian state-owned companies. In the implementation stage, the Georgian government used the financial resources that Russia provided irrespective of the tense political situation that had been referred to in order to push through the tariff increase. The evidence presented above hence suggests that the difference between the pre-2004 and the post-2004 reform process was the change in government and the relative political costs linked to the restructuring of the hydropower sector.

In a nutshell, the case of hydropower development in Georgia suggests that the interplay of preferential fit and the use of negative incentives by Russia helped the incumbent government to divert potentially negative political costs, while using grants, loans and investments of all external donors including Russian state-led companies to implement the reform of the hydropower sector in Georgia.

Renewable energy

Apart from hydropower resources that were increasingly developed after the rise to power of Mikheil Saakashvili in 2004, other sources of renewable energy, such as wind, solar and biomass, were also supposed to be developed in the framework of the PCA and the ENP. These renewable energy sources, including also small hydropower plants usually defined by a generation capacity of below 10 or 30 MW, were renowned for their small socio-ecological impact (US Department of Energy 2011). The EU had supported the development of renewable energy and energy efficiency in Georgia since 1998. At the time, a TACIS project created the Energy Efficiency Center Georgia (EEC) at the Ministry of Energy of Georgia which has conducted studies and drafted reports on renewable energy sources and energy efficiency ever since (European Commission 1999). However, the EEC lacked the institutional and legal framework to significantly shape the ministry's policies (Energy Charter Secretariat

2012: 15; Transparency International Georgia 2007) and was reportedly treated as a 'foreign body' within the Ministry of Energy.[7] The EEC operates as an independent NGO in Georgia (Energy Charter Secretariat 2012: 61).

Despite the failure of the EEC to develop major policies with the Ministry of Energy at the time, amendments to the 1997 Law on Electricity and Natural Gas of Georgia were enacted in 2005, 2006 and 2007, some of which aimed at deregulating the operation of small hydropower plants to enhance their attraction to investors (President of Georgia 1997). This entailed that hydropower plants with up to 10 MW capacity could be operated without being officially licensed. In addition, a more comprehensive energy strategy was passed by the Georgian parliament in 2006 defining the 'Main Directions of the State Policy in the Power Sector of Georgia' (Parliament of Georgia 2006). It foresaw the development of hydropower generation units, ranging from small to large power stations. The strategy, however, did not include or specify any legal, economic or financial mechanisms for explicitly strengthening renewable energy assets with little environmental impact, which were in general less competitive and needed feed-in tariffs to survive on the energy market. The strategy rather considered that the alternative sources of energy would be utilized only 'on the conditions that [the] application of traditional and alternative sources of energy shall be treated equally' (Parliament of Georgia 2006). As a report of Transparency International reveals, an additional energy efficiency clause mentioned in the parliamentary resolution did not match the agenda of the Ministry of Energy at the time, which ruled out any legislative regulation of renewable energies or energy efficiency to promote their development (Transparency International Georgia 2007). The strategy rather suggested a deregulation of the entire sector, which was in line with the overall fight against corruption and efforts to reduce bureaucracy in the Saakashvili government.[8] The resolution hence addressed the development of renewable energy, but failed to provide for economic incentives or legislation in this area required by the ENP action plan.

International development banks raise their voices

In 2007, the issue of a law on renewable energy and energy efficiency was put on the agenda again (Energy Charter Secretariat 2012: 56). The KfW, the EIB and the EBRD, supported by the Neighborhood Investment Facility, provided credit for the Georgian government to build a new electricity transmission line with an anticipated cost of €220 million. The 500 kilovolt (KV) line was supposed to connect Georgia to the Turkish market and promised beneficial export opportunities for Georgian electricity producers, which had started to generate excess energy seasonally from the country's large hydropower sources since 2007 (Government of Georgia 2008a). Yet, while the financial institutions agreed to grant the loan, the Georgian government consented to the development of legislation in the area of renewable energy and energy efficiency by 2012.[9] The commitment formed part of the overall agreement, but as the loan was provided prior to the adoption of legislation, it did not qualify as the classic quid pro quo form of policy conditionality.

Still, the work on a draft law on renewable energy and energy efficiency started in 2008 when the Ministry of Energy approached USAID for help. In the framework of its 'rural energy program', USAID engaged a subcontractor who worked on a draft law jointly with experts from Georgian energy NGOs, including the EEC.[10] Several workshops and meetings of the contractors with staff of the Ministry of Energy were conducted (USAID Georgia 2008), and subsequently a first draft law was tabled, which included the creation of an energy efficiency agency, the introduction of an obligatory purchase and feed-in tariff for renewable resources, including biomass, solar, wind and small hydro.[11] The Ministry of Energy, however, rejected the first draft as too demanding and requested a less regulation-intense text. An official of the Ministry of Energy called the law proposal a form of 'luxury' for a developing economy such as Georgia, claiming that 'you are killing generation business on the one side and you are putting forcing by law of consumers to invest in energy efficienc[y]'.[12] The contractors tried to relax the requirements of the draft law further and finally had a document that was ready for parliamentary discussion, at which point Prime Minister Lado Gurgenidze reportedly wrote a letter to USAID stating that this draft law was currently not on the governmental agenda and that the government believed the introduction of more regulations would complicate the area (cf. Energy Charter Secretariat 2012: 55).[13] Non-governmental observers concluded that the legislative attempt to promote renewable energy and energy efficiency was stopped by the dominant liberal fraction in the Georgian government,[14] while representatives of the Ministry of Energy criticized that the only reason put forward for drafting the law at the time was that experts had recommended doing so. The government refused to engage in 'copy-pasting whatever regulation [was] existing somewhere', which 'is completely not relevant and adequate to the Georgia[n] reality'.[15]

Still, a document on renewable energy was passed in 2008: the State Program 'Renewable Energy 2008' (Government of Georgia 2008b). It established a purchase guarantee for newly constructed power plants below a generation capacity of 100 MW to 'support new renewable energy sources construction in Georgia by attracting foreign investments' (Government of Georgia 2008b). The program hence anchored the same economic incentives for small, medium-sized and large power stations alike. At the same time it confronted small hydro and alternative renewable power plant owners with fierce competition on the Georgian energy market.[16] The program thus failed to introduce the regulatory regime required to incentivize the development of purely renewable energy (Transparency International Georgia 2008c: 12f.).

Capacity building increases, but non-compliance remains

In January 2011, renewable energy and energy efficiency were once more on the agenda. The Ministry of Economy founded a department for sustainable development under its auspices. International donors, among them GIZ and UNDP, subsequently organized workshops and drafted reports on Georgia's green market potential jointly with the newly established unit, but faced a clear prescription from the Georgian government. As one of the participating consultants remembers, 'the condition was: no legislative regulations and no subsidies and it came from the ministry itself'.[17] Despite the fact that some formal institutions were created and a legal process was started, supposedly due to the KfW agreement, the development of a Georgia-wide legal, economic or financial framework to promote environmentally friendly, purely renewable energy was not established (Energy Efficiency Task Force 2008; INOGATE 2012).

Sub-national entities, however, proved more receptive to the idea of working more bindingly on renewable energy development and energy efficiency. The municipality of Tbilisi joined the 'Covenant of Mayors', a Europe-wide initiative to promote renewable energy and energy efficiency in order to improve on the official goal of the EU to reduce its CO_2 emissions by 20 percent by 2020. Prior to the municipal elections in May 2010, Tbilisi's incumbent Mayor Giorgi Ugulava (UNM) signed the Covenant on 30 March 2010, despite the fact that the national government reportedly opposed the idea (Hunter Christie et al. 2012: 18).[18] The municipalities of Rustavi, Kutaisi and Batumi, and further smaller cities soon joined in as well. With the support of GIZ the municipality of Tbilisi worked on a sustainable action plan which foresaw the development of thermal and solar power available in Tbilisi and work on energy efficiency in buildings and public infrastructure (Government of Tbilisi City 2011).

In addition, market-based or donor-funded projects indeed helped to develop sporadic renewable energy projects on the ground, where they proved generally in line with the liberal governmental agenda. First, some private investors indeed increasingly asked for the development of small hydropower plants in Georgia. In addition, donor-funded projects supported the development of small hydropower plants. In April 2011, UNDP provided financial support to the KfW, directed toward the development of small hydropower plants in Georgia, and emerged as the only source for low-interest rate loans for renewable energy developers in Georgia (UNDP 2011).

USAID helped the small mountainous region of Tusheti in northeastern Georgia to generate its own energy via micro-hydropower plants – a project that was also supported by the Georgian government (USAID Georgia 2011). However, this project targeted one of the main pillars of the incumbent government's economic strategy, namely to enhance Tusheti's standing as a tourist magnet. Other projects, such as an attempt by the GIZ in 2008 to promote energy efficiency in buildings, were straightforwardly rejected.[19] This evidence is substantiated by data on total non-hydro renewable electricity net generation from the US Energy Information Administration (2015b), suggesting that unlike Armenia, Georgia had not achieved a measurable amount of non-hydro renewable energy electricity generation by 2012.

This overall development did not change with the rise to power of the GD coalition. Even though the new government had promised to develop renewable energies and more generally to promote sustainable development in Georgia, it arguably failed to live up to its promises by 2014 (Green Alternative 2015). Initially, the new governments applied for accession to the European Energy Community in January 2013 – a membership that would have required Georgia, amongst other things, to strategically develop renewable energy. Yet accession negotiations reportedly were delayed and lacked prioritization (EC and HR 2015a) and Georgia's progress report notes that legislation on renewables and energy efficiency was still missing by 2014 (EC and HR 2015a).

Renewable energy development and governmental resistance

In short, while some projects with a view to renewable energy development were sporadically developed by private investors or donor support, the Georgian government both under UNM and GD rule failed to provide for a sound legislative, economic or financial framework to promote purely renewable energy or strengthen related institutions on a governmental level. As the framework agreements of the KfW did not provide for a quid pro quo-based policy conditionality, compliance has so far been unnecessary to thwart the threat of suspension of the loan. Taken together, the evidence suggests a misfit of preferences over outcomes that prevented any instrumental usage of the capacity by the EU or other external actors.

A lack of capacity building seemingly fails to provide for plausible explanations for non-compliance in this case. Indeed, the creation of the EEC in the Ministry of Energy in 1998 was an attempt to constantly provide the Georgian government with information and policy-specific advice on this issue. While the EEC developed as one of the most renowned energy think tanks in Georgia, the government has rarely made use of it. Likewise, the ministry received assistance from USAID in 2008, when it asked for support in the creation of a renewable energy law. While the capacity was provided, the reform attempt was stopped for not being in line with the prevailing governmental agenda. Attempts by donors, such as the GIZ, to work on energy efficiency encountered either outright rejection from the governmental ministries responsible,[20] or the range of the appropriate norms to promote was clearly identified by the ministry beforehand, as has been the case with the Department of Sustainable Energy in the Ministry of Economy. Thus the Georgian government seemingly did not suffer from a lack of capacity that prevented the government from making a strategic choice in the first place. The intense investment in human resources and knowledge by external donors equipped the government with the capacity to introduce the relevant financial and economic mechanisms, but it chose not to do so. While this evidence cannot support or reject any claims on whether the individuals participating in some of the externally provided transgovernmental networks in this case indeed internalized externally promoted norms, it suggests that any potential socialization process has so far remained without policy effects. Arguing from a more rationalist perspective, the capacity building did not sustainably empower any lower-level officials who then successfully lobbied for change on the governmental level.

Regional diversification

President Eduard Shevardnadze had lobbied for Georgia's role as a transit country since 1993, not least to garner support from the West for consolidating Georgia's independence and EU integration (Alieva 2000: 19). By 1999, however, when the PCA entered into force, Georgia was still largely dependent on energy supplies from Russia, particularly with a view to natural gas. In addition, the energy sector figured as a hotspot of corruption and theft controlled by government-connected clans and regional governors (Closson 2009).

At around the same time, though, regional energy diversification efforts started to take shape when large volumes of natural gas were discovered on the Shah Deniz gas fields in Azerbaijan. Georgia's participation in the infrastructural projects seemingly benefited the Shevardnadze regime: FDI that flooded the Georgian economy during the period of pipeline construction fueled the growth of the Georgian economy despite a lack of structural anti-corruption reforms (EIU 2002). Consequently, a strategic agreement, the so-called 'Istanbul Protocol', was signed by President Shevardnadze and his Azerbaijani, Kazakh and Turkish counterparts in November 1999, which initiated the beginning of one of the central Caucasian energy projects, the Baku–Tbilisi–Ceyhan (BTC) oil pipeline, and lay the groundwork for the formation of a Eurasian transport corridor (Nichol 2011: 43).

More important for Georgia's diversification of gas supply were discussions about the BTC's sister South Caucasus gas pipeline (SCP) or Baku–Tbilisi–Erzurum (BTE) pipeline. The BTE aimed at delivering gas via Georgia to the Turkish town of Erzurum, supplying Georgia with gas from Azerbaijan as a complement to Russian supplies. Several agreements on transit and sale of natural gas were signed by Georgian and Azerbaijani officials in 2001 and 2002 which established the formal basis of the SCP to be operated from 2006 onward (British Petroleum 2014). Construction started in 2003 (EIU 2004b) and was supported only indirectly by the EU's infrastructural assistance of INOGATE and TRACECA (Transport Corridor Europe–Caucasus–Asia), while the participation of EU-based companies equally indirectly promoted the application of EU internal market rules in the infrastructure projects (Sierra 2010: 190).

Rivaling incentives from Russia

The gas diversification attempts were, however, accompanied by what some analysts termed consistent counter-action by Russian state-owned and private companies (Teurtrie 2010: 194). In 2001, Georgia was still fully dependent on natural gas supplied by Itera, a Russian company that controlled Russia's gas supply to some former Soviet Union countries. Itera seemingly figured as the main private rival to the state-controlled Gazprom on the Russian market, but its *de facto* connection to the government remained opaque and subject to intense discussion in the early 2000s (Belton and Carney 2001; Tsereteli 2002).

In 2001, several gas supply cuts reportedly aimed at sanctioning Georgia's main distribution company AES Telasi for negotiating with competing gas suppliers (Belton and Carney 2001). Additionally, Itera attempted to pressure the Georgian government into a takeover of one of the state-owned gas networks in 2002. High government debt to Itera and the political costs of a potentially unstable energy supply prior to the 2003 parliamentary election supposedly informed the decision-making rationale of the government at the time (Devdariani 2003; Jervalidze 2006: 28; Zaharova 2003). After intense negotiations in late August 2002, a Memorandum of Understanding was signed which paved the way for an agreement to transfer to Itera a controlling stake in Georgia's state-owned gas pipelines, the Azot chemical plant and the Gardabani thermal power station (Jervalidze 2006: 27).

However, trips by government officials to Moscow in summer and fall 2002 provided the Georgian authorities with a seemingly more attractive deal in July 2003. Gazprom, Itera's Russian state-led rival, offered the Georgian government a long-term strategic partnership on gas supplies. Gazprom suggested investing more than $250 million in the rehabilitation of infrastructure and secure stable energy supplies (Zaharova 2003), against the right of supplying 'natural gas to the Georgian customers, [...] use of the Georgian infrastructure for transit purposes and use of gas for electricity production which would be jointly sold by Georgia and Gazprom' (Sepashvili 2003). Shevardnadze consented to the agreement with Russia's Gazprom. While this quid pro quo deal was fiercely criticized by the US Administration, it did not immediately foresee any provisions of ceding ownership or control of the existing pipelines on Georgian territory, nor the construction of new ones (Nygren 2008: 150). Observers feared, however, that the opaque deal might open the door to further transfers of assets to Gazprom that might ruin the projects of energy diversification as they were supported by the US Administration (Baran 2003). In addition to the conditional offer of rewards to Georgia, Russia lobbied Azerbaijan to use Russia's existing infrastructure for gas supplies to Turkey instead of building a new route via Georgia – a proposal that, if accepted, would have put an end to the BTE endeavor, but Azerbaijan refused to cooperate (Teurtrie 2010: 195).

Despite the fact that the gas agreement with Gazprom seemingly secured the energy supply prior to the election, the deals turned out to be politically costly for President Shevardnadze. His already weak government came under fierce attack from domestic opponents. The opposition accused Shevardnadze of selling out Georgia's independence to Russia in return for political support in the upcoming election. Zurab Zhvania attacked the concluding agreement as 'inadmissible' and called for the impeachment of the negotiating minister of energy (Sepashvili 2003).

By November 2003 the rigged parliamentary elections triggered the start of the Rose Revolution, which brought to power the triumvirate of Mikheil Saakashvili, Nino Burjanadze and Zurab Zhvania. Due to the change in power and strong parliamentary opposition to the deal, the agreement that Shevardnadze had concluded was never ratified by parliament (Nygren 2008: 150). While it remains a point of speculation to what extent the absence of the revolution might have subverted the *de facto* diversification endeavor and undermined compliance, the evidence presented above suggests that the initial preferential fit for diversification coupled with rivaling policy conditionality by Russia's state-led gas company hollowed the initial diversification effort.

A new government and multiple offers (not) to diversify energy flows

After having been elected president in January 2004, Mikheil Saakashvili immediately confirmed his participation in the US-supported trans-Caspian energy projects. His administration also propagated the reintegration of the breakaway territories into Georgia proper and a quick economic recovery. The participation in infrastructural projects entailed both economic and political opportunities for the newly inaugurated government, as it still attracted large amounts of FDI and figured prominently on the agenda of foreign actors.

At the same time President Saakashvili offered 'a friendly hand to Russia' (Donaldson and Nogee 2009: 186). Indeed, this friendly gesture was reciprocated by Russia's help to restore Georgia's territorial integrity in Adjaria in 2004. Cooperation also targeted the energy sphere. In November 2004, the Saakashvili administration, many of whom had opposed the deal with Gazprom in 2003, started talks with the Russian state-led company about the potential sale of its north–south gas pipeline (Socor 2004). The pipeline was delivering gas to Armenia and required urgent but costly repairs, which Gazprom promised to conduct in exchange for a potential transfer of ownership. The quid pro quo deal was very much in line with and initially supported by the rigid privatization agenda connected predominantly to Kakha Bedukidze, the head of the Ministry of Economic Reforms and the ideological brain of the new radical liberalism that emerged in Georgia at the time (Petriashvili 2005; Sierra 2010: 195). However, the proposal again raised significant opposition in the US Administration, with warnings to Georgia not to endanger the BTE project. When Energy Minister Nika Gilauri traveled to Washington to discuss the issue, the US Administration promised to allocate $295 million for infrastructural projects under the Millennium Challenge Program in exchange for confirmation that the Georgian government would not sell the pipeline at least until April 2011 (RFE/RL 2010). Facing in addition increasingly loud internal opposition from domestic allies and renowned energy experts such as speaker of parliament Nino Burjanadze and former Minister of Economy Vladimir Papava, the government agreed to the

US proposal (Civil Georgia 2006a; Petriashvili 2005). The justification strategies of Minister of Energy Gilauri, however, suggest that while this decision was largely welcomed by the Georgian population, he was in need of justification toward the libertarian fraction in the Georgian ruling party. In March, he declared:

> This position is based not on some specific attitude towards Russia, but on the principle of preventing a monopoly. [...] We are working at establishing a competitive environment in the country's energy market.
> (Gilauri, quoted in Petriashvili 2005)

Unconditional, negative incentives by Russia, whether due to the failed pipeline sale or not, followed promptly. By late 2005, disagreements about Russia's peace-keeping forces in the separatist regions, Georgia's outspoken North Atlantic Treaty Organization (NATO) and EU integration foreign policy and – targeting the core of Saakashvili's electoral agenda – Russia's more open support of the secessionist regions had aggravated the Russian-Georgian relationship, which also extended to energy cooperation. The announcement by Gazprom of a rise in the subsidized gas price for Georgia from $63 to $110 per thousand cubic meters was taken as a politically motivated step by the government at the time – an accusation that seemed to be difficult to maintain as the move also targeted the 'Russian-friendly' Armenia (Teurtrie 2010: 195). Falling short of alternatives, the Georgian side accepted the gas price, which did not come with further strings attached.

Yet, the relationship between Georgia and Russia was rapidly deteriorating throughout 2006. Two gas pipelines, a main and a reserve branch of the Mozdok–Tbilisi pipeline in North Ossetia, exploded in January 2006 in the northern Caucasus and cut Georgia off from Russian energy supplies for several days (BBC 2006). However, unlike the increase in gas prices, the pipeline explosions could not unambiguously be traced to a foreign policy decision of the Russian government. The Georgian side suspected Moscow of using the interruption of gas supplies through the explosions as a political tool (Saakashvili 2006b), whereas the Russian government talked about an act of terrorism (Civil Georgia 2006e). Likewise, the spy scandal, Russia's economic sanctions against Georgian agricultural products, and a massive expulsion of ethnic Georgians from Russia pushed the diplomatic crisis to a peak. This coincided with the announcement of Gazprom to more than double gas prices for Georgia from $110 to the market price of $230 from 2007 onward. The threat of withholding former subsidies, which was interpreted by the Georgian government as a sanction, was tied to clear conditions this time and functioned as a form of rivaling policy conditionality. Gazprom offered the Georgian government a mitigation of the price hike if they handed over parts of their pipeline infrastructure to Gazprom in return (Schulze 2008: 191).

At the time Georgia had, however, already made a decisive step towards the diversification of energy supply. In 2006 the BTE pipeline was commissioned and Azerbaijan offered a non-Russian alternative to gas supply in Georgia from March 2007.

The reaction of the Georgian president to Gazprom's moves was clear. Mikheil Saakashvili had already published an article in *The Washington Post* in early 2006, in which he stated that Georgia, having experienced gas leverage from Russia for decades, had decided 'aggressively to diversify [its] energy sources and transportation networks' (Saakashvili 2006f). He refused to accept what was perceived as a 'political' gas price. The rivaling policy conditionality by Russia also coincided with ever more bellicose rhetoric from President Saakashvili and his defense minister, Irakli Okruashvili, toward the breakaway territories, and the marginalization of pragmatists toward conflict resolution surrounding former Prime Minister Zurab Zhvania, who had passed away in 2005 (EIU 2006). Internally and internationally, Saakashvili used Russia's gas price increase and cut-offs to remind his audience of Georgian pride and independence prior to local elections in October 2006.[21] Similarly, Saakashvili openly warned the EU not to give up the attempt to diversify its own energy resources via the Southern energy corridor in order not to expose itself to the 'mercy of Gazprom' (Civil Georgia 2007a).

According to international reports, by late 2006 almost all opposition parties fully supported Saakashvili's reintegration agenda and considered Russia an 'imperial aggressor in Georgian affairs' (EIU 2006: 15). The rhetoric was accompanied by concrete steps toward the diversification of Georgia's gas supply. In June 2006, the Georgian parliament passed a resolution on the 'Main Directions of the State Policy in the Power Sector', which declared as its first goal to achieve economic independence and provide security to the sector, among other political factors (Parliament of Georgia 2006). In addition, Saakashvili started requesting the help of Turkey and Azerbaijan (Fuller 2007). Furthermore, the Georgian government and some of the Georgian distribution companies started to negotiate with Iranian gas suppliers on alternative supply, which was, however, critically observed by US officials in Tbilisi. Reportedly, Russia again tried to lobby Azerbaijan not to provide gas to Georgia, but when President Ilham Aliev visited Moscow in November 2006, he refused to comply (Baev 2008: 134). On the contrary, Azerbaijan was indeed willing to provide gas supplies at a cheaper price than Russia to Georgia and an agreement was reached according to which the State Oil Company of Azerbaijan supplied 238 million cubic meters of natural gas for $120 per thousand cubic meters to Georgia starting in spring 2007 (Transparency International Georgia 2008b: 7). The agreement was resumed several times. As a result of the increased gas prices from Russia, Georgia hence agreed to be supplied with alternative gas from Azerbaijan in 2006 and formally complied with the EU prescription of diversified energy supplies.

The implementation of the agreement followed suit. By 2007, the gas imports of Georgia were diversified to the extent that 45 percent of consumed gas was imported from Azerbaijan (Transparency International Georgia 2008d: 8). Domestic companies could choose their gas supplying company in open competition between gas from Azerbaijan and Russia. The reform success was once more taken by Saakashvili to stress its pivotal transit role in the region for the EU. He stated:

> So we have already solved our energy problem [...] Now we are helping Europe to solve its problem, which in turn will increase Georgia's importance.
> (Saakashvili, quoted in Civil Georgia 2007c)

The new GD administration has so far not changed the policy of the UNM, even though it has very recently started talks with Gazprom about possibilities to re-increase supplies from Russia to a certain extent (Stratfor 2015).

Compliance as a result of a new government facing multiple external incentives

This evidence suggests that the assumed interplay of preferential fit and rivaling policy conditionality by Russia did not result in shallow compliance, because the incumbent government was able to find non-EU alternatives that served the incumbent government to rally domestic and international support; particularly against the background of the heated conflict with Russia about the breakaway territories.

An alternative reading of the case could suggest that political survival was indeed at stake in this case, as the increase in gas prices needed to be followed by increased consumer prices, which could easily have encouraged people to take to the streets, as suggested by Saakashvili himself (Saakashvili 2006d). If these had been the anticipated costs, the preferential fit hypothesis would be falsified for this case, as I would expect the Georgian government to accept the Russian conditions and hand over the pipeline in order to stay in power. The regulatory commission indeed increased tariffs for electricity in May 2006 and for gas in 2007, yet without provoking a major governmental crisis at the time. Some experts questioned the economic need for an increase in consumer tariffs as a result of Russia's threatened sanctions. Gas held only a marginal share of 20 to 23 percent in overall electricity generation and almost half of it was already imported at a lower price from Azerbaijan at the time (Transparency International Georgia 2008a). Russian gas providers were even identified as the winners of the Georgian-Azerbaijani gas deal:

> As a result [of the Georgian-Azeri gas agreement], a significant misbalance was caused between the prices of Russian and Azerbaijan gas, which should have forced the Russian side to decrease the gas price for the purpose of competing with Azerbaijani gas. If the companies established with Russian partners incurred losses, they would be forced to negotiate with GazExport. If they failed to do so, they would probably become bankrupt and be forced to sell the assets [...] The government decided to purchase the entire volume of gas supplied from Azerbaijan and Russia and sell it to large consumers at a weighted price [...] instead

of importing cheap gas on its own with the assistance of the parent companies, the Russian-Georgian and Russian-Kazakh gas companies acting in Georgia became beneficiaries of cheap Azerbaijani gas.

(Transparency International Georgia 2008b: 8)

Therefore, Georgia not only had the possibility to prevent consumer tariffs from rising, but also to 'force' Russian companies back into adjustments of their prices to the Azerbaijani market price. Both the financial and political costs of the increase in gas prices have hence been questioned and may rather be linked to the attempt to render the entire sector more cost efficient and attractive to investors.

In addition, capacity building as an explanation only exerts limited explanatory power for this case. First, the EU did not play a significant role with a view to capacity building in the gas diversification project. Some technical assistance was provided by INOGATE and TRACECA, but the lion's share of financial capacity for the project was contributed by the international consortium (Sierra 2010: 190). The USA indeed provided Georgia with immense assistance, but this was financial assistance only and formed part of the conditional agreement under the Millennium Challenge Program not to sell the Georgian pipeline infrastructure to Russia. Instances of socialization in transgovernmental networks via capacity building have thus not been detected in the case of Georgia and its energy diversification, and seemingly fail to account for the compliance effort in the case at hand.

This evidence rather suggests that both the Shevardnadze and the Saakashvili administrations indeed shared a preference for energy diversification to secure economic growth despite a lack of structural reforms (Shevardnadze), to enhance the international standing of Georgia as a transit hub (both), and to rally the Georgian population behind an anti-Russian discourse that served the fulfillment of the incumbent's reintegration agenda (Saakashvili). While the application of rivaling policy conditionality by Russia in 2003 indeed supposedly questioned the *de facto* long-term compliance with the aim of energy diversification, this effect was subverted by the Rose Revolution in November 2003. Russia's rivaling policy conditionality in 2005 was countered by the better offer of the USA in the framework of its Millennium Challenge Program. The subsequent quid pro quo invocation of sanctions by Russia was alleviated by alternative offers by Azerbaijan, which additionally provided the Georgian government with the opportunity to enhance the domestic and international legitimacy for its increasingly anti-Russian reintegration agenda at the time. Despite the lack of EU policy conditionality, the evidence presented here hence suggests that the involvement of multiple actors allowed the Georgian government to pick its most preferred option by 2006.

Energy diversification in Armenia

Chapter 3 showed that Armenia scores slightly worse than Georgia with a view to compliance with EU energy prescriptions, despite an overall positive assessment. The next section traces to what extent this compliance pattern can be explained by the interplay of preferential fit and external incentives or capacity building. In order to reduce redundancy in the case studies of hydropower and further renewable energy development, these cases are presented as one.

Hydropower and renewable energy development

With the start of the war against Azerbaijan in 1992 Armenia experienced a severe energy crisis. The subsequent full economic blockade by Azerbaijan and Turkey virtually cut off Armenia from its energy supplies until 1996. In addition, an earthquake in 1988 forced the government to close the nuclear power station near the town of Medzamor, which had provided Armenia with roughly one third of its electricity before (Sargsyan et al. 2006). In the early 1990s, Armenia was thus left with its electricity supply generated by domestic hydropower resources, mostly stemming from Lake Sevan, which simultaneously figured as one of the most precious sites of Armenia's national heritage. Other hydro plants were operational, but were often highly indebted to the distribution company and their operation was not cost efficient. Until 1996, electricity generated by domestic resources or Russian gas delivered via Georgia provided for a maximum of two hours of electricity a day (Sargsyan et al. 2006). In short, new sources of energy generation and investments were needed to rehabilitate the sector.

International capacity building and autonomy benefits support reforms

As early as 1996 the EU provided capacity to the Armenian government supporting legal reforms to promote hydro and renewable energy development. Mirroring similar attempts in Georgia, an Energy Strategy Center was established with TACIS funding within the Ministry of Energy (PEEREA 2005). The center intended to support the government of Armenia in policy development and the creation of strategic documents for the energy sector (European Commission 2011a). Again, as was the case in Georgia, the World Bank and the IMF supported the energy sector reform in Armenia, helped to establish an independent regulatory commission and pushed the privatization process. Consequently, the Armenian government passed a law on privatization in 1997, which announced some state assets to be privatized, among them 25 small hydropower plants (Sargsyan et al. 2006: 5).

The international reform recipe seemingly coincided with the political agenda of the incumbent government, both under Levon Ter-Petrosyan and Robert Kocharyan, which World Bank representatives considered 'paramount' for the reform outcome in retrospective (Sargsyan et al. 2006: xv). According to statements by international observers, the efforts of the Armenian government to enhance its energy security via the diversification of its domestic resources largely stemmed from the lessons learned from the severe energy crisis in the early 1990s, which was caused by the Turkish-Azerbaijani blockade (PEEREA 2005: 3f.).

After Ter-Petrosyan's ouster, the major hydropower generation units on Lake Sevan needed to be closed down in 1999 due to their severely harmful environmental impact on the lake (Republic of Armenia 2002). The new Armenian government under President Kocharyan subsequently established the legal basis for renewable energy development in Armenia. In 2001 the National Assembly revised the 1997 Law on Energy, which defined the main principles of the state policy in the Armenian energy sector and laid the regulatory basis for the development of renewable energy, including hydropower (President of Armenia 2001). The justification given within the document corresponded to the experts' assessment: it mentions an increase in the country's autonomy in the energy sector, citing the 'enhancement of the energy independence of the Republic, including the differentiation of domestic and imported energy resources and ensuring the maximum utilization of generating capacities' as one of the basic state policies to guide the Armenian energy policy (President of Armenia 2001). Toward this end the law introduced a purchase guarantee for electricity generated by small hydropower plants and other renewable energy sources for 15 years.

Subsequently, USAID's Municipal Network for Energy Efficiency Program established the Armenian Energy Efficiency Council in 2002 which brought together stakeholders from ministries, NGOs, donors and businesses, and acted as a steering committee to supervise legislative processes (Pasoyan 2005). With the help of their various reports and assessments for the Armenian government on renewable energy and energy efficiency development (European Commission 2004a; USAID Armenia 2002), the Law on Energy Efficiency and Alternative Energy was passed in 2004 aiming at promoting the development of renewable energy. Again, the government justified its legal initiative via autonomy benefits: raising energy independence via energy efficiency and renewable energy development was directly linked to the security of the country (Sargsyan et al. 2006: 67). In addition, the Public Service Regulatory Commission introduced fixed and preferential feed-in tariffs for renewable energy units in February 2004 (Danish Energy Management 2011).

Russia's negative incentives facilitate reforms again

By mid-2000, the development of hydro and renewable energies was well on track, at least on paper. Evidence suggests that this process was further catalyzed by negative, unconditional incentives from Russia at the time. Against the background of a cut in fuel supply by Russia in 2002, the 'Energy Sector Development Strategy' of the Armenian government was developed in 2005. It foresaw the development of all kinds of renewable energy resources, including small hydro, biomass, solar and wind power, and identified energy conservation as an important means to this end, stating that: 'the least costly and most sustainable way to enhance energy supply is to stop wasting it' (Government of Armenia 2005: 5.2). The strategy also defined concrete development targets and suggested steps toward their attainment. To justify these efforts, the strategy referred to the historical events of the 1990s, as well as to interruptions in fuel supply at the time which occurred also due to a lack of payment capability to Russia (Government of Armenia 2005: 5).

Likewise in 2007, again with the assistance of USAID, the Armenian government adopted a 'National Program on Energy Saving and Renewable Energy', which prescribed the actions to take in order to implement energy-saving mechanisms and develop renewable energy (IFC 2010). It mentions as its goal to 'decrease the dependence on foreign energy suppliers and avoid interruptions in the Armenian fuel supply' (Government of Armenia 2007b). While Russia was thus absent as an active external actor at the policy formulation stage, unlike the EU and USAID, it indirectly functioned as a point of reference within the legislative processes to justify legal changes made toward compliance with EU requirements. The national program was subsequently complemented by an action plan in 2010 for its implementation, and in 2011 by a roadmap for renewable energy development (Arzumanyan and Abovyan 2014), as well as a strategic development program for the hydropower sector (International Energy Agency and International Renewable Energy Agency 2015). To what extent was this formal output translated into the *de facto* development of hydro and renewable energy, and what role did external actors play in the implementation process?

First, the privatization process of small hydropower plants was implemented rather smoothly. While larger privatization deals were allegedly designed to reward those loyal to President Levon Ter-Petrosyan with cheap state assets and failed to increase the state budget significantly (Astourian 2000; Freedom House 1998), the privatization process of small hydropower plants was not obstructed by vested interests. The small hydropower plants privatized between 1997 and 2002 were mainly sold to local Armenians, who were striving for their own generation units (Sargsyan et al. 2006). Unlike in most other sectors of the economy, which were dominated by oligarchic elites (Astourian 2000), the renewable energies, to which the plants belonged, seemed to lack attraction for them. As the small hydropower plants were used by locals to match their energy needs, they were also rehabilitated in order to serve their purpose profitably. Hence, the privatization of the plants did not imply larger power shifts within the oligarchy-structured Armenian elite, but rather functioned as a niche to improve energy security.

Russian state companies support reform implementation

While investment in the small generation assets was flourishing, the larger generation units were less attractive, particularly for Western investors due to the fragile macro-economic situation in the country, despite the fact that the Armenian government had increased the tariff for energy consumption, abolished subsidies and raised the bill collection rates in January 1999 (Lampietti et al. 2007a). European investors shied away from investing in a country that was marked by corruption and uncertain legal standards, but Russia figured as the largest source of FDI at the time. In the first half of 2001, 55 percent of all FDI originated from Russia, most of which was going into the energy, water and gas sectors and hence significantly contributed to its economic development (EIU 2002).

Yet Armenia was highly indebted to Russia. Due to lack of payment capacity of the Armenian government, Russian state-owned companies frequently delayed or stopped their fuel supplies which were needed to run some of the largest power plants. In order to settle some of the government debt, a subsidiary of Russia's RAO UES acquired the ownership of the Hrazdan thermal power plant and the Sevan-Hrazdan hydropower cascade, which consisted of six larger hydropower plants, in 2003. The Hrazdan plant was traded for $31 million, and the cascade was transferred to RAO Nordic, a subsidiary company of RAO UES in 2003 (Sargsyan et al. 2006). The debt for equity agreement supported Armenia's goal to develop its hydropower resources: the company financed the company's shortfall, raised salaries by 20 to 30 percent and increased electricity generation by 15 percent (Sargsyan et al. 2006). In total, Armenia managed to increase its hydroelectricity net generation by more than 80 percent from 2000 to 2012 (US Energy Information Administration 2015a). Similarly, the preferential tariffs for purely renewable energy spurred investment in the sector (Danish Energy Management 2011). In addition to small hydropower plants, wind farms were set up, also jointly implemented with the Iranian government (REEEP 2012). Investments from the Armenian diaspora and the EBRD further facilitated the *de facto* implementation of the formally adopted laws and strategies. Assistance was channeled into the sector by international donors and the Armenian diaspora to support the rehabilitation and development of renewable energy in Armenia. The EBRD invested €1.1 million in small hydropower plants along the Yeghegis River and the Armenian diaspora additionally supported small hydropower, usually without demanding state guarantees (Sargsyan et al. 2006). By 2010, outcome compliance with the provision to develop purely renewable energies was established, too. The generation of non-hydro renewable energy, such as wind, solar or biomass, had increased from 0 to 4 million kilowatt hours in 2012 (US Energy Information Administration 2015b) and the electricity output of small hydropower plants subsequently increased as well (EC and HR 2013b).

Enhancing energy autonomy with the help of multiple external actors

The evidence presented above suggests that since the early 2000s Armenia has attempted to further enhance its renewable energy and hydropower potential to reap autonomy benefits. The memory of the energy crisis from 1992 to 1996 as well as the experience of insecure fuel supply from Russia accelerated the adoption of legal and strategic measures to promote the development of hydro and alternative resources (output). Hence, Russia indirectly encouraged Armenia's output compliance through negative but unconditional incentives.

In addition, the government used the capacity provided by the EU and Russian state-owned companies and international donors in terms of investments and debt for equity swaps to implement its policies (outcome), which increased autonomy vis-à-vis external energy supply and did not cause major power shuffles with regard to the distribution of power within the oligarchically-structured market.

Medzamor

The fate of the Medzamor nuclear power plant has been an issue of salience in the relationship between Armenia and the EU ever since the Armenian government under Ter-Petrosyan's presidency decided to reopen one unit of the plant in November 1995. The restart of the NPP has often been cited as having ended the energy crisis in Armenia, despite the fact that this interpretation is disputed by international observers (Sargsyan et al. 2006). Unlike the Armenian authorities, the EU became increasingly concerned about the fact that an old, rundown Soviet power plant was working in a seismic zone in its neighborhood and started to lobby for its closure even prior to the entry into force of the PCA. On 17 December 1998 the EU and Armenian delegations in Yerevan agreed to establish a Medzamor working group between the European Commission and the government of Armenia to discuss the costs of closure, the enhancement of alternative forms of energy supply and a comprehensive financing plan in order to be able to close the plant by 2004 (RAPID 1998). In 1999, the Armenian government also signed a preliminary agreement with the EU to close the NPP by 2004 (EIU 2001a). Conditional on the signature of a Memorandum of Understanding entailing a binding early closure date, the EU offered €100 million to help Armenia develop alternative power resources, including hydroelectric power and gas. In addition to the policy conditionality and together with other international donors, the EU provided TACIS support to help the Armenian authorities develop strategic documents to allow for a substitution of the Medzamor power plant by 2004 (European Commission 2004a). It funded the elaboration of a strategy paper for the design of an energy security and diversification plan to develop alternative capacities beyond Armenia's nuclear energy in 2001 and 2002 (European Commission 2004a).

The fear of autonomy losses and prevailing non-compliance

In 2002, however, the authorities rowed back from the preliminary agreement with the EU and suggested postponing the final closure of the plant to an undetermined point of time after 2004 on the condition that alternative energy supplies were to be secured (EIU 2002). The Armenian government continuously stressed that they were committed to an early decommissioning of the plant, but that they did not want to 'see Armenia go back to the 1992/1993 situation' (EU-Armenia Cooperation Council 2002: 22), or to implement a solution that would decrease their energy independence or increase electricity prices (EU-Armenia Cooperation Council 2005: 26). In addition, the substitution of nuclear energy with alternative supplies was presented as economically costly. In 2002, government representatives stressed that 'the 100 million euros pledged by the European Union is clearly not sufficient to address the existing problems. In the near future, the Government of Armenia will not be able to come up with funds necessary to decommission the ANPP, which is preliminarily estimated at about USD 1.5 billion' (Margaryan 2002).

This assessment was supported by the 'least-cost plan' USAID published in 2003. The report recommended investment in safety upgrades and estimated the economic losses of an early closure for the Armenian government to be immense: 'Retiring the plant in late 2008 rather than late 2014 carries an economic penalty of about $250 million on cumulative Net Present Value basis ($2003)' (Delphia and Keyan 2003: iii). Against these calculations, the benefit of €100 million for alternative energy development seemed marginal indeed. In addition, safety upgrades that were needed to continuously run the plant proved rather easy to finance. The EU in particular funded the increase in security standards at the plant, and provided €29 million to the Armenian government to increase nuclear safety from 1996 to 2006 (European Commission 2005a).

Russian state companies increase the costs of compliance

Likewise, Russian state-owned companies contributed to the fact that the nuclear power plant enhanced its economic performance, making its shutdown ever more costly. Prior to 2003, the cost-effective operation of the NPP was constrained by its dependence on outside supplies. The nuclear fuel to run the plant had to be provided by Russia – a costly exercise that confronted the debt-ridden Armenia in the early 2000s with financial sorrows. From 2001 to 2003 the fuel supply was frequently delayed, because Armenia was unable to pay its bills to Russia. This triggered electricity supply interruptions, which again negatively affected the industrial output of the country (EIU 2001a, 2003a). By September 2003, the plant had accrued $40 million in debt to Russia for fuel supply. In order to settle the debt, the Armenian government agreed to a quid pro quo agreement with Russia and transferred the financial control of Medzamor to the Russian state-owned UES for five years (EIU 2003a).

UES was not only responsible for overseeing payments made by domestic consumers and paying the imported nuclear fuel, but was also in charge of the operational safety of the plant (EIU 2003a). The move triggered irritation among the European partners, who called for clarification on the issue (EU-Armenia Cooperation Council 2002), while it seemingly served the Armenian economic interests of cheap electricity generation without fully abandoning control of the plant. In 2004, the NPP produced 'a record volume of electricity [...], balanced its books for the first time since its 1995 restart, and avoided the refueling delays that had plagued its operations in past years'

(Sargsyan et al. 2006: 10). In addition, the cooperation with the EU on safety upgrades seemingly went smoothly, as did the provision of nuclear safety measures that the EU provided under its TACIS Nuclear Safety Instrument.[22]

Having secured the operation of the plant despite its low state budget with the help of Russia and safety assistance from the EU TACIS funding, the Armenian government raised the 'theoretically possible' option to replace the old and seemingly insecure nuclear power station with new nuclear capacity at the 2004 EU-Armenia Cooperation Council (2005: 26). Soon the nuclear option also shaped the government's strategic documents. The Armenian regulatory commission extended Medzamor's operating license to 2016 in 2004, as the former 15-year license was expiring (EIU 2004a). Similarly, a new nuclear option was more prominently discussed within Armenia. Robert Kocharyan cited a new power plant as an important pillar for Armenia's energy security and reminded his audience that:

> speaking of the Armenian Nuclear Power Plant one should remember the faces of those people, who in their time stopped the ANPP – there could have not been a greater damage to Armenia: dark days, energy and economic crisis were not the consequences of the war in Karabakh, but the closing of the ANPP.
> (Kocharyan, quoted in PanArmenian.net 2005)

The governmental energy diversification strategy of 2005 hence included a nuclear option to replace the old Medzamor power plant (Government of Armenia 2005: 6.4). In 2006, the Armenian National Assembly passed a law that allowed for full privatization of new nuclear units in order to attract investment into the project (ARKA News Agency 2010). The Armenian authorities now considered substituting the installed nuclear capacity with an 800 MW plant. The idea of doubling Armenia's nuclear capacity was dismissed by the EU as 'something we cannot sell to donors or internally within the European Union' (EU-Armenia Cooperation Council 2007: 27). As a result, the EU was becoming more pronounced in its possible refusal to grant support:

> We are running out of time with regard to our commitment on this, because you will remember that we have committed 100 million euros for the decommission[ing] under the condition obviously that the plant would be closed much earlier than what has now been announced.
> (EU-Armenia Cooperation Council 2007: 27)

The invocation of policy conditionality, however, did not trigger substantial results. In 2007, an energy action program was adopted by the Armenian government, which foresaw the building of a new nuclear unit immediately after the shutdown of the old reactor (IAEA 2011). With TACIS support, a decommissioning strategy was passed in 2007 which, however, far exceeded the EU's initially envisaged closure date (Government of Armenia 2007a). In May 2009, the Armenian government selected the company Worley Parsons to manage the construction of the new nuclear power plant and prepare all the necessary documents to get investors involved in the project (IAEA 2011). To finalize the legal process, the National Assembly adopted the 'law on construction of a new NPP' in October 2009, regulating the construction of a new nuclear reactor of double the capacity of the old plant and costing an estimated $5 billion (Danielyan 2009; European Commission 2010: 14). While some domestic criticism was launched by environmental groups due to the seismic location of the new plant (EIU 2010), the protest seemed to be marginal. As one interviewee stated, '[i]t is a concern of the population, but because they have inherited the fear of the early 90s, they are willing to pay almost any price for energy security, because the memory is very vivid of these dark years'.[23] Finally, in 2012 the government extended the license of the NPP to operate beyond 2016 (Danielyan 2012b; Shoghikian 2012). With the refusal to agree on a binding early closure date and the establishment of a legal basis for a new, bigger NPP, the Armenian government failed to formally comply with the ENP provision.

Russia's rivaling policy conditionality cements non-compliance

Unsurprisingly, the implementation of the NPP project fell equally short of mirroring EU demands, which was further encouraged by the invocation of rivaling policy conditionality by Russia. Due to the global financial and economic crisis, attracting investors in the project proved difficult, despite the fact that an agreement on electricity trade between Turkey and Armenia in September 2008 provided attractive export possibilities for the new NPP's surplus energy (EIU 2008a).

The only partner that showed interest in the endeavor was Russia. On 3 December 2009, a closed joint stock company was established by governmental decree to construct the new NPP. Both the Armenian government and Atomstroyexport, headed by the Russian state corporation Rosatom, were involved in the company that was set up to finance no less than 40 percent of the construction costs of the new NPP. The Russian side consented to contribute half, which constituted a financial incentive that was indeed entirely linked to the implementation of a policy that undermined the EU demands. However, as the financing of the remaining 60 percent was still to be secured, the company was open to other investors as well (ARKA News Agency 2010). Subsequently, an agreement between Russia and Armenia on the construction of a nuclear power plant was signed in August 2010 and the Armenian government announced plans to further delay the decommissioning of the old plant for several years, given that the new facility would need more time to be built (EIU 2010). After the Fukushima incident in early 2011, nuclear energy development in seismic zones remained a point of concern for many investors. Hence, Armenia twice postponed an investors' conference planned for the end of April 2011.[24] The difficult search for investors was ongoing at the time of writing. The Armenian authorities also promised to review safety issues with regard to their own plant when confronted with criticism by Armenian environmentalists that the plant was situated in a similar seismic zone to the Japanese one and referred to the extensive safety measures that had been implemented with the help of Russia, the EU and the USA since 1995, which amounted to $130 million of assistance (Asbarez 2011). In addition, they agreed to participate in an EU-supported comprehensive risk and safety assessment of the plant – the so called 'stress test' (EC and HR 2013b).

Preferential misfit and rivaling policy conditionality

The economic and autonomy costs that the Armenian government feared to encounter due to the implementation of the non-nuclear scenario seemingly caused a pronounced preferential misfit, both in the Armenian government and society. Despite the fact that the EU attached conditionality to the plant's early closure, the *de facto* output and outcome compliance was subverted by rivaling policy conditionality of Russia. Alternative explanations, such as a lack of capacity, fall short of fully accounting for non-compliance in this case. A lack of capacity in terms of financial means to build a new power plant indeed delayed compliance with the prescription to close the outdated plant, but this was due only to the strong preference of the Armenian government to stick to a nuclear substitute. On the contrary, the EU had intensely and over a long period of time supported the closure of the Medzamor power plant financially and through human resources, which would have been expected to empower decommissioning advocates in the government or trigger socialization effects. The transgovernmental networks that had been established as early as 1998 hence seemingly failed to impact the government's policy choice in this case.

Regional diversification

In 1994 the Armenian government considered diversifying its energy supplies for the first time by building a gas pipeline with Iran. It was deemed to be a way out of the problems that Armenia increasingly faced due to the unreliable transit of Russian gas through Georgia caused by attacks on gas pipelines by secessionist groups. In 1995, the Armenian and Iranian governments signed an agreement to construct a pipeline that would deliver Iranian gas to Armenia, but its realization encountered massive resistance by the USA, which froze the project for several years (Teurtrie 2010: 197f.). During this time, Armenia was hence fully relying on Russia as its main supplier of gas, which was shipped at prices well below the world market level.

Evidence suggests that unconditional negative incentives stemming from Russian companies encouraged the reconsideration of the project in the early 2000s. In 2002, Armenia fell short of paying its bills for the gas supplied by the Russian gas company Itera. Subsequently, the company threatened to reduce the amount of supplied gas in 2002 – a prospect that reportedly made the Armenian government seek alternatives in negotiations with Turkmenistan (EIU 2002: 50). The energy sector development strategy passed in June 2005 underscores this effect. In the document the pipeline to Iran figures as one of the central activities 'targeted at mitigating the country's dependence' caused by fuel supply interruptions (Government of Armenia 2005). After several rounds of negotiations with their Turkmen counterparts, the Armenian government announced the conclusion of an agreement with Iran over the construction of a gas pipeline to supply the Armenians with Turkmen gas via Iran (CACI Analyst 2002). Finally, in May 2004, Armenia and Iran signed an intergovernmental agreement about the 141-kilometer gas pipeline (Nygren 2008: 117). The total cost of the project was estimated to be $220 million and a first financing agreement was signed in September 2004. The agreement foresaw that Iranian companies would carry out the construction of the pipeline section on Armenian territory. It also prescribed that the Iranian National Gas Company committed itself to providing 36 billion cubic meters of gas to Armenia over a 20-year period, which Armenia paid by delivering electricity in return (EIU 2004a).

This was likely to provide enormous economic opportunities for both Armenia and Iran, as Georgia also announced its interest in being connected to the pipeline, allowing for potential transport of Iranian gas via Armenia and Georgia to European markets (EIU 2004a). Also, the progress in the cooperation with Iran gave Armenia the opportunity to counter increasing concerns about the hegemonic standing of Russian state-owned companies on the Armenian market which had occurred after two debt for equity swaps and the takeover of the Armenian distribution company in 2003 and 2005, respectively (EIU 2005a). The EU – as opposed to the USA – diplomatically supported the pipeline project as a welcome means of Armenia's energy diversification which was supposed to facilitate the closure of the Armenian nuclear power plant.[25] When Russia increased its gas price to Armenia to $110 per thousand cubic meters from 2006 onwards, the decision of the Armenian authorities to diversify its supplies was further vindicated: the cooperation with Iran not only broke Gazprom's monopolistic standing in terms of gas supply, but also Iran reportedly agreed to supply Turkmen gas at a lower price than Russia in 2005 (Socor 2006b). Accelerated by Russia's unconditional increase in gas prices, the pipeline was inaugurated in March 2007. In short, at the time Armenia had managed to diversify its gas sources from one to two suppliers.

Russia's rivaling policy conditionality challenges compliance

The intended outcome of the pipeline construction, however – namely, to make Armenia less dependent on one supplier of natural gas and thus fully comply with one of the provisions in the ENP Action Plan – was never fully implemented due to the invocation of rivaling policy conditionality by Russia.

Since 2002, ArmRosGazprom, the national gas company, had largely expanded its market and triggered an immense gasification of the Armenian energy sector that boosted Armenia's economic growth (EIU 2007a, 2008a). ArmRosGazprom, which was a joint company of Gazprom, Itera and the Armenian state, soon emerged as Armenia's leading corporate taxpayer and enjoyed a beneficial monopolistic standing in the Armenian gas market (EIU 2007a). In 2005, Gazprom reportedly became concerned about the gas pipeline project with Iran that had been launched in 2004. Alexander Ryazanov, vice-president of Gazprom, was quoted warning that 'if we do not participate in the Iranian-Armenian gas pipeline, nobody knows where this gas will end up' (Minassian 2008). Evidence suggests that Russia actively tried to counter this scenario. First, rumors spread about Russian pressure to reduce the diameter of the planned pipeline. Reportedly, Russia had urged the Armenian authorities to reduce the pipeline's diameter from 1,420 mm to 700 mm – a size large enough to satisfy Armenia's gas demand, but too small to allow for further exports to Europe (Cheterian 2006; Minassian 2008; Socor 2007). While this instance of pressure is hardly verifiable, an official agreement reached between Russia and Armenia in April 2006 is.

Just as had been the case in Georgia, Gazprom announced a gas price increase to $110 for Armenia from 2006 onward, with further increases anticipated. In spring 2006, however, Vladimir Putin offered his Armenian counterpart, Robert Kocharyan, a freeze in gas prices until 2009 if Gazprom were granted the ownership of the Armenian section of the newly operated Armenia–Iran gas pipeline in return (Asbarez 2007; EIU 2007a). After lengthy negotiations, the Armenian government consented to this quid pro quo offer and fully transferred the ownership of the newly inaugurated gas pipeline to ArmRosGazprom, in which Gazprom held the majority of assets by then (Socor 2006a; Socor 2006c; Teurtrie 2010: 198). Thereby Russian state-led companies also controlled the Armenian distribution network, which – taken together – put them in 'control over the access of gas from a third-country supplier' (Socor 2007), and hence undermined the original diversification intent of the Armenian government, which did not go unnoticed by Western observers (Lobjakas 2006).

The agreement to this deal may appear irrational at first sight, given the limited timeframe of the gas price guarantee and the fact that Iran had offered to provide gas at cheaper prices. Yet, the Armenian government justified the deal as stimulating the Armenian economy against critics who alleged the government to sell off Armenia's national security (RFE/RL 2006). This economic argument is supported by the fact that at the beginning of its operation the amount of gas supplied through the newly operated pipeline was unable to fully substitute Russian-provided gas (Socor 2006b). In addition, the price of gas deliveries from Iran was by no means fixed and likely to increase significantly by 2006. At the same time, it became clear that US pressure on Georgia made a scenario of Iranian gas being shipped to Georgia via Armenia ever more unlikely (Fuller 2007). More importantly, however, 2006 was the pre-election period for the parliamentary election in 2007 and a gas price increase threatened to significantly strengthen the position of the nationalist and left-wing opposition. Taken together, Kocharyan's agreement to the deal seems to be largely interpretable as a precautionary measure against anticipated economic and particularly political costs of increased gas prices.

Rivaling policy conditionality and shallow compliance

All in all, evidence suggests that the Armenian government considered diversification of regional suppliers a means to increase its autonomy vis-à-vis gas and fuel supplies from Russia via Georgia. However, Russia threatened to increase the political costs for the *de facto* implementation of the project by raising gas prices. Being confronted with costly rivaling policy conditionality from Russia prior to an election, the Armenian government complied shallowly: it built a pipeline with Iran (output), which carried low levels of gas and was owned by a Russian-dominated company, which prevented the *de facto* diversification (outcome). Alternative explanations, such as a lack of strategic capacity or possible socialization effects via capacity building, seem to exert little explanatory power in this case. First, Russia's offer to keep gas prices constant in exchange for pipeline assets was by no means without unknown strategic alternatives for Armenia. The pipeline to Iran was already in place and would have allowed for compensating shipments from Russia in a few years' time at temporarily higher prices, which Georgia had accepted at the time. Second, attempting to explain this outcome by socialization or pressure through international diplomacy also leaves some questions unanswered. The USA and Russia would probably have outweighed the diplomatic power of the EU, which may thus rather have resulted in a constant freeze on the project, comparable to the pre-2004 situation.

Comparative analysis

The case studies on energy diversification (Table 5.1) again suggest that preferential fit is a sufficient condition for domestic change, yet it is not always followed by full, but also by shallow compliance. Full compliance with energy diversification reform was achieved whenever domestic incumbents in Georgia and Armenia were able to use the reform prescriptions for their own purposes. This was the case with regional diversification efforts in Armenia before 2006, when the Armenian government sought cooperation with Iran as a means to potentially boost growth and increase its independence vis-à-vis ever more unstable fuel supplies from Russia via Georgia. Evidence suggests that the same mechanism was at work when Armenia decided to accelerate the development of its own domestic energy sources, both hydropower and other renewable energy. In both cases, compliance was established, despite the fact that in the case of cooperation with Iran it lacked implementation at the time.

Table 5.1 Overview of cases: energy diversification

Case	Preferential fit	EU – policy conditionality	RUS – policy conditionality	RUS – uncond.	EU – capacity	RUS – capacity	Com-pliance
AM RD pre-2006	1	0	0	1	0	0	Full
AM hydro, renew.	1	0	0	1	1	Con-certed	Full
GEO hydro post-2004	1	0	0	1	1	Con-certed	Full
AM RD post-2006	1	0	Rivaling	0	0	0	Shallow
GEO RD pre-2004	1	0	Rivaling	0	0	0	Shallow
GEO RD post-2004	1	0	Rivaling	1	0	0	Full
AM NPP	0	1	Rivaling	0	1	Rivaling	None
GEO renew.	0	0	0	0	1	0	None
GEO hydro pre-2004	0	0	0	0	0	0	None

Note: RD – regional diversification; NPP – nuclear power plant; AM – Armenia; GEO – Georgia; RUS – Russia. 0 stands for the absence, 1 the presence of a condition.

Similarly, Georgia started to put massive efforts into the development of its hydropower sources from 2004 onward. The required privatization and breakup of informal power structures stemming from the Shevardnadze era supposedly consolidated the power of the newly inaugurated administration. All these reforms were conducted under the impression of increasingly negative incentives by Russia. The withholding of former energy subsidies, gas cuts or insecurities related to energy imports accelerated the reform dynamics in the countries. The distinct feature of these, in some cases most likely unintended incentives provided by Russia, was a lack of rivaling policy conditionality. Gas prices were raised at the beginning of 2006, but not made conditional upon specific behavioral changes in the countries. Thus, Russia did not offer a quid pro quo arrangement that may have altered preferences over strategies of the incumbent government in a direction of non-compliance. Rather, they encouraged the countries to seek further autonomy and independence vis-à-vis external actors. In short, these unconditional negative incentives had a positive effect on compliance with the EU-prescribed policy change.

On the flipside, preferential misfit resulted in non-compliance whenever it did not encounter specific conditionalities from external actors. Under Shevardnadze, for instance, the Georgian government failed to develop its hydropower resources, falling short of the required investment, which was constrained by the overall corrupt power system that secured Shevardnadze's power base. Likewise, the Saakashvili government rallied behind an ultra-liberal reform consensus that proved at odds with the development of renewable energy via stronger regulation. In this case, the domestic costs that were

182 Energy diversification

anticipated by the Georgian government were both economic and ideological in kind and triggered non-compliance.

The cases also support the hypothesized interaction effect of preferential fit and external incentives. As Table 5.1 shows, policy conditionality invoked by the EU in the sphere of energy diversification is rare, but Russia indeed provides for policy conditionality in four different cases. In line with the hypothesis, compliance with regional diversification requirements after the invocation of Russian conditionality in Armenia in 2006 and in Georgia before 2004 triggered shallow compliance. The process outlined above documents to what extent the invocation of conditionality increased the costs for incumbent regimes: prior to elections in both countries, Russia offered the 'candy' of fixed energy prices in return for the takeover of strategic pipeline infrastructure. Both governments indeed consented to the deal at the time. In Georgia, however, a change of government made the arrangement null and void, while Armenia was stuck with the decision, which hollowed its compliance efforts. Preferential fit hence does not necessarily result in full, but can also trigger shallow domestic change, if rivaling policy conditionality by a second external actor is invoked.

The case of regional diversification in Georgia represents the typical 'great game scenario'. In 2005, when Russia offered the libertarian government under Mikheil Saakashvili to heavily invest in the urgently needed rehabilitation of its pipeline infrastructure and to freeze its gas price in return for the handover of the pipeline net, the administration indeed considered accepting the deal. The offer was in line with the prevailing liberal ideology and promised some economic benefits, while it was under attack from the opposition for security reasons. However, the US Administration, not the EU, was alarmed by what seemed to counter the development of alternative energy routes to the Caspian basin. While EU policy conditionality was absent, the USA indeed offered the Georgians an alternative, and domestically more beneficial, arrangement.

The case of the Medzamor nuclear power plant mirrors this. While the EU applied policy conditionality, Russia provided for rivaling, and seemingly more beneficial, policy conditionality for the Armenian government, which allowed it to elude EU demands. As the closure of the nuclear power plant entailed multiple costs for the Armenian government, the Russian offer to link financial support to the construction of an even bigger plant helped the Armenian government fulfill its initial policy preferences. The two latter cases thus show the impact of two or more external actors involved in rule transfer processes in one region: target regimes are faced with more choice and alternatives to potentially costly pressure from outside and can thus pick and choose whatever serves their preferences best.

The evidence presented above again largely confirms the hypothesis on the interplay of preferential fit and external capacity building for the cases at hand. In cases of preferential fit and capacity building, the external resources helped to develop strategies or to finance the implementation of EU policies, while it remained without effect in cases of preferential misfit. This finding

Energy diversification 183

hints at a usage of externally provided capacity and thus leads to the conclusion that a manipulation of utility costs of the central government can indeed account more plausibly for domestic change in the neighborhood than socialization effects or the empowerment of specific bureaucrats in the administration via capacity building can.

This has been illustrated in the comparison of the development of renewable energy in Georgia and Armenia. Armenia and Georgia were both included in similar networks and targeted by the same assistance provided by USAID and TACIS, and should hence have, ceteris paribus, similarly internalized the externally promoted policies. In the case of Armenia, the development of renewable energy proved politically cheap and compatible with the oligarchically-structured Armenian market. Subsequently, the externally provided capacity was indeed channeled into policy output and outcome. The Georgian case study showed the open resistance of the Georgian government to these reform attempts, which originated in the government's fear of losing economic benefits. The very same assistance, again TACIS and USAID funded, drained away in Georgia without any effect.

Capacity has also been provided by Russia, but not in the form of financial or technical assistance, but primarily as investment by state-led companies. The investment was crucial for the implementation of some of the reforms, as Russian companies provided the capital that other investors were unable or unwilling to bring to the region. They invested in Georgian hydropower plants after 2004 and provided Armenia with some of the capital needed to develop renewable energy. Despite policy divergence between Russia and the EU in this case, Russia has thus also enabled some of the ENP-prescribed reforms in the energy sector by providing the respective financial capacity for their implementation.

Notes

1 Parts of the material presented in this chapter draw on Ademmer and Börzel (2013) and on Ademmer (2015).
2 Renewable energies are usually defined as 'renewable non-fossil energy sources [comprising] wind, solar, geothermal, wave, tidal, hydropower, biomass, landfill gas, sewage treatment plant gas and biogases' (European Parliament and Council of the European Union 2001). However, as only small hydropower generation units below a capacity of 10 megawatts (MW) can be considered to have a small socio-ecological impact (European Commission 2008c; US Department of Energy 2011), the development of larger hydropower stations is not discussed under the heading of renewable energy here.
3 In the ENP Action Plans, the ENC are asked to 'further develop the National Energy Regulatory Commission in line with the principles of the Electricity and Gas Directives 2003/54 and 2003/55' (European Commission 2006b, 2006c).
4 Interview with a local energy expert, USAID Georgia, Tbilisi, 09.10.2010.
5 Russia acquired the majority of shares in the Georgian electricity market in 2003 with a purchase of the American company AES-Telasi, which owned 75 percent of the Georgian electricity network and numerous power stations (Baran 2003).

6 Interview with an official of the Ministry of Energy and Natural Resources of Georgia (MENR), Tbilisi, 05.10.2010.
7 Interview with a consultant on energy issues in Georgia, Deutsche Gesellschaft für Internationale Zusammenarbeit (GIZ), Berlin, 15.11.2011, own translation.
8 Interview with a local energy expert, USAID Georgia, Tbilisi, 09.10.2010.
9 Interview with an official of the MENR, Tbilisi, 05.10.2010; interview with a local energy expert, Energy Efficiency Center Georgia (EEC), Tbilisi, 05.10.2010.
10 Interview with a local energy expert, USAID Georgia, Tbilisi, 09.10.2010; follow-up interview with a local energy expert, EEC, Tbilisi, 27.09.2011.
11 Follow-up interview with a local energy expert, EEC, Tbilisi, 27.09.2011.
12 Interview with an official of the MENR, Tbilisi, 05.10.2010.
13 Interview with a local energy expert, USAID Georgia, Tbilisi, 09.10.2010.
14 Interview with an energy expert for Armenia and Georgia, KfW, Tbilisi, 12.10.2010; interview with a consultant on energy issues in Georgia, GIZ, Berlin, 15.11.2011.
15 Interview with an official of the MENR, Tbilisi, 05.10.2010.
16 Interview with a local energy expert, EEC, Tbilisi, 05.10.2010.
17 Interview with a consultant on energy issues in Georgia, GIZ, Berlin, 15.11.2011, own translation.
18 Follow-up interview with a local energy expert, EEC, Tbilisi, 27.09.2011; interview with a consultant on energy issues in Georgia, GIZ, Berlin, 15.11.2011.
19 Interview with a consultant on energy issues in Georgia, GIZ, Berlin, 15.11.2011.
20 Ibid.
21 For example, in 2006 Saakashvili said: 'those people who [...] cut off completely gas and electricity supplies are deceiving themselves if they think that Georgia will break up, collapse, be brought to its knees and then crawl back to Russia on all fours. Speaking to us like that – our dear friends and partners in the Kremlin – has never worked and will never work, nor will it work for you' (Saakashvili 2006a). Likewise, he declared energy independence from Russia one of the 'main elements of Georgia's independence' (Saakashvili 2006d), and infrastructural projects the 'condition of laying the firm foundation of liberty, independence and future successes of our country, which have a historical importance' (Saakashvili 2006e).
22 Phone interview with an EU official, EC (DG Energy), 05.09.2011; phone interview with an EU official, EC (DG DEVCO), 30.08.2011.
23 Interview with a local energy expert, Revolving Fund for Renewable Energy (R2E2) Armenia, Yerevan, 19.10.2010.
24 Interview with a local energy expert, USAID Armenia, Yerevan, 18.10.2011; interview with an official of the Nuclear Department of the Ministry of Energy of Armenia, Yerevan, 20.10.2011.
25 In 2007, members of the European Parliament in the EU-Armenian Parliamentary Cooperation Council declared: 'referring to the recent energy supply difficulties in Armenia, that highlighted Armenia's dependence on gas imports from the Russian Federation, takes note of the need to diversify the country's energy sources; in this context, notes the ongoing construction of the Iran-Armenia gas pipeline and hopes that this project will help Armenia diversify its energy supplies' (Council of the European Union 2007).

6 Anchoring policy change in times of crisis

Since the end of 2013, the post-Soviet neighborhood has witnessed an unprecedented crisis between the EU and Russia, taking Europe to the brink of war. Both Armenia and Ukraine rowed back from initialing or signing a new AA with the EU at the Eastern Partnership summit in Vilnius in November 2013. Armenia subsequently joined the CU, while Ukraine lapsed into outright war with thousands of casualties in its wake. The crisis originated in an apparent choice that neighboring countries had to make between two so far incompatible integration regimes and their associated policies. The events that unfolded in the aftermath of the Vilnius summit have ever since unsettled the entire region: mass demonstrations on Ukraine's Independence Square eventually forced the Ukrainian President Victor Yanukovych to flee the country and Russia soon annexed Crimea. Moldova and Georgia indeed signed the AA with the EU, but Moldova plummeted into a political crisis and Georgia has gone through an era of deep political polarization. All these developments were accompanied by invocations of trade embargos, offers of assistance and loans, and threats and promises by Russia and the EU.

The recent developments in the increasingly contested neighborhood therefore provide valuable insights into the link between external competition and the effectiveness of the EU's policy transfer – the central theme of this book. How does the EU manage to anchor its policies in a crisis-ridden neighborhood? Are choices in favor of or against AA with the EU still a function of the interplay of preferential fit and multiple policy conditionalities, as argued in the previous chapters?

In order to answer these questions, the first part of this chapter elaborates on why these choices may be analyzed through the theoretical prism originally chosen for the explanation of specific policy changes. It argues that the decisions (not) to sign AA with the EU can be well understood as a form of policy transfer under multiple external constraints. The AA entail a set of highly specific policies with detailed and binding commitments. While their implementation involves various state and non-state actors in multiple sectors, the decision to conclude and sign the AA in the first place rests with the incumbent administration. The gains in power, security or welfare that incumbents anticipate from the AA – labeled preferential fit – are thus likely to matter in the explanation for ENCs' recent integration choices. In addition, the manifold incentives Russia and the EU apply to further shape the incumbents' integration strategies provide a relevant test case to the argument that the interplay of preferential fit with multiple external incentives impacts neighborhood Europeanization.

The second part of the chapter then applies this framework to the recent developments in Armenia, Moldova, Georgia and Ukraine. I argue that the same factors that made ENC pick individual policies in the area of energy diversification and migration management can largely explain the decisions to sign the AA with the EU. Russia's quid pro quo bargaining frequently made ENC turn down the EU association offer, even though integration into the CU alternative also initially remained shallow, as in Armenia. Russia's sanctions to punish ENC for their broader foreign policy strategy, however, often speeded up their EU integration process, as seen in Georgia and Moldova, for instance. The case studies once again stress the importance of preferential fit for explaining whether ENC opt for integration with the EU or its Eurasian alternative.

The choice between competing integration regimes

For the first time the EU (apart from its accession policy) and Russia suggest the integration of post-Soviet states into a comprehensive, legally binding, and so far mutually exclusive regime. The EU's AA go far beyond the previous PCA or the ENP Action Plans, as they require a massive takeover of the EU's acquis communautaire by the ENC (Delcour and Kostanyan 2014: 3). The AA cover a large variety of sectors, such as energy, transport, public health, consumer protection, to name but a few, in which ENC agree to approximate to EU law. The agreements additionally come with a detailed timeline and institutional structures for the implementation of relevant legislation. The DCFTA forms part of the AA and not only prescribes the reduction of tariffs, but also foresees the reduction of non-tariff barriers by approximating ENCs' legislation and standards to that of the EU in trade and trade-related areas. The DCFTA covers food safety regulations and intellectual property rights, for instance, but also addresses highly sensitive issues, such as public procurement and competition law. As a result, the AA offers a closer political association and economic integration to ENC that is much more binding and rule based than previous cooperation agreements.

The CU and its successor EEU also strongly differ from previous paper tigers such as the CIS or EurAsEC. They are also rule bound, densely institutionalized and have some mechanisms in place to safeguard the implementation of rules (Dragneva and Wolczuk 2012, 2014). The EEU equally foresees the harmonization of national legislation to further the economic and political integration of its members (Eurasian Economic Commission 2015). The increase in competition results especially from the fact that the trade regimes included in both integration templates are currently mutually exclusive, despite the fact that the EU as such has figured as the blueprint for the

EEU (Dreyer and Popescu 2014). The DCFTA binds signatory states or organizations to reduce their tariff and non-tariff barriers to trade – a right that members of a customs union, however, pool on a supranational level. In order to be compatible, a DCFTA would thus need to be signed directly between the EU and the CU/EEU (Libman and Vinokurov 2012). Hence, the ENC needed to make tough choices between signing an AA with the EU, acceding to the CU/EEU, or maintaining a status quo of non-association with either regime.

It is especially this new quality and mutual exclusivity that renders the ENC decision for or against the AA an instance of EU policy transfer under multiple external constraints. The conclusion of international agreements based on EU rules is usually considered a form of rule selection that precedes domestic rule adoption and subsequent implementation (Lavenex and Schimmelfennig 2009), but as the AA contain highly specific EU policies, timelines and institutional structures for their implementation, signatories commit themselves more strongly to binding domestic changes than in the case of the previous ENP AP or PCA. The decision (not) to sign or ratify the AA with the EU hence qualifies as a crucial first step toward output compliance.

In addition, as in the areas of migration and energy policy, the decision to sign the AA privileges state over non-state actors. Neighborhood Europeanization in Armenia's and Georgia's energy policy and migration management has been portrayed as a domestic, executive-driven process. The evidence of Chapters 4 and 5 suggested that preferential fit was a sufficient condition for full or shallow compliance with EU policies in the Eastern neighborhood. Preferential fit was defined as the compatibility of the EU policy with the incumbent's preferences over outcomes, in terms of power, welfare and security (see Chapter 2). I showed that whenever incumbents and their connected elites in the ENC anticipated losses in power, security or welfare from ENP requirements, compliance regularly did not occur or remained shallow. Changes in preferential fit were driven by changes of incumbents and their power bases in the ENC, via electoral or, more often, non-electoral ways. Unlike the implementation of the AA, which relies on diverse stakeholders in various sectors, it is the incumbent administration of an ENC that decides whether to sign or not to sign an AA. The preferences of incumbents are consequently likely to matter considerably for this relatively discretionary and sovereignty-laden decision.

Instead of focusing on individual policies, this chapter thus investigates the specific gains and losses that incumbents and their specific power bases encounter from this broader integration choice. The chapter does not claim to provide for an exhaustive analysis in this regard, but relies on secondary literature to identify powerful executive and executive-related political and economic groups in the ENC and to sketch their gains and losses from the AA.

The decision (not) to sign the AA is made in an environment marked by multiple external incentives. As argued in Chapter 2, multiple external incentives do not change the incumbents' preferences over outcomes, but they may affect their preferences over strategies. In this vein, the previous chapters showed that the outcome of the compliance process in a context of multiple external actors depended on the interplay of the incumbents' initial preferential fit with policy conditionalities imposed by the EU and Russia: if ENC were faced with conditional incentives from the EU or Russia in cases of preferential misfit, they tended to decouple formal from *de facto* compliance in order to reap external benefits, while circumventing domestic costs. If both the EU and Russia applied rivaling policy conditionalities, incumbents reverted to a pick-and-choose strategy, in which they chose the conditional offer that best fitted their agenda.

The empirical evidence also suggested that whenever Russia clearly linked specific incentives to a policy that countered EU requirements *and* the EU itself did not incentivize policy change, full compliance with ENP requirements was unlikely. On the contrary, negative incentives by Russia that were not tied to specific policy changes in a quid pro quo manner frequently made compliance with EU demands more attractive.

The current crisis in the Eastern neighborhood has also been characterized by the provision of various incentives by the EU and Russia to shape integration choices. Russia has largely been considered an 'active saboteur' of the ENC AA endeavor (Delcour and Kostanyan 2014: 3), using a variety of economic, political, military and societal incentives. It has reverted to conditional offers of loans and gas price reductions for abandoning plans to sign the AA with the EU, but also has employed trade embargos and other sanctions, largely without leaving room for quid pro quo bargaining. Likewise, the EU has responded to Russia's foreign policy by committing itself to sign the AA as soon as possible with those ENC that had initialed them at the Vilnius summit (European Council 2013).

However, to what extent can the interplay of preferential fit and multiple policy conditionalities, the ingredients of neighborhood Europeanization identified in this book, indeed explain the decisions of incumbents in Georgia, Armenia, Moldova and Ukraine (not) to sign an AA and DCFTA with the EU? In order to answer this question, the next sections provide more detailed analyses of the developments in the four countries that eventually led to the decision to sign the AA or to accede to the CU/EEU.

Georgia

Georgia started to negotiate the AA with the EU in July 2010 and since then has been committed to further integration into the EU. The AA, including the DCFTA, was signed in June, ratified in July, and has been provisionally applied since September 2014. In 2012, however, Georgia witnessed a change in power: Bidzina Ivanishvili was sworn in as prime minister. He had been a businessman in Russia, had held Russian citizenship, and advocated for a normalization of ties with Georgia's northern neighbor. However, despite frequent allegations of compromising Georgia's EU integration, the new government progressed with signing the AA – a result of a substantial preferential fit by the new government with the EU's integration template and a lack of rivaling conditionality by Russia.

New cooperation possibilities and domestic politics

Like Moldova, Georgia had also witnessed trade embargos, a suspension of the bilateral visa-free regime and even outright war with Russia. However, unlike the cases of other Eastern Partnership countries, these developments had already taken place in 2008 – mostly seen as a reaction to the rise to power of Mikheil Saakashvili after the Rose Revolution. By 2013, Georgia had diversified its trade, FDI and energy supplies away from Russia and had coped with the absence of bilateral diplomatic ties (Cenusa et al. 2014; see also Chapter 5). Only a few channels of influence were left for Russia in 2013 to inflict economic costs on Georgia and hence to incentivize alternative integration regimes.

At the same time, the former UNM government had been replaced by the GD coalition as a result of the parliamentary election of 2012. Unlike the strongly anti-Russian UNM, the coalition included parties that lobbied for a greater rapprochement and a normalization of ties with Russia. The new government hence relied on a different power base from the previous one (see also Chapter 3), and adopted a less aggressive tone toward its northern neighbor. Evidence suggests that the new government tried to reap political benefits by increasing economic cooperation with Russia, while staying firmly committed to the EU's integration offer. As one of its first foreign policy initiatives, it appointed a special envoy for relations with Russia who regularly met with Russia's deputy foreign minister (Fix 2014). The GD's more cooperative stance began to bear fruit: Russia lifted the embargo on Georgian wine, water and fruit in summer and autumn 2013, which provided Georgian producers with more export opportunities. There were also discussions about potentially easing the tight visa regime by Russia (RFE/RL 2013f) – a highly attractive prospect for many Georgians. This cooperation was only partially hampered during the period of so-called cohabitation of the GD government and the UNM president: remarks by President Saakashvili had, for instance, insulted Russian officials invited to conduct wine inspections in February 2013 (RFE/RL 2013g). Yet, the embargo was eventually lifted.

At the same time, however, there was little talk of considering integration into the ECU. Shortly after Armenia's U-turn, Bidzina Ivanishvili said that he would not rule out Georgia's membership in the EEU, but only if this were compatible with European integration (RFE/RL 2013e). The commitment to European integration also largely prevailed among the Georgian population, despite the fact that it had grown more Eurosceptic (Apriashvili 2015). Yet, the GD needed to delegitimize claims by the still vocal UNM opposition alleging that it would compromise on Georgia's Western policy orientation or its territorial integrity (RFE/RL 2013c). The GD government hence presented its approach to Russia as a break with the style of Saakashvili's, as Ivanishvili put it, 'hysteric' and 'saber-rattling' foreign policy-making (Ivanishvili, quoted in RFE/RL 2013e), but not with the overall Western orientation, nor the commitment to Georgia's territorial integrity. An important signal in that regard was a bipartisan parliamentary resolution shortly after the resumption of Georgia's wine exports to Russia in March 2013. The resolution stipulated that Georgia would not have 'diplomatic relations or be in a military, political, customs alliance' with states that recognized or occupied Georgia's breakaway territories (RFE/RL 2013b). It also specified that:

> The Georgian authorities will provide implementation of all those conditions, which will allow Georgia to successfully complete negotiations with the European Union on [the] Association Agreement; Deep and Comprehensive Free Trade Agreement and Visa Liberalization Agreement.
> (Civil Georgia 2013)

Georgia's commitment to sign the AA and the DCFTA was hence firmly locked in – seemingly driven by domestic politics rather than external developments. Cooperating with Russia economically, while progressing toward the conclusion of an AA with the EU, hence allowed the new government to cater for its own constituency and to take the wind out of the sails of the UNM opposition. At the same time, there was little possibility of Russia enacting a form of rivaling conditionality to sweeten Georgia's prospect of joining the CU.

Negative incentives further EU integration

After Georgia and the EU had signed the AA and DCFTA, there were meetings of Georgia's special representative and Russia's deputy foreign minister, as well as of Russian and Georgian experts to discuss the DCFTA impact on Georgian-Russian new trade relations (RFE/RL 2014b). Despite declarations of fruitful dialogue, Russia still threatened to suspend the Georgian-Russian 1994 free trade agreement shortly afterwards. The threat did not materialize, but as exports to Russia still accounted for a relatively low share of total Georgian exports at the time, it also would not have hit Georgia that hard (Menabde 2014). The Georgian parliament unanimously ratified the DCFTA on 18 July 2014 (RFE/RL 2014b).

In addition, even though cooperation in the economic sphere was progressing, Russia actively furthered its ties with Georgia's breakaway regions. In March 2013, shortly after the passage of the resolution in parliament, there were rumors that President Putin would meet Aleksandr Ankvab, the leader of Georgia's breakaway region Abkhazia, in Moscow (RFE/RL 2013h). In June and September 2013, Russia also engaged in so-called 'borderization', establishing physical borders between Georgia and its secessionist territories, thereby also moving the border further into the territory previously controlled by the central government (Delcour and Kostanyan 2014; Socor 2013).

Russia's support for secessionist strife culminated after Georgia's AA and DCFTA with the EU provisionally entered into force in September 2014: in November 2014 and March 2015, Russia signed treaties to enhance bilateral integration and cooperation with Abkhazia and South Ossetia, respectively. Even though the GD government had tried to downplay these developments, arguably to safeguard the normalization process in its ties with Russia (Caucasian House 2014; Socor 2013), it was still vocal about EU and NATO integration being the main recipe for addressing Georgia's territorial integrity concerns. In summer 2013, Ivanishvili stressed that Georgia wanted to join NATO as soon as possible (RFE/RL 2013d). In October 2014, then Prime Minister Garibashvili openly acknowledged that the process of normalizing political ties with Russia had failed (RFE/RL 2014a), and in July 2015, the Georgian defense minister was quoted saying that Georgia could only achieve territorial integrity by further EU integration (*The Moscow Times* 2015). This evidence suggests that Russia's engagement in Georgia's breakaway regions further pushed Georgia's EU and NATO integration agenda.

The case of Georgia's commitment to signing the AA with the EU shows that despite the change of government, the AA still proved beneficial. It helped to sideline allegations by the main opposition party without contradicting the improvement of economic relations with Russia, resulting in a substantial preferential fit of the AA with the incumbent's political agenda. Russia's increased cooperation with Georgia's breakaway regions strengthened a vocal embrace of EU and NATO integration in Georgia, and hence encouraged rather than undermined further EU integration.

Armenia

Armenia surprised the international community when it announced in September 2013 that it would join the ECU instead of initialing the AA with the EU. Armenia's U-turn indeed resulted from an initial preferential fit with the EU's integration template that was then coupled with strong rivaling conditionality applied by Russia in 2013. This conditionality eventually made the Armenian government decide to join the CU – even though it sought to do so in a rather 'shallow' way.

Preferential fit and 'the big surprise'

Armenia and the EU had negotiated new contractual relations, as promised with the launch of the Eastern Partnership, from 2010 onward. Negotiations on the AA started in July that year and reportedly progressed 'at a good pace' (EC and HR 2012b: 2). Armenia also advanced relatively smoothly with regard to specific domestic reforms, the so-called 'key recommendations', which were necessary to start negotiations of a DCFTA with the EU (Delcour and Wolczuk 2015b). DCFTA talks were subsequently launched in February 2012. At the time Armenia officially figured jointly with Georgia and Moldova as the most advanced reformer among the Eastern Partners (EC and HR 2013a). The negotiations about the DCFTA were consequently concluded rapidly, together with negotiations on the AA in July 2013. At the Vilnius Eastern Partnership summit of November 2013, Armenia and the EU originally intended to initial both agreements – a plan that was crossed by Armenia's decision to join the CU instead.

The smooth negotiations and especially Armenia's compliance with EU rules and regulations in this area have mostly been attributed to a strong fit between governmental preferences and the AA and DCFTA prescriptions. The prospect of an AA with the EU seemingly served the incumbent government to gain legitimacy and reap economic benefits. The EU's reform requests met a dire need for modernization of the incumbent administration which was seeking to enhance its legitimacy after the political crisis of 2008. Also, against the backdrop of a strong economic downturn in the late 2000s, Armenia opted for an economic modernization agenda to get the economy back on track – an agenda that became a 'survival strategy' for Armenia's incumbent government (Delcour and Wolczuk 2015b: 498). Armenia additionally envisaged profiting substantially from a trade agreement with the EU: trade with the EU accounts for roughly one third of Armenia's overall trade balance and slightly exceeds the Armenian-Russian bilateral and overall CIS turnover (Eurasian Development Bank 2013: 14). In the long run, a study carried out for the European Commission hence forecast an additional 2.3 percent GDP growth for Armenia once the DCFTA was in place and remaining tariff as well as non-tariff barriers to trade were removed (ECORYS and CASE 2013). While forecasts of the Eurasian Development Bank also projected positive economic effects of a potential CU membership (Eurasian Development Bank 2013), the necessary increase in Armenia's very low external tariff toward non-CU members was expected to divert trade away from its main non-CU trading partners (see Dreyer and Popescu 2014: 4, for similar effects in other CU member states). In addition, Armenian authorities had ruled out CU membership early on due to the lack of a common border with other CU members. As Armenia's then Prime Minister Tigran Sargsyan put it:

> The whole point of a customs union is to have commercial exchanges without customs control [...] In our case, that is impossible as we have to pass through the territory of a neighboring state and twice undergo customs administration [...] Our Russian colleagues understand this situation. We are looking for ways of cooperation without the Customs Union.
> (Tigran Sargsyan, quoted in Danielyan 2012a)

The statement suggests that the Armenian government initially seemed to hope for closer economic integration into the EU coupled with a strong strategic partnership with Russia (Delcour 2014). Consequently, President Serzh Sargsyan's announcement on 3 September 2013 that Armenia would not initial the DCFTA with the EU, but join the CU instead, took most people by surprise. The decision was seemingly at odds with the assumed and also the declared policy preferences of the Armenian government at the time. Yet, there was relatively little opposition from other political or societal forces against the move (Kostanyan 2015). What had happened?

Rivaling conditionality and shallow integration attempts

Already in late 2012 Russia had asked several CIS countries to join the ECU, offering lower energy prices, economic support or further military cooperation in return (EIU 2013a). Also in Armenia, rumors spread in summer 2012 that Armenia's refusal to join the CU would provoke an increase in prices for Russian energy supplies. Price negotiations between the Armenian and Russian presidents were held, but no official increase in energy prices was announced (EIU 2013a). Allegations spread that the government had tried to conceal a *de facto* increase in gas prices prior to the presidential and municipal elections in early 2013 (EIU 2013a). Armenian customs data indeed indicated that Russian gas prices had already increased in 2012, but it was only two weeks after the elections in May 2013 that Gazprom also officially announced the price increase from US$190 to $270 per thousand cubic meters (EIU 2013b).

Were these price increases indeed used as a bargaining chip by Russia to further Armenia's CU aspirations? The developments after Armenia's announcement to join the CU lend some support to this hypothesis. Very shortly after the Vilnius Eastern Partnership summit in November, Vladimir Putin visited Yerevan to sign a number of energy agreements, which *inter alia* fixed the gas price at the original $190 (Asbarez 2014). In addition, Armenia agreed to hand over its remaining shares in the Armenian gas network ArmRosGazprom to Gazprom, reportedly to pay the debt it had accumulated when concealing the previous price hike (Asbarez 2014; EIU 2013b).

The more decisive set of rivaling conditionalities, however, occurred in the realm of Russian and Armenian security cooperation (Delcour 2014; Emerson and Kostanyan 2013). Security cooperation and arms supplies had figured high on the Russian-Armenian agenda from late 2012 onwards, when Armenia became increasingly worried about the 'horrendous quantity' of arms in Azerbaijan (EIU 2013b). According to the Armenian government, a deal was made in April 2013 to increase Russia's military presence by the deployment of Russian combat helicopters later that year (Shoghikian 2013). In summer 2013, Armenia and Russia also signed a new agreement about military cooperation (EIU 2013b). Yet, at around the same time, Russia delivered a large amount of weapons to Azerbaijan (EIU 2013b). In addition, a high-level meeting of Russian and Azerbaijani delegations in Baku in August reportedly made many Armenians nervous (De Waal 2013; Kucera 2013). Even though high-ranking Russian and CSTO officials reassured the Armenian leadership that the military balance in the region would not be changed by this delivery, the Armenian media and the opposition openly expressed their concerns (EIU 2013b). The timing of events and the justification given by Serzh Sargsyan suggest that it was especially the potential loss of Russian security guarantees that informed the decision to join the CU. At a working visit in Moscow on 3 September 2015, relatively shortly after the Russian-Azerbaijani meeting, Armenia's president announced and justified Armenia's CU accession:

> When you are part of one system of military security it is impossible and ineffective to isolate yourself from a corresponding economic space.
> (Sargsyan, quoted in RFE/RL 2013a)

Tying CU membership to Russian security guarantees drastically increased the price for Armenia's plan to initial the DCFTA. Previous Armenian presidents had lost political power whenever they were perceived as compromising on the status of Nagorno-Karabakh, the ethnic Armenian enclave in Azerbaijan. Indeed, even though the decision to join the CU was a relatively big surprise to society and parts of the elite (Delcour and Wolczuk 2015b), it failed to stir protests comparable to those in Ukraine later that year. Only about 200 protestors took to the streets after the announcement, and most major political parties kept silent, with some acknowledging the importance of Russia's security guarantees (Hayrumyan 2013). After the announcement, the Armenian authorities sought a new mode of complementarity in their integration regimes. Evidence suggests that they tried to integrate more shallowly into the CU while upholding important trade flows and cooperation with the EU.

The response of Štefan Füle, the EU's commissioner for enlargement and the European Neighborhood Policy, to Sargsyan's decision was clear: Armenia's CU membership would be incompatible with signing a DCFTA (Charap and Troitskiy 2013: 56). Serzh Sargsyan still sought to initial the non-DCFTA parts of the AA at the Vilnius summit, but the EU refused (Kostanyan 2015). Instead, there was a formal declaration at the summit that the EU and Armenia would elaborate alternative ways of cooperation, resulting in the start of a scoping exercise for a new agreement in late 2014.

Armenia was also in the course of negotiating its terms of accession to the CU. A roadmap was adopted in December 2013 and a subsequent action plan in January 2014. Yet Armenia's enthusiasm toward the new integration scheme seemed to be limited. Prime Minister Sargsyan still openly raised concerns with regard to the economic consequences of the required increase in Armenian tariffs and the reconsideration of WTO commitments (Delcour 2014: 44). Indeed, the Armenian side negotiated exemptions from the CU's external tariff for more than 800 products until 2020 (EIU 2015). This suggests that Armenia's incumbent administration sought to limit threats to its outright political survival in seeking closer economic integration with Russia, while averting costly trade effects by a more shallow integration into the CU.

Governmental reshuffle and Karabakh again

After President Sargsyan had officially decided to opt for membership in the CU, however, Armenia's domestic political scene changed, hinting at a shift of the incumbent's power base. In mid-2013, observers still noted that there was:

> a reform-minded team in place, including the prime minister, Tigran Sargsyan [who ...] is now well placed to oversee reforms. Nonetheless, the president will probably be fairly cautious with the introduction of the reform agenda, in order to ensure that he does not alienate the wealthy government-linked tycoons, who have played an important role in supporting his position.
>
> (EIU 2013b)

In early 2014, a controversial pension reform – supported by the IMF – entered into force and united opposition forces in their pledge to ask the government of Prime Minister Tigran Sargsyan to resign (EIU 2014b). With rising pressure on the incumbent administration, Tigran Sargsyan stepped down in April 2014. The subsequent governmental reshuffle removed many other reform-oriented ministers from their posts. Hovik Abrahamyan, the parliamentary speaker and a wealthy oligarch, was appointed as the new prime minister (EIU 2014b). Abrahamyan held personal ties to Gagik Tsarukyan, a business tycoon and head of the Prosperous Armenia Party, and a close associate of former President Robert Kocharyan, both of whom had emerged as major opponents of the incumbent president (EIU 2014b). The shift in power suggests a deviation from Armenia's previous modernization agenda as a political survival strategy and was followed by further steps toward CU accession.

Russia was arguably interested in Armenia's quick accession to the CU (Hayrumyan 2013) – a process that was yet delayed by negotiations about the status of Nagorno-Karabakh in the treaty (Garcés de los Fayos 2014). Kazakhstan's President Nazarbayev – on good terms with his Azerbaijani counterpart – insisted on including a reference to Armenia's internationally recognized borders in the treaty, thereby *de facto* suspending the treaty's application to the territory of Nagorno-Karabakh (EIU 2014a). An outright exclusion of Karabakh, however, would have created a dividing line between Armenia's mainland and the ethnic Armenian enclave – a red line for the Armenian negotiators. Observers suggested that it was thanks to pressure from Russia that the parties eventually signed a treaty in October 2014 that abstained from mentioning Armenia's international borders (EIU 2014a). Armenia had been thus fully integrated into the CU and its successor EEU.

This evidence suggests that the interplay of preferential fit and rivaling conditionality by Russia can largely explain why Armenia chose to integrate with the CU and the EEU. The threat of losing Russian security guarantees and subsidized gas prices changed the government's integration strategy: it first tried to keep Russia's support without fully diverting non-CU trade relations by means of a more shallow form of integration into the CU. The government reshuffle finally gave rise to full integration into the EEU from 2015 onward. This integration choice, however, limits the room for maneuver of the Armenian government to a greater extent than has been the case with previous choices for individual policies. Russian rivaling policy conditionality made Armenia integrate into a hard law trade regime in which it cedes its sovereignty to determine external tariffs and hence constrains its future ability to decouple formal from *de facto* change in this policy area.

Moldova

For a long time, Moldova has figured as the Eastern Partnership's poster child. The pro-EU coalition government, Alliance for European Integration (AEI), embarked on a reform agenda to quickly conclude negotiations on an AA, including a DCFTA, and visa liberalization with the EU. From early 2013 onward, however, Moldova was not only subject to a manifest domestic political crisis, but also to trade embargos and other sanctions by Russia. Unlike Armenia, however, Moldova remained firmly committed to European integration and eventually signed the AA in June 2014. Russia's subsequent sanctions did not undermine this agenda as they were largely neutralized by the EU. Instead, Russia's assertive foreign policy helped to speed up the EU's integration offers, which in return provided substantial, even though short-lived, political benefits to a domestically contested ruling coalition.

A bullied poster child?

Shortly after the launch of the Eastern Partnership in May 2009, Moldova witnessed a change in government. The Communist Party under the leadership of Vladimir Voronin had lost its majority in a snap parliamentary election in July 2009. A coalition of four parties, the AEI, formed a new government, led by Vlad Filat of the Liberal Democratic Party (LDP). The new ruling coalition was mainly glued together by its opposition to the Communist Party and a strong focus on European integration (Parmentier 2014). A closer political association with the EU, as foreseen in the Eastern Partnership, was very much in line with the new government's agenda and a DCFTA promised further benefits to Moldova's highly liberalized economy, especially in comparison with a more protectionist CU (Radeke et al. 2013).

The AEI soon emerged as the frontrunner in the Eastern Partnership process (Paul 2014; Rinnert 2013). The coalition implemented austerity measures, tried to improve the business climate and reformed the police (Secrieru 2014). Reform activism showed especially in areas that were linked to tangible EU benefits, such as the opening of the DCFTA negotiations or the visa liberalization dialogue (EC and HR 2012a). By 2012 Moldova had made sufficient progress on the EU's 'key recommendations' to start DCFTA negotiations. They were concluded in June 2013 and the EU and Moldova initialed the AA including the DCFTA at the Vilnius summit in November 2013. Since spring 2014 Moldova has been the first Eastern Partnership country to profit from visa liberalization, and since September that year the DCFTA and the AA have been provisionally applied.

Throughout this process, however, Moldova had been subject to intense pressure by Russia, arguably to sanction Moldova's EU integration drive (see Cenusa et al. 2014 for a detailed overview). However, trade embargos, support for separatist strife or restrictions for Moldovan labor migrants seemingly failed to discourage the Moldovan government from concluding the AA. Instead, further European integration was one of the few straws the incumbent government coalition could clutch to safeguard its political survival in a homemade political crisis.

Domestic power struggles and Russian incentives

By mid-2013 at the latest, Moldova's poster child image had suffered a serious blow. An illegal hunting trip by judges and public officials in late 2012 left one participant dead. The incident triggered a severe domestic political crisis and revealed the pervasiveness of corruption among the ruling AEI (Rinnert 2013). The political infighting occurred especially between Prime Minister Vlad Filat (LDP) and the wealthy businessmen and politician Vlad Plahotniuc of the coalition partner Democratic Party (DP). A vote of no confidence in parliament in spring 2013 dissolved the AEI, and Vlad Filat was removed from his post of prime minister (Knott 2013). Early elections, however, were an unattractive prospect both to the incumbent coalition and to the EU shortly prior to the Vilnius summit: due to the corruption scandals, the AEI was unlikely to be reelected, so an early election would threaten to alter the balance of power in favor of the Communist Party and its popular leader Vladimir Voronin (Rinnert 2013). Voronin had openly shown interest in the CU, risking to deprive the EU of Moldova as its 'success story' at the summit in November 2013. The unpopular incumbency was also in dire need of political windfalls from progressing with the European integration process (cf. Minzarari 2013). As a result, a new pro-European coalition government without Vlad Filat was formed in May 2013 – united once again in its goal to strengthen ties with the EU and to prevent a return of the Communist Party to power (Freedom House 2014b; Knott 2013).

The fragile government coalition indeed quickly progressed with regard to further European integration, which was at least indirectly facilitated by Russian sanctions. Russia had threatened to cut energy supplies and denied work permits for 20,000 migrant workers (Paul 2014). From January 2014 Moldovans were only allowed to stay for 90 days in Russia, resulting in an increase of illegal Moldovan migrants on Russian territory (Ademmer and Delcour 2016; Całus 2014). Russia also helped to organize a referendum in Gagauzia on CU integration in February 2014 (Delcour and Kostanyan 2014: 6).

The Gagauz population voted 98.4 percent in favor of the CU, but the referendum was declared illegal by Moldovan authorities (Paul 2014).

Most of Russia's sanctions, however, occurred in the area of trade policies. In September 2013, Russia had already banned Moldovan wine imports, arguably because of a violation of quality standards (Charap and Troitskiy 2013; Emerson and Kostanyan 2013). In the following months, it enacted an embargo on Moldovan meat, fruit and vegetables (Cenusa et al. 2014; Delcour and Kostanyan 2014), and in August 2014 it suspended the CIS free trade agreement for 19 product categories, including agro-food items, and strengthened intra-Moldovan tensions by exempting Gagauzia from many of these restrictions (Cenusa et al. 2014). While the embargos sensitively affected the Moldovan economy, their consequences were alleviated by loopholes in their application, a set of measures implemented by the incumbent government and, importantly, by a more speedy provision of benefits by the EU. First, as Belarus initially refused to join the Russian embargo, Moldovan wine and fruit were directly or indirectly traded to Belarus, or even via Belarus to Russia (Całus 2014; Cenusa et al. 2014). Second, the Moldovan government tried to boost internal demand and alleviate the burden on individual farmers with the help of subsidies, additionally trying to tap alternative markets (Paul 2014). Third, the Russian sanctions led to further political and economic support by the EU and individual member states: from January 2014 onward, Moldovan wine was imported to the EU duty free, and Denmark, for instance, provided further financial assistance (European Parliament 2013; Paul 2014). In August 2014, the EU lifted quotas for Moldovan fruit products. Some Moldovan producers had difficulties adjusting to EU standards and hence exploiting the EU as an alternative market, but there has still been a substantial reorientation of trade toward the EU (Cenusa et al. 2014). The case of Moldova hence suggests that there was a substantial preferential fit in place, as the progress toward the AA promised political benefits to an increasingly contested ruling coalition. As a most likely unintended side effect, the non-negotiable Russian sanctions further speeded up the Moldovan economic EU integration process.

External rivalry and a lack of domestic reform

The usage of the EU's integration offer for furthering the political survival of a contested ruling coalition, however, has proven unsustainable. Despite its EU integration efforts, the AEI failed to fight, and rather furthered the prevalence of corruption in Moldova. Consequently, the November 2014 election substantially strengthened the opposition, even though the LDP and the DP still managed to form a pro-EU minority government in February 2015 (EPRS 2015).

The domestic political crisis was aggravated in September 2015, when it became clear that $1 billion had disappeared from the state budget under the AEI coalition government. The scandal triggered massive protests by diverse

Moldovan groupings that called for the government to resign. Ever since, external actors have loomed large in the debate about these protests, also to legitimize the ruling coalition's grip on power. In September 2015, then Prime Minister Valeriu Strelets, for instance, justified his refusal to step down, arguing that 'there are too many forces interested in destabilizing the situation in order to divert the country away from its strategic course to European integration' (Strelets, quoted in Puiu 2015). A month later, the Moldovan parliament eventually dismissed the pro-European government over the corruption scandal. Vlad Filat, who had figured as the most prominent EU-oriented reformer, was subsequently arrested for his involvement in the banking scandal. His arrest was widely interpreted as further strengthening the DP-connected oligarchs (Socor 2015), raising questions about the prospect of sustainable implementation of the AA in Moldova.

Apart from stressing the importance of preferential fit and negative incentives by Russia for explaining Moldova's choice to sign the AA, the case of Moldova also shows that incumbent governments have frequently only paid lip service to EU policies that threaten their illicit power bases. The increased rivalry between the EU and Russia catered for these semi-democratic incumbents, which have emerged as a key factor of instability in the neighborhood.

Ukraine

The case of Ukraine shows most vividly the EU–Russian competition on integration offers and their consequences. The decision by President Yanukovych not to sign the AA and DCFTA in November 2013 drove protestors onto the Ukrainian Maidan. Why did Yanukovych decide to suspend his signature? Why did the new administration reverse his course? Yanukovych tried to play Russia and the EU against each other to safeguard his political survival – a strategy that eventually failed with devastating consequences for the entire country. For the new administration that emerged from the protests, the signing of the AA subsequently figured as a *raison d'être*.

Playing the status quo

After Viktor Yanukovych was elected president in 2010, he continued the negotiations with the EU on an AA and DCFTA, which had started in 2007 and 2008, respectively. He pursued a pragmatic economic foreign policy that sought to combine free trade agreements with the EU and the CIS (Samokhvalov 2015). Yanukovych also embraced the deep-rooted, albeit declarative agenda on European integration that had characterized the foreign policy of various ruling elites in Ukraine since the early 2000s (Dragneva and Wolczuk 2015). The DCFTA was expected to be beneficial for the Ukrainian economy, but gains for Yanukovych and associated businessmen were less clear. While most assessments concluded that a DCFTA with the EU would boost Ukraine's economy in general (Åslund 2013), benefits from tariff reductions were unevenly spread across different sectors and, hence, businessmen profited to different degrees (Langbein 2014). Some Ukrainian oligarchs, such as the confectionery giant Petro Poroshenko, and other food producers were to gain substantially from DCFTA tariff reductions (Kościński and Vorobiov 2013), but those oligarchs had been increasingly sidelined in Ukrainian politics, as Yanukovych expanded the political and economic power of 'the family', comprising Yanukovych's relatives and associated friends who also reigned over important ministries (Konończuk 2015; Kościński and Vorobiov 2013).

The 'family' and other still politically influential oligarchs were assumed to be rather indifferent. The DCFTA eventually required the creation of transparent public procurement procedures and anti-monopoly legislation that undermined established oligarchic business models (Kościński and Vorobiov 2013). In addition, many oligarchs located in eastern Ukraine and dominating Yanukovych's Party of the Regions had a strong economic interest not to endanger trade with Russia (Konończuk 2015; Kościński and Vorobiov 2013). At the same time, however, Yanukovych and some of his connected political and business elite seemingly preferred the DCFTA over the CU alternative (Samokhvalov 2015): they were active in European markets, and the CU was expected to unduly favor Russian over Ukrainian businesses. The agreement was also popular among Ukrainians and considered to insulate Ukrainian oligarchs from Russian trade measures that had previously affected them negatively (Åslund 2015). In addition, the DCFTA prospect fitted Yanukovych's declared economic modernization agenda, which, however, seemed merely to cater for oligarchic interests (Åslund 2015; Dragneva and Wolczuk 2015). Finally, Ukraine's negotiations on the AA and the DCFTA proved cheap for the Ukrainian government: unlike Moldova, Georgia and Armenia, Ukraine did not have to comply with the EU's 'key recommendations' to start DCFTA negotiations in the first place (Delcour and Wolczuk 2013). Domestic change was hence only necessary after the agreements entered into force. All this suggests that Yanukovych preferred to uphold the status quo: he had an interest in furthering negotiations on the AA with the EU, while trying to keep the CU and *de facto* domestic reforms at bay. Hence, in late 2011, negotiations on the DCFTA were concluded, followed by those on the overall AA in spring 2012.

Balancing multiple incentives

Yanukovych also tightened his political power, increased control over the judiciary and started to persecute political opponents, most prominently shown in the imprisonment of Yulia Tymoshenko, whom he feared would endanger his reelection in 2015 (Freedom House 2014a). Dominated by the Party of the Regions, Ukraine's parliament also became firmly submissive to Yanukovych's rule, as he secured the party's support for winning elections in eastern and southern Ukraine by allowing for the personal enrichment of party leaders in return (Dragneva and Wolczuk 2015). The EU responded to these developments, as well as to the rigged parliamentary election in late 2012 (Delcour and Wolczuk 2015a): the signature of the AA was put on hold and Yanukovych was faced with a comprehensive list of conditions by the EU in order to unfreeze the process, including a reform of the electoral code and the judiciary, as well as a tougher fight against corruption – all of which sensitively challenged Yanukovych's power base at the time. Progress toward the AA and the DCFTA hence became increasingly costly for the incumbent.

At the same time, Russia arguably intensified its lobbying for the CU, asserting that Ukraine had to make a choice between the DCFTA and the CU (Åslund 2013). Ukraine agreed to become an observer to the CU in May 2013 – a status that did not trigger any legal commitments and was still in line with signing a DCFTA with the EU (Åslund 2013).

Over the summer, Russia also applied trade sanctions. From July to October 2013, there was a ban on Ukrainian chocolates and railway carriages, and an increase in customs controls that *de facto* stopped Ukrainian exports into Russia (Cenusa et al. 2014; Charap and Troitskiy 2013; Emerson and Kostanyan 2013). These measures came without room for negotiations and, at least at first sight, did not change Yanukovych's commitment to sign the AA. Quite the contrary: he consequently decided 'to go "full speed to Europe"' (Dragneva and Wolczuk 2015). In August 2013 Yanukovych announced that he wanted to sign the AA and fulfill the EU's conditions for the Vilnius summit (Åslund 2015). Some of the EU conditions were indeed fulfilled when the Ukrainian parliament adopted some of the so-called 'European laws' in September 2013, suggesting that Russia's negative incentives rather provided further stimulus to foster cooperation with the EU. However, two crucial and politically costly issues – the reform of the Prosecutor's Office and the release of Yulia Tymoshenko – remained pending (Konończuk 2013).

By October 2013, Yanukovych's gamble to foster cooperation with the EU without enacting these costly reforms, and showing goodwill to Russia without acceding to the CU, became increasingly untenable. Ukraine urgently needed financial assistance as the country was about to default on its foreign debt (Freedom House 2014a). Support from the IMF, however, was tied to domestic reforms (Åslund 2015; Hoffmann et al. 2014). Yanukovych hence looked both ways. First, he tried to condition his signature of the AA on EU financial support. He reportedly asked the EU for €160 billion and the abandonment of the condition to release Yulia Tymoshenko, which the EU initially refused (Hoffmann et al. 2014; Samokhvalov 2015). In addition, there were several negotiations between the Ukrainian and Russian sides prior to the summit in Vilnius: Russia – concerned that Ukraine would indeed sign the AA – reportedly offered financial help, gas price reductions or, in case Ukraine signed the AA, a full-fledged trade war (Hoffmann et al. 2014). On 21 November Yanukovych announced that he would not sign the AA in Vilnius, even though the EU made a last-minute offer to relax the Tymoshenko condition (Delcour and Wolczuk 2015a; Hoffmann et al. 2014). Shortly after the Vilnius summit, Russia granted a $15 billion loan to Ukraine, as well as gas price reductions, and investments, but Ukraine's potential accession to the CU and EEU remained unclear. As Åslund (2015: Chapter 6) summarizes:

> This deal was also a personal victory for Yanukovych [...] By pretending to be serious about negotiating accession, Yanukovych had convinced Moscow to provide the international financing he needed to sustain Ukraine's debts until the presidential elections, and the Russians did not ask him to pursue any pesky reforms.

This evidence indeed suggests that Yanukovych tried to use the external rivalry between the EU and Russia to further his political survival. However, his personal victory proved to be short lived.

A new incumbency and an Association Agreement (partly) put on hold

The events that unfolded after Yanukovych's decision have filled worldwide news. Mass demonstrations started on Independence Square (Maidan Nezalezhnosti) in Kiev, which became known as the 'Euromaidan'. The peaceful protests radicalized after their violent dispersal through the police (Samokhvalov 2015). Yanukovych's power base eroded, despite EU member states brokering a compromise between Yanukovych and the opposition (Dragneva and Wolczuk 2015). The defection of several deputies of Yanukovych's Party of the Regions finally shifted the power in parliament and eventually ended Yanukovych's rule (Åslund 2015). In late February 2014, he fled Ukraine for Russia. The Party of the Regions soon collapsed as well (Dragneva and Wolczuk 2015). Yulia Tymoshenko was released, a provisional new president was elected and a new government installed. A presidential election took place in May 2014 and brought Petro Poroshenko, one of Ukraine's wealthiest businessmen, to power. Parliamentary elections in October were equally won by his party and a new coalition government started its work, headed by the former interim Prime Minister Arseniy Yatsenyuk (Freedom House 2015b).

Rather than disempowering the oligarchic elite, however, Ukraine subsequently witnessed a change in oligarchs (Melnykovska 2014): the 'family' was stripped of its power in favor of the previously sidelined oligarchs – such as Petro Poroshenko – who had actively supported the Euromaidan protests. The new executive hence relied on a vastly different, yet still business-connected power base that originated in a movement against Yanukovych's refusal to sign the AA with the EU. Shortly after Poroshenko's inauguration, in late June 2014, he signed the AA including the DCFTA.

After the interim government had taken over, separatist strife erupted in eastern Ukraine and Crimea. Crimea voted for accession to Russia in a referendum that the central government declared unconstitutional, and was annexed by Russia in March 2014. Russia also supported separatist strife in eastern Ukraine by so-called 'hybrid warfare' and intensified trade embargos.

It cut gas supplies to Ukraine, which, – as had been the case in Georgia in the mid-2000s – induced the country 'to diversify energy sources [...] and to engage further in energy savings' (Delcour and Kostanyan 2014: 7). In addition, Russia announced an end to tariff-free trade under a bilateral CIS free trade agreement, which was estimated to reduce Ukraine's exports to Russia by $3 billion; an extent that corresponded to roughly 1.7 percent of Ukraine's GDP (Cenusa et al. 2014: 2f.).

In order to counter the increasing confrontation, trilateral talks between Ukraine, Russia and the EU were launched about the DCFTA, and a postponement of its application until January 2016 was agreed. In return, Russia agreed not to suspend the CIS free trade agreement until then (Cenusa et al. 2014). The DCFTA postponement implied that only tariffs for Ukrainian goods into the EU would be initially abolished, whereas existing non-tariff barriers and Ukrainian tariffs for EU products would be upheld for a longer period (Langbein 2014). Whether the new Ukrainian leadership is indeed committed to implementing the new agreement after its entry into force has yet to be ascertained.

The developments in Ukraine hence suggest that Yanukovych tried to play the increased rivalry between integration offers of the EU and Russia to further his own political survival, underlining the processes of usage that have also shaped more specific policy change in the region, as shown in the previous chapters. Negative incentives by Russia that failed to be clearly linked to a bargaining process did not prevent Ukrainian incumbents from signing the AA. Instead, it was the negotiation offer that Yanukovych received after he announced the signing of the AA that diverted him from selecting the EU integration template. It was a bottom-up induced change in government that paved the way for the signature in the end.

Conclusion

The developments that led to the AA being signed or not in Moldova, Georgia, Ukraine and Armenia underline that it is especially the interplay of preferential fit and multiple policy conditionalities that accounts for the selection of integration schemes. AA were signed when they promised to increase the incumbent's hold on power. To be sure, the power bases of ENC incumbents are highly diverse and complex phenomena, and Ukraine and Moldova have only been glanced at in this chapter (but see e.g. Åslund 2015; Buzogány 2013; Dragneva and Wolczuk 2015). However, the broader line of events provides some evidence for this claim.

In Moldova, European integration had come to be one of the few remaining common denominators of an increasingly contested ruling coalition. Likewise, the new Georgian government used further EU integration steps to sideline the political opposition, while at the same time promoting an economic rapprochement toward Russia. In Ukraine, it was only the change of the ruling elite and its power base that opened up the possibility to sign the

AA, despite the refusal of the previous administration to do so. Whether the initial preferential (mis)fit toward an integration regime translated into its outright choice was yet shaped by its interplay with multiple external conditionalities. Armenia – initially set to sign an AA – was confronted with rivaling conditionality by Russia that the EU was unable to balance, showcasing the weakness of the EU to engage with the protracted security situations in many ENC. Armenia consequently altered its integration strategy and chose not to sign the AA, while trying to integrate rather shallowly into the CU in order not to thwart benefits from its trade relations with the EU. Viktor Yanukovych seemingly favored the status quo of not being associated with either regime and tried to play the EU and Russia against each other to safeguard his political survival: he first signaled his commitment to domestic reform after the EU invoked strong conditionalities, only to eventually opt for a more attractive offer from Russia. Evidence also shows that negative incentives from Russia that are not clearly linked to quid pro quo bargains do not prevent ENC from following their preferred integration path. Trade sanctions against Moldova and Ukraine have mostly speeded up the integration process. The same occurred in Georgia with Russia's threats to suspend a free trade agreement and its support for separatism.

In addition, the case studies show that interdependence with Russia as such has trouble accounting for the ENC integration choices. Patterns of interdependence with Russia differed across countries, especially in the area of trade that should have altered the strategy (not) to sign the DCFTA part of the AA with the EU: Georgia was hardly dependent on trade with Russia and unsurprisingly signed the AA, but Moldova and Ukraine held close trade ties to Russia and incurred economically costly losses from its trade embargos, yet eventually opted for the AA. Armenia's trade patterns, however, were more directed to the EU. It had also been dependent on Russia's security guarantees throughout the entire period that it had negotiated the AA with the EU.

The integration choices are thus better explained by the usage of this interdependence by Russia in form of quid pro quo negotiations and their interplay with the political preferences of domestic incumbents. The Moldovan ruling coalition profited politically from European integration and was not targeted by concrete quid pro quo offers by Russia. Russia's success in the case of Armenia can only be explained against the background of the outright linkage of trade integration with security guarantees and the domestic political costs for Armenian incumbents associated with compromising on the security of Karabakh.

While this is broadly in line with the patterns found for policy changes in the previous chapters, there are also some remarkable differences: first, while the fit of integration templates with political preferences of incumbents proves highly relevant, the developments in Ukraine from 2013 onward have shown that integration choices have become more than just an intra-elite struggle (Dragneva and Wolczuk 2015). The mass protests on Ukraine's Maidan have been bottom-up constraints on the executive that dramatically changed the course of regional integration. These developments may hint at a more diverse and less centralized dispersion of political power of Ukraine (see e.g. Buzogány 2013; Dimitrova and Dragneva 2013), but they also show that under conditions of increasing external rivalry the selection of integration regimes is no longer perceived as a choice for a set of policies only. Rather it has come to figure as a symbol for the overall direction of political development and ultimately the choice of Ukraine's political regime (Dragneva and Wolczuk 2015).

The case of Armenia's choice to integrate into the CU has also shown that the associated transfer of sovereignty is likely to limit the incumbent's room for maneuver in the future and consequently the use of shallow compliance strategies. Even though the AA are also more binding and specific than previous agreements, they do not imply a transfer of sovereignty to the EU. It is hence far from clear to what extent Georgia, Moldova and Ukraine will indeed translate their commitments for further European integration into *de facto* political and policy change. Previous developments in the region show that the formal reform commitment of ENC allows for few inferences about *de facto* behavioral change. Shallow compliance with EU templates may be a strategy available to incumbents in hybrid or semi-democratic regimes in the years to come – especially in a context of increasing external rivalry.

The competition between the EU and Russia may additionally limit the use of conditionality as an instrument to press for domestic reforms. The (military) escalation of external competition made the EU condition its support on Russia's foreign policy actions instead of domestic change in ENC, as exemplified in the decision to speed up the ENC integration processes and to include Russia in trilateral talks about Ukraine's DCFTA. Such a reactive EU foreign policy that may come at the expense of consistently pushing for reforms in ENC, however, also risks 'tarnish[ing] [...] the EU's image as a value-based community' (Dragneva and Wolczuk 2015: Chapter 8, n.p.). The dilemma that may emerge from these developments has already been well demonstrated by the case of Moldova, where the ruling elite's vocal embrace of the European integration process without enacting domestic reforms worsened the perception of the EU, instead of improving the country's political and economic development (Rinnert 2013: 6).

7 Conclusion

> Many of the challenges that need to be tackled by the EU and its neighbours together, cannot be adequately addressed without taking into account, or in some cases co-operating with, the neighbours of the neighbours.
>
> (EC and HR 2015b)

In its call for a review of the ENP in 2015, the EU – echoing many other observers – admitted that the ENP had failed in many respects. Russia's foreign policy was perceived as having contributed its fair share to the instability and conflict in a region that the ENP initially envisioned transforming into a 'ring of friends' (Prodi 2002) in which stability and prosperity prevailed. When looking more closely into the successes and failures of the ENP, however, it shows that the EU managed at least partially to deliver on one of the ENP's goals, namely to transfer specific EU policies to neighboring countries. Unlike what was previously assumed in the literature, this policy transfer occurred even in areas in which neighboring countries were more dependent on Russia than on the EU, and in which Russia reverted to an increasingly assertive foreign policy (Ademmer et al. 2016; Hagemann 2013; Langbein 2015). This book set out to explain this puzzling finding and asked whether, how and under what conditions Russia indeed impacts the transfer of EU policies to the post-Soviet space. By identifying concrete conditions under which different degrees of policy transfer occur and specifying the circumstances under which Russia exerts either supportive or constraining effects on this process, this book adds to the academic debate about neighborhood Europeanization and the heated public and emerging academic discussion about the impact of competing integration attempts on domestic developments in the EU's and Russia's contested neighborhood.

In order to do so, this book systematically included Russia in the analysis of EU policy transfer to post-Soviet states. I developed a theoretical framework that adjusted the rationalist-institutionalist approach of Europeanization research to the context of the ENC which is characterized by multiple external actors and semi-democratic regimes. I suggested that full, shallow or non-compliance with prescriptions of the ENP Action Plans, the bilateral reform program of the EU and the ENC, may be the result of rational and strategic choices of domestic incumbents in ENC under constraints of the structural, institutional and especially the agency-based characteristics of their relationships with both the EU and Russia. The book consequently explored whether it is the structural condition of interdependence, the density of institutional ties, the compatibility of domestic economic and administrative structures, or the concrete foreign policy actions in the form of incentives and capacity building of both the EU and Russia that drive domestic policy change in the region. Furthermore, I investigated how important these external factors are in relation to domestic ones for anchoring EU-demanded policies in neighboring states.

Based on a comparative analysis of Georgia's and Armenia's compliance in the area of Justice, Liberty and Security, and energy policy, this book argued that instead of institutions or structural interdependence, 'preferential fit', defined as the compatibility of the EU policy with the domestic incumbent's preferences over outcomes, in terms of power, welfare and security (see also Ademmer and Börzel 2013), figured as a sufficient condition for at least formal EU-demanded policy change. Whether incumbents could fully realize their preferences over outcomes by adopting or neglecting EU policies additionally depended on the multitude of external incentives with which they were confronted, comprising *inter alia* visa liberalization offers from the EU, the distribution of Russian passports in secessionist regions, or increases in gas prices by Gazprom. However, the book argued that these external incentives remained limited in their success in introducing or hampering *de facto* changes in behavior: even if policies were externally imposed by strong conditionalities and high-value bargaining chips, target governments in the context of the semi-democratic ENC could elude costly external requirements by hollowing out the policies at the implementation stage. Furthermore, I showed that strong incentives by Russia do not necessarily constrain EU policy transfer: negative incentives that were not clearly linked to specific demands frequently made third countries seek shelter in compliance with EU policies to be eligible for (geo)political and economic alternatives. I suggested that the dominant mechanism of EU policy transfer to the contested neighborhood was a form of strategic lesson drawing or usage of external policies by incumbent governments in the ENC. The book showed that the interplay of preferential fit and different external incentives could also largely account for the more recent decisions of incumbents in Georgia, Armenia, but also in Moldova and Ukraine (not) to sign the Association Agreement with the EU.

Russia's impact on EU policy transfer in the post-Soviet space

The evidence presented in this book portrays neighborhood Europeanization as a domestic, executive-driven process within the ENC that is only shallowly constrained by the fact that not only the EU, but also Russia, provide the Eastern neighborhood with distinct quid pro quo incentives. This finding implies that instead of being a function of multiple structural and institutional constraints, full, shallow or non-compliance with the ENP AP is best explained by the interplay of two agency-related factors, namely preferential fit and policy conditionalities of multiple external actors.

First, the findings of this book show that preferential fit is a sufficient condition for full or shallow compliance with EU policies in the Eastern neighborhood. In assessing the fit of an EU policy with the preferences of an incumbent government, I focused on the specific power bases of executives in the ENC, which largely depend on the co-optation of distinct political and economic elites, and the security forces (Stefes 2010). This was based on two considerations. First, as opposed to fully democratic states, the semi-democratic ENC are unlikely to host strong non-governmental veto players, given their weak civil society, fragile political opposition and powerful executive (Börzel 2011; Hale 2015). A differential empowerment of various domestic political and societal actors by EU policies is rather unlikely in such an environment (cf. Schimmelfennig and Sedelmeier 2005a: 17). Second, semi-democratic governments may also have positive preferences for EU-induced policy change, as EU policies frequently target the effectiveness of governance arrangements or provide incumbents with resources to fulfill previously held agendas (Ademmer and Börzel 2013; Börzel and Pamuk 2012; Börzel and Risse 2012b). I consequently hypothesized that it was particularly likely that EU policies were adopted if they provided opportunities to empower domestic executives and executive-connected elites to fulfill their preferences in terms of welfare, security and power.

In order to test this hypothesis, Chapter 3 investigated the veto power potential stemming from within the ENC executive and its closely connected elites to assess the comparative costs or benefits to be expected from adaptation to EU policies, and hence establish the preferential prevailing in Armenia and Georgia in the realm of JLS and energy policy. The chapter first provided clues that there was a larger number of veto players who needed to be co-opted for policy changes in Armenia. This was supposed to account for Armenia's weaker compliance with energy policy demands by the EU. However, the chapter also argued that not only the sheer number of intra-elite veto players, but their specific preferences toward individual EU policies would need to be analyzed, which was carried out in Chapters 4 and 5. These in-depth case studies on the transfer of individual policies in the area of migration management and energy diversification showed that whenever incumbents and their connected elites in the ENC anticipated power, security or welfare losses from ENP requirements, compliance either did not occur at all or it remained shallow. In cases of preferential fit, full or shallow compliance followed suit. Apart from a few outlier cases, which suggest alternative, though less frequented pathways to change, preferential fit has thus been identified as the condition that tips compliance outcomes regularly in one or the other direction. Chapter 6 additionally indicated that the gains and losses of crucial executive actors also helped to explain whether incumbents opted to sign or not sign an AA with the EU. Preferential fit is not a static category, though. Incumbents and their connected elites in the ENC change over time, via electoral or, more often, non-electoral ways. As the examples of power transition in Georgia from Eduard Shevardnadze to Mikheil Saakashvili, or changes in the governmental coalition in Armenia in 2009 have shown, when incumbents and their power base changed, so did their gains and losses from EU policies and their respective compliance efforts.

The in-depth case studies also highlighted the causal mechanisms that link preferential fit to compliance and preferential misfit to non-compliance. In cases of preferential fit, instances of usage of external incentives and capacity building occurred, in which the incumbent governments referred to EU prescriptions or utilized EU and Russian capacity to implement formerly held agendas. In cases of preferential misfit, capacity building remained without effect. In these cases, financial assistance was contracted and training was carried out, but the targeted policy was not adopted. Lower-level policy initiatives were prevented by higher state officials, by governmental degrees, letters from the prime minister to implementing agencies or because of simple ignorance when high-level decisions were needed.

Second, this book suggested that the absence of exclusive rivaling policy conditionality by Russia figures as a necessary condition for full compliance with EU policies in the Eastern neighborhood. In other words, whenever Russia clearly linked specific incentives to a policy that countered EU requirements *and* the EU itself did not incentivize policy change, full compliance with ENP requirements was not achieved. Whenever policy change was unilaterally incentivized and the change entailed losses of power, welfare or security for incumbents, the required policies were formally adopted to reap benefits, but their *de facto* application either did not happen at all or only shallowly. Conditional incentives that Russia and the EU attached to policy change thus made a difference to domestic change in the ENC, but rather a superficial one.

The in-depth case studies of Chapters 4 and 5 highlighted the causal mechanisms that led to shallow compliance: formally adopted rules were hollowed out by additional provisions that the executive introduced side by side with the EU-required change. Likewise, governments at times only implemented a policy change in geographically limited areas or formally scheduled the application of rules for a later point in time. Formal rule application was also frequently undermined by informal side deals in the ENC. An exception to the rule was Georgia's full compliance with the EU's demand to conclude readmission agreements that occurred despite an initial preferential misfit and EU-inflicted policy conditionality. Here, however, the outright implementation of readmission agreements was made an additional condition to proceed further in the visa liberalization process.

The empirical analysis also showed which path EU policies took once governments were faced with rivaling policy conditionalities by both the EU and Russia. Incumbents reverted to a pick-and-choose strategy, in which they took what best fit their agenda. In light of the public debate on Russia and neighborhood Europeanization, it is surprising that cases in which the EU

210 *Conclusion*

and Russia directly incentivized different forms of policy change, remained very few. Only in the case of Armenia's decommissioning of the Medzamor nuclear power plant did we see a simultaneous application of conditionality by the EU and Russia, in which Armenia indeed decided to opt for its preferred outcome and remained inert with a view to EU-prescribed domestic change. Georgia's continuous diversification effort despite rivaling policy conditionality inflicted by Russia showed that also non-EU actors, such as the USA, can step in to counter Russian conditionality in favor of full EU compliance. This shows that the strategic interaction in the neighborhood is not only limited to the ENC, Russia and the EU.

The interaction effect of preferential fit and multiple policy conditionalities can be illustrated in a decision tree. Figure 7.1 portrays the pathways that lead to full, shallow or non-compliance. The Figure suggests that the path to different compliance outcomes is predetermined by the initial preferential fit or misfit with the EU policy prevailing in an ENC, and then (shallowly) affected by (rivaling) policy conditionalities invoked by the EU and Russia.

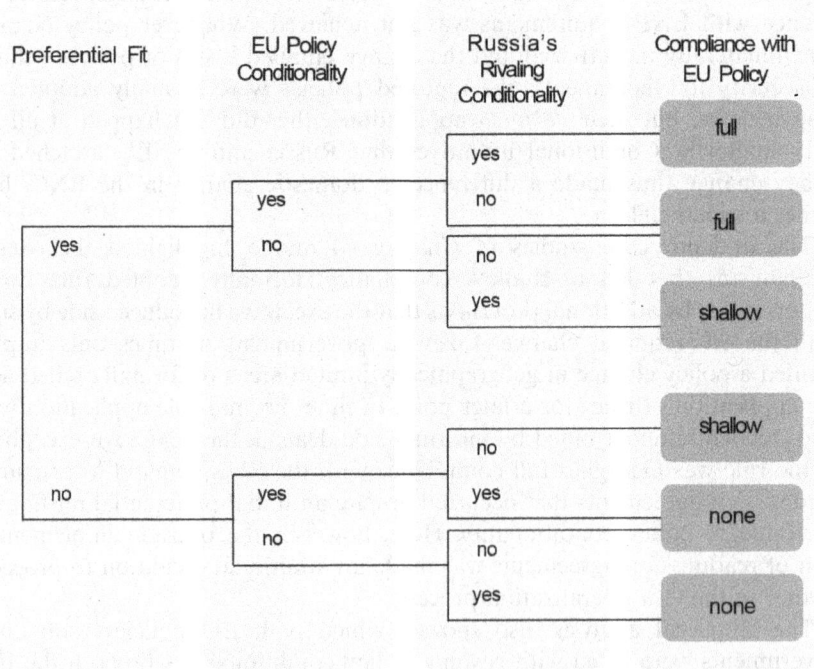

Figure 7.1 Decision tree for neighborhood Europeanization East

Russia's negative incentives and multiple capacity building

The findings of the book also provide important insights into the discussion of other conditions under which Russia has been considered to impact EU policy transfer to the post-Soviet space.

First, I hypothesized that Russian threats and sanctions that fail to specify the policy they target, but supposedly aim at punishing a neighborhood country for its broader foreign policy strategy, may figure as additional stimuli for compliance with EU policies. The evidence presented in the case studies on migration management and energy diversification provided ample support for this hypothesis. Adopting ENP requirements in these two areas frequently presented a way to gain autonomy vis-à-vis Russia. This was the case, for instance, when Georgia sought quick visa liberalization in order to reduce the political costs caused by Russian passportization in its secessionist territories, and complied shallowly with the conditions that the EU set toward this end. Chapter 6 also illustrated this effect with regard to the developments that preceded the decisions (not) to sign the AA with the EU.

Negative incentives by Russia, however, amplified rather than changed the ingredients of the compliance process outlined above. For instance, Russia's passportization policy in Georgia increased the attractiveness of EU benefits and thus strengthened the policy conditionality attached to policy change. This amplifier effect is relevant, as Russia's increasingly assertive foreign policy toward neighboring countries has usually been considered to undermine EU integration attempts by the ENC. On the contrary, the findings of this book suggest that students of neighborhood Europeanization need to distinguish between specific policy conditionalities and incentives that are not clearly linked to a specific policy to understand Russia's countervailing or stimulating effect on EU policy transfer in the post-Soviet space.

Second, capacity building has been considered to help governments make strategic choices in the first place (Chayes and Chayes 1993), to empower reform-minded actors within an administration (Andonova 2008: 485), or – in cases in which capacity is provided in transgovernmental networks – to socialize lower-level bureaucrats into EU policies (Freyburg 2012). The same effect should occur with regard to functional equivalents to formal capacity building provided by Russia. I hypothesized, however, that the effect of capacity building was likely to hinge on the preferential fit or misfit that prevailed in an ENC. The in-depth case studies largely confirmed this hypothesis. The EU provided immense capacity building to both countries and in both sectors, but whether this fostered compliance varied with the willingness of the target regime. In cases of preferential fit, capacity building was used as a financial resource to implement an often previously held governmental agenda. In cases of preferential misfit, capacity-building efforts, including training, reporting and financial support, often drained away without any effect.

Furthermore, Russia provided additional support for the implementation of reforms in a few cases, especially in the energy sector. Its efforts mostly targeted the implementation stage and were provided by Russian state-owned companies. Unlike the EU's formal state-to-state capacity building, Russia's 'assistance' hence mostly came in the form of business transactions. Yet, it helped ENC governments to implement EU-demanded reforms, despite the hesitation of other investors to engage. Rivaling capacity was only provided in the case of Armenia's Medzamor nuclear power plant. Here, Russian state-owned companies improved the management and operation of the power plant which made its closure ever more costly. Likewise, they rewarded Armenia with a large portion of the capital needed to finance its preferred solution of building a new power plant, instead of opting for the EU-envisaged non-nuclear scenario. Again, these instances of rival capacity building crucially relied on the respective domestic governments seeking alternative policy solutions. Armenia's hesitation in the closure of the power plant preceded Russia's offer to help build a new one. In addition, the fact that Georgia allowed Russian state-owned companies to invest in Georgia was highly criticized domestically, but fitted the liberal governmental agenda and helped to implement it at the time. In a nutshell, the effect of capacity building was hence strongly contingent on preferential fit in the cases under scrutiny here and did not individually alter the compliance outcome.

The findings of the book also highlighted the underlying causal mechanisms associated with capacity building and policy change. While I am methodologically unable to confirm or disprove any instances of socialization of individuals who participated in EU-initiated transgovernmental networks, the case studies showed that any policy change that bureaucratic actors tried to foster, but that was at odds with the overall governmental agenda, was prevented, at times even before it found its way into discussions at the governmental level. This was the case with the national action plans on migration in both Georgia and Armenia before 2009. It also happened to the draft law on energy efficiency and data protection in Georgia.

An exception to the rule was capacity building that supported policy change once the EU applies policy conditionality. In the case of Georgia's readmission agreements and the introduction of biometric passports, the EU basically took over the implementation process by funding relevant projects on the ground. This suggests that policy transfer may also be facilitated by a combination of external instruments that diversify demand for regulatory changes, as argued by Langbein (2015) for the transfer of market rules to Ukraine. Unlike in a setting where conditionality and capacity building create local demand among various private and public actors, however, the sustainability of the empowerment of individual state actors in this case remains questionable, once external donors retreat from the implementation process.

Interdependence, institutions and domestic resonance

The empirical findings of this book also qualify some of the prominent structural and institutional arguments about the impact Russia and the EU have on neighborhood Europeanization.

First, the transfer of EU norms and policies has been considered less likely, if a country is more dependent on Russia than on the EU (Cameron and Orenstein 2011; Dimitrova and Dragneva 2009). This hypothesis is usually based on a subtle or open assumption of policy divergence between these two external actors. As research shows, however, Russia and the EU do not necessarily compete in all sectors and issue areas (Casier 2012; Dragneva and Dimitrova 2007). Consequently, this book set out to evaluate whether there was indeed a negative structural impact of Russia on compliance with EU demands if Russia and the EU promote or at least represent divergent policies. The macro-qualitative analysis in Chapter 3 showed that Georgia and Armenia were more dependent on Russia than on the EU in the energy sector and in the area of JLS. In addition, in the realm of energy, I detected a substantial difference in policies promoted by the EU and Russia, while the issue area of JLS policies displayed a large policy overlap. The analysis of compliance patterns, however, showed that Georgia and Armenia displayed better results with the adoption and implementation of EU energy policies than with JLS issues. At the same time, despite a comparable degree of interdependence with Russia, Armenia complied better with JLS policies, while Georgia outdid Armenia in the case of energy policies. This evidence suggested that interdependence as a structural feature of the relationship of the ENC with Russia and the EU fell short of presenting a valuable explanatory factor to account for cross-country and cross-sectoral differences in compliance patterns for the cases at hand. The empirical evidence presented in this book rather suggested that it is not simply the possibility of using bilateral asymmetries for foreign policy purposes that makes a difference in the ENC, but its *de facto* usage in quid pro quo negotiations. This even holds true for the area of energy policy, the 'textbook case of high interdependence' (Dimitrova and Dragneva 2009: 585).

Second, external rules are usually considered to travel better, the more institutionalized the cooperation of external actors with third countries. This hypothesis has been most prominently discussed in the literature on the EU's external governance (Freyburg et al. 2009), but can also be transferred to Russian-dominated institutions, such as the CIS for the cases under scrutiny here. In order to measure the institutional setting in which external rules are promoted, I compared the different degrees of codification, internationalization and institutionalization across countries and issue areas. I found that EU policies were on average more codified, more internationalized and better institutionalized than Russian- or CIS-promoted rules. However, the degree of all three characteristics did not vary between Georgia and Armenia, and between the policy fields of energy and JLS. While the institutional setting could hence account for the fact that EU rules travel at all under conditions of multiple interdependence, it did not explain variation between country- or sector-specific compliance.

Third, the resonance of the domestic structures of the ENC with those of external actors has been considered important to explain the success or failure of compliance with the ENP in the literature (Lavenex and Schimmelfennig 2009). Well-resonating domestic structures are usually assumed to reduce the costs of adaptation, if argued from a more rationalist perspective or, in a more constructivist vein, enhance the legitimacy of externally promoted rules. This argument can also apply to the ENC and Russia, as the former might seek to adhere to Russian or CIS-originating rules if they resonate better with their domestic status quo than the policies promoted by the EU.

In order to investigate this hypothesis, in Chapter 3 I compared the domestic structures of the ENC, Russia and the EU in terms of rule of law, economic freedom, transition to a market economy, and state capacity. The comparison confirmed the hypothesis insofar as the ENC and the EU countries were marked by roughly the same degree of economic freedom, while Russia scored significantly worse. This resonance may account for the positive compliance outcome in the field of energy policies. However, the resonance of Armenia and the EU was slightly greater than that of Georgia, which was at odds with the measured compliance outcome. In addition, in all other categories, Georgia and Armenia on average resonated better with Russia than with the EU. While the resonance hypothesis may thus partly explain the comparably better compliance in the energy sector, it cannot account for any other cross-country variation in compliance.

Taken together, I suggested that full, shallow or non-compliance with the ENP AP in the contested neighborhood is best explained as a function of the interplay of preferential fit and policy conditionalities by the EU and Russia. The book showed that unlike other structural or institutional factors, Russia's foreign policy actions impact EU policy transfer in two ways. They undermine EU policy transfer if Russia applies rivaling policy conditionalities that are not balanced by more attractive EU incentives to incumbent governments in the ENC. Russia frequently also supports EU policy transfer if it provides the ENC with negative incentives that fail to specify the policy change they target. Policy-specific conditional incentives therefore enable both the EU and Russia to introduce policy change formally in the ENC. Yet the ability of both external actors to inflict domestic change in the ENC remains largely restricted to cosmetic reforms. Profound behavioral changes or full compliance with EU policies that contradict governmental preferences or challenge incumbent regimes did not occur, as domestic governments remained the gatekeepers of domestic reform and stagnation.

Generalizability of the findings

This book argued that in order to explain EU policy transfer to the contested neighborhood, the interaction of powerful domestic agents with specific incentives provided by both the EU and Russia need to be taken into account. Consequently, it encourages the careful study of domestic politics in target countries and the disentangling of the structural power potential of external actors from their *de facto* usage in the form of policy conditionalities and other incentives. This argument was backed by a comprehensive study of policy transfer to Georgia and Armenia in the area of JLS and energy policy – two sovereignty-laden policy areas. Chapter 6 additionally showed that the interplay of preferences of powerful executive actors in ENC with multiple policy conditionalities and other incentives could also largely explain the relatively discretionary choices of ENC incumbents (not) to sign the AA with the EU. However, can these findings also travel beyond the rather small universe of the cases under scrutiny in this book?

First, the findings of this book can principally travel to world regions beyond the post-Soviet space. This book argued that much of the background noise that is related to Russian foreign policy in the CIS, in terms of economic embargos, boycotts, but also political support for incumbent regimes that fails to come with a quid pro quo approach, does not seem to exert significant effects on the target countries in terms of EU policy transfer. This is not to say that Russia is not able to increase instability, or strengthen incumbents, both by directly providing political or financial support or by indirectly serving as a reference point to the incumbents' strive for domestic support on anti-Russian agendas. However, the evidence presented here suggests that Russia, just like the EU, is limited in its ability to introduce domestic policy changes in third countries bypassing the powerful domestic agents that guard reform and stagnation. In this regard, Russia hence loses its role as a highly specific third country beyond comparison to other external actors. Generally, the argument presented here is therefore likely to be relevant for a much larger number of cases than those studied in this book. The EU engages in policy transfer with countries in a variety of world regions. Many of the targeted countries do not qualify as democracies and are equally addressed by other, often competing foreign policies of other external actors. Further research hence needs to show the extent to which this model of neighborhood Europeanization can indeed travel to other regions, including the Mediterranean neighbors and other African countries, in which China, for instance, is establishing itself as an alternative external actor that provides attractive opportunities to domestic, non-democratic incumbents (Hackenesch 2013).

Second, the findings of this book can also apply to other countries and sectors within the post-Soviet space. In this book, I constructed most likely cases for Russia to impact EU policy transfer and found that their various incentives had an impact on domestic change that was, however, strongly contingent on domestic preferences of the incumbent executive. The countries and policies in this book were *inter alia* chosen on the grounds of their highly asymmetric dependence on Russia and their semi-democratic, hybrid regime types. As the post-Soviet space is characterized by many other states that are strongly dependent on Russia in various policy sectors, the argument is likely to apply to a wider range of countries and policies in the region. Evidence from other case studies lends support to a greater generalizability of the findings presented here. Studies on EU policy transfer to Moldova (Hagemann 2013) and Ukraine (Langbein 2015) show that trade embargos enacted by Russia, which were not tied to clear quid pro quos but were rather perceived to reflect demands by Russian producers in the case of Ukraine, or to punish the overall Western orientation of Moldova, furthered the EU integration process rather than stalling it. Likewise, Russia's current conflict with Ukraine encouraged rather than undermined a further alignment with EU rules in the country, also in diverse issue areas such as environmental (Buzogány 2016) or energy policy (Wolczuk 2016).

The (shallow) success of the application of policy conditionalities by both the EU and Russia in the cases under scrutiny in this book is likely to be contingent on high degrees of asymmetric interdependence that equip external actors with sufficient bargaining power to apply conditionality in the first place (cf. Schimmelfennig and Sedelmeier 2004: 673). Lower levels of interdependence or more symmetry in the triangular relations between Russia, the EU and ENC, should then strengthen the argument that incumbents remain gatekeepers of policy change and stagnation: in these cases incumbent governments are even less likely to be constrained by quid pro quo bargaining by the EU or Russia, because the costs inflicted and benefits promised are lower, or the expectation to successfully play one external actor against the other is greater (see Wolczuk 2016, for some related evidence on energy sector reform in Ukraine).

Most EaP countries also qualify – just like Armenia and Georgia – as consolidated, hybrid regimes that are located somewhere between the more autocratic Central Asian countries and the much more liberal Baltic states in the post-Soviet space (Wheatley and Zürcher 2008). However, while Belarus and Azerbaijan are more autocratic and closed systems, Ukraine and Moldova show a greater dispersion of political power, both across political institutions and within the executive (Buzogány 2013; Dimitrova and Dragneva 2013; Langbein 2015). Hence, unlike in Georgia and Armenia, where political power has mostly been highly concentrated in the presidential administration and its connected elite fractions for the period under investigation in this book (Wheatley and Zürcher 2008), a wider power dispersion in 'weaker authoritarian states', as Way (2006) calls them, may consequently result in more competition over policy outcomes, also within semi- or outright non-democratic contexts. Such a weaker power vertical may result in a certain blockade of EU-demanded reforms that target state actors, as shown in a study on the Ukrainian asylum system prior to Yanukovych's re-election in 2010 (Wetzel 2016). In policy areas less sovereignty-laden than those analyzed in this book, however, a greater competition of state actors coupled with powerful non-state actors, such as businesses, can also help the EU to diversify domestic reform demands and promote EU policy change (Langbein 2015). Further comparative studies of other policy areas and countries that systematically vary these differences could help identify the degree and type of power dispersion within semi-democratic systems that is necessary to turn the processes of usage described in this book into processes of differential empowerment, even in such unfavorable contexts.

Finally, the question arises to what extent these findings can travel to a neighborhood in which competing integration attempts are more legalized and backed by strong institutions of the Eurasian Economic Union (Dragneva and Wolczuk 2012). I have shown that the institutionalization of policies with the EU was much higher than with Russia or the CIS in the period, the countries and the policy sectors studied in this book. I argued that the degree of institutionalization consequently explained why EU policies traveled at all to the neighborhood, but that it failed to account for variation in compliance across countries and sectors. With the rise of the EEU, this pattern is likely to change. Studying countries, such as Armenia, in sectors in which both the EU and the EEU provide for highly institutionalized relationships may hence allow for a more nuanced assessment of how these diverse patterns of institutionalization (do not) shape EU policy transfer in the future.

So what? Policy implications and outlook

The findings of this book also entail implications for practically designing EU policy transfer to the contested Eastern neighborhood, with regard to the actors the ENP targets, the application of policy conditionality and, most importantly, the opening of the ENP for concerns of the neighbors' neighbors. These implications are especially relevant in light of the review process of the ENP that the EU launched in 2015.

First, as opposed to recent literature on the subject, the findings of this book draw a gloomier picture of the effect of sectoral cooperation of the EU and state actors in the current ENP. The external governance literature considers the EU's functional cooperation with neighboring administrations as a means to promote democracy 'between the lines' (Freyburg et al. 2007). Lower state officials may internalize democratic governance provisions by cooperating with peers from EU member states on a regular basis in transgovernmental networks (Freyburg 2015). In line with the more conventional view on the subject that scrutinizes polity-level effects of functional cooperation (Freyburg 2012), I argued, however, that instead of challenging or reducing the incumbent's power, functional cooperation and capacity building in the cases under scrutiny here have strengthened incumbent executives in rendering their governance arrangements more effective, while attempts to increase accountability or transparency were frequently hollowed out. Such instances of usage of external incentives and capacities for domestic purposes indeed feed the rivaling notion of the democracy-stability dilemma, in which external actors are (ab)used by semi-democratic or semi-authoritarian regimes to increase their political power (Börzel and Pamuk 2012; Van Hüllen 2015). In order to promote profound compliance with the ENP, the EU should hence channel more support into the creation of a more level playing field for a variety of domestic political actors and local civil society.

First steps in this direction have been made with the setup of the Civil Society Facility, an EU support scheme to non-governmental actors in its neighboring countries, in response to criticism after the Arab Spring in May 2011. Likewise, since 2013 the European Endowment for Democracy has supported civil society actors in ENC. The latest discussions associated with the review of the ENP (EC and HR 2015b, 2015c) also feature proposals to increase the ownership of reforms of non-governmental actors that may consequently act as watchdogs on governmental behavior. In order to mobilize reform-oriented actors for EU policy transfer, however, the EU would also need to acquire more profound knowledge about the diverse domestic actors and their vested interests – knowledge that has too often been lacking (see also Langbein 2015).

Second, this book has shown that policy conditionality is one of the few effective foreign policy instruments to enact at least formal policy change in target states (see also Ademmer and Börzel 2013; Langbein and Wolczuk 2012). Migration management reforms in Georgia, for instance, were substantially advanced after the EU tied the promise of visa facilitation and visa liberalization to domestic reforms, even though the incumbent government had previously opposed policy changes. Furthermore, when the EU made benefits contingent on the *de facto* implementation of reforms, as was the case with readmission agreements in Georgia, this strategy proved successful to enact full compliance, too. The findings of this book suggest that the EU would hence be well advised to strengthen rather than weaken this instrument in the neighborhood. In this vein, an increase in monitoring of domestic developments in ENC would also be required to assess whether reforms are only formally adopted, or give rise to behavioral changes too. However, while the principle of differentiation and 'more for more' that underlies the instrument of policy conditionality featured prominently in the ENP review of 2011 (European Commission 2011e), the current reflection has also been critical of a too prescriptive and inflexible ENP that fails to respect the diverse integration aspirations of ENC (EC and HR 2015c). It remains to be seen how the new ENP will manage to combine such greater flexibility toward various integration choices of ENC with clear and conditional offers to further domestic change in ENC.

Third, this book calls for a clearly defined and differentiated opening of the ENP to the concerns of the neighbors' neighbors. The conclusions of the EU's recent consultation process about the ENP recommend the inclusion of the neighbors' neighbors in the ENP in policy areas where interdependence is high, stating that:

> Where connections and interdependencies with other partners require broader formats of cooperation, third countries should be involved [...] Thematic Frameworks will be used to provide a regular forum to discuss joint policy approaches, programming and investment that reach beyond the neighbourhood [...] Migration, energy and security will be particular priorities.
>
> (EC and HR 2015c: 18)

While such a framework certainly helps to overcome a lack of cooperation and prevent conflict between all parties involved, it should be used cautiously with regard to issues of EU policy transfer, especially in the areas of migration and energy. The findings of this book have shown that a high interdependence with third countries as such is unlikely to impede EU policy transfer to the neighborhood in these policy areas. Rather, it is the exploitation of the power potential arising from asymmetric interdependence that matters. The principle of involving third parties in areas where 'connections and interdependence with other partners require broader formats of cooperation' may consequently become a self-fulfilling prophecy: if third parties gain a say in policy approaches, programming and investment of the ENP and have a strategic interest in being involved, the exploitation of asymmetric interdependencies may be incentivized to create areas 'that require broader formats of cooperation' in the first place. The EU would thus be well advised to specify the conditions for the inclusion of third parties by clearly defining the policy approaches that reach beyond the neighborhood, and by sketching out the scope of the third party's involvement with regard to decisions about EU policy transfer into ENC.

This book argued that both the EU and Russia are limited in their effectiveness to shape domestic developments in ENC. While Russia is obviously a crucial actor in the neighborhood that needs to be taken into account to adequately address many of the challenges that the EU and its neighbors face, as suggested by the quote at the beginning of this chapter, this book also showed that the greatest hurdle for EU policy transfer lies within the ENC themselves. The semi-democratic incumbents in the neighborhood have frequently used the heightened geopolitical rivalry between the EU and Russia to divert attention from a lack of domestic reform and to safeguard their political survival, as seen in the cases of Ukraine under Yanukovych or Moldova and its recent political crisis. The ENP's greater sensitivity to broader regional developments and security interests of alternative regional powers should hence not divert but go hand in hand with a greater focus on domestic developments in ENC. Relaxing the approach to demand domestic changes for EU integration benefits risks further increasing disillusionment with the ENP. This is especially the case among the citizens in ENC, whose empowerment is yet needed to further the long-term goals of the ENP, including not only stability, but also democracy and good governance.

Appendix I: Interviews

Number	Date	Interview partner	Documentation
1.	04.10.2010	Local expert, International Organization for Migration (IOM) Georgia, Tbilisi	Recorded, notes
2.	05.10.2010	Local expert, Energy Efficiency Center Georgia, Tbilisi	Recorded, notes
3.	05.10.2010	Advisor, Georgian-European Policy and Legal Advice Center (GEPLAC), Tbilisi	Recorded, notes
4.	05.10.2010	Official, Ministry of Energy and Natural Resources of Georgia, Tbilisi	Recorded, notes
5.	06.10.2010	Local expert, Eurasia Partnership Foundation, Georgia, Tbilisi	Recorded, notes
6.	06.10.2010	Member of the Committee on European Integration, Parliament of Georgia, Tbilisi	Recorded, notes
7.	06.10.2010	Staff member, Georgian Foundation for Strategic and International Studies, Tbilisi	Notes
8.	06.10.2010	Official, State Office for Euro-Atlantic Integration, Tbilisi	Recorded, notes
9.	07.10.2010	Official, International Relations Department, Ministry of Energy Georgia, Tbilisi	Recorded, notes
10.	07.10.2010	Local expert, Center for Strategic Research and Development, Tbilisi	Recorded, notes
11.	08.10.2010	Official, Civil Registry Agency, Tbilisi	Recorded, notes
12.	08.10.2010	Expert on migration issues, Delegation of the European Union (EU) to Georgia, Tbilisi	Recorded, notes
13.	09.10.2010	Expert on energy issues, United States Agency for International Development (USAID) Georgia, Tbilisi	Partly recorded, notes

Appendix I 221

Number	Date	Interview partner	Documentation
14.	11.10.2010	Local experts, Caucasus Institute for Peace, Democracy and Development (CIPDD), Tbilisi	Recorded, notes
15.	11.10.2010	Official, Ministry of Internally Displaced Persons, Refugees and Accommodation, Tbilisi	Recorded, notes
16.	11.10.2010	Local expert, International Labour Organization (ILO), Tbilisi	Recorded, notes
17.	12.10.2010	Energy expert for Armenia and Georgia, Kreditanstalt für Wiederaufbau (KfW), Tbilisi	Recorded, notes
18.	12.10.2010	Official, International Relations Department, Ministry of Foreign Affairs Georgia, Tbilisi	Recorded, notes
19.	13.10.2010	Legal expert, GEPLAC, Georgia, Tbilisi	Recorded, notes
20.	13.10.2010	Official, Department of European Integration, Ministry of Foreign Affairs Georgia, Tbilisi	Recorded, notes
21.	13.10.2010	Energy expert, Georgian Foundation for Strategic and International Studies, Tbilisi	Recorded, notes
22.	15.10.2010	Local expert, Georgian Foundation for Strategic and International Studies, Georgia, Tbilisi	Recorded, notes
23.	15.10.2010	Official, Consular Department, Ministry of Foreign Affairs Georgia, Tbilisi	Recorded, notes
24.	15.10.2010	Official, State Office for Euro-Atlantic Integration, Georgia, Tbilisi	Recorded, notes
25.	15.10.2010	Lawyer, Georgian Young Lawyers' Association (GYLA), Tbilisi	Recorded, notes
26.	18.10.2010	Staff member, Ecolur, environmental non-governmental organization (NGO), Yerevan	Recorded, notes
27.	18.10.2010	Staff member, IOM Armenia, Yerevan	Recorded, notes
28.	19.10.2010	Local expert, European Bank for Reconstruction and Development (EBRD), Armenian branch, Yerevan	Recorded, notes
29.	19.10.2010	Official, Consular Department of the Ministry of Foreign Affairs Armenia, Yerevan	Partly recorded, notes
30.	19.10.2010	Local energy expert, Revolving Fund for Renewable Energy (R2E2) Armenia, Yerevan	Recorded, notes

Appendix I

Number	Date	Interview partner	Documentation
31.	20.10.2010	Official, Renewable Energy Department, Ministry of Energy of Armenia, Yerevan	Recorded, notes
32.	20.10.2010	Legal advisor, Armenian-European Policy and Legal Advice Center (AEPLAC), Yerevan	Recorded, notes
33.	20.10.2010	Staff member, Organization for Security and Co-operation in Europe (OSCE) Armenia, Yerevan	Recorded, notes
34.	21.10.2010	Staff member, Ecoteam, environmental NGO, Yerevan	Recorded, notes
35.	22.10.2010	Official, International Department, Ministry of Energy in Armenia, Yerevan	Recorded, notes
36.	25.10.2010	Official, European Department, Ministry of Foreign Affairs, Armenia, Yerevan	Notes
37.	25.10.2010	Official, Nuclear Department, Ministry of Energy, Armenia, Yerevan	Recorded, notes
38.	26.10.2010	Member of the National Assembly of the Republic of Armenia, Prosperous Armenia Party, Yerevan	Recorded, notes
39.	26.10.2010	Official, State Migration Service of Armenia, Ministry of Territorial Administration, Yerevan	Recorded, notes
40.	26.10.2010	Local energy expert, USAID, Mission to Armenia, Yerevan	Notes
41.	26.10.2010	Staff member, e-Governance Infrastructure Implementation Unit (EKENG), Yerevan	Recorded, notes
42.	27.10.2010	Official, Passport and Visa Department of the Police of the Republic of Armenia, Yerevan	Recorded, notes
43.	28.10.2010	Local experts, ILO, Mission to Armenia, Yerevan	Recorded, notes
44.	28.10.2010	EU official, EU Delegation to Armenia, Yerevan	Notes
45.	09.08.2011	EU official, EU Delegation to Georgia (phone)	Recorded
46.	11.08.2011	EU official, European Commission, Directorate-General (DG) Home (phone)	Recorded
47.	30.08.2011	EU official, European Commission, DG Development and Cooperation (Devco) (phone)	Recorded

Number	Date	Interview partner	Documentation
48.	30.08.2011	EU official, European Commission, DG Justice (phone)	Recorded
49.	01.09.2011	EU official, European External Action Service, (phone)	Recorded
50.	05.09.2011	EU official, European Commission, DG Energy (phone)	Recorded
51.	09.09.2011	EU official, European Commission, DG Devco (phone)	Recorded
52.	26.09.2011	Local expert, Eurasian Partnership Foundation (follow up), Georgia, Tbilisi	Recorded, notes
53.	27.09.2011	Energy expert, Energy Efficiency Center Georgia (follow up), Tbilisi	Recorded, notes
54.	28.09.2011	Official, Department for European Integration, Ministry of Foreign Affairs Georgia (follow up), Tbilisi	Recorded, notes
55.	29.09.2011	Local expert, Georgian Foundation for Strategic and International Studies (follow up), Tbilisi	Recorded, notes
56.	29.09.2011	Staff member, Targeted Initiative Georgia, Tbilisi	Recorded, notes
57.	29.09.2011	Energy expert for Armenia and Georgia, KfW, Tbilisi	Recorded, notes
58.	30.09.2011	Local expert, IOM Georgia (follow up), Tbilisi	Recorded, notes
59.	30.09.2011	Expert on migration issues, Delegation of the EU to Georgia (follow up), Tbilisi	Notes
60.	30.09.2011	Expert on energy issues, Delegation of the EU to Georgia, Tbilisi	Notes
61.	01.10.2011	Member of the Georgian National Security Council, Tbilisi	Notes
62.	03.10.2011	Official, International Relations Department, Ministry of Energy Georgia (follow up), Tbilisi	Recorded, notes
63.	03.10.2011	Local experts, Danish Refugee Council, Georgia, Tbilisi	Recorded, notes
64.	03.10.2011	Lawyers, GYLA, Tbilisi	Recorded, notes
65.	04.10.2011	Official, State Office for Euro-Atlantic Integration, Georgia (follow up), Tbilisi	Recorded, notes
66.	04.10.2011	Official, Ministry of the Interior, Georgia, Tbilisi	Notes
67.	04.10.2011	Local expert, Deutsche Gesellschaft für Internationale Zusammenarbeit (GIZ), Tbilisi	Partly recorded, notes

Appendix I

Number	Date	Interview partner	Documentation
68.	05.10.2011	Official, Civil Registry Agency of Georgia, Tbilisi	Recorded, notes
69.	05.10.2011	Local expert on European Integration Issues, Georgian Foundation for Strategic and International Studies (GFSIS), Tbilisi	Recorded, notes
70.	05.10.2011	Professor, Migration Center, Tbilisi State University, Tbilisi	Recorded, notes
71.	05.10.2011	Official, Ministry of IDPs, Refugees and Accommodation, Georgia (follow-up), Tbilisi	Recorded, notes
72.	06.10.2011	Officials, CIS Department, Ministry of Foreign Affairs Georgia, Tbilisi	Notes
73.	06.10.2011	Local expert, Center for Strategic Research and Development of Georgia (CSRDG), Georgia, Tbilisi	Recorded, notes
74.	06.10.2011	Local migration expert, Eurasia Partnership Foundation, Georgia, Tbilisi	Recorded, notes
75.	06.10.2011	Official, Office of the State Minister for Diaspora Issues, Tbilisi	Recorded, notes
76.	11.10.2011	Local expert, IOM Armenia, Yerevan	Recorded, notes
77.	11.10.2011	Official Delegation of the EU to Armenia, Yerevan	Recorded, notes
78.	12.10.2011	Staff member, OSCE Mission to Armenia, Yerevan (follow up)	Recorded, notes
79.	12.10.2011	Migration expert, GIZ, Armenia, Yerevan	Recorded, notes
80.	12.10.2011	Official, Consular Department, Ministry of Foreign Affairs of Armenia, Yerevan	Notes
81.	13.10.2011	Local expert, EU Advisory Group to Armenia, Yerevan	Recorded, notes
82.	13.10.2011	Local energy expert, R2E2 Armenia, Yerevan (follow up)	Recorded, notes
83.	13.10.2011	Official, State Migration Service of Armenia, Yerevan (follow up)	Recorded, notes
84.	14.10.2011	Official, Ministry of Foreign Affairs Armenia, Yerevan	Notes
85.	14.10.2011	Local expert, EBRD, Armenian branch, Yerevan (follow up)	Recorded, notes
86.	14.10.2011	Local energy expert, R2E2 Armenia, Yerevan	Recorded, notes
87.	17.10.2011	Official, Delegation of the EU to Armenia, Yerevan	Notes

Number	Date	Interview partner	Documentation
88.	18.10.2011	Staff member, EKENG, Yerevan (follow up)	Recorded, notes
89.	18.10.2011	Local experts, ILO, Mission to Armenia, Yerevan (follow up)	Notes
90.	18.10.2011	Local energy expert, USAID, Mission to Armenia, Yerevan (follow up)	Notes
91.	19.10.2011	Local expert, GIZ, Yerevan	Recorded, notes
92.	19.10.2011	Official, Passport and Visa Department, Police of Armenia, Yerevan (follow up)	Notes
93.	19.10.2011	Staff member, IOM Armenia, Yerevan	Recorded, notes
94.	20.10.2011	Official, Renewable Energy Department, Ministry of Energy of Armenia, Yerevan (follow up)	Notes
95.	20.10.2011	Official, Nuclear Department of the Ministry of Energy, Armenia, Yerevan (follow up)	Notes
96.	21.10.2011	Economic advisor, Embassy of France to the Republic of Armenia, Yerevan	Recorded, notes
97.	10.11.2011	Expert on Justice, Liberty and Security in EU external relations, European University Institute (EUI), Florence (phone)	Notes
98.	15.11.2011	Consultant on energy issues in Georgia, GIZ, Berlin	Recorded

References

A1+ (2012) 'Whoever supports Serzh, supports emigration', www.a1plus.am/en/politics/2012/03/01/manukyan.
Abushov, K. (2009) 'Policing the near abroad: Russian foreign policy in the South Caucasus', *Australian Journal of International Affairs* 63(2): 187–212.
Ademmer, E. (2013) *A Third Rejoices: Russia, the EU, and Policy Transfer to the Post-Soviet Space*, PhD thesis, Berlin: Freie Universität Berlin.
Ademmer, E. (2015) 'Interdependence and EU-demanded policy change in a shared neighbourhood', *Journal of European Public Policy* 22(5): 671–689.
Ademmer, E. and Börzel, T.A. (2013) 'Migration, energy and good governance in the EU's eastern neighbourhood', *Europe-Asia Studies* 65(4): 581–608.
Ademmer, E. and Delcour, L. (2016) 'With a little help from Russia? The European Union and visa liberalization with post-Soviet states', *Eurasian Geography and Economics* 57(1): 89–112.
Ademmer, E., Delcour, L. and Wolczuk, K. (2016) 'Beyond geopolitics: An introduction to the impact of the EU and Russia in the "contested neighborhood"', *Eurasian Geography and Economics* 57(1): 1–18.
Aghajanian, L. (2011) *Armenia: Private Project Plays Up Repatriation*, www.eurasianet.org/node/64435.
Albrecht, H. and Frankenberger, R. (2010) 'Autoritarismus Reloaded: Konzeptionelle Anmerkungen zur Vergleichenden Analyse politischer Systeme', in R. Frankenberger and H. Albrecht (eds) *Autoritarismus Reloaded: Neuere Ansätze und Erkenntnisse der Autokratieforschung*, Baden-Baden: Nomos, pp. 37–59.
Alieva, L. (2000) *Reshaping Eurasia: Foreign Policy Strategies and Leadership Assets in Post-Soviet South Caucasus*, Berkeley Program in Soviet and Post-Soviet Studies Working Paper, Berkeley, CA: UC Berkeley.
Altmann, F.-L. (2007) *Südosteuropa und die Sicherung der Energieversorgung der EU*, SWP-Studie No. S1, Berlin: Stiftung Wissenschaft und Politik.
Alturki, F., Espinosa-Bowen, J. and Ilahi, N. (2009) *How Russia Affects the Neighborhood: Trade, Financial and Remittance Channels*, IMF Working Paper No. 277, Washington, DC: IMF.
Ambrosio, T. (2010) 'Constructing a framework of authoritarian diffusion: Concepts, dynamics, and future research', *International Studies Perspectives* 11(4): 375–392.
Andonova, L.B. (2008) 'The climate regime and domestic politics: The case of Russia', *Cambridge Review of International Affairs* 21(4): 483–504.

Apriashvili, M. (2015) *Implementation of the DCFTA by Georgia*, Riga: Latvian Institute of International Affairs.

Arakelyan, A. (2011) *The Victims of Serzh Sargsyan's Drive to Consolidate Power*, hetq. am/eng/opinion/6078/the-victims-of-serzh-sargsyans-drive-to-consolidate-power.html.

ARKA News Agency (2010) 'Russia, Armenia seal agreement on cooperation in nuclear unit construction', www.arka.am/en/news/economy/21117/.

Armenian National Congress (2010) *Speech by Levon Ter-Petrosyan at the meeting in September 17, 2010*, www.anc.am/en/speeches/432/.

Armenian News (2010) 'Increased money transfers and migration in Armenia', news. am/eng/news/35200.html.

Armenian News (2011a) 'Armenian Government elaborates migration control strategy', news.am/eng/news/49952.html.

Armenian News (2011b) 'Armenian Parliament ratifies Readmission Agreement with Czech Republic', news.am/eng/news/47474.html.

Armenian UN Association (2009) 'Reinforcement of management of migratory flows in Armenia', auna.am/index.php?option=com_content&view=article&id=34&Item id=44&lang=en.

Arzumanyan, T. and Abovyan, M. (2014) *Country Report Armenia*, Vienna: Centre for Social Innovation (ZSI).

Asbarez (2007) 'Russian control of Iran-Armenia pipeline confirmed', 12 September, asbarez.com/55793/russian-control-of-iran-armenia-pipeline-confirmed/.

Asbarez (2011) 'Armenia to review nuclear plant safety after Japan crisis', 21 March, asbarez.com/94304/armenia-to-review-nuclear-plant-safety-after-japan-crisis/?utm_source=feedburner&utm_medium=feed&utm_campaign=Feed:+Asbarez+(Asba rez+News).

Asbarez (2014) 'Gazprom completes Armenian gas takeover', asbarez.com/118554/ga zprom-completes-armenian-gas-takeover/#.

Åslund, A. (2013) *Ukraine's Choice: European Association Agreement or Eurasian Union?*, Policy Brief No. PB13-22, Washington, DC: Peterson Institute for International Economics.

Åslund, A. (2015) *Ukraine: What Went Wrong and How to Fix It*, Washington, DC: Peterson Institute for International Economics.

Aspinwall, M.D. and Schneider, G. (2000) 'Same menu, separate tables: The institutionalist turn in political science and the study of European integration', *European Journal of Political Research* 38(1): 1–36.

Astourian, S.H. (2000) *From Ter-Petrosian to Kocharian: Leadership Change in Armenia*, Berkeley Program in Soviet and Post-Soviet Studies Working Paper, Berkeley, CA: UC Berkeley.

Babayan, N. (2015) 'Democratization: The return of the empire? Russia's counteraction to transatlantic democracy promotion in its near abroad', *Democratization* 22(3): 438–458.

Baev, P.K. (2008) *Russian Energy Policy and Military Power: Putin's Quest for Greatness*, London and New York: Routledge.

Baldwin, D.A. (1980) 'Interdependence and power. A conceptual analysis', *International Organization* 34(4): 471–506.

Baldwin, D.A. (2002) 'Power and international relations', in W. Carlsnaes, T. Risse and B.A. Simmons (eds) *Handbook of International Relations*, London: SAGE, pp. 177–191.

Banisar, D. (2006) *Freedom of Information Around the World*, London: Privacy International.
Baran, Z. (2003) 'Deals give Russian companies influence over Georgia's energy infrastructure', 17 August, www.eurasianet.org/departments/business/articles/eav081803.shtml.
Barbé, E., Costa, O., Herranz, A., Johansson-Nogués, E. and Sabiote, M.A. (2009) 'Drawing the neighbours closer ... to what?: explaining emerging patterns of policy convergence between the EU and its neighbours', *Cooperation and Conflict* 44(4): 378–399.
BBC (2006) 'Russia blamed for "gas sabotage"', news.bbc.co.uk/2/hi/europe/4637034.stm.
Bedevian, A. (2012) 'Ruling party sees fewer businessmen in new parliament', *Radio Free Europe/Radio Liberty Armenia*, www.armenialiberty.org/content/article/24479156.html.
Beichelt, T. (2007) 'Externe Demokratisierungsstrategien der Europäischen Union: Die Fälle Belarus, Moldova, Ukraine', in M. Knodt and A. Jünemann (eds) *Externe Demokratieförderung durch die Europäische Union*, Baden-Baden: Nomos, pp. 207–230.
Belton, C. and Carney, D. (2001) 'Russia's shadowy giant: Gas supplier Itera's clout extends across the old Soviet empire', *Bloomberg Businessweek*, 1 April, www.businessweek.com/magazine/content/01_14/b3726147.htm.
Bendeliani, K. (2012) 'Irakli Melashvili: Lack of correct voters' list is state mistake', humanrights.ge/index.php?a=main&pid=14493&lang=eng.
Bennett, C.J. (1991a) 'How states utilize foreign evidence', *Journal of Public Policy* 11(1): 31–54.
Bennett, C.J. (1991b) 'Review article: What is policy convergence and what causes it?', *British Journal of Political Science* 21: 215–233.
Berry, J.M. (2002) 'Validity and reliability issues in elite interviewing', *Political Science and Politics* 35(4): 679–682.
Bertelsmann Foundation (2006) *BTI 2006 Status Index Ranking*, Gütersloh: Bertelsmann Foundation.
Bertelsmann Foundation (2015) *Bertelsmann Transformation Index: BTI 2003–2014 Ergebnisse*, Gütersloh: Bertelsmann Foundation, www.bti-project.de/index/.
Bilgin, M. (2011) 'Energy security and Russia's gas strategy: The symbiotic relationship between the state and firms', *Communist and Post-Communist Studies* 44(2): 119–127.
Blank, S. (2012) 'Whither the new great game in Central Asia?', *Journal of Eurasian Studies* 3: 147–160.
Bogner, A. and Menz, W. (2009) 'Das theoriegenerierende Experteninterview: Erkenntnisinteresse, Wissensformen, Interaktion', in A. Bogner, B. Littig and W. Menz (eds) *Experteninterviews: Theorien, Methoden, Anwendungsfelder*, Wiesbaden: VS Verlag für Sozialwissenschaften, pp. 61–98.
Boniface, J., Wesseling, M., Connell, K.O., Servent, A.R. and Krauss, S. (2008) *Visa Facilitation versus Tightening of Control – Key Aspects of the ENP*, Brussels: European Parliament.
Börzel, T.A. (2000) 'Why there is no "southern problem". On environmental leaders and laggards in the European Union', *Journal of European Public Policy* 7(1): 141–162.
Börzel, T.A. (2010) *The Transformative Power of Europe Reloaded: The Limits of External Europeanization*, KFG Working Paper No. 11, Berlin: Freie Universität Berlin.

References

Börzel, T.A. (2011) 'When Europe hits ... beyond its borders: Europeanization and the near abroad', *Comparative European Politics* 9(4/5): 394–413.
Börzel, T.A. (2015) 'The noble west and the dirty rest? Western democracy promoters and illiberal regional powers', *Democratization* 22(3): 519–535.
Börzel, T.A. and Langbein, J. (2014) *Explaining Policy Change in the European Union's Eastern Neighbourhood*, London and New York: Routledge.
Börzel, T.A. and Lebanidze, B. (2015) *European Neighbourhood Policy at the Crossroads Evaluating the Past to Shape the Future*, MAXCAP Working Paper No. 12, Berlin: Freie Universität Berlin.
Börzel, T.A. and Pamuk, Y. (2012) 'Pathologies of Europeanisation: Fighting corruption in the Southern Caucasus', *West European Politics* 35(1): 79–97.
Börzel, T.A., Pamuk, Y. and Stahn, A. (2008) *The European Union and the Promotion of Good Governance in its Near Abroad One Size Fits All?*, SFB-Governance Working Paper No. 18, Berlin: Freie Universität Berlin.
Börzel, T.A. and Risse, T. (2000) 'When Europe hits home: Europeanization and domestic change', *European Integration Online Papers* 4(15): 1–20.
Börzel, T.A. and Risse, T. (2002) 'Die Wirkung internationaler Institutionen: Von der Normanerkennung zur Normeinhaltung', in M. Jachtenfuchs and M. Knodt (eds) *Regieren in Internationalen Institutionen*, Opladen: Leske und Budrich, pp. 141–181.
Börzel, T.A. and Risse, T. (2009) *The Transformative Power of Europe: The European Union and the Diffusion of Ideas*, KFG Working Paper No. 1, Berlin: Freie Universität Berlin.
Börzel, T.A. and Risse, T. (2012a) 'From Europeanisation to diffusion: Introduction', *West European Politics* 35(1): 1–19.
Börzel, T.A. and Risse, T. (2012b) 'When Europeanisation meets diffusion: Exploring new territory', *West European Politics* 35(1): 192–207.
Börzel, T.A. and van Hüllen, V. (2011) *Good Governance and Bad Neighbors? The Limits of the Transformative Power of Europe*, KFG Working Paper No. 35, Berlin: Freie Universität Berlin.
Brandstetter, R. and Zakoyan, H. (2012) *IFES Evaluation Report*, Vienna, VA: USAID Armenia.
Braun, D. and Gilardi, F. (2006) 'Taking "Galton's problem" seriously: Towards a theory of policy diffusion', *Journal of Theoretical Politics* 18(3): 298–322.
British Petroleum (2014) 'Shah Deniz: Project timeline', www.bp.com/en_az/caspian/op erationsprojects/Shahdeniz/projecthistory.html.
Brunarska, Z., Nestorowicz, J. and Markowski, S. (2014) 'Intra- vs. extra-regional migration in the post-Soviet space', *Eurasian Geography and Economics* 55(2): 133–155.
Brusis, M. (2005) 'The instrumental use of European Union conditionality: Regionalization in the Czech Republic and Slovakia', *East European Politics & Societies* 19(2): 291–316.
BSEC Permanent International Secretariat (2010) *Report of the Twenty Third Meeting of the Council of Ministers of Foreign Affairs of the BSEC Member States, BS/FM/R (2010)2*, Istanbul: Organization of the Black Sea Economic Cooperation.
BTI (2003) *BTI Armenia Country Report 2003*, Gütersloh: Bertelsmann Foundation.
BTI (2006) *BTI Georgia Country Report 2006*, Gütersloh: Bertelsmann Foundation.
BTI (2008) *BTI Georgia Country Report 2008*, Gütersloh: Bertelsmann Foundation.
BTI (2010) *BTI Georgia Country Report 2010*, Gütersloh: Bertelsmann Foundation.
BTI (2014a) *BTI 2014 Armenia Country Report*, Gütersloh: Bertelsmann Foundation.
BTI (2014b) *BTI 2014 Georgia Country Report*, Gütersloh: Bertelsmann Foundation.

230 References

Bugajski, J. (2010) 'Russia's pragmatic reimperialization', *Caucasian Review of International Affairs* 4(1): 3–19.

Bundesamt für Migration der Schweizerischen Eidgenossenschaft (2010) *Rückkehrhilfeprogramm Armenien*, Bern-Wabern: Bundesamt für Migration der Schweizerischen Eidgenossenschaft.

Buzogány, A. (2013) 'Selective adoption of EU environmental norms in Ukraine. Convergence à la carte', *Europe-Asia Studies* 65(4): 609–630.

Buzogány, A. (2016) 'EU-Russia regulatory competition and business interests in post-Soviet countries: the case of forestry and chemical security in Ukraine', *Eurasian Geography and Economics* 57(1): 138–159.

Byford, A. (2012) 'The Russian diaspora in international relations: "Compatriots" in Britain', *Europe-Asia Studies* 64(4): 715–735.

Bzhalava, D. (2008a) 'Mirtskhulava sustains Strasbourg court case while passing up political career', *The Georgian Times*, www.geotimes.ge/index.php?m=home&newsid=9349.

Bzhalava, D. (2008b) 'Will Strasbourg consider the cases of Molashvili and Mirtskhulava?', *The Georgian Times*, www.geotimes.ge/index.php/uploads/pub.swf?m=home&newsid=8714.

CACI Analyst (2002) 'Armenian minister announces new accord for proposed Iran-Armenia pipeline', www.cacianalyst.org/?q=node/632.

Całus, K. (2014) *Russian Sanctions against Moldova: Minor Effects, Major Potential*, OSW Commentary No. 152, Warsaw: Center for Eastern Studies.

Cameron, D.R. and Orenstein, M.A. (2011) *Post-Soviet Authoritarianism: The Impact of International Actors, Linkages and Alliances*, in Paper presented at the 2011 annual meeting of the American Political Science Association, 3 September, Seattle.

Casier, T. (2007) 'The clash of integration processes? The shadow effect of the enlarged EU on its eastern neighbours', in K. Malfliet, E. Vinokurov and L. Verpoest (eds) *The CIS, the EU and Russia: The Challenges of Integration*, Basingstoke: Palgrave Macmillan, pp. 73–94.

Casier, T. (2011a) 'The EU's two-track approach to democracy promotion: The case of Ukraine', *Democratization* 18(4): 956–977.

Casier, T. (2011b) 'To adopt or not to adopt: Explaining selective rule transfer under the European Neighbourhood Policy', *Journal of European Integration* 33(1): 37–53.

Casier, T. (2012) 'Are the policies of Russia and the EU in their shared neighbourhood doomed to clash?', in R.E. Kanet and M.R. Freire (eds) *Competing for Influence: The EU and Russia in Post-Soviet Eurasia*. Dordrecht: Republic of Letters Publishing BV, pp. 31–55.

Cassarino, J.-P. (2011) *Beyond Asymmetries: Cooperation on Readmission in the Neighbourhood*, in EUSA Twelfth Biennial International Conference, 3–5 March, Boston.

Caucasian House (2014) *Georgia's EU Integration Agenda and Normalization Process with Russia*, Tbilisi: Caucasian House.

Cenusa, D., Kovziridse, T. and Movchan, V. (2014) *Russia's Punitive Trade Policy Measures towards Ukraine, Moldova and Georgia*, CEPS Working Document No. 400, Brussels: Centre for European Policy Studies.

Charap, S. and Troitskiy, M. (2013) 'Russia, the West and the integration dilemma', *Survival* 55(6): 49–62.

Chayes, A. and Chayes, A.H. (1993) 'On compliance', *International Organization* 47(2): 175–205.

References

Checkel, J.T. (2001) 'Why comply? Social learning and European identity change', *International Organization* 55(3): 553–588.
Chelea, N. (2011) 'Opposition-6 reinstates issue of biometric passports', *Weekly Georgian Journal*, www.georgianjournal.ge/index.php/politics/5705-opposition-6-reinstates-issue-of-biometric-passports-.
Cheterian, V. (2006) 'Armenien, Iran und die Gaspipeline', www.caucaz.com/home_de/breve_contenu.php?id=144.
Cheterian, V. (2009) 'The August 2008 war in Georgia: From ethnic conflict to border wars', *Central Asian Survey* 28(2): 155–170.
Chiaberashvili, Z. and Tevzadze, G. (2005) 'Power elites in Georgia', in P.H. Fluri and E. Cole (eds) *From Revolution to Reform: Georgia's Struggle with Democratic Institution Building and Security Sector Reform*, Vienna and Geneva: Bureau for Security Policy at the Austrian Ministry of Defence; National Defence Academy and Geneva Centre for the Democratic Control of Armed Forces, pp. 186–207.
Chindea, A., Majkowska-Tomkin, M., Mattila, H. and Pastor, I. (2008) *Migration in Armenia: A Country Profile 2008*, Geneva: International Organization for Migration.
Chobanyan, H. (2012) *On the Institutional Structure of Migration in the Republic Armenia*, Yerevan: European University Institute and Robert Schuman Centre for Advanced Studies.
CIS Council of Heads of Governments (2007) *Soglashenie o formirovanii obshchego elektroenergeticheskogo rynka gosudarstv – uchastnikov Sodruzhestva Nezavisimykh Gosudarstv, No. 02191, adopted on 25.11.2007*, Minsk: CIS Register of Legal Acts and Documents.
CIS Council of Heads of Governments (2010) *Protokol ob etapakh formurovaniya obshchego elektroenergeticheskogo rynka gosudarstv – uchastnikov SNG, No. 02848, adopted on 21.5.2010*, Minsk: CIS Register of Legal Acts and Documents.
CIS Council of Heads of States (2010) *Reshenie o Plane meropriyatii pa realizatsii Kontseptsii soglasovannoi nogranichnoi politiki gosydarstv – uchastnikov Sodruzhestva Nezavisimykh Gosudarstv na 2011–2015 gody, No.02984, adopted on 10.12.2010*, Minsk: CIS Register of Legal Acts and Documents.
CIS Economic Council (2005) *Reshenie ob Osnovnykh napravleniyakh i printsipakh vzaimodeistviya gosudarstv – uchastnikov Sodruzhestva Nezavisimykh Gosudarstv v oblasti obespecheniya energoeffektivnosti, No.01705, adopted on 11.03.2005*, Minsk: CIS Register of Legal Acts and Documents.
CIS Electric Power Council and Eurelectric (2005) *Summary Report of the CIS EPC-EURELECTRIC Joint Working Groups 'Markets' and 'Environment', Ref: 2005-030-1268*, Brussels: CIS Electric Power Council, Eurelectric.
CIS Executive Committee (2011a) 'Obshchaya informatsiya Sotrudnichestvo v sfere borby s prestupnostyu', cis.minsk.by/page.php?id=18780.
CIS Executive Committee (2011b) 'Sotrudnichestvo v sfere migratsii i borby s torgovlei lyudmu', cis.minsk.by/page.php?id=18752.
Civil Development Agency (2015) 'Migration', in *Two Years in Government: Georgian Dream's Performance Review*, Tbilisi: Transparency International Georgia, pp. 107–111.
Civil Georgia (2005) 'Government launches program to overcome energy crisis, www.civil.ge/eng/article.php?id=9189&search=Gilauri.
Civil Georgia (2006a) 'Burjanadze slams energy minister', www.civil.ge/eng/_print.php?id=12083.
Civil Georgia (2006b) 'Energy facilities' privatization results unclear', www.civil.ge/eng/_print.php?id=12867.

Civil Georgia (2006c) 'Opposition targets electricity tariff debate', www.civil.ge/eng/article.php?id=12562.
Civil Georgia (2006d) 'PM: Russian investments pose no threat', www.civil.ge/eng/_print.php?id=12574.
Civil Georgia (2006e) 'Russian ambassador comments on gas crisis', www.civil.ge/eng/article.php?id=11576&search=Russian Ambassador comments on gas crisis.
Civil Georgia (2007a) 'Focusing on trans-Caspian pipes to diversify supplies', www.civil.ge/eng/article.php?id=14845.
Civil Georgia (2007b) 'New cabinet nominated', www.civil.ge/eng/article.php?id=15692.
Civil Georgia (2007c) 'Saakashvili: Georgia has guaranteed energy security', www.civil.ge/eng/_print.php?id=15336.
Civil Georgia (2011a) 'Biometric voter registry cost debated', civil.ge/eng/_print.php?id=23213.
Civil Georgia (2011b) 'Six opposition parties reject ruling party's electoral proposals', civil.ge/eng/_print.php?id=23671.
Civil Georgia (2012) 'EU, Georgia launch visa liberalisation talks, civil.ge/eng/article.php?id=24845.
Civil Georgia (2013) 'Parliament adopts bipartisan resolution on foreign policy', www.civil.ge/eng_old/_print.php?id=25828.
Civil Georgia (2014) 'PM reaffirms support for Khudoni HPP project', www.civil.ge/eng/article.php?id=27150.
Civil Registry Agency Georgia (2007) *Civil Registry Agency Strategic Plan 2007–2011, adopted on September 26, 2007, revised on December 23, 2008*, Tbilisi: Civil Registry Agency of the Government of Georgia.
Civil Registry Agency Georgia (2010) 'The first biometric passport was issued in Georgia', www.cra.gov.ge/index.php?lang_id=ENG&sec_id=49&info_id=1245.
Closson, S. (2009) 'State weakness in perspective: Strong politico-economic networks in Georgia's energy sector', *Europe-Asia Studies* 61(5): 759–778.
Corso, M. (2005a) 'Privatization in Georgia: Solving the sensitive issues', www.eurasianet.org/departments/business/articles/eav071905.shtml.
Corso, M. (2005b) 'Promises still power Georgia's electricity system', www.eurasianet.org/departments/insight/articles/eav012405.shtml.
Corso, M. (2010) 'Georgia: Judges try to get in shape for courtroom', www.eurasianet.org/departments/insight/articles/eav031010c.shtml.
Council of Europe (1981) *Convention for the Protection of Individuals with Regard to Automatic Processing of Personal Data, ETS No.108*, Strasbourg: Council of Europe.
Council of Europe (2001) *Additional Protocol to the Convention for the Protection of Individuals with Regard to Automatic Processing of Personal Data Regarding Supervisory Authorities and Transborder Data Flows*, Strasbourg: Council of Europe.
Council of the European Union (2004) 'Press release: 2590th Council Meeting General Affairs and External Affairs, Luxembourg, 14 June 2004', 10189/04 (Presse 195), Luxembourg: Council of the European Union.
Council of the European Union (2005) *Note from the Permanent Representatives Committee to the Delegations, Common Approach on Visa Facilitation, 16030/05, adopted on 21.12.2005*, Brussels: Council of the European Union.

Council of the European Union (2007) 'Note on ninth meeting of EU-Armenia parliamentary cooperation committee', 6247/07, 12 February, Brussels: Council of the European Union.

Council of the European Union (2008) *Cover Note from the Presidency to the Delegations, Extraordinary European Council, Brussels, 1 September 2008, Presidency Conclusions, 12594/2/08, adopted on 6.10.2008*, Brussels: Council of the European Union.

Council of the European Union (2009a) *Gemeinsame Erklärung des Prager Gipfeltreffens zur Östlichen Partnerschaft, 8435/09 (Presse 78), adopted 7.05.2009*, Brussels: Council of the European Union.

Council of the European Union (2009b) *Joint Declaration of the Prague Eastern Partnership Summit, Prague, May 7, 8435/09 (Presse 78)*, Brussels: Council of the European Union.

Council of the European Union (2010) *Note from the General Secretariat of the Council to the Delegations, EU-Ukraine Visa Dialogue – Action Plan on Visa Liberalisation, 17883/10, adopted on 14.12.2010*, Brussels: Council of the European Union.

Council of the European Union (2011a) *Conclusion of Two EU Agreements with Georgia on Visa Facilitation and Readmission, 5412/11 (Presse 5), adopted on 18.01.2011*, Brussels: Council of the European Union.

Council of the European Union (2011b) *Note from the General Secretariat of the Council to Delegations, Provisional Agenda for Council Meetings, during the second semester of 2011 (Polish Presidency), 12324/11, adopted on 30.06.2011*, Brussels: Council of the European Union.

CSTO (2002) *Charter of the Collective Security Treaty Organization*, Madrid: Spanish Institute for Strategic Studies.

Cutler, D. (2008) 'Factbox: Who is Badri Patarkatsishvili?', *Reuters*, www.reuters.com/article/2008/01/10/us-georgia-tycoon-patarkatsishvili-idUSL1070390020080110.

Danielyan, E. (2006) 'Armenian Oligarchs Makes Bid for Power with New Political Party', *Eurasia Daily Monitor* 3(9).

Danielyan, E. (2009) 'Armenia presses ahead with nuclear power plant construction', *Eurasia Daily Monitor* 6(103).

Danielyan, E. (2012a) 'Armenia again rules out membership in Russian-led customs union', *Eurasia Daily Monitor* 9(78).

Danielyan, E. (2012b) 'UN nuclear chief meets Armenian leaders, inspects Metsamor Plant', 18 April, *Radio Free Europe/Radio Liberty Armenia*, www.azatutyun.am/content/article/24552816.html.

Danielyan, E. (2012c) 'Yerevan announces dates for free-trade, visa talks with EU', *Radio Free Europe/Radio Liberty Armenia*, www.azatutyun.am/content/article/24464377.html.

Danielyan, E. and Martirosian, A. (2009) 'Dashnaks quit Armenia's ruling coalition', *Radio Free Europe/Radio Liberty Armenia*, www.armenialiberty.org/content/article/1616799.html.

Danish Energy Management (2011) 'Development of small hydro power in Armenia – The success story', www.renewableenergyarmenia.am/index.php?option=com_content&task=view&id=34&Itemid=113http://www.renewableenergyarmenia.am/index.php?option=com_content&task=view&id=36&Itemid=114.

Dean, J.P. and Whyte, W.F. (2006) 'What kind of truth do you get?', in L.A. Dexter (ed.) *Elite and Specialized Interviewing*, Oxford: ECPR Press, pp. 100–114.

Delcour, L. (2014) 'Faithful but constrained? Armenia's half-hearted support for Russia's regional integration policies in the post-Soviet space', in D. Cadier (ed.) *Geopolitics of Eurasian Integration*, London: LSE Ideas Reports, pp. 38–45.

Delcour, L. (2016) 'Multiple external influences, policy conditionality and domestic change: The case of food safety', *Eurasian Geography and Economics* 57(1): 43–65.

Delcour, L. and Kostanyan, H. (2014) *Towards a Fragmented Neighbourhood: Policies of the EU and Russia and their Consequences for the Area that Lies in Between*, CEPS Essay No. 17, Brussels: Centre for European Policy Studies.

Delcour, L. and Wolczuk, K. (2013) *Beyond the Vilnius Summit: Challenges for Deeper EU Integration with Eastern Europe*, EPC Policy Brief (31 October), Brussels: European Policy Centre.

Delcour, L. and Wolczuk, K. (2015a) 'Spoiler or facilitator of democratization?: Russia's role in Georgia and Ukraine', *Democratization* 22(3): 459–478.

Delcour, L. and Wolczuk, K. (2015b) 'The EU's unexpected "ideal neighbour"? The perplexing case of Armenia's Europeanisation', *Journal of European Integration* 37(4): 491–507.

Delegation of the EU to Armenia (2009) 'Project fiche: EU advisory group to the Republic of Armenia', eeas.europa.eu/delegations/armenia/projects/list_of_projects/219290_en.htm.

Delegation of the EU to Armenia (2011) *ENPI 2011 Twinning Contract Support the State Migration Service for Strengthening of Migration Management in Armenia, No. AM11/ENP-PCA/JH/12*, Yerevan: Delegation of the EU to Armenia.

Delegation of the EU to Armenia (2012) 'EU launches negotiations on visa facilitation and readmission agreements with Armenia', 27 February, eeas.europa.eu/delegations/armenia/press_corner/all_news/news/2012/2012.27.02_en.htm.

Delegation of the EU to Georgia (2012a) 'Simplified visa requirements for Georgian citizens', eeas.europa.eu/delegations/georgia/travel_eu/visa/index_en.htm.

Delegation of the EU to Georgia (2012b) 'Technical and financial co-operation', eeas.europa.eu/delegations/georgia/eu_georgia/tech_financial_cooperation/index_en.htm.

Delphia, M.J. and Keyan, M. (2003) *Armenian Power Sector 2002 Least Cost Plan*, Washington, DC: PA Consulting Group.

Devdariani, J. (2003) 'Potential deal with Russian gas conglomerate sparks controversy in Georgia', www.eurasianet.org/departments/business/articles/eav060603.shtml.

De Waal, T. (2013) 'An offer Sargsyan could not refuse', *Eurasia Outlook*, 4 September, carnegie.ru/eurasiaoutlook/?fa=52841.

Dexter, L.A. (2006) *Elite and Specialized Interviewing*, Colchester: ECPR Press.

Dilanyan, H. (2011) 'Consultation on migration at the president's office, 20 July, GAB International Business Network for Armenia and the Caucasus, www.gab-ibn.com/IMG/pdf/Ar21-_Consultation_On_Migration_At_The_President.pdf.

Dimitrova, A. and Dragneva, R. (2009) 'Constraining external governance: Interdependence with Russia and the CIS as limits to the EU's rule transfer in the Ukraine', *Journal of European Public Policy* 16(6): 853–872.

Dimitrova, A. and Dragneva, R. (2013) 'Shaping convergence with the EU in foreign policy and state aid in post-orange Ukraine: Weak external incentives, powerful veto players', *Europe-Asia Studies* 65(4): 658–681.

Doggart, C. (2009) *Russian Investments in Georgia's Electricity Sector: How Georgia's Institutional Framework Encouraged High Levels of Russian Investment*, USAEE-IAEE Working Paper No.09-035, Cleveland: USAEE, IAEE.

References

Donaldson, R.H. and Nogee, J.L. (2009) *The Foreign Policy of Russia: Changing Systems, Enduring Interests*, Armonk, NY and London: M.E Sharpe.

Dragneva, R. and Dimitrova, A. (2007) 'Patterns of integration and regime compatibility: Ukraine between the CIS and the EU', in K. Malfliet, L. Verpoest and E. Vinokurov (eds) *The CIS, The EU and Russia: The Challenges of Integration*, Basingstoke: Palgrave Macmillan, pp. 171–201.

Dragneva, R. and Wolczuk, K. (2012) 'Russia, the Eurasian customs union and the EU: Cooperation, stagnation or rivalry?', Chatham House Briefing Paper REP BP 2012/01, London: Chatham House.

Dragneva, R. and Wolczuk, K. (2013) *Eurasian Economic Integration: Law, Policy and Politics*, Cheltenham: Edward Elgar Publishing Limited.

Dragneva, R. and Wolczuk, K. (2014) 'Eurasian economic integration: Institutions, promises and faultlines', in *The Geopolitics of Eurasian Economic Integration*, LSE Ideas Report, London: London School of Economics, pp. 8–15.

Dragneva, R. and Wolczuk, K. (2015) *Ukraine between the EU and Russia: The Integration Challenge*, Basingstoke: Palgrave Macmillan.

Dreyer, I. and Popescu, N. (2014) *The Eurasian Customs Union: The Economics and the Politics*, ISS Brief No. 11, Paris: European Union Institute for Security Studies.

Drezner, D.W. (2001) 'Globalization and policy convergence', *International Studies Review* 3(1): 53–78.

EaP Community (2012) 'Supplies for the production of e-passports in Georgia', www.easternpartnership.org, www.easternpartnership.org/programmes/supplies-production-e-passports-georgia.

EC and HR (2012a) *Implementation of the European Neighbourhood Policy in the Republic of Moldova, Progress in 2011 and recommendations for action, SWD (2012)118 final, adopted on 15.5.2012*, Brussels: European Commission.

EC and HR (2012b) *Joint Staff Working Document 'Implementation of the European Neighbourhood Policy in Armenia, Progress in 2011 and recommendations for action, SWD (2012) 110 final, adopted on 15.5.2012*, Brussels: European Commission.

EC and HR (2013a) *Joint Communication to the European Parliament, the Council, The European Economic and Social Committee and the Committee of the Regions 'European Neighbourhood Policy: Working Towards a Stronger Partnership', JOIN (2913) 4 final, adopted 20.3.2013*, Brussels: European Commission.

EC and HR (2013b) *Joint Staff Working Document 'Implementation of the European Neighbourhood Policy in Armenia: Progress in 2012 and recommendations for action' SWD(2013) 79 final, adopted 20.03.2013*, Brussels: European Commission.

EC and HR (2014a) *Joint Staff Working Document 'Implementation of the European Neighbourhood Policy in Armenia Progress in 2013 and recommendations for action', SWD(2014) 69 final, adopted on 27.3.2014*, Brussels: European Commission.

EC and HR (2014b) *Joint Staff Working Document 'Implementation of the European Neighbourhood Policy in Georgia' Progress in 2013 and recommendations for action, SWD(2014) 72 final, adopted on 27.3.2014*, Brussels: European Commission.

EC and HR (2015a) *Implementation of the European Neighbourhood Policy in Georgia Progress in 2014, SWD(2015) 66 final, adopted 25.3.2015*, Brussels: European Commission.

EC and HR (2015b) *Joint Consultation Paper: Towards a new European Neighbourhood Policy, JOIN(2015) 6 final, adopted on 4.3.2015*, Brussels: European Commission.

EC and HR (2015c) *Review of the European Neighbourhood Policy, JOIN(2015) 50 final, adopted on 18.11.2015*, Brussels: European Commission.

The Economist (2004) 'A different sort of oligarch', www.economist.com, www.economist.com/node/2963216.
The Economist (2014) 'Europe's ring of fire: The European Union's neighbourhood is more troubled than ever', *The Economist*, www.economist.com/news/europe/21618846-european-unions-neighbourhood-more-troubled-ever-europes-ring-fire.
ECORYS and CASE (2013) *Trade Sustainability Impact Assessment in Support of Negotiations of a DCFTA between the EU and the Republic of Armenia*, Final Report, Rotterdam.
EIU (1999) *Country Report Georgia and Armenia*, 3rd quarter, London: The Economist Intelligence Unit.
EIU (2000a) *Country Report Georgia and Armenia*, August 2000, London: The Economist Intelligence Unit.
EIU (2000b) *Country Report Georgia and Armenia*, November 2000, London: The Economist Intelligence Unit.
EIU (2001a) *Country Report Georgia and Armenia*, August 2001, London: The Economist Intelligence Unit.
EIU (2001b) *Country Report Georgia and Armenia*, November 2001, London: The Economist Intelligence Unit.
EIU (2002) *Country Report Georgia and Armenia*, May 2002, London: The Economist Intelligence Unit.
EIU (2003a) *Country Report Armenia*, November 2003, London: The Economist Intelligence Unit.
EIU (2003b) *Country Report Georgia*, May 2003, London: The Economist Intelligence Unit.
EIU (2003c) *Country Report Georgia*, November 2003, London: The Economist Intelligence Unit.
EIU (2004a) *Country Report Armenia*, November 2004, London: The Economist Intelligence Unit.
EIU (2004b) *Country Report Georgia*, August 2004, London: The Economist Intelligence Unit.
EIU (2004c) *Country Report Georgia*, May 2004, London: The Economist Intelligence Unit.
EIU (2005a) *Country Report Armenia*, November 2005, London: The Economist Intelligence Unit.
EIU (2005b) *Country Report Georgia*, August 2005, London: The Economist Intelligence Unit.
EIU (2006) *Country Report Georgia*, September 2006, London: The Economist Intelligence Unit.
EIU (2007a) *Country Report Armenia*, November 2007, London: The Economist Intelligence Unit.
EIU (2007b) *Country Report Georgia*, September 2007, London: The Economist Intelligence Unit.
EIU (2008a) *Country Report Armenia*, November 2008, London: The Economist Intelligence Unit.
EIU (2008b) *Country Report Georgia*, September 2008, London: The Economist Intelligence Unit.
EIU (2009) *Georgia Country Report*, September 2009, London: The Economist Intelligence Unit.

EIU (2010) *Country Report Armenia*, November 2010, London: The Economist Intelligence Unit.
EIU (2011) *Country Report Georgia*, December, London: The Economist Intelligence Unit.
EIU (2013a) *Country Report Armenia*, 1st Quarter, London: Economist Intelligence Unit.
EIU (2013b) *Country Report Armenia*, 3rd Quarter, London: Economist Intelligence Unit.
EIU (2014a) *Armenia Joins Eurasian Union*, London: Economist Intelligence Unit.
EIU (2014b) *Country Report Armenia*, 2nd Quarter, London: Economist Intelligence Unit.
EIU (2015) *Country Report Armenia*, 2nd Quarter, London: Economist Intelligence Unit.
EKENG (2010) 'Roland Berger consultants are in Armenia', www.ekeng.am/?p=141.
Ekiert, G., Kubik, J. and Vachudova, M.A. (2007) 'Democracy in the post-communist world: An unending quest?', *East European Politics & Societies* 21(7): 7–30.
Elkins, Z. and Simmons, B. (2005) 'On waves, clusters, and diffusion: A conceptual framework', *The Annals of the American Academy of Political and Social Science* 598(1): 33–51.
Emerson, M. (2005) *EU-Russia: Four Common Spaces and the Proliferation of the Fuzzy*, CEPS Policy Brief No. 71, Brussels: Centre for European Policy Studies.
Emerson, M. et al. (2005) *The Reluctant Debutante in its Neighbourhood*, CEPS Working Document No. 223, Brussels: Centre for European Policy Studies.
Emerson, M. and Kostanyan, H. (2013) *Putin's Grand Design to Destroy the EU's Eastern Partnership and Replace it with a Disastrous Neighbourhood Policy of his Own*, CEPS Commentary, Brussels: Centre for European Policy Studies.
Energy Charter Secretariat (2004) *In-depth Review of Energy Efficiency Policies and Programmes: Georgia*, Brussels: Energy Charter Secretariat.
Energy Charter Secretariat (2012) *In-depth Review of Energy Efficiency Policies and Programmes: Georgia*, Brussels: Energy Charter Secretariat.
Energy Community (2012) 'Facts and figures', www.energy-community.org/portal/page/portal/ENC_HOME/ENERGY_COMMUNITY/Facts_and_Figures.
Energy Efficiency Task Force (2008) *Report on Energy Efficiency in the Contracting Parties and Observer Countries to the Treaty Establishing the Energy Community*, Brussels: Energy Community.
Epress.am (2011) 'So that critical mass remains here and revolution happens? Armenia PM on emigration', www.epress.am/en/2011/06/28/so-that-critical-mass-remains-here-and-revolution-happens-armenia-pm-on-emigration.html.
EPRS (2015) 'Moldova's political parties: Caught between the EU and Russia', *At a Glance* (March), Brussels: European Parliamentary Research Service.
Escobales, R., Attewill, F. and Harding, L. (2008) 'Police investigate death of Georgian oligarch', *The Guardian*, www.guardian.co.uk/world/2008/feb/13/internationalcrime.georgia.
EU-Armenia Cooperation Council (2002) *Draft Minutes of the third meeting of the EU-Armenia Cooperation Council, UE-AM 4552/02, adopted on 18.09.2002*, Brussels: Council of the European Union.
EU-Armenia Cooperation Council (2005) *Draft Minutes of the sixth meeting of the EU-Armenia Cooperation Council, UE-AM 4553/05, adopted on 5.12.2005*, Brussels: Council of the European Union.

EU-Armenia Cooperation Council (2007) *Minutes of the seventh meeting of the EU-Armenian Cooperation Council, UE-AM 4552/07, adopted on 1.10.2007*, Brussels: Council of the European Union.

EU-Georgia Cooperation Council (2001) *Minutes of the second meeting of the EU-Georgia Cooperation Council, UE-GE 4651/01, adopted on 12.10.2001*, Brussels: Council of the European Union.

EurActiv (2011a) 'Pipeline politics? Russia and the EU's battle for energy', www.euractiv.com/energy/pipeline-politics-russia-eu-battle-energy/article-177579.

EurActiv (2011b) 'Russia-EU energy politics', www.euractiv.com/energy/russia-eu-energy-politics-analysis-508992.

Eurasian Development Bank (2013) *Armenia and the Customs Union: Impact of Economic Integration*, Saint Petersburg: EDB Center for Integration Studies.

Eurasian Economic Commission (2015) *Eurasian Economic Integration: Facts and Figures*, Moscow: Eurasian Economic Commission.

European Bank for Reconstruction and Development (2012) 'Georgia country profile', www.ebrdrenewables.com/sites/renew/countries/Georgia/default.aspx.

European Commission (1999) *Bericht der Kommission, Tacis-Jahresbericht 1998, KOM (1999) 380 endg., 23 July*, Brussels: European Commission.

European Commission (2000) *Report from the Commission, The TACIS Programme Annual Report 1999, COM (2000) 835 final, adopted on 21.12.2000*, Brussels: European Commission.

European Commission (2001) *Country Strategy Paper 2002–2006, National Indicative Programme 2002–2003, Republic of Armenia, adopted on 27.12.2001*, Brussels: European Commission.

European Commission (2003a) *Communication from the Commission to the Council and the European Parliament, Wider Europe – Neighbourhood: A New Framework for Relations with our Eastern and Southern Neighbours, COM (2003) 104 final, adopted 11.03.2003*, Brussels: European Commission.

European Commission (2003b) *Country Strategy Paper 2003–2006, TACIS National Indicative Programme 2004–2006 Georgia, adopted on 23.09.2003*, Brussels: European Commission.

European Commission (2004a) *Action programme 2004/2005 Armenia*, Brussels: European Commission.

European Commission (2004b) *Annex 2 – Statements by participating countries, ministerial conference on energy co-operation between the EU, the Caspian littoral states and their neighbouring countries*, 13 November, Baku: European Commission.

European Commission (2005a) *Commission Staff Working Paper, Annex to: European Neighbourhood Policy – Country Report Armenia, SEC (2005) 285/3, adopted on 2.3.2005*, Brussels: European Commission.

European Commission (2005b) *Commission Staff Working Paper, annex to: European Neighbourhood Policy – country report Georgia, SEC (2005)288/3*, Brussels: European Commission.

European Commission (2005c) *Common Spaces Roadmap*, Brussels: European Commission.

European Commission (2006a) *Communication from the Commission to the Council and the European Parliament on Strengthening the European Neighbourhood Policy, COM(2006)726 final, adopted 4.12.2006*, Brussels: European Commission.

European Commission (2006b) *EU/Georgia Action Plan*, 14 November, Brussels: European Commission.

European Commission (2006c) *EU/Armenia Action Plan*, 14 November, Brussels: European Commission.
European Commission (2007a) *Communication from the Commission, On Circular Migration and Mobility Partnerships between the European Union and Third Countries, COM(2007) 248 final, adopted on 16.5.2007*, Brussels: European Commission.
European Commission (2007b) *ENPI Armenia Country Strategy Paper 2007–2013*, Brussels: European Commission.
European Commission (2007c) *ENPI Armenia National Indicative Programme 2007–2010*, Brussels: European Commission.
European Commission (2007d) *ENPI Georgia Country Strategy Paper 2007–2013*, Brussels: European Commission.
European Commission (2007e) *ENPI Georgia National Indicative Programme 2007–2010*, Brussels: European Commission.
European Commission (2007f) *Mitteilung der Kommission, Anwendung des Gesamtansatzes zur Migration auf die östlichen und südöstlichen Nachbarregionen der Europäischen Union, KOM (2007), 247 endgültig/2, adopted 8.06.2007*, Brussels: European Commission.
European Commission (2008a) *Commission Staff Working Document 'Implementation of the European Neighbourhood Policy in 2007' Progress Report Armenia, SEC (2008) 392, adopted 3.4.2008*, Brussels: European Commission.
European Commission (2008b) *Commission Staff Working Document 'Implementation of the European Neighbourhood Policy in 2007' Progress Report Georgia, SEC (2008) 393, adopted 3.04.2008*, Brussels: European Commission.
European Commission (2008c) *Commission Staff Working Document, the Support of Electricity from Renewable Energy Sources, SEC (2008) 57, adopted on 23.1.2008*, Brussels: European Commission.
European Commission (2008d) *Communication from the Commission to the Council and the European Parliament: Report on the First Year of Implementing the Black Sea Synergy, COM (2008) 391 final, adopted 19.06.2008*, Brussels: European Commission.
European Commission (2008e) *Communication from the Commission to the European Parliament and the Council – Eastern Partnership, COM(2008) 823 final, adopted 3.12.2008*, Brussels: European Commission.
European Commission (2008f) *Communication from the Commission to the European Parliament, the Council, the European Economic and Social Committee and the Committee of the Regions, Second Strategic Energy Review, an EU Energy Security and Solidarity Action Plan, COM (2008) 781 final*, Brussels: European Commission.
European Commission (2009a) *Commission Staff Working Document 'Implementation of the European Neighbourhood Policy in 2008' Progress Report Armenia, SEC (2009) 511/2, adopted 23.04.2009*, Brussels: European Commission.
European Commission (2009b) *Commission Staff Working Document 'Implementation of the European Neighbourhood Policy in 2008', Progress Report Georgia, SEC (2008) 513/2, adopted on 23.4.2009*, Brussels: European Commission.
European Commission (2009c) *Memorandum on an Early Warning Mechanism in the Energy Sector within the Framework of the EU-Russia Energy Dialogue*, Brussels: European Commission.
European Commission (2010) *Commission Staff Working Document 'Implementation of the European Neighbourhood Policy in 2009' Progress Report Armenia, SEC (2010) 516, adopted 12.05.2010*, Brussels: European Commission.

European Commission (2011a) 'Energy strategy centre', www.managenergy.net/actors/561.
European Commission (2011b) *ENPI Armenia National Indicative Programme 2011–2013*, Brussels: European Commission.
European Commission (2011c) *ENPI Georgia National Indicative Programme 2011–2013*, Brussels: European Commission.
European Commission (2011d) 'EU-Russian energy dialogue', eeas.europa.eu/delegations/russia/eu_russia/fields_cooperation/energy/index_en.htm.
European Commission (2011e) *Joint Communication to the European Parliament, the Council, the European Economic and Social Committee and the Committee of the Regions – A New Response to a Changing Neighbourhood, COM (2011)303, adopted on 25.05.2011*, Brussels: European Commission.
European Commission (2011f) *Joint Staff Working Paper 'Implementation of the European Neighbourhood Policy in 2010' Country Report: Armenia, SEC(2011) 639, adopted 25.05.2011*, Brussels: European Commission.
European Commission (2011g) *Joint Staff Working Paper 'Implementation of the European Neighbourhood Policy in 2010' Country Report: Georgia, SEC (2011)649, adopted on 25.05.2011*, Brussels: European Commission.
European Commission (2011h) 'Justice, freedom and security', eeas.europa.eu/delegations/russia/eu_russia/fields_cooperation/justice_freedom/index_en.htm.
European Commission (2011i) 'Overview of TAIEX projects in Armenia', ec.europa.eu/enlargement/taiex/dyn/taiex-events/index_en.jsp.
European Commission (2011j) 'Overview of TAIEX projects in Georgia', ec.europa.eu/enlargement/taiex/dyn/taiex-events/index_en.jsp.
European Commission (2011k) 'Visas and readmission', eeas.europa.eu/delegations/russia/eu_russia/fields_cooperation/visas_readmission/index_en.htm.
European Commission (2012a) *Annual Action Programme 2012 for Georgia*, Brussels: European Commission.
European Commission (2012b) *Annual Action Programme 2012 in Favour of Armenia – Action Fiche*, Brussels: European Commission.
European Commission (2012c) *Annual Programmes 2007–2012*, Brussels: European Commission, ec.europa.eu/europeaid/work/ap/index_en.htm.
European Commission (2012d) *Annual Programmes East 2002–2007*, Brussels: European Commission.
European Commission (2012e) *Joint Staff Working Document 'Implementation of the European Neighbourhood Policy in 2011' Regional Report: Eastern Partnership, SWD (2012) 112 final, adopted 15.05.2012*, Brussels: European Commission.
European Commission (2012f) *Nuclear Safety Programme: Projects Search*, Joint Research Centre – Institute for Energy and Transport, nuclear.jrc.ec.europa.eu/tacis-insc/index.php?option=com_content&view=article&id=46&lang=en&s=reset.
European Commission (2012g) *Promoting investment through the Neighbourhood Investment Facility (NIF)*, Development and Cooperation – Europeaid, ec.europa.eu/europeaid/where/neighbourhood/regional-cooperation/irc/investment_en.htm.
European Commission (2013a) *Commission Implementing Decision Modifying the Commission Implementing Decision C(2013) 5182 on the Annual Action Programme 2013 in Favour of Armenia to be Financed from the General Budget of the European Union*, Brussels: European Commission.
European Commission (2013b) *Commission Implementing Decision on the Annual Action Programme 2013 in Favour of Armenia to be Financed from the General*

References

Budget of the European Union, C(2013)5182, adopted 2.8.2013, Brussels: European Commission.
European Commission (2013c) *Commission Implementing Decision on the Annual Action Programme 2013 in Favour of Georgia to be Financed from the General Budget of the European Union, C(2013)5181 final, adopted on 2.8.2013*, Brussels: European Commission.
European Commission (2013d) *First Progress Report on the Implementation by Georgia of the Action Plan on Visa Liberalisation, COM(2013)808 final, adopted on 15.11.2013*, Brussels: European Commission.
European Commission (2013e) *Neighbourhood Investment Facility Operational Report 2013*, Brussels: European Commission.
European Commission (2015a) *Review of the European Neighbourhood Policy, JOIN (2015) 50 final, adopted 18.11.2015*, Brussels: European Commission.
European Commission (2015b) *Third Progress Report on Georgia's Implementation of the Action Plan on Visa Liberalisation, COM(2015) 199 final, adopted 8.5.2015*, Brussels: European Commission.
European Communities (1997) *Agreement on Partnership and Cooperation Establishing a Partnership between the European Communities and their Member States, of one part, and the Russian Federation, of the other part, L 327, published on 28.11.1997*, Brussels: Official Journal of the European Communities.
European Communities (1999a) *Partnership and Cooperation Agreement between the European Communities and their Member States, of the one part, and Georgia, of the other part, L 205/3, 4 August*, Brussels: Official Journal of the European Communities.
European Communities (1999b) *Partnership and Cooperation Agreement between the European Communities and their Member States, of the one part, and the Republic of Armenia, of the other part, L 239, 9 September*, Brussels: Official Journal of the European Communities.
European Council (2013) *European Council 19/20 December 2013 Conclusions, EUCO 217/13*, Brussels: European Council.
European Investment Bank (2011a) *Factsheet: EIB Financing in the EU's Eastern Neighbours*, Luxembourg: European Investment Bank.
European Investment Bank (2011b) *Georgia: EIB Supports Rehabilitation of Enguri and Vardnili Hydropower Plant Cascade, Press Release, BEI/11/1, issued 7.1.2011, Tbilisi*, Luxembourg: European Investment Bank.
European Parliament (2013) *MEPs Back Freeing Wine Trade with Moldova to Offset Russian Trade Sanctions*, Brussels: European Parliament.
European Parliament and Council of the European Union (2001) *Directive 2001/77/EC of the European Parliament and of the Council of 27 September 2001, on the Promotion of Electricity Produced from Renewable Energy Sources in the Internal Market, L 283/33, published on 27.10.2001*, Brussels: Official Journal of the European Communities.
European Stability Initiative (2010a) *Georgia's Libertarian Revolution Part One: Georgia as a Model*, Berlin, Brussels, Istanbul: European Stability Initiative.
European Stability Initiative (2010b) *Georgia's Libertarian Revolution Part Three: Jacobins in Tbilisi*, Berlin, Brussels, Istanbul: European Stability Initiative.
European Union (2011) *Agreement between the European Union and Georgia on the Readmission of Persons Residing without Authorisation, L 52/47, published on 25.02.2011*, Brussels: Official Journal of the European Union.

References

Europol (2004) *European Union Organised Crime Report*, Brussels: Europol.
Eurostat (2011) 'Extra-trade of mineral fuel, lubricates and related materials per partner country', *Eurostat Database*, epp.eurostat.ec.europa.eu/tgm/table.do?tab=table&init=1&language=de&pcode=tet00043&plugin=1.
Eurostat (2015) *Eurostat Statistics Explained: Energy Production and Imports*, Brussels: Eurostat.
Evans, M. (2004a) 'Introduction: Is policy transfer rational policy-making?', in M. Evans (ed.) *Policy Transfer in Global Perspective*, Aldershot: Ashgate, pp. 1–9.
Evans, M. (2004b) 'Understanding policy transfer', in M. Evans (ed.) *Policy Transfer in Global Perspective*, Aldershot: Ashgate, pp. 10–44.
Fairbanks, C.H. and Gugushvili, A. (2013) 'A new chance for Georgian democracy', *Journal of Democracy* 24(1): 116–127.
Fischer, S. (2006) *Die EU und Russland: Konflikte und Potential einer schwierigen Partnerschaft, SWP-Studie No. S 34*, Berlin: Stiftung Wissenschaft und Politik.
Fix, L. (2014) *Georgia Knocking on Europe's Door: Russia, Georgia, and the EU Association Agreement*, Berlin: DGAP.
Freedom House (1998) *Nations in Transit – Armenia*, Washington, DC: Freedom House.
Freedom House (2011a) *Freedom in the World – Country Report Armenia*, Washington, DC: Freedom House.
Freedom House (2011b) *Freedom in the World – Country Report Georgia*, Washington, DC: Freedom House.
Freedom House (2013) *Freedom in the World – Country Report Armenia*, Washington, DC: Freedom House.
Freedom House (2014a) *Freedom in the World 2014: Ukraine*, Washington, DC: Freedom House.
Freedom House (2014b) *Nations in Transit: Moldova*, Washington, DC: Freedom House.
Freedom House (2015a) *Freedom in the World – Country Report Georgia*, Washington, DC: Freedom House.
Freedom House (2015b) *Freedom in the World 2015: Ukraine*, Washington, DC: Freedom House.
Freedom House (2015c) 'Freedom in the world comparative and historical data, individual country ratings and status, FIW 1973–2015', www.freedomhouse.org/report-types/freedom-world.
Freire, M.R. and Simão, L. (2007) *The Armenian Road to Democracy – Dimensions of a Tortuous Process, CEPS Working Document No. 267*, Brussels: Center for European Policy Studies.
Freitag-Wirminghaus, R. (1999) 'Südkaukasus und die Erdöl-Problematik am Kaspischen Meer', in G. Mangott (ed.) *Brennpunkt Südkaukasus- Aufbruch trotz Krieg, Vertreibung und Willkürherrschaft*, Wien: Braumüller, pp. 247–282.
Freyburg, T. (2012) 'The two sides of functional cooperation with authoritarian regimes: A multi-level perspective on the conflict of objectives between political stability and democratic change', *Democratization* 19(3): 575–601.
Freyburg, T. (2015) 'Transgovernmental networks as an apprenticeship in democracy? Socialization into democratic governance through cross-national activities', *International Studies Quarterly* 59: 59–72.
Freyburg, T., Lavenex, S., Skripka, T. and Wetzel, A. (2009) 'EU promotion of democratic governance in the neighbourhood', *Journal of European Public Policy* 16(6): 916–934.

Freyburg, T., Lavenex, S., Skripka, T. and Wetzel, A. (2011) 'Democracy promotion through functional cooperation? The case of the European neighbourhood policy', *Democratization* 18(4): 1026–1054.

Freyburg, T., Skripka, T. and Wetzel, A. (2007) *Democracy between the Lines? EU Promotion of Democratic Governance via Sector-specific Co-operation'*, NCCR Working Paper No.5, Zurich: National Centre of Competence in Research.

Frieden, J.A. (1999) 'Actors and preferences in international relations', in D.A. Lake and R. Powell (eds) *Strategic Choice and International Relations*, Princeton, NJ: Princeton University Press, pp. 39–76.

Frontex (2011) *Frontex Press Pack May 2011*, Warsaw: Frontex.

Fuller, L. (2007) 'Caucasus: Georgia, Azerbaijan seek alternatives to Russian gas', *Radio Free Europe/Radio Liberty*, fb.rferl.org/content/article/1073826.html.

Garbis, C. (2012) 'Garbis: Notes on emigration', 22 March, *Armenian Weekly*, www.armenianweekly.com/2012/03/22/garbis-notes-on-emigration/.

Garcés de los Fayos, F. (2014) *The Signature of the Eurasian Union Treaty: A Difficult Birth, an Uncertain Future*, Brussels: European Parliament.

Gawrich, A., Melnykovska, I. and Schweickert, R. (2009) *Neighbourhood Europeanization through ENP: The Case of Ukraine*, KFG Working Paper No.3, Berlin: Freie Universität Berlin.

Gawrich, A., Melnykovska, I. and Schweickert, R. (2010) 'Neighbourhood Europeanization through ENP: The case of Ukraine', *Journal of Common Market Studies* 48(5): 1209–1235.

Genov, N. and Savvidis, T. (2011) *Transboundary Migration in the Post-Soviet Space: Three Comparative Case Studies*, Frankfurt am Main: Peter Lang.

George, A.L. and Bennett, A. (2005) *Case Studies and Theory Development in the Social Sciences*, Cambridge, MA: MIT Press.

The Georgia Times (2009) 'Another oppositional ombudsman?', www.georgiatimes.info/en/articles/24811-2.html.

The GeorgiaTimes (2010) 'CDM objects unaffordable price of biometric passports', geotimes.ge/index.php?m=home&date=2010.04.26.

Gevorgyan, S. (2012) 'ID matters: Justice minister says only passports will enable Armenia citizens to vote, www.armenianow.com/news/35708/armenia_passports_ids_elections.

Gevorgyan, V. (2008) 'Part 1 – Policy for combating irregular migration in the Republic of Armenia', in L. Zanfrini, W. Kluth, V. Gevorgyan, T. Kavounidē and I. Ivakhnyuk (eds) *Policies on Irregular Migrants – Volume II Republic of Armenia, Greece and Russian Federation*, Strasbourg: Council of Europe Publishing.

Ghazanchyan, S. (2013) 'European Union supports return and reintegration of Armenians', *Public Radio of Armenia*, www.armradio.am/en/2013/03/21/european-union-supports-return-and-reintegration-of-armenians/.

GHN News Agency (2011) 'Georgian authorities are not willing to accept money from Ivanishvili for financing biometric passports', www.eng.ghn.ge/print-4619.html.

Goble, P.A. (2008) 'Russian "passportization"', *The New York Times*, topics.blogs.nytimes.com/2008/09/09/russian-passportization/.

Goldthau, A. and Geden, O. (2007) 'Europas Energieversorgungssicherheit – Ein Plädoyer für einen pragmatischen Ansatz', *Internationale Politik und Gesellschaft Online* (4): 58–73.

Gordadze, T. (2014) 'Georgia', in *The Geopolitics of Eurasian Economic Integration*, LSE Ideas Report, London: London School of Economics, pp. 54–59.

Government of Armenia (2004) *Republic of Armenia Concept Paper on State Regulation of Population Migration, Appendix to Republic of Armenia Government Session Record, Decree No.24, adopted 25.06.2004*, Florence: Consortium for Applied Research on International Migration.

Government of Armenia (2005) *Energy Sector Development Strategy in the Context of Economic Development in Armenia, N1 resolution of N 24 protocol, 23 June*, Yerevan: Government of Armenia.

Government of Armenia (2007a) *Armenian Nuclear Power Plant Decommissioning Strategy, Attachment to the Decree of the Government of RA*, Yerevan: Ministry of Energy of the RA.

Government of Armenia (2007b) *National Program on Energy Saving and Renewable Energy of Republic of Armenia*, Yerevan: Ministry of Energy and Natural Resources of the Republic of Armenia.

Government of Armenia (2010) *Concept for the Policy of the State Regulation of Migration in the Republic of Armenia, Protocol Decision N.51, approved on 30.12.2010*, Yerevan: Government of Armenia.

Government of Armenia (2011) *Decision on Approving the 2012–2016 Action Plan for Implementation of the Concept for the Policy of State Regulation of Migration in the Republic of Armenia, N 1593-N, adopted on 10.11.2011*, Yerevan: EU Advisory Group.

Government of Armenia (2012) *Draft Law of the Republic of Armenia on the Protection of Personal Data*, Florence: Consortium for Applied Research on International Migration.

Government of Georgia (2008a) *Overview of the Georgian Electricity Sector*, Tbilisi: Ministry of Energy of the Republic of Georgia.

Government of Georgia (2008b) *State Program 'Renewable Energy 2008' about Approval of the Rule to Enable the Construction of Renewable Energy Sources in Georgia, government decree no. 107, 18 April*, Tbilisi: Ministry of Energy of the Republic of Georgia.

Government of Georgia (2010a) *Draft Law on Personal Data Protection*, Tbilisi: provided by IOM Georgia to the author.

Government of Georgia (2010b) *Mobility Partnership Report*, Tbilisi: provided by a government official to the author.

Government of Georgia (2010c) *State Commission on Migration Provision, Resolution No. 314, adopted on 13.10.2010*, Tbilisi: Government of Georgia.

Government of Moldova (2010) *EU-Republic of Moldova Visa Dialogue, Action Plan on Visa Liberalization, adopted on 16.12.2010*, Chişinău: Government of Moldova.

Government of the Russian Federation (2003) *The Summary of the Energy Strategy of Russia for the Period of up to 2020*, Moscow: Ministry of Energy of the Russian Federation.

Government of Tbilisi City (2011) *Sustainable Energy Action Plan City of Tbilisi for 2011–2020, Decision No. 07.10.237, adopted on 28.3.2011*, Brussels: Covenant of Mayors Office.

Government of Ukraine (2007) 'Ukraine believes CIS electric power energy market to be unprofitable, 30.05.2007', web portal of the Ukrainian Government, www.kmu.gov.ua/control/en/publish/article?art_id=80744921&cat_id=244315154.

Green Alternative (2015) 'Environmental protection, natural resources and energy', in *Two Years in Government: Georgian Dream's Performance Review*, Tbilisi: Transparency International Georgia, pp. 69–78.

Grigoryan, A. (2011a) *EU-Armenia: Visa Facilitation Possibilities, EU Frontiers Policy Paper No.4*, Budapest: Center for EU Enlargement Studies.

Grigoryan, M. (2011b) 'Armenia: Russian guest worker program highlights population drain', www.eurasianet.org/node/63157.

Hackenesch, C. (2013) 'Aid donor meets strategic partner? The European Union's and China's relations with Ethiopia', *Journal of Current Chinese Affairs* 42(1): 7–36.

Hagemann, C. (2013) 'External governance on the terms of the partner? The EU, Russia and the Republic of Moldova in the European Neighbourhood Policy', *Journal of European Integration* 35(7): 767–783.

Hale, H.E. (2006) 'Democracy or autocracy on the march? The colored revolutions as normal dynamics of patronal presidentialism', *Communist and Post-Communist Studies* 39: 305–329.

Hale, H.E. (2015) *Patronal Politics: Eurasian Regime Dynamics in Comparative Perspective*, Cambridge: Cambridge University Press.

Hanf, T. and Nodia, G. (2000) *Georgia Lurching to Democracy: From Agnostic Tolerance to Pious Jacobinism – Societal Change and People's Reactions*, Baden-Baden: Nomos.

Hardabkhadze, V. and Kvernadze, L. (2006) 'Georgia', in J. McNamee (ed.) *Final Report: Monitoring of Russia and Ukraine (priority 1) and Armenia, Azerbaijan, Belarus, Georgia, Kazakhstan and Moldova (priority 2): Telecommunications and the Information Society*, Brussels: European Commission.

Hayrumyan, N. (2011) 'Elections 2012: Opposition leader says "dead souls" are main guarantee of this government's existence', www.armenianow.com/news/politics/32788/armenia_ections2012_electoral_code.

Hayrumyan, N. (2013) 'Armenian leadership meets little opposition over customs union decision despite opinions about "shameful decision"', armenianow.com/commentary/analysis/48309/armenia_eu_customs_union_russia.

Hedenskog, J. and Larsson, R. (2007) *Russian Leverage on the CIS and the Baltic States*, Stockholm: Swedish Defence Research Agency.

Henderson, J. and Mitrova, T. (2015) *The Political and Commercial Dynamics of Russia's Gas Export Strategy*, Oxford: The Oxford Institute for Energy Studies.

The Heritage Foundation (2015) *2015 Index of Economic Freedom*, Washington, DC: The Heritage Foundation, www.heritage.org/index/explore?view=by-region-country-year.

Hernandez i Sagrera, R. (2010) 'The EU-Russia readmission-visa facilitation nexus: An exportable migration model for Eastern Europe?', *European Security* 19(4): 569–584.

Hoffmann, C. et al. (2014) 'Summit of failure: How the EU lost Russia over Ukraine', *Spiegel Online*, www.spiegel.de/international/europe/war-in-ukraine-a-result-of-misunderstandings-between-europe-and-russia-a-1004706-2.html.

Hofmann, T. (2009) 'From irredenta to independence and back: Armenia and Nagorno-Karabakh 1986–1997', in E. Jahn (ed.) *Nationalism in Late and Post-Communist Europe – Volume 2: Nationalism in the Nation States*, Baden-Baden: Nomos, pp. 267–289.

Holtved, O. (2011) *Biometrics in Elections – Georgia: De-duplication or Voter Register and Verification of Voter Identity Using Biometrics*, Tbilisi: USAID/ IFES.

Holzinger, K., Jörgens, H. and Knill, C. (2007) 'Transfer, Diffusion und Konvergenz: Konzepte und Kausalmechanismen', in K. Holzinger, H. Jörgens and C. Knill (eds) *Transfer, Diffusion und Konvergenz von Politiken*, Wiesbaden: VS Verlag, pp. 11–35.

References

Holzinger, K. and Knill, C. (2007) 'Ursachen und Bedingungen internationaler Politikkonvergenz', in C. Knill, K. Holzinger and H. Jörgens (eds) *Transfer, Diffusion und Konvergenz von Politiken*, Wiesbaden: VS Verlag, pp. 85–106.

Hovhannisian, K. (2011) *Visa Liberalization Baseline Study: Armenia*, Yerevan: PASOS, Open Society Foundations.

Human Dynamics (2012) 'Capacity building in support of rule of law in Georgia', www.humandynamics.org, www.humandynamics.org/reference/capacity-building-support-rule-law-georgia.

Hunter Christie, E., Lussay, S. and Wolczuk, K. (2012) *The EU and its Eastern Partners: Energy needs and future prospects*, Brussels: European Parliament.

IAEA (2011) 'Armenia, 2011, country nuclear power profiles', www.pub.iaea.org/MTCD/Publications/PDF/CNPP2011_CD/countryprofiles/Armenia/Armenia2011.htm.

ICHD (2012) *Final Narrative Report (2007–2009)*, Yerevan: provided by ICHD to the author.

ICHD (2013) 'Support to migration management policies and institutions', www.ichd.org/?laid=1&com=module&module=static&id=245.

ICMPD (2005) *Overview of the Migration Systems in the CIS Countries*, Vienna: International Centre for Migration Policy Development.

ICMPD (2012) 'Budapest process', www.icmpd.org/Budapest-Process.1528.0.html.

IFC (2010) *Energy Efficiency: A New Resource for Sustainable Growth*, Washington, DC: International Finance Corporation.

ILO (2008) *Migrant Remittances to Armenia*, Yerevan: ILO.

ILO (2009) 'Gevorg Petrosyan appointed as labour and social affairs minister of Armenia', www.ilo.org/public/english/region/eurpro/moscow/news/2009/0512_2.htm.

IMF (2012) *Direction of Trade Statistics*, Washington, DC: IMF.

INOGATE (2011a) 'Armenia – energy sector review: Renewable energy', *Energy Portal*, www.inogate.org/index.php?option=com_inogate&view=countrysector&id=1&Itemid=63&lang=en.

INOGATE (2011b) 'Partner countries – Georgia: Energy sector review', *Energy Portal*, www.inogate.org/index.php?option=com_inogate&view=countrysector&id=19&Itemid=63&lang=en.

INOGATE (2012) 'Georgia – energy sector review: Renewable energy and energy efficiency', *Energy Portal*, www.inogate.org/index.php?option=com_inogate&view=countrysector&id=19&Itemid=63&lang=en.

International Crisis Group (2007) *Georgia: Sliding Towards Authoritarianism, Europe Report No.189*, Brussels: International Crisis Group.

International Energy Agency and International Renewable Energy Agency (2015) 'IEA/IRENA joint policies and measures database', www.iea.org/policiesandmeasures/renewableenergy/?country=ARMENIA.

IOM (2008) *Review of Migration Management in Georgia – Assessment Mission Report*, Tbilisi: IOM.

IOM (2010a) 'IOM hands over migrant resource centre to Armenian government authorities', www.iom.int/jahia/Jahia/media/press-briefing-notes/pbnEU/cache/offonce/lang/en?entryId=28505.

IOM (2010b) 'IOM supports government implementation of biometric identity and travel documents in Armenia', www.iom.int/jahia/Jahia/media/press-briefing-notes/pbnEU/cache/offonce?entryId=28103.

IOM (2012) *Readmission to Georgia: Annual Newsletter*, Tbilisi: IOM.

References

IOM, UNHCR, OSCE and ODIHR (2000) *Assessment Report of the Conference Process 1996–2000*, Geneva: IOM.
Iskandaryan, A. (2008) 'Der Südkaukasus', in W. Schneider-Deters, P.W. Schulze and H. Timmermann (eds) *Die Europäische Union, Russland und Eurasien – Die Rückkehr der Geopolitik*, Berlin: Berliner Wissenschaftsverlag, pp. 519–568.
Iskandaryan, A. (2011a) 'Armenia-Russia relations: Geography matters', in A. Hug (ed.) *Spotlight on Armenia*, London: Foreign Policy Centre, pp. 54–57.
Iskandaryan, A. (2011b) *Nations in Transit: Country Report Armenia*, Washington, DC: Freedom House.
Iskandaryan, A. (2013) *Nations in Transit 2013: Armenia*, Washington, DC: Freedom House.
Iskandaryan, A. (2014) *Nations in Transit 2014: Armenia*, Washington, DC: Freedom House.
Ivakhnyuk, I. (2009) *Russian Migration Policy and its Impact on Human Development*, Hum Dev Research Paper No.14, New York: UNDP.
Jacoby, W. (2006) 'Inspiration, coalition, and substitution: External influences on postcommunist transformations', *World Politics* 58(04): 623–651.
Jacquot, S. and Woll, C. (2003) 'Usage of European integration – Europeanisation from a sociological perspective', *European Integration Online Papers* 7(12): 1–18.
Jahn, D. and Müller-Rommel, F. (2010) 'Political institutions and policy performance: A comparative analysis of Central and Eastern Europe', *Journal of Public Policy* 30(1): 23–44.
Jamestown Foundation (1998) 'Yerkrapah turns into political party', *Eurasia Daily Monitor*, www.jamestown.org/single/?no_cache=1&tx_ttnews[tt_news]=16730&tx_ ttnews[backPid]=212.
Jawad, P. (2007) 'The European Union as an external democracy promoter in the South Caucasus', in M. Knodt and A. Jünemann (eds) *Externe Demokratieförderung durch die Europäische Union*, Baden-Baden: Nomos, pp. 269–292.
Jervalidze, L. (2006) *Georgia: Russian Foreign Energy Policy and Implications for Georgia's Energy Security*, London: GMB Publishing Ltd.
Jgamadze, N. and Markarashvili, M. (2009) *Testing New Channels and Products to Maximize the Development Impact of Remittances for the Rural Poor in Georgia: Assessment of Banking Institutions*, Tbilisi: International Organization for Migration.
Kabeleova, H., Mazmanyan, A. and Yeremyan, A. (2007) *Assessment of the Migration Legislation in the Republic of Armenia*, Yerevan: OSCE.
Katznelson, I. and Weingast, B.R. (2005) 'Intersections between historical and rational choice institutionalism', in I. Katznelson and B.R. Weingast (eds) *Preferences and Situations*, New York: Russell Sage Foundation, pp. 1–26.
Kekic, L. (2006) *The Economist Intelligence Unit's Index of Democracy*, London: Economist Intelligence Unit.
Kelley, J. (2006) 'New wine in old wineskins: Promoting political reforms through the New European Neighbourhood Policy', *Journal of Common Market Studies* 44(1): 29–55.
Keohane, R.O. and Nye, J.S. (1977) *Power and Interdependence: World Politics in Transition*, Boston, MA and Toronto: Little, Brown and Company.
Keohane, R.O. and Nye, J.S. (1987) 'Power and interdependence revisited', *International Organization* 41(04): 725–753.
Ketting, J. (2008) 'The end of the Russian electricity sector', *European Energy Review* (3): 94–97.

Khachatrian, H. (2002) 'Yerkrapah: "Lightning rod" or political force in postwar Armenia?', www.eurasianet.org/departments/insight/articles/eav051302a.shtml.

Khasson, V., Vasilyan, S. and Vos, H. (2008) '"Everybody needs good neighbours": The EU and its neighbourhood', in J. Orbie (ed.) *Europe's Global Role: External Policies of the European Union*, Burlington, VT: Ashgate, pp. 217–238.

Khojoyan, S. (2011) 'Identity reform: Parliament starts discussions on introducing ePassport in Armenia', www.armenianow.com/news/31771/biometric_passport_armenia.

Khutsidze, N. (2007) 'Georgia brings Russia to European court over deportations', www.civil.ge/eng/article.php?id=1486812.

King, G., Keohane, R.O. and Verba, S. (1994) *Designing Social Inquiry*, Princeton, NJ: Princeton University Press.

King, N. (1994) 'The qualitative research interview', in C. Cassell and G. Symon (eds) *Qualitative Methods in Organizational Research: A Practical Guide*, London: SAGE, pp. 14–36.

Kipiani, M. (2011) 'Konfliktporträts – Georgien, Bundeszentrale für politische Bildung: Innerstaatliche Konflikte', www.bpb.de/themen/7C6KIQ,0,0,Georgien.html.

Kirtzkhalia, N. (2010) 'Georgia will issue biometric passports today', *Trend*, en.trend.az/regions/scaucasus/georgia/1669937.html.

Knill, C. and Lenschow, A. (1998) 'Change as "appropriate adaptation": Administrative adjustment to European environmental policy in Britain and Germany', *European Integration Online Papers* 2(1): 1–22.

Knott, E. (2013) 'Moldova is at the crossroads between Russia and the EU ahead of the Eastern Partnership summit in Vilnius', EUROPP Blog, London: London School of Economics, bit.ly/17E90uX.

Kocharyan, R. (2003) 'Robert Kocharian – election campaign program', robertkocharian.am, forum.hyeclub.com/showthread.php/67-ROBERT-KOCHARIAN-Election-Campaign-Program.

Kocharyan, R. (2008) *Concept Paper for the Republic of Armenia Migration System and Introduction of System of Electronic Passport and Identification Cards Containing Biometric Characteristics in the Republic of Armenia, NK-53-A, adopted on 15.3.2008*, Yerevan: President of the Republic of Armenia.

Kononćzuk, W. (2013) 'Ukraine withdraws from signing the Association Agreement in Vilnius: The motives and implications', OSW Analyses, Warsaw: Center for Eastern Studies.

Kononćzuk, W. (2015) 'Oligarchs after the maidan: The old system in a "new" Ukraine', OSW Commentary No. 162, Warsaw: Centre for Eastern Studies.

Konoplyanik, A. (2009) 'A common Russia-EU energy space: The new EU-Russia partnership agreement, acquis communautaire and the energy charter', *Journal of Energy & Natural Resources Law* 27(2): 258–291.

Korneev, O. (2008) *Primus Inter Pares? The EU's Justice and Home Affairs Policies in its Eastern European Neighborhood*, Baillet Latour Working Papers No. 32, Leuven: Chair InBev – Baillet Latour.

Korneev, O. (2011) 'Pushing the burden to the East: Russia's involvement in the EU migration management strategy and its consequences for Central Asia', in EUSA Conference, 3–5 March, Boston.

Kościński, P. and Vorobiov, I. (2013) 'Do oligarchs in Ukraine gain or lose with an EU association agreement?', *PISM Bulletin* 86(536): 1–2.

Kostanyan, H. (2015) *The Rocky Road to an EU-Armenia Agreement: From U-turn to Detour*, CEPS Commentary, Brussels: Centre for European Policy Studies.

Kramer, A.E. (2011) 'Riot police break up opposition protest in Georgia', *The New York Times*, www.nytimes.com/2011/05/27/world/europe/27georgia.html.
Krastev, I. and Leonard, M. (2010) *The Spectre of a Multipolar Europe*, London: European Council on Foreign Relations.
Kubicek, P. (1999) 'Russian foreign policy and the West', *Political Science Quarterly* 114(4): 547–568.
Kucera, J. (2011) 'Central Asia, Caucasus: "Putinization" blamed for hampering democratization', www.eurasianet.org/node/62717.
Kucera, J. (2013) 'In Baku, Putin brings gunboats along with diplomacy', www.eurasianet.org/node/67392.
Kuntz, P. (2011) *Unlikely Revolutions: Popular Uprising Against Electoral Authoritarian Rule in Serbia, Georgia and Ukraine*, PhD thesis, Erlangen, Nürnberg: Friedrich-Alexander Universität.
Lambach, D. and Göbel, C. (2010) 'Die Responsivität autoritärer Regime', in H. Albrecht and R. Frankenberger (eds) *Autoritarismus Reloaded: Neuere Ansätze und Erkenntnisse der Autokratieforschung*, Baden-Baden: Nomos, pp. 79–92.
Lampietti, J.A., Banerjee, S.G. and Branczik, A. (2007a) 'Electricity sector reforms and the poor in Europe and Central Asia', *Beyond Transition* (7–9): 19–20.
Lampietti, J.A., Banerjee, S.G. and Branczik, A. (2007b) *People and Power: Electricity Sector Reforms and the Poor in Europe and Central Asia*, Washington, DC: The World Bank.
Langbein, J. (2011) *Organizing Regulatory Convergence Outside the EU: Setting Policy-specific Conditionality and Building Domestic Capacities*, KFG Working Paper No. 33, Berlin: Freie Universität Berlin.
Langbein, J. (2014) 'Regeltransfer ohne Elitenkonsens? Vorschläge zur Umsetzung des Assoziierungsabkommens mit der Ukraine', *ukraine-analysen* (137): 2–3.
Langbein, J. (2015) *Transnationalization and Regulatory Change in the EU's Eastern Neighbourhood*, London: Routledge.
Langbein, J. and Wolczuk, K. (2012) 'Convergence without membership? The impact of the European Union in the neighbourhood: Evidence from Ukraine', *Journal of European Public Policy* 19(6): 863–881.
Larionova, M., Rakhmangulov, M. and Berenson, M.P. (2014) *The Russian Federation's International Development Assistance Programme: A State of the Debate Report*, Brighton: Institute of Development Studies.
Lavenex, S. (2004) 'EU external governance in "wider Europe"', *Journal of European Public Policy* 11(4): 680–700.
Lavenex, S. (2008) 'A governance perspective on the European neighbourhood policy: Integration beyond conditionality?', *Journal of European Public Policy* 15(6): 938–955.
Lavenex, S. and Schimmelfennig, F. (2009) 'EU rules beyond EU borders: Theorizing external governance in European politics', *Journal of European Public Policy* 16(6): 791–812.
Lavenex, S. and Wichmann, N. (2009) 'The external governance of EU internal security', *Journal of European Integration* 31(1): 83–102.
Lehne, S. (2014) *Time to Reset the European Neighborhood Policy*, Washington, DC: Carnegie Endowment for International Peace.
Leonard, M. and Popescu, N. (2007) *A Power Audit of EU-Russia Relations*, ECFR Policy Paper No. 02/11, Berlin: European Council on Foreign Relations.
Levitsky, S. and Way, L.A. (2006) 'Linkage versus leverage: Rethinking the international dimension of regime change', *Comparative Politics* 38(4): 379–400.

Libman, A. and Vinokurov, E. (2012) 'Eurasian economic union: Why now? Will it work? Is it enough?', *The Whitehead Journal of Diplomacy and International Relations* 13(2): 29–44.
Lobjakas, A. (2006) 'Armenia: Making the best of a difficult neighborhood', *Radio Free Europe/Radio Liberty*, fb.rferl.org/articleprintview/1072914.html.
Lynch, D. (2006) *Why Georgia Matters*, Chaillot Paper No. 86, Paris: Institute for Security Studies.
Manaseryan, T. (2004) *Diaspora: The Comparative Advantage for Armenia*, Working Paper No. 4, Yerevan: Armenian International Policy Research Group.
Manutscharjan, A. (1999) 'Das Regierungs- und Parteiensystem Armeniens', in G. Mangott (ed.) *Brennpunkt Südkaukasus: Aufbruch trotz Krieg, Vertreibung und Willkürherrschaft?*, Vienna: Braumüller, pp. 19–60.
Marat, E. and Murzakulova, A. (2007) 'The CSTO seeks to build new sub-structures', CACI Analyst, www.cacianalyst.org/newsite/newsite/?q=node/4708.
March, J.G. and Olsen, J.P. (1998) 'The institutional dynamics of international political orders', *International Organization* 52(4): 943–969.
Marcus, S. (2010) 'Georgia shifts leaders' powers, but some see a political ploy', *The New York Times*, www.nytimes.com/2010/10/16/world/europe/16georgia.html.
Margaryan, A. (2002) 'Speech of the RoA Prime Minister Andranik Margaryan in the round table on energy issues during the World Summit on Sustainable Development in Johannesburg on September 3, 2002', www.gov.am/enversion/premier_2/primer_home_A.Margaryan.htm?mat=225.
Marsh, D. and Sharman, J.C. (2009) 'Policy diffusion and policy transfer', *Policy Studies* 30(3): 269–288.
Martens, K. and Brüggemann, M. (2006) *Kein Experte ist wie der Andere: Vom Umgang mit Missionaren und Geschichtenerzählern*, TranState Working Papers No. 39, Bremen: Universität Bremen.
Martirosian, A. (2011) 'Armenia's visa facilitation talks with EU delayed', *Radio Free Europe/Radio Liberty Armenia*, www.armenialiberty.org/articleprintview/24180302.html.
Matusiak, M. (2014) *Georgia – Between a Dream and Reality*, OSW Commentary No. 133, Warsaw: Centre for Eastern Studies.
Medvedev, D.A. (2008) *The Foreign Policy Concept of the Russian Federation, approved by the President of the Russian Federation on 12.7.2008*, Brussels: Permanent Mission of the Russian Federation to the European Union.
Melnykovska, I. (2014) 'Die Oligarchen und die Politik in Kriegs- und Krisenzeiten. Wie kann das eherne Gesetz der Oligarchie in der Ukraine gebrochen werden?', *ukraine-analysen* (143): 18–22.
Melnykovska, I., Plamper, H. and Schweickert, R. (2012) 'Do Russia and China promote autocracy in Central Asia?', *Asia Europe Journal* 10(1): 75–89.
Menabde, G. (2014) 'Is Russia resuming a trade war against Georgia?', *Eurasia Daily Monitor* 11(144).
The Messenger (2011) 'Deadlock in the negotiations', *The Messenger Online*, www.messenger.com.ge/issues/2333_april_7_2011/2333_edit.html.
Michaletos, I. (2009) 'Organized crime in the Caucasus', *International Analyst Network*, www.analyst-network.com/article.php?art_id=3237.
Milov, V., Coburn, L.L. and Danchenko, I. (2006) 'Russia's energy policy, 1992–2005', *Eurasian Geography and Economics* 47(3): 285–313.

Minassian, G. (2008) *Armenia, a Russian Outpost in the Caucasus?*, Russie.Nei.Visions No. 27, Paris: Ifri.
Ministry of Foreign Affairs of the Republic of Armenia (2009a) 'Foreign minister of Armenia delivered speech at the 35th session of the UNESCO's General Conference', www.mfa.am/en/press-releases/item/2009/10/08/france/.
Ministry of Foreign Affairs of the Republic of Armenia (2009b) 'The ambassador of Netherlands presents copies of his credentials to Deputy Foreign Minister of Armenia Karine Kazinian', www.mfa.am/en/press-releases/item/2009/11/03/netherlands/.
Ministry of Foreign Affairs of the Republic of Armenia (2010a) 'A preparatory meeting before the launch of the association agreement between Minister of Foreign Affairs Edward Nalbandian and EU officials', www.mfa.am/en/press-releases/item/2010/07/06/raul/.
Ministry of Foreign Affairs of the Republic of Armenia (2010b) 'Negotiations on the association agreement started between the Republic of Armenia and the European Union', www.mfa.am/en/press-releases/item/2010/07/19/association_negotiations/.
Ministry of Foreign Affairs of the Republic of Armenia (2010c) 'The Deputy Foreign Minister Karine Kazinian participates at the informal meeting of the EU and Eastern partnership countries', www.mfa.am/en/press-releases/item/2010/05/24/kazinyan/.
Ministry of Foreign Affairs of the Republic of Armenia (2010d) 'The interview of Edward Nalbandian, foreign affairs minister of Armenia, to the program "realpolitik" of the public TV', www.mfa.am/en/interviews/item/2010/12/30/realpolitic1/.
Ministry of Foreign Affairs of the Republic of Armenia (2011) 'Bilateral relations', www.mfa.am/en/country-by-country/.
Ministry of Justice of Georgia (2010) 'First session of state commission on migration issues was held at Ministry of Justice of Georgia', justice.gov.ge/index.php?lang_id=ENG&sec_id=146&info_id=2918.
Ministry of Justice of Georgia (2011) 'State commission on migration issues holds its regular session', 19 May, www.justice.gov.ge/index.php?lang_id=ENG&sec_id=23&info_id=3406.
Ministry of Justice of Georgia (2012a) 'Ministry's history: Gia Kavtaradze', www.justice.gov.ge/index.php?sec_id=185&lang_id=ENG.
Ministry of Justice of Georgia (2012b) 'Personal data protection', www.justice.gov.ge/index.php?lang_id=ENG&sec_id=675.
Minzarari, D. (2013) 'EU-Moldova association agreement may yield huge political windfall for Filat's party', *Eurasia Daily Monitor* 10(58).
Molodikova, I. (2010) 'Contradictions of disintegration: Two decades of CIS countries' migration system', in M. Tukhashvili and I. Molodikova (eds) *Migration*, Vol.4, Tbilisi: Tbilisi State University, pp. 7–35.
Monaghan, A. (2006) *Russia-EU Relations: An Emerging Energy Security Dilemma*, Washington, DC: Carnegie Endowment for International Peace.
The Moscow Times (2015) 'Georgian defense minister calls for greater EU integration as Russia denies territory violations', www.themoscowtimes.com/news/article/georgian-defense-minister-calls-for-greater-eu-integration-as-russia-denies-territory-violations/526045.html.
Myers, S.L. (2006) 'Russian officials pledge more sanctions to cut off cash to Georgia', *The New York Times*, www.nytimes.com/2006/10/04/world/europe/04georgia.html?n=T…&_r=0.

National Assembly of Armenia (2011) 'Parliamentary hearings in the national assembly', www.parliament.am/news.php?do=view&cat_id=2&day=31&month=10&year=2011&NewsID=4827&lang=eng.

National Assembly of Armenia (2012) 'Sittings of the RA NA standing committees were held', www.parliament.am/news.php?do=view&cat_id=2&day=03&month=02&year=2012&NewsID=4980&lang=eng.

Nichol, J. (2011) *Armenia, Azerbaijan, and Georgia: Political Developments and Implications for U.S. Interests*, Washington, DC: Congressional Research Service.

Noutcheva, G. (2009) 'Fake, partial and imposed compliance: The limits of the EU's normative power in the Western Balkans', *Journal of European Public Policy* 16(7): 1065–1084.

Nygren, B. (2008) *The Rebuilding of Greater Russia*, London and New York: Routledge.

Oliker, O., Crane, K., Schwartz, L.H. and Yusupov, C. (2009) *Russian Foreign Policy-Sources and Implications*, Santa Monica, Arlington, Pittsburgh: RAND Corporation.

Open Society Georgia Foundation (2011) *Implementation of EU-Georgia Action Plan: Progress Report on Georgia 2011*, Tbilisi: Open Society Georgia Foundation.

Orttung, R.W. and Overland, I. (2011) 'A limited toolbox: Explaining the constraints on Russia's foreign energy policy', *Journal of Eurasian Studies* 2: 74–85.

OSCE (2010) *OSCE Office in Yerevan – Newsletter No. 2*, Yerevan: OSCE.

OSCE (2011) *OSCE Annual Security Review Conference, Statement by S. Mkrtchian, Director Arms Control and International Security Department, Ministry of Foreign Affairs of the Republic of Armenia, PC.DEL/726/11, published on 8.07.2011*, Vienna: OSCE.

OSCE and ODIHR (2004) *Georgia Parliamentary Elections, 2 November 2003, OSCE/ODIHR Election Observation Mission Report, Part 1*, Warsaw: OSCE/ODIHR.

OSCE and ODIHR (2006) *Georgia: Municipal Elections 5 October 2006, OSCE/ODIHR Limited Election Observation Mission Final Report*, Warsaw: OSCE.

OSCE and ODIHR (2007) *Republic of Armenia Parliamentary Election 12 May 2007, OSCE/ODIHR Election Observation Mission Report, adopted on 10.09.2007*, Warsaw: OSCE.

OSCE and ODIHR (2008) *Georgia Parliamentary Elections 21 May 2008, OSCE/ODIHR Election Observation Mission Final Report, adopted on 9.09.2008*, Warsaw: OSCE.

OSCE and ODIHR (2012) *Republic of Armenia Parliamentary elections, 6 May 2012, OSCE/ODIHR Election Observation Mission Final Report*, Warsaw: OSCE/ODIHR.

PanArmenian.net (2005) 'Kocharian: I do not rule out opportunity of building new nuclear power plant in Armenia', www.panarmenian.net, www.panarmenian.net/eng/politics/news/12773/.

PanArmenian.net (2007) 'Euroatom allocated 200 mln euros for closing Metsamor NPP', www.panarmenian.net, www.panarmenian.net/eng/world/news/23381/.

PanArmenian.net (2010) 'Yerevan hosts sitting of EU-Armenia Justice, Freedom and Security Subcommittee', www.panarmenian.net, www.panarmenian.net/eng/politics/news/50987/.

PanArmenian.net (2011a) 'Armenia to cooperate on migration issues with Sweden, Lichtenstein from 2011', www.panarmenian.net, www.panarmenian.net/eng/society/news/59472/.

PanArmenian.net (2011b) 'Departures from Armenia exceed arrivals by 67000 in 1st halfyear of 2011', www.panarmenian.net, www.panarmenian.net/eng/news/74771/.

PanArmenian.net (2011c) 'PM explains growing migration by Armenian people's mobility', www.panarmenian.net, www.panarmenian.net/eng/news/74882/.
Panossian, R. (2005) 'Homeland-diaspora relations and identity differences', in E. Herzig and M. Kurkchiyan (eds) *The Armenians: Past and Present in the Making of National Identity*, London and New York: Routledge, pp. 229–243.
PAO Armenia (2007) 'TAIEX events for 2007', www.pao-armenia.am, www.pao-armenia.am/en/taiex_pline.
Papava, V. (2006) 'The political economy of Georgia's rose revolution', *East European Democratization* (Fall): 657–667.
Parliament of Georgia (2006) *Resolution of the Parliament of Georgia on 'Main Directions of State Policy in the Power Sector of Georgia'*, N3190-IS, 7 June, Tbilisi: Parliament of Georgia.
Parmentier, F. (2014) 'Moldova', in *The Geopolitics of Eurasian Economic Integration, LSE Ideas Report*, London: London School of Economics, pp. 46–53.
Pasoyan, A. (2005) *Alliance to Save Energy Armenia, Municipal Network for Energy Efficiency (MUNEE): Accomplishments*, Yerevan: USAID, MUNEE.
Pataraia, T. (2011) *Prospects for Visa Liberalization between the EU and Georgia: An Assessment of Georgia's Readiness, CIPDD Policy Brief*, Tbilisi: Caucasus Institute for Peace, Democracy and Development.
Paul, A. (2014) *Moldova – Heading into a Hot Autumn*, EPC Policy Brief, Brussels: European Policy Centre.
PEEREA (2005) *Armenia: Regular Review of Energy Efficiency Policies*, Brussels: Energy Charter Secretariat.
Perovic, J. (2005) 'From disengagement to active economic competition: Russia's return to the South Caucasus and Central Asia', *Demokratizatsiya* 13(1): 61–85.
Petriashvili, D. (2005) 'Georgia: No gas pipeline sale for now', www.eurasianet.org/departments/business/articles/eav030905.shtml.
Pollack, M.A. (2006) 'Rational choice and EU politics', in K.E. Jorgensen, M.A. Pollack and B. Rosamond (eds) *Handbook of European Union Politics*, London: Sage, pp. 31–56.
Pop, V. (2011) 'Georgia to EU: Don't neglect eastern neighbourhood', *EU Observer*, euobserver.com/892/32246.
Popescu, N. and Wilson, A. (2009) *The Limits of Enlargement-Lite: European and Russian Power in the Troubled Neighbourhood*, Policy Report, London: European Council on Foreign Relations.
Potemkina, O. (2010) 'EU-Russia cooperation on the common space of freedom, security and justice – a challenge or an opportunity?', *European Security* 19(4): 551–568.
Potts, A. (2011) 'Visa-free travel to Europe inches closer', *The Moscow News*, themoscownews.com/international/20110425/188609946.html.
Prange-Gstöhl, H. (2009) 'Enlarging the EU's internal energy market: Why would third countries accept EU rule export?', *Energy Policy* (37): 5296–5303.
President of Armenia (2001) *Energy Law of the Republic of Armenia*, 11 April, Budapest: Energy Regulators Regional Association.
President of Georgia (1997) *Georgian Law on Electricity and Natural Gas*, 27 June, Tbilisi: Electric System Commercial Operator Georgia (ESCO).
President of Georgia (2011) *Law of Georgia on Personal Data Protection, No. 5669-RS*, adopted on 28.12.2011, unofficial translation, Tbilisi: Government of Georgia.
Probert, D.E. (2009) *Roadmap for Real-time Armenia: e-Government, e-Commerce and e-Security*, Yerevan: USAID, CAPS.

Prodi, R. (2002) *A Wider Europe – A Proximity Policy as the Key to Stability, Speech Given at the Sixth ECSA-World Conference, 5–6 December, SPEECH/02/619*, Brussels: European Commission.

Provost, C. (2012) 'The rebirth of Russian foreign aid', *The Guardian*, www.guardian.co.uk/global-development/2011/may/25/russia-foreign-aid-report-influence-image.

Public Radio of Armenia (2008) 'Working consultations at RA President's Office', www.armradio.am/news/?part=off&id=12163; agbu.org/newsbulletin/2008-03-0314.pdf.

Puiu, V. (2015) 'Moldova: Examining the Russian media factor in protests', www.eurasianet.org/node/75046.

Putin, V. (2000a) *The Foreign Policy Concept of the Russian Federation, approved by the President of the Russian Federation on 28.06.2000*, Washington, DC: Federation of American Scientists.

Putin, V. (2000b) *The National Security Concept of the Russian Federation, Presidential Decree No.24, adopted on 10.01.2000*, Moscow: The Ministry of Foreign Affairs of the Russian Federation.

Radaelli, C.M. (2003) 'The Europeanization of public policy', in K. Featherstone and C.M. Radaelli (eds) *The Politics of Europeanization*, Oxford: Oxford University Press, pp. 27–57.

Radeke, J., Giucci, R. and Lupusor, A. (2013) *Moldova's Trade Policy: Strategy, DCFTA and Customs Union*, Policy Paper Series (PP/03/2013), Berlin and Chi: German Economic Team Moldova.

RAPID (1998) *EU Grants Assistance: Armenia an Exceptional Financial, IP/98/1160*, Brussels: European Union.

RAPID (2008) *Commission Recommends the Negotiation of Visa Facilitation and Readmission Agreements with Georgia, IP/08/1406*, Brussels: European Union.

RAPID (2010) *European Union Signs Visa Facilitation Agreement with Georgia, IP/10/737*, Brussels: European Union.

RAPID (2011) *EU Starts Negotiations on Caspian Pipeline to Bring Gas to Europe, IP/11/1023*, Brussels: European Commission.

REEEP (2012) *Policy DB Details: Armenia*, Vienna: Renewable Energy and Energy Efficiency Partnership (REEEP).

Reisner, O. (2009) 'Georgia and its new national movement', in E. Jahn (ed.) *Nationalism in Late and Post-Communist Europe – Volume 2: Nationalism in the Nation States*, Baden-Baden: Nomos, pp. 240–266.

Reisner, O. and Kvatchadze, L. (2005) *Studien zur Länderbezogenen Konfliktanalyse: Georgien*, Berlin: Friedrich-Ebert-Stiftung.

Republic of Armenia (2002) *World Summit on Sustainable Development, National Assessment Report, Johannesburg*, Yerevan: Lusabats Publishing House.

RFE/RL (2006) 'Armenian president defends deals with Gazprom', *Radio Free Europe/Radio Liberty*, fb.rferl.org/articleprintview/1067518.html.

RFE/RL (2010) 'Georgia's main gas pipeline up for grabs', *Radio Free Europe/Radio Liberty*, www.rferl.org/articleprintview/2095528.html.

RFE/RL (2011a) 'Armenian president signals new delay in nuclear plant closure', *Radio Free Europe/Radio Liberty*, www.rferl.org/articleprintview/24414196.html.

RFE/RL (2011b) 'EU hopes for resumption of Georgian election reform talks', *Radio Free Europe/Radio Liberty*, www.rferl.org/content/eu_hopes_resumption_georgian_election_reform_talks/4746282.html.

References

RFE/RL (2011c) 'Georgia hails "successful completion" of election law talks', *Radio Free Europe/Radio Liberty*, www.rferl.org/content/georgia_hails_successful_completion_of_election_law_talks/24253417.html.

RFE/RL (2012a) 'Armenia, Russia plan new military deal', *Radio Free Europe/Radio Liberty*, www.armenialiberty.org/content/article/24479171.html.

RFE/RL (2012b) 'Georgian parliament ignores election-law recommendations', *Radio Free Europe/Radio Liberty*, www.rferl.org/content/georgia_ignores_election-law_suggestions/24441200.html.

RFE/RL (2013a) 'Armenia to join Russian-led customs union', *Radio Free Europe/Radio Liberty*, www.rferl.org/content/armenia-customs-union/25094560.html.

RFE/RL (2013b) 'Georgian lawmakers adopt resolution reaffirming Western course', *Radio Free Europe/Radio Liberty*, www.rferl.org/articleprintview/24923035.html.

RFE/RL (2013c) 'Georgian PM criticizes Saakashvili, pledges to restore Russian relations', *Radio Free Europe/Radio Liberty*, www.rferl.org/articleprintview/24893497.html.

RFE/RL (2013d) 'Georgian PM meets Rasmussen, discusses NATO and Russia', *Radio Free Europe/Radio Liberty*, www.rferl.org/articleprintview/25028737.html.

RFE/RL (2013e) 'Interview: Georgian PM still aiming for EU, but doesn't rule out Eurasian union', *Radio Free Europe/Radio Liberty*, www.rferl.org/articleprintview/25100642.html.

RFE/RL (2013f) 'Officials say Moscow could ease visa rules for Georgians', *Radio Free Europe/Radio Liberty*, www.rferl.org/articleprintview/24917108.html.

RFE/RL (2013g) 'Russian wine inspectors may withdraw over Saakashvili remarks', *Radio Free Europe/Radio Liberty*, www.rferl.org/articleprintview/24914219.html.

RFE/RL (2013h) 'Tbilisi denounces talks between Putin, breakaway Abkhaz leader', *Radio Free Europe/Radio Liberty*, www.rferl.org/articleprintview/24926600.html.

RFE/RL (2014a) 'Georgian PM: No progress normalizing relations with Moscow', *Radio Free Europe/Radio Liberty*, www.rferl.org/articleprintview/26641744.html.

RFE/RL (2014b) 'Russia hits back at Georgia over trade agreement with European Union', *Radio Free Europe/Radio Liberty*, www.rferl.org/articleprintview/25478788.html.

RIA Novosti (2007) 'CIS council to consider common electricity market concept', www.en.rian.ru, en.rian.ru/business/20071012/83607550.html.

RIA Novosti (2011) 'Russia eyes legal opportunities to challenge EU's third energy package', 18 November, www.en.rian.ru, en.rian.ru/world/20111118/168813105.html.

Rinnert, D. (2013) *The Republic of Moldova in the Eastern Partnership: From 'Poster Child' to 'Problem Child'*, Berlin: Friedrich-Ebert-Stiftung.

Rogowski, R. (1999) 'Institutions as constraints', in D.A. Lake and R. Powell (eds) *Strategic Choice and International Relations*, Princeton, NJ: Princeton University Press, pp. 115–136.

Roig, A. (2007) 'EC readmission agreements: A re-evaluation of the political impasse', *European Journal of Migration and Law* 9(3): 363–387.

Rose, R. (1991) 'What is lesson-drawing?', *Journal of Public Policy* 11(1): 3–30.

Saakashvili, M. (2005) *President Saakashvili Calls Emergency Government Meeting on Energy Crisis in Georgia, Speech given on 25.02.2005*, Tbilisi: The Administration of the President of Georgia.

Saakashvili, M. (2006a) *Emergency Statement by President Saakashvili, Speech given on 22.01.2006*, Tbilisi: Administration of the President of Georgia.

Saakashvili, M. (2006b) *President Saakashvili's Comments on Pipeline Explosion to BBC News, Speech given 22.01.2006*, Tbilisi: Administration of the President of Georgia.

Saakashvili, M. (2006c) *President Saakashvili Holds Energy Commission Meeting, speech given on 25.04.2006*, Tbilisi: Administration of the President of Georgia.

Saakashvili, M. (2006d) *President Saakashvili Seeks to Diversify Energy Sources, Speech given on 19.01.2006*, Tbilisi: Administration of the President of Georgia.

Saakashvili, M. (2006e) *Public Appearance of the President of Georgia Michael Saakashvili at the Presentation of the Baku – Tbilisi – Ceykhan Oil Pipeline, 13.07.2006*, Tbilisi: Administration of the President of Georgia.

Saakashvili, M. (2006f) 'The path to energy security', *The Washington Post*, www.washingtonpost.com/wp-dyn/content/article/2006/01/08/AR2006010801167_pf.html.

Saakashvili, M. (2010) *Mikheil Saakashvili met the Students and Professors of Tbilisi Free University, Speech given on 11.08.2010*, Tbilisi: The Administration of the President of Georgia.

Saghabalian, A. (2008) 'Baghdasarian returns to Armenian government', www.armtown.com/news/en/rfe/20080229/200802292/.

Sakwa, R. (2010) 'Senseless dreams and small steps: The CIS and CSTO between integration and cooperation', in M.R. Freire and R.E. Kanet (eds) *Key Players and Regional Dynamics in Eurasia: The Return of the Great Game*, Basingstoke: Palgrave Macmillan, pp. 195–213.

Sakwa, R. and Webber, M. (1999) 'The Commonwealth of Independent States, 1991–1998: Stagnation and survival', *Europe-Asia Studies* 51(3): 379–415.

Samadashvili, S. (2007) 'EU visa policy endangers Georgia peace effort', *EU Observer*, euobserver.com/9/24255.

Samokhvalov, V. (2015) 'Ukraine between Russia and the European Union: Triangle revisited', *Europe-Asia Studies* 67(9): 1371–1393.

Sandukhchyan, D. (2006) 'Armenia', in J. McNamee (ed.) *Final Report: Monitoring of Russia and Ukraine (priority 1) and Armenia, Azerbaijan, Belarus, Georgia, Kazakhstan and Moldova (priority 2): Telecommunications and the Information Society*, Brussels: European Commission, pp. 1–38.

Sandukhchyan, D. and Misnikov, Y. (2004) *Evaluation Report of UNDP Armenia ICT-for-Development Programme*, Yerevan, Bratislava: UNDP.

Sargsyan, G., Balabanyan, A. and Hankinson, D. (2006) *From Crisis to Stability in the Armenian Power Sector: Lessons Learned from Armenia's Reform Experience*, World Bank Working Paper No. 74, Washington, DC: World Bank.

Sasse, G. (2008) 'The European Neighbourhood Policy: Conditionality revisited for the EU's eastern neighbours', *Europe-Asia Studies* 60(2): 295–316.

Sasse, G. (2013) 'Linkages and the promotion of democracy: The EU's eastern neighbourhood', *Democratization* 20(4): 553–591.

Savvidis, T. (2011) 'Comparing out-migration from Armenia and Georgia', in N. Genov and T. Savvidis (eds) *Transboundary Migration in the Post-Soviet Space: Three Comparative Case Studies*, Frankfurt am Main: Peter Lang, pp. 175–242.

Scharpf, F.W. (2000) 'Institutions in comparative policy research', *Comparative Political Studies* 33(6/7): 762–790.

Schimmelfennig, F. (2007) 'European regional organizations, political conditionality, and democratic transformation in Eastern Europe', *East European Politics & Societies* 21(1): 126–141.

Schimmelfennig, F. (2012) 'Europeanization beyond Europe', *Living Reviews in European Governance* 7(1): 1–31.
Schimmelfennig, F., Engert, S. and Knobel, H. (2003) 'Costs, commitment and compliance: The impact of EU democratic conditionality on Latvia, Slovakia and Turkey', *Journal of Common Market Studies* 41(3): 495–518.
Schimmelfennig, F. and Scholtz, H. (2010) 'Legacies and leverage: EU political conditionality and democracy promotion in historical perspective', *Europe-Asia Studies* 62(3): 443–460.
Schimmelfennig, F. and Sedelmeier, U. (2004) 'Governance by conditionality: EU rule transfer to the candidate countries of Central and Eastern Europe', *Journal of European Public Policy* 11(4): 661–679.
Schimmelfennig, F. and Sedelmeier, U. (2005a) 'Introduction: Conceptualising the Europeanization of Central and Eastern Europe', in F. Schimmelfennig and U. Sedelmeier (eds) *The Europeanization of Central and Eastern Europe*, Ithacam NY and London: Cornell University Press, pp. 1–28.
Schimmelfennig, F. and Sedelmeier, U. (Eds) (2005b) *The Europeanization of Central and Eastern Europe*, Ithaca, NY and London: Cornell University Press.
Schmidtke, O. and Chira-Pascanut, C. (2011) 'Contested neighbourhood: Toward the "Europeanization" of Moldova?', *Comparative European Politics* 9(4–5): 467–485.
Schulze, P.W. (2008) 'Die Russische Föderation', in W. Schneider-Deters, P.W. Schulze and H. Timmermann (eds) *Die Europäische Union, Russland und Eurasien – Die Rückkehr der Geopolitik*, Berlin: Berliner Wissenschaftsverlag, pp. 57–238.
Secrieru, S. (2006) *Russia's Foreign Policy Under Putin: 'CIS Project' Renewed*, UNISCI Discussion Paper No. 10, Bucharest: UNISCI.
Secrieru, S. (2014) 'Can Moldova stay on the road to Europe?', ECFR Policy Memo, Brussels: European Council of Foreign Relations.
Sedelmeier, U. (2011) 'Europeanisation in new member and candidate states', *Living Reviews in European Governance* 6(1).
Sepashvili, G. (2003) 'Georgia-Gazprom deal signed', www.civil.ge/eng/_print.php?id=4642.
Shain, Y. (2007) *Kinship and Diasporas in International Affairs*, Ann Arbor: University of Michigan Press.
Shoghikian, H. (2012) 'Armenian nuclear plant operations officially extended', *Radio Free Europe/Radio Liberty Armenia*, www.armenialiberty.org/articleprintview/24554019.html.
Shoghikian, H. (2013) *Russia Widens Military Presence in Armenia*, www.armenialiberty.org/content/article/25176068.html.
Sierra, O.P. (2010) *The Governance of the European Union in its Eastern Neighbourhood: The Impact of the EU on Georgia*, PhD thesis, University of Birmingham.
Simão, L. and Freire, M.R. (2008) 'The EU's neighborhood policy and the South Caucasus: Unfolding new patterns of cooperation', *Caucasian Review of International Affairs* 2(4): 225–239.
SIPRI (Stockholm International Peace Research Institute) (2015) *SIPRI Military Expenditure Database*, www.sipri.org/databases/milex.
Snidal, D. (2002) 'Rational choice and international relations', in W. Carlnaes, B. Simmons and T. Risse (eds) *Handbook of International Relations*, London: Sage, pp. 73–94.
Socor, V. (2004) 'Gazprom or Sha-Deniz? Georgia's choice of strategic partners', *Eurasia Daily Monitor* 1(126).

Socor, V. (2006a) 'Armenia's giveaways to Russia: From property-for-debt to property-for-gas', *Eurasia Daily Monitor* 3(76).
Socor, V. (2006b) 'Gas from Iran to break Gazprom's monopoly in Armenia', *Eurasia Daily Monitor* 3(14).
Socor, V. (2006c) 'Russia cements control of Armenia's energy system', *Eurasia Daily Monitor* 3(204).
Socor, V. (2007) 'Iran-Armenian gas pipeline: Far more than meets the eye', *Eurasia Daily Monitor* 4(56).
Socor, V. (2013) 'Russia accelerates "borderization" in Georgia on war's 20th anniversary', *Eurasia Daily Monitor* 10(175).
Socor, V. (2015) 'Moldovan billionaire Plahotniuc gaining more political power', *Eurasia Daily Monitor* 12(188).
Soghomonyan, V. (2007) *Europäische Integration und Hegemonie im Südkaukasus. Armenien, Aserbaidschan und Georgien auf dem Weg nach Europa*, Baden-Baden: Nomos.
Solonenko, I. (2008) 'European neighborhood policy after four years: Has it had any impact on the reform process in Ukraine', *International Issues & Slovak Foreign Policy Affairs* XVII(4): 20–40.
Spendzharova, A.B. and Vachudova, M.A. (2012) 'Catching up? Consolidating liberal democracy in Bulgaria and Romania after EU accession', *West European Politics* 35(1): 39–58.
Stefes, C.H. (2006) *Understanding Post-Soviet Transitions- Corruption, Collusion and Clientelism*, Basingstoke: Palgrave.
Stefes, C.H. (2010) 'Regimebeständigkeit und "Revolution": Armenien und Georgien im Vergleich', in S. Frech (ed.) *Der Bürger im Staat – Autoritäre Regime*, Stuttgart: Landeszentrale für politische Bildung Baden-Württemberg, pp. 32–38.
Stent, A.E. (2008) 'Restoration and revolution in Putin's foreign policy', *Europe-Asia Studies* 60(6): 1089–1106.
Stewart, S. (2009) 'The interplay of domestic contexts and external democracy promotion: Lessons from Eastern Europe and the South Caucasus', *Democratization* 16(4): 804–824.
Stratfor (2015) 'Despite fears, Georgia is still the West's partner', www.stratfor.com/analysis/despite-fears-georgia-still-wests-partner.
Stulberg, A.N. and Lavenex, S. (2007) 'Connecting the neighborhood: Energy and environment', in K. Weber, M.E. Smith and M. Baun (eds) *Governing Europe's Neighbourhood – Partners or Periphery*, Manchester: Manchester University Press, pp. 134–155.
Sushko, O. (2012) *Ukraine's Progress Towards Visa Liberalisation with the EU*, Kiev: PASOS, Open Society Foundations.
Tallberg, J. (2002) 'Paths to compliance: Enforcement, management, and the European Union', *International Organization* 56(3): 609–643.
Tchirakadze, N. (2007) 'Die geopolitische Interessenpolitik im Kaspischen Raum: Die Rolle interner und externer Akteure', in H.-D. Wenzel (ed.) *Der kaspische Raum – Ausgewählte Them zu Politik und Wirtschaft*, Bamberg: Bamberg University, pp. 19–40.
The Telegraph (2008) 'Badri Patarkatsishvili', www.telegraph.co.uk/news/obituaries/1578596/Badri-Patarkatsishvili.html.
Teurtrie, D. (2010) *Géopolitique de la Russe: Intégration régionale, enjeux énergétiques, influence culturelle*, Paris: L'Harmattan.

Tishkov, V., Zayinchkovskaya, Z. and Vitkovskaya, G. (2005) *Migration in the Countries of the Former Soviet Union*, Geneva: Global Commission on International Migration (GCIM).
Tolstrup, J. (2009) 'Studying a negative external actor: Russia' s management of stability and instability in the "near abroad"', *Democratization* 16(5): 922–944.
Tolstrup, J. (2013) 'When can external actors influence democratization? Leverage, linkages, and gatekeeper elites', *Democratization* 20(4): 716–742.
Tolstrup, J. (2014) *Russia vs. the EU: The Competition for Influence*, Boulder, CO: Lynne Rienner Publishers.
Transparency International Georgia (2007) *Georgia's Energy Policy: Overview of Main Directions*, Tbilisi: Transparency International Georgia.
Transparency International Georgia (2008a) *Georgia's State Policy in the Electricity Sector: Brief History and Ongoing Processes*, Tbilisi: Transparency International Georgia.
Transparency International Georgia (2008b) *Georgia's State Energy Policy in the Natural Gas Sector*, Tbilisi: Transparency International Georgia.
Transparency International Georgia (2008c) *National Policy of Georgia on Developing Renewable Energy Sources*, Tbilisi: Transparency International Georgia.
Transparency International Georgia (2008d) *State Policies of Georgia in the Energy Sector: Tariffs on Electricity and Gas*, Tbilisi: Transparency International Georgia.
Transparency International Georgia (2014) *Challenges of New Immigration Policies of Georgia*, Tbilisi: Transparency International Georgia.
Trauner, F. and Kruse, I. (2008a) 'EC visa facilitation and readmission agreements: A new standard EU foreign policy tool?', *European Journal of Migration and Law* 10(4): 411–438.
Trauner, F. and Kruse, I. (2008b) *EC Visa Facilitation and Readmission Agreements: Implementing a New EU Security Approach in the Neighbourhood*, CEPS Working Document No. 290, Brussels: Centre for European Policy Studies.
Trenin, D. (1999) 'Conflicts in the South Caucasus', in G. Mangott (ed.) *Brennpunkt Südkaukasus: Aufbruch trotz Krieg, Vertreibung und Willkürherrschaft*, Wien: Braumüller, pp. 293–306.
Trenin, D. (2005) *Russia, the EU and the Common Neighbourhood*, Centre for European Reform Essays, London: Centre for European Reform.
Trenin, D. (2009) 'Russia's spheres of interest, not influence', *The Washington Quarterly* 32(4): 3–22.
Tsebelis, G. (1995) 'Decision making in political systems: Veto players in presidentialism, parliamentarism, multicameralism and multipartyism', *British Journal of Political Science* 25(3): 289–325.
Tsereteli, M. (2002) *Russia Close to Regaining Control Over Strategic Georgian Assets*, CACI Analyst, www.cacianalyst.org/newsite/?q=node/116.
Tsotniashvili, E. (2007) 'Saakashvili warns ministers to pay for own medical expenses', *The Messenger Online*, www.messenger.com.ge/issues/1409_july_27_2007/n_1409_2.html.
Tudoroiu, T. (2007) 'Rose, orange, and tulip: The failed post-Soviet revolutions', *Communist and Post-Communist Studies* (40): 315–342.
UNDP (2011) 'Georgia: Hydro power boosts development in the country's poorest regions', europeandcis.undp.org/news/show/0FD6952A-F203-1EE9-BBB55B1EDF297336.
UN Economic and Social Council (2011) *Steering Committee of the Energy Efficiency 21 Programme, ECE/Energy/WP.4/2011/4*, New York: United Nations.

UNESCAP (2002) 'Electric power in Asia and the Pacific 2001–2002: Armenia', www.unescap.org/esd/energy/information/electricpower/2001-2002/html/armenia.htm.

UNHCR and IOM (2007) 'Danish Refugee Council to help Georgia develop its migration policy', soderkoping.org.ua/page15513.html?template=print#.

UNHCR, IOM, CIM and Migrationsverket (2012) *The Söderköping Process*, soderkoping.org.ua/page2864.html.

USAID Armenia (2002) *USAID Armenia FY 2002 Annual Report*, Arlington: USAID.

USAID Georgia (2008) *Policy Recommendations for Renewable Energy and Energy Efficiency Development in Georgia*, Tbilisi: USAID Georgia.

USAID Georgia (2011) 'U.S. ambassador celebrated opening of hydropower plant in Tusheti', georgia.usaid.gov/news/press-releases/2011/08/30/988.

USAID, UNDP and DFID (2007) *USAID, DFID, UNDP to Support Civil Registry Reform in Georgia*, Tbilisi: UNDP.

US Bureau for International Narcotics and Law Enforcement Affairs (2005) *Major Money Laundering Countries: International Narcotics Control Strategy Report*, Washington, DC: US Department of State.

US Department of Energy (2011) 'Energy basics: Large-scale hydropower', www.eere.energy.gov/basics/renewable_energy/large_scale_hydropower.html.

US Department of State (2000) *1999 International Narcotics Control Strategy Report*, Washington, DC: US Department of State.

US Department of State (2002) *Victims of Trafficking and Violence Protection Act – Trafficking in Persons Report*, Washington, DC: US Department of State.

US Department of State (2003) *Victims of Trafficking and Violence Protection Act – Trafficking in Persons Report*, Washington, DC: US Department of State.

US Department of State (2004a) *2003 International Narcotics Control Strategy Report Part I: Drug and Chemical Control*, Washington, DC: US Department of State.

US Department of State (2004b) *Victims of Trafficking and Violence Protection Act – Trafficking in Persons Report*, Washington, DC: US Department of State.

US Department of State (2006) *International Narcotics Control Strategy Report Volume II: Money Laundering and Financial Crimes*, Washington, DC: US Department of State.

US Department of State (2008) *International Narcotics Control Strategy Report Volume II: Money Laundering and Financial Crimes*, Washington, DC: US Department of State.

US Department of State (2009) *2009 International Narcotics Control Strategy Report, Volume I: Drug and Chemical Control*, Washington, DC: US Department of State.

US Department of State (2010) *2010 International Narcotics Control Strategy Report, Volume II: Money Laundering and Financial Crimes*, Washington, DC: US Department of State.

US Energy Information Administration (2015a) 'International energy statistics: Hydroelectricity net generation', www.eia.gov/cfapps/ipdbproject/iedindex3.cfm?tid=2&pid=33&aid=12&cid=AM,GG,&syid=2000&eyid=2012&unit=BKWH.

US Energy Information Administration (2015b) 'International energy statistics: Total non-hydro renewable electricity net generation', eia.gov, 205.254.135.7/cfapps/ipdbproject/iedindex3.cfm?tid=2&pid=34&aid=12&cid=AM,GG,&syid=1999&eyid=2012&unit=BKWH.

Uzbekistan Daily (2008) 'CSTO officials to discuss fight against illegal migration', www.uzdaily.com/articles-id-2342.htm.

Vachudova, M.A. (2001) *The Leverage of International Institutions on Democratizing States: Eastern Europe and the European Union*, EUI Working Paper No.2001/33, Florence: European University Institute.

Vachudova, M.A. (2005) *Europe Undivided: Democracy, Leverage, and Integration After Communism*, Oxford: Oxford University Press.

Van Hüllen, V. (2012) *It Takes Two to Tango. The European Union and Democracy Promotion in the Mediterranean*, PhD thesis, Berlin: Freie Universität Berlin.

Van Hüllen, V. (2015) *EU Democracy Promotion and the Arab Spring: International Cooperation and Authoritarianism*, Basingstoke: Palgrave Macmillan.

Venice Commission (2011) *Opinion No. 611/2011: Electoral Code of Armenia, adopted on 26 May 2011, CDL-REF(2011)029*, Strasbourg: Council of Europe.

Venice Commission and OSCE/ODIHR (2011a) *Joint Final Opinion on the Electoral Code of Armenia, CDL-AD(2011)032, adopted on 26.05.2011*, Strasbourg: Council of Europe.

Venice Commission and OSCE/ODIHR (2011b) *Joint Opinion on the Draft Election Code of Georgia, CDL-AD(2011)043, adopted on 19.12.2011*, Strasbourg, Warsaw: Council of Europe.

Vertlib, V. (1999) 'Die wirtschaftliche Dimension des Südkaukasus', in G. Mangott (ed.) *Brennpunkt Südkaukasus: Aufbruch trotz Krieg, Vertreibung und Willkürherrschaft*, Wien: Braumüller, pp. 139–214.

Vinokurov, E. (2008) *The CIS Common Electric Power Market: Sector Report*, Almaty: Eurasian Development Bank.

Way, L.A. (2006) 'Authoritarian failure: How does state weakness strengthen electoral competition', in *Electoral Authoritarianism: The Dynamics of Unfree Competition*, London: Lynne Rienner Publishers, pp. 167–180.

Way, L.A. and Levitsky, S. (2006) 'The dynamics of autocratic coercion after the Cold War', *Comparative Politics* 39(4): 387–410.

Weekly Georgian Journal (2011) 'Bidzina Ivanishvili – I don't want to hear the word "revolution"', www.georgianjournal.ge/index.php?option=com_content&view=article&id=6217:bidzina-ivanishvili-i-dont-want-to-hear-the-word-revolution&catid=9:news&Itemid=8.

Westphal, K. (2006) 'Energy policy between multilateral governance and geopolitics: Whither Europe?', *Internationale Politik und Gesellschaft Online* (4): 44–62.

Wetzel, A. (2016) 'From halt to hurry: external and domestic influences on Ukrainian asylum policy', *Eurasian Geography and Economics* 57(1): 66–88.

Wetzinger, J. (2011) 'Georgiens Außenpolitik unter Michail Saakaschwili: ein riskantes Spiel im Spannungsfeld zwischen Washington und Moskau', *Internationale Politik und Gesellschaft* (1): 66–79.

Wheatley, J. (2010) 'Georgia at a crossroads: After the post-war', www.opendemocracy.net/jonathan-wheatley/georgia-at-crossroads-after-post-war.

Wheatley, J. and Zürcher, C. (2008) 'On the origin and consolidation of hybrid regimes: The state of democracy in the Caucasus', *Taiwan Journal of Democracy* 4(I): 1–31.

Wierzbowska-Miazga, A. and Kaczmarski, M. (2011) *Russia's Development Assistance*, OSW Commentary No. 62, Warsaw: Centre for Eastern Studies.

Willerton, J.P. and Beznosov, M.A. (2007) 'Russia's pursuit of its Eurasian security interests: Weighing the CIS and alternative bilateral-multilateral arrangements', in K. Malfliet, L. Verpoest and E. Vinokurov (eds) *The CIS, the EU and Russia: The Challenges of Integration*, Basingstoke: Palgrave Macmillan, pp. 47–72.

Wilson, A. and Popescu, N. (2009) 'Russian and European neighbourhood policies compared', *Southeast European and Black Sea Studies* 9(3): 317–331.

Woehrel, S. (2009) *Russian Energy Policy Toward Neighboring Countries*, Washington, DC: Congressional Research Service.

Wolczuk, K. (2016) 'Managing the flows of gas and rules: Ukraine between the EU and Russia', *Eurasian Geography and Economics* 57(1): 113–137.

Woll, C. and Jacquot, S. (2010) 'Using Europe: Strategic action in multi-level politics', *Comparative European Politics* 8(1): 110–142.

World Bank (2005) *Progress Report, Economic Development and Poverty Reduction Program*, Tbilisi: The World Bank.

World Bank (2010a) *Bilateral Migration Matrix 2010*, Washington, DC: The World Bank, go.worldbank.org/JITC7NYTT0.

World Bank (2010b) *Bilateral Remittance Estimates for 2010 Using Migrant Stocks, Host Country Incomes, and Origin Country Incomes (millions of US$) (May 2013 Version)*, Washington, DC: The World Bank, go.worldbank.org/092X1CHHD0.

World Bank (2011) *Global Bilateral Migration Database*, Washington, DC: The World Bank, data.worldbank.org/data-catalog/global-bilateral-migration-database.

World Bank (2012) *Fighting Corruption in Public Services: Chronicling Georgia's Reforms*, Washington, DC: The World Bank.

World Bank (2013) 'Russia as a donor: Infographic', www.worldbank.org/content/dam/Worldbank/Highlights&Features/eca/russia/russia-donor-ig-eng-full.jpg.

World Bank (2014) *The Worldwide Governance Indicators, 2014 Update: Aggregate Indicators of Governance 1996–2013*, Washington, DC: The World Bank, www.govindicators.org.

World Bank (2015) *World Development Indicators*, databank.worldbank.org/data/.

WTO (2010) *Trade Policy Review: Georgia, WT/TPR/S/224*, Geneva: World Trade Organization.

Yeganyan, G. (2003) *45th Meeting of the European Committee on Migration, Statement of Gagik Yeganyan, Head of the State Department for Migration and Refugees of the Republic of Armenia*, www.dmr.am/admr/ELUJTNER/Meuropcomang.HTML.

Yeganyan, G. (2006) *Cluster Process Meeting on May 10–11 in Brussels, Statement of Mr. Gagik Yeganyan, Head of Migration Agency, Ministry of Territorial Administration of the Republic of Armenia*, www.dmr.am/ADMR/ELUJTNER/U_3.htm.

Zaharova, T. (2003) 'US-Gazprom clash over pipelines in Georgia', neftegaz.ru/en/analisis/view/6099.

Index

AA (Association Agreements) 12, 31, 38–9, 185, 186, 205; 2013 Vilnius Eastern Partnership Summit 185, 188, 192, 194, 197; choosing between competing integration regimes 186–8, 199 (mutual exclusivity 186–7, 194); EEU,CU/AA, DCFTA choice 12, 186, 186–7, 188, 189, 195, 196, 202; DCFTA 186–7, 188, 190–4, 196–7, 199–203, 204, 205; declining to sign AA 4, 9, 38–9, 43, 100, 185, 199, 201–202, 204, 215; multiple external constraints 12, 185, 187; multiple external incentives 31, 187; 'preferential fit/external incentives' interplay 9, 12, 185–6, 188, 203, 204, 207; preferential fit of domestic actor/elite 12, 187, 204, 208–209, 215; signing AA 185, 189–91, 196–7, 203; *see also* Armenia and the AA; Georgia and the AA; Moldova; Russia and the AA; Ukraine

Abashidze, Aslan 93, 95, 98

Abkhazia 56, 82, 91, 93, 101, 155, 190–1; Georgian hydropower plant 62

Abrahamyan, Hovik 134, 135, 195

Adeishvili, Zurab 120–1

Adjaria 79, 91, 93, 95, 98, 164

AENEAS (financial/technical assistance program for migration and asylum) 81, 115, 126, 133, 134

AEPLAC (Armenian-European Policy and Legal Advice Center) 139, 140

agency 3–4, 6; agency-centered factors and compliance 20; agency-centered perspective 3, 6, 7, 16; neighborhood Europeanization in agency-centered framework 27–36, 45, 206–207; *see also* external incentives; preferential fit

ARF (Armenian Revolutionary Federation–Dashnaktsutyun) 89, 90, 124, 133–4, 136, 138, 142

Armenia 1, 2, 39–42; Nagorno-Karabakh conflict 56–7, 88, 89, 91, 126, 169, 193–6; assistance/ capacity building 57, 80–3; CIS 23; CSTO 23, 132; EEU 23, 42, 195, 196; external incentives 41–2; JLS 47, 57–60, 64–5, 68, 69, 72, 79, 81, 213; Russian military involvement in 56–7, 193–4; *see also the entries below for* Armenia

Armenia and the AA 12, 42, 100, 191–6; CU 12, 43, 185, 191, 192–6 (shallow compliance with 12, 186, 191, 194, 204, 205); declining to sign AA 100, 185, 204; preferential fit 191–3, 204; Russia, rivaling policy conditionality 191, 193–4, 196, 204; *see also* AA

Armenian domestic structures: authoritarian tendencies 40–1; civil society 87, 101; corruption 59, 76, 79; democratic transition 41; domestic compatibility with Russia 79; economic freedom and transition to a market economy 74–7; government-associated elite constellation 87–91, 98–9; hybrid regime 30, 39, 79, 87, 216; nationalism: hay dat, Araratism, Miazum 91, 98, 124; rule of law 74, 75, 79; state capacity 77–9, 129; *see also* Armenia; Armenian elections

Armenian elections 209; 1990 parliamentary elections 41; 2003 presidential election 40, 90; 2007 parliamentary elections 40, 90; 2008 presidential election 40, 90; 2012 parliamentary elections 40–1; 2013 presidential election 41; biometric passport 131–2

Index

Armenian energy diversification 2, 11–12, 52, 168–80, 208; Armenia/Georgia comparison 180–3; ArmRosGazprom 179, 193; capacity building 169–70, 173, 183; electricity 62, 150, 151–2, 169–74; ENP, full compliance 149, 180–1; ENP, non-compliance 66, 149, 168–9, 173–4, 176–7; ENP, shallow compliance 179, 180, 182; Hrazdan thermal power plant 86, 172, 179; hydropower 51, 151, 169–73, 181, 183; Iranian–Armenian gas pipeline 86, 177–80, 184; Kocharyan, Robert 169, 170, 175, 179, 180; Lake Sevan 169, 170; Medzamor nuclear power 62, 173–7, 182, 210 (closure of 12, 50, 52, 66, 83, 85–6, 87, 149, 150, 151, 173, 176; costs of closure 174, 182; new NPP 173, 175–7, 212); policies, polities and politics misfits 150–2; policy conditionality 173, 175–6, 210; preferential fit 180, 183; preferential misfit 177; privatization 169, 171, 175; regional diversification 150, 177–80, 182; renewable energy 51, 65, 73, 83, 149, 151–2, 169–73, 181, 183; Ter-Petrosyan, Levon 169, 170, 171, 173; USAID 170, 171, 174, 183; *see also* Armenian energy diversification and Russia; energy diversification

Armenian energy diversification and Russia 183; asymmetric interdependence favoring Russia 60–1, 62–3, 149, 184, 213; debt owed to Russia 86, 172, 174, 178, 193; gas supply 86, 149, 150, 165, 177–8, 179, 180; Gazprom 86, 178, 179, 193; negative incentives facilitating reform 12, 86, 170–1, 173; non-compliance regarding Medzamor 174–7, 212; rivaling policy conditionality 176–7, 178–80, 182, 210; Russian state companies supporting reform implementation 171–2; strategic investments in infrastructure 149; *see also* Armenian energy diversification

Armenian migration management 2, 11, 102, 103, 133, 123–40; Armenia/Georgia comparison 140–4; capacity building 128–9, 130–1, 132–3, 137–8, 139, 140, 144, 212; Compatriots Program 11, 136–7, 143; CSTO 132; data protection 47, 105–106, 138–40; Department for Refugees and Migration 105; DMR 124, 125, 126; document security 65, 104, 129–33 (biometric passport 129–32, 138, 140, 143, 144); ENP, full compliance 11, 123, 126, 127, 132, 135, 138, 140; ENP, shallow compliance 102, 139–40; external incentives 127–8, 129, 132; FMS 127, 136, 143; emigration, reduction of 11, 124–5, 129, 140; IOM 72, 126, 127, 130, 133, 138, 140; JLS sub-committee 127, 131, 138; Kocharyan, Robert 124, 129, 130, 134–5, 138, 140; MFA 128, 133; Migration Agency 104, 126, 133–4, 135; national action plans on migration and asylum 133–8, 212; policy and politics misfits 103–106; policy conditionality, lack of 131–2; preferential fit 124–5, 127, 128–9, 132, 138; preferential misfit 140; readmission 11, 65, 102, 103, 124–9, 140–1; Russia 126–7, 136–7, 138, 140, 142, 143, 144; Sargsyan, Serzh 129, 130, 134–5, 136, 140; visa facilitation 42, 81, 127–8, 137; visa liberalization 42, 125, 128, 131, 137; *see also* migration management

Åslund, Anders 202

authoritarian regime 9, 15, 216; Armenia 40–1; compliance with EU policies 16; domestic change 16; Georgia 41; interest to stay in power 15–16; Russia 40, 41; *see also* semi-democratic regime

Azerbaijan 71, 91, 128, 150, 193, 216; Nagorno-Karabakh conflict 56–7, 88, 89, 91, 126,169, 193–6; gas supply 162, 163, 165–8, 169; ; Shah Deniz gas fields 162

Belarus 13, 59, 198, 216
Bendukidze, Kakha 93, 95–6, 97, 154, 155
Bertelsmann Foundation 30; BTI 27, 76–7
Black Sea Synergy Initiative 71
Bogner, Alexander 44
BOMCA (Border Management Program for Central Asia) 46
Börzel, Tanja A. 34
BSEC (Organization of the Black Sea Economic Cooperation) 71
Burjanadze, Nino 93, 94–5, 96, 164

capacity building 34–6, 80, 207, 211; Armenia 80–3 (energy diversification 169–70, 173, 183; migration

Index 265

management 128–9, 130–1, 132–3, 137–8, 139, 140, 144, 212); definition 34, 36; energy policy 12, 82–3; ENP, full compliance 35; ENP, non-compliance 36; EU 36, 80; explaining variation in compliance patterns 11, 66, 81–3, 100; Georgia 80–3 (energy diversification 155–7, 158–62, 168, 183; migration management 110, 114, 119, 120, 123, 143–4, 212); JLS 81–2; measurement of 36; migration management 11, 143–4; preferential fit 35, 211–12; preferential misfit 36, 211; 'reinforcement by support' 34; rivaling capacity building 35; Russia 35, 80, 81–2, 83 (CIS agreements 36, 81); socialization 34, 80; Ukraine 34
CEEC (Central and Eastern European countries) 1, 5, 25, 29
CIS (Commonwealth of Independent States) 8, 13, 57, 213, 215; Armenia 23; capacity building 36, 81; CIS Charter 46; energy policy 50–2, 55, 68, 71, 73; Georgia 23, 92; institutionalization 24; JLS 46–7, 69–70, 72, 85; migration management 46–7; policy convergence/divergence 23; rule codification 66–7, 68; Ukraine 6, 203; visa-free regime with Russia 59, 85
civil society 87, 101, 119, 217–18; weak civil society 28, 29, 87, 208
Civil Society Facility 217–18
CNC (Caucasian neighborhood countries) 48, 58, 59, 60
CoE (Council of Europe): Convention and additional protocol on supervisory authorities 139; Convention on Laundering, Search, Seizure and Confiscation of the Proceeds from Crime 46, 67; Convention for the Protection of Individuals with regard to the Automatic Processing of Personal Data 47, 68, 105–106, 120
compliance 17–19; agency-centered factors 20, 27–36; capacity building 11, 34–36, 66, 80–3, 100; compliance with ENP Action Plans 3–4, 14, 17–19; 'convergence' 17–18; definition 19; domestic compatibility 66, 74–80, 100; emerging compliance 19, 43, 63–65; external incentives 11, 27, 30–34, 66, 83–7, 100, 110, 116, 120, 123, 124, 129, 137, 142, 143, 167, 182, 188, 207, 209; ENP, full compliance 19, 32, 33, 35, 63, 206–207 (Armenia [energy diversification 149, 180–1; migration management 11, 123, 126, 127, 133, 135, 138, 140]; Georgia [energy diversification 149, 154–6, 167–8, 180, 210; migration management 109–10, 112, 114, 218]); institutional setting 66–74, 100; ENP, non-compliance 3, 4, 19, 26, 32–35, 63, 206–207, 209, 2010 (Armenia [energy diversification 66, 149, 168–9, 173–4, 176–7; JLS 64]; Georgia [energy 65–6; energy diversification 152, 160–1, 181–2; JLS 64, 106; migration management 110, 115–16, 119, 141]); policy conditionality 3–4, 11, 14, 31, 32, 83–7, 100, 108, 120, 142, 161, 188, 207, 209; preferential fit/ preferential misfit 3–4, 11, 14, 27–30, 31, 32, 35, 87–99, 100, 119, 129, 140–143, 164, 180, 208, 209; 'preferential fit/policy conditionality' interplay 3, 4, 32, 33, 207, 208, 210, 214; Russia, rivaling policy conditionality 4, 9, 32, 164, 167, 168, 176–178, 180–182, 209, 210; ENP, shallow compliance 3, 9, 19, 32, 43, 63, 205, 206–209 (Armenia [energy diversification 179, 180, 182; JLS 64, 102; migration management 102]; Georgia [energy diversification 180, 182; JLS 64, 102; migration management 11, 102, 118–19, 120, 122–3, 142]); rationalist institutionalism 15–17, 19–20; a result of cost-benefit analysis 5, 16, 19–20; see also energy policy, compliance patterns; JLS, compliance patterns; 'preferential fit/ policy conditionality' interplay
constructivism 5, 16, 214
Cooperation Council 69, 70, 184
Copenhagen Criteria 5, 74
corruption 1, 48, 76; Armenia 59, 76, 79; control of 27, 78; Georgia 59, 76, 79, 93, 94, 150, 152, 153, 155, 156, 158, 162, 182; Moldova 197, 198–9; Ukraine 200–201
Council of the European Union 41, 43, 84, 108, 121
Crimea, annexed by Russia 185, 201–202
CSTO (Collective Security Treaty Organization) 13; Armenia 23, 132; JLS 46, 47; migration management 47, 132; policy convergence/divergence 23

266 *Index*

CU (Eurasian Customs Union) 2; AA/CU choice 12, 186; Armenia 12, 43, 185, 191, 192–6 (shallow compliance with 12, 186, 191, 194, 204, 205); Georgia 43; Ukraine 201
CUG (Citizen's Union of Georgia) 93, 94
Czech Republic 27, 76, 109, 125, 127

data protection 11, 103; 1981 Convention on Protection of Individuals Regarding Automatic Processing of Personal Data 47, 68, 105–106, 120; 2001 Additional Protocol to the Data Protection Convention 105, 122; Armenia 47, 105–106, 138–40; ENP Action Plans 68, 105; Georgia 47, 105–106, 120–3, 142, 143, 212; policy and politics misfits 105; *see also* migration management
DCFTA (Deep and Comprehensive Free Trade Area) 31, 38, 186–7, 188, 190–4, 196–7; Armenia 42, 81; Georgia 42; Ukraine 199–201, 202, 203, 205
DCI (Development Cooperation Instrument) 80, 81, 82, 83
Demirchyan, Karen 89, 91
democracy 74, 217, 219; democratic transition 1, 39, 41; democratization 5, 16; EU member states 39–40; Freedom House Index 39–40; 'partly free' country 39, 41; *see also* semi-democratic regime
document security 11, 103; Armenia 65, 104, 129–33 (biometric passport 129–32, 138, 140, 143, 144); biometric passport 46, 47, 84, 111–14; Georgia 104, 110–14 (biometric passport 111–14, 143–4, 145, 212); readmission 104; *see also* migration management
domestic actor 14, 206–207, 208, 217; empowerment of 3, 8, 28, 35, 115, 162, 177, 183, 211, 212; preferences over outcomes 15–16; *see also* ENC; executive actor; veto player
domestic compatibility 25–7, 207; administrative system compatibility 26; Armenia's/Georgia's greater compatibility with Russia 79; democracy 74; domestic resonance hypothesis 26, 74, 213–14; Eastern ENC's greater compatibility with Russia 25, 79, 214; economic freedom and transition to a market economy 74–7, 79, 100; economic system compatibility 26, 27;

ENC 3, 7, 14, 26; explaining variation in compliance patterns 66, 74–9, 100; measurement of 26–7, 44; policy-specific misfit 26, 27–8; regime type 26–7; rule of law 27, 74, 75, 79, 89, 100, 214; state capacity 26, 27, 77–9, 100, 212, 214
DRC (Danish Refugee Council) 110, 115, 119, 126
drug trafficking 22, 46, 47, 48, 49, 81; *see also* JLS

EaP (Eastern Partnership) 31, 69, 81, 189, 191; Eastern Partnership Summit 116,185, 188, 192, 194, 197; Moldova 196–7; state actors, focus on 28–9; visa liberalization 84, 116, 122, 128; *see also* visa liberalization
EBRD (European Bank for Reconstruction and Development) 73, 82, 155, 158, 172
EEC (Energy Efficiency Center Georgia) 157–8, 161
EEU (Eurasian Economic Union) 13, 24, 33, 217; AA/EEU choice 186–7, 188, 189, 195, 196, 202; Armenia 23, 42, 195, 196
EIB (European Investment Bank) 82, 115, 155, 158
EIU (Economist Intelligence Unit) 30, 37, 195
EKENG (e-Governance Infrastructure Implementation Unit) 130, 139
EMCDDA (European Monitoring Center for Drugs and Drug Addiction) 49
ENC (European neighborhood countries) 3, 6, 7, 219; domestic compatibility 3, 7, 14, 26; empowerment of reform coalitions 10; furthering the domestic agenda 4, 7, 32; institutional context 3, 7, 10, 14, 16; interdependence with EU/Russia 3, 7, 14, 16 (ENC's asymmetric interdependence with Russia and CIS 6, 21, 56–7); semi-democratic regime 2, 206, 219
Energy Community 70–1, 85, 161
energy diversification 49, 54, 55, 63, 65, 66, 68, 149; capacity building 82–3; ENP Action Plans 52, 150, 151, 152, 157; EU demands 2, 52, 87, 173; EU/Russia policy divergence 52–3; PCA 52, 150, 151, 157; 'preferential fit/

Index 267

policy conditionality' interplay 157, 183; socialization 12, 161–2, 168, 177, 180; *see also* Armenian energy diversification; energy policy; Georgian energy diversification
energy interdependence 22, 60–3; Armenia 60–1, 62–3, 149, 184, 213; asymmetric interdependence 22; asymmetric interdependence favoring Russia 42, 61–3, 149, 162, 184, 213; EU 60–1; Georgia 60–1, 62–3, 149, 162, 213; symmetric interdependence 22; *see also* energy policy
energy policy 2, 7, 12, 42, 149, 208; 1994 Energy Charter Treaty 50, 51, 53, 54, 55, 68; CIS 50–2, 55, 68, 71, 73; energy efficiency 49, 51–2, 53, 54, 55, 63, 65, 68, 73, 83; Energy Efficiency Protocol 50, 53, 54; ENP Action Plans 52, 83; EU 49, 51, 53, 60–1, 70, 83, 85–6, 87; EU/Russia cooperation 53–5; EU/Russia policy divergence 49, 52–3, 54–5, 63, 99, 149, 183, 213; PCA 50, 52, 53, 68, 70; regulatory convergence 49, 50–1, 53, 54–5, 63, 65, 68, 83, 149; renewable energy 11, 49, 51, 65, 70, 73, 83, 149; Russia 50–1, 52–3, 83, 86–7, 211–12, 213; Ukraine 51, 55; USA 73; *see also* energy diversification; energy interdependence; energy policy, compliance
energy policy, compliance patterns 63, 65–6, 99, 100; capacity building 12, 82–3; emerging compliance 65, 79, 149; institutionalization 70–2; internationalization 72–4; non-compliance 65–6; policy conditionality 85–7; rule codification 68; *see also* compliance
ENI (European Neighborhood Instrument) 80
ENP (European Neighborhood Policy) 1, 2; an alternative to enlargement 17; countries included in 13; Eastern dimension 13, 39; EU membership perspective, absence of 1, 5, 6, 15, 29, 31; failure 1, 206; review 1, 206, 217, 218; socialization 6, 7; state actors, focus on 28–9; Ukraine 6; *see also the entries below for* ENP; neighborhood Europeanization
ENP Action Plans 3, 43; compliance with 3–4, 14, 17–19; data protection 68, 105; energy diversification 52, 150, 151, 152, 157; energy policy 52, 83; JLS 46, 47, 67, 69, 81, 84; migration management 2, 11, 103, 104, 115; neighborhood Europeanization 10; not legally binding agreements 17; *see also* ENP
ENPI (European Neighborhood and Partnership Instrument) 36, 80, 81, 82, 111, 121, 155
EPC (Electric Power Council) 50–1
EU (European Union) 1; capacity building 36, 80; economic potential and military capacity 56, 57, 101; energy policy 49, 51, 53, 60–1, 70, 83, 85–6, 87; as external actor/foreign policy agent 4, 16, 43; interdependence 56–7, 101 (energy interdependence 60–1; JLS interdependence 57–9); policy conditionality 3, 5, 31, 84, 85–6; *see also* ENP; EU policy transfer; EU/Russia rivalry; neighborhood Europeanization; PCA
EU policy transfer 3, 206, 215, 219; agency-centered approach 27–36; a bottom-up process 10; domestic actor 3, 10, 15; executive actor 9, 28–9, 207, 208, 215; failed implementation 8; lesson drawing 4, 7, 11, 12, 29, 133, 207; practical implications for designing EU policy transfer 217–19; 'preferential fit/policy conditionality' interplay 14, 27, 35–6, 37; Russia, impact on EU policy transfer in the ENC 6–7, 42, 208–10, 214, 215, 219; semi-democratic regime 2, 3, 208; a strategic choice under multiple constraints 3, 4, 7, 10, 14, 15; structural and institutional approach 20–7; successful EU rule transfer 206; *see also* domestic compatibility; ENP; external incentives; institutional context; interdependence; neighborhood Europeanization; policy conditionality; preferential fit; 'preferential fit/policy conditionality' interplay; Russian constraining effects on EU policy transfer; Russian supportive effects on EU policy transfer
EU/Russia rivalry 9, 10, 219; AA 198–9, 202, 203, 204, 205; competition over policy change 1–2, 7–8; *see also* Russia, rivaling policy conditionality
EurAsEc (Eurasian Economic Community) 13, 186
Eurasian integration 2, 9, 13

Eurojust (European Union Judicial Cooperation Unit) 48, 105
European Community 50, 80, 126
Europol (European Police Office) 22, 47, 48, 49, 59, 60, 105
Eurostat 22, 37
Evans, Mark 18
executive actor 3, 9, 215; AA, preferential fit of domestic actor/elite 12, 187, 204, 208–209, 215; Armenia, government-associated elite constellation 79, 87–91, 98–9; constraining domestic change 10, 209, 214, 215; empowerment of 28–9, 208, 217; gatekeeper 9, 214, 216; Georgia, government-associated elite constellation 79, 91–9, 123, 152; EU policy transfer 9, 28–9, 207, 208, 215; hybrid regime 28, 208; *see also* domestic actor; ENC; veto player
external actor 16, 214; competition of external actors 15; EU and Russia as external actors 16, 18, 43; *see also* EU; Russia
external incentives 2, 3, 6, 7, 30–4, 187–8, 207; AA 12, 31, 187, 203, 204; Armenia 41–2 (migration management 127–8, 129, 132); ENC 2, 3, 7; EU membership incentive, absence of 1, 5, 6, 15, 29, 31; explaining variation in compliance patterns 11, 66, 83–7, 100, 188; Georgia 41–2 (migration management 108–10, 116–17, 121–2, 123); migration management 11, 143; provided by EU/Russia 2, 3, 7, 9, 31; 'reinforcement by reward or punishment' 34; *see also* agency; EU policy transfer; policy conditionality; 'preferential fit/policy conditionality' interplay; sanction; visa facilitation; visa liberalization

FATF (Financial Action Task Force) 48
Filat, Vlad 196, 197, 199
FMS (Federal Migration Service) 127, 136, 143
Freedom House 26, 30, 37, 44; Freedom House Index 39–40
Freyburg, Tina 24, 25
Frieden, Jeffrey 15, 30
FRONTEX (European Agency for the Management of Operational Cooperation at the External Borders of the Member States of the European Union) 22, 46, 49
Füle, Štefan 194

Gachechiladze, Levan 96
Gamsakhurdia, Zviad 91–2
Gazprom 54, 55; Armenia 86, 178, 193; Georgia 86, 163–7 *passim*; *see also* Russia
GD (Georgian Dream) 41, 57, 93, 96–7, 114, 161, 167; AA 189–90, 191; reconciliatory policy toward Russia 98, 99, 189; *see also* Ivanishvili, Bidzina
Georgia 2, 39–42; 2003 Rose Revolution 41, 80, 92, 164, 168; 2006 Georgian-Russian spy crisis 85, 165; 2008 war with Russia 33, 55, 80, 107, 128, 144; assistance/ capacity building 57, 80–3; CIS 23, 92; CU 43; external incentives 41–2; JLS 47, 57–60, 64, 65, 67, 68, 69, 72, 81; Russian military involvement in 56, 92, 93, 98; *see also the entries below for* Georgia
Georgia and the AA 12, 42, 100, 188–91, 203–204; PCA 19; political polarization 185; preferential fit 189, 191; Russian sanctions and the speeding up of EU integration 12, 186, 190–1, 204; signing AA 185, 189–91; *see also* AA
Georgian domestic structures: anti-Russian rhetoric 96, 98, 99, 154; authoritarian tendencies 41; civil society 87, 101, 119; corruption 59, 76, 79, 93, 94, 150, 152, 153, 155, 156, 158, 162, 182; democratic transition 41; domestic compatibility with Russia 79; economic freedom and transition to a market economy 75; government-associated elite constellation 91–9, 152; hybrid regime 30, 39, 79, 87, 91, 216; liberalism 75, 95–6, 106, 115; reconciliatory policy toward Russia 98, 99, 189; rule of law 74, 75; state capacity 77–9; territorial integrity 97–8, 117, 190–1; *see also* Georgia; Georgian elections
Georgian elections: 1990 presidential election 41; 2003 parliamentary elections 94–5, 164; 2004 presidential election 92; 2006 elections 110; 2008 elections 96; 2012 parliamentary elections 41, 91, 93, 119; 2013 presidential election 41, 91, 123; biometric ID/

Index 269

passport 112–13, 145; *see also* Georgia
Georgian energy diversification 2, 11–12, 52, 152–68; Armenia/Georgia comparison 180–3; Azerbaijan 162, 163, 165–8; BTC pipeline 162; BTE pipeline 162, 163, 164, 165–6; capacity building 155–7, 158–62, 168, 183; corruption 150, 152, 153, 155, 156, 158, 162, 182; electricity 62, 150, 151–7, 167, 184; energy efficiency 158–61, 212; Enguri hydropower plant 62, 82, 86, 155; ENP, full compliance 149, 154–5, 156, 167–8, 180, 210; ENP, non-compliance 152, 160–1, 181–2; ENP, shallow compliance 180, 182; hydropower 51, 151, 152–7, 181–2, 183; Khudoni hydropower project 156; Mozdok–Tbilisi pipeline 165; policies, polities and politics misfits 150–2; preferential fit 11, 157, 164, 167, 168, 180, 182, 183; preferential misfit 161–2, 181–2; privatization 153, 154, 155–6, 164, 181; regional diversification 150, 162–8, 182; renewable energy 51, 65, 73, 83, 149, 151–2, 157–62, 183; Saakashvili, Mikheil 153–4, 155–6, 157, 158, 164, 166–7, 168, 182, 184; SCP 162; Shevardnadze, Eduard 12, 152–3, 155, 156, 157, 162, 163, 164, 168, 181–2; USA 12, 163, 164, 168, 182, 210; USAID 155, 159, 160, 161, 183; *see also* energy diversification; Georgian energy diversification and Russia
Georgian energy diversification and Russia 167–8, 183, 184, 212; asymmetric interdependence favoring Russia 60–1, 62–3, 149, 162, 213; debt owed to Russia 86, 163; gas supply 86–7, 150, 153, 162, 165–6, 167; Gazprom 86, 163–7 *passim*; negative incentives facilitate reform 12, 87, 153–5, 156, 157, 165–6, 181; rivaling policy conditionality 162–4, 167, 168, 182, 210; *see also* Georgian energy diversification
Georgian migration management 2, 11, 103, 106–23; Armenia/Georgia comparison 140–4; capacity building 110, 114, 119, 120, 123, 143–4, 212; CRA 110–14, 116–19, 121, 131; data protection 47, 105–106, 120–3, 142, 143, 212; document security 104, 110–14 (biometric passport 111–14, 143–4, 145, 212); ENP, full compliance 109–10, 111, 114, 218; ENP, non-compliance 110, 115–16, 120, 141; ENP, shallow compliance 11, 102, 118–19, 120, 122–3, 142; external incentives 108–10, 116–17, 121–2, 123; IOM 107, 109, 110, 115, 118; MFA 109, 111, 115; MIA 109, 115; MRA 105, 109, 115, 116, 118, 120; national action plan on migration and asylum 115–20, 142, 212; policy conditionality 107–108, 110, 111–12, 114, 120, 142, 143–4, 218; policy, polity, politics misfits 103–106; 'preferential fit/policy conditionality' interplay 120; preferential misfit 116, 120, 123, 142, 143–4; readmission 81, 103–104, 106–10, 142, 143–4, 212, 218 (implementation of 106–107, 108–10, 142, 209); Russia, passportization as negative incentive 11, 107, 110, 111, 114, 116, 120, 142, 211; Saakashvili, Mikheil 106, 107, 114, 115, 119, 123, 141; Shevardnadze, Eduard 106; visa facilitation 42, 81, 107–108, 110, 111, 116, 121, 128, 142, 211, 218; visa liberalization 42, 109, 114, 116, 119, 123, 142, 209, 218; VLAP 109, 114, 116, 119, 122; *see also* migration management
Gevorgyan, Armen 135
Gilauri, Nika 96, 164–5
GIZ (Deutsche Gesellschaft für Internationale Zusammenarbeit) 160, 161
governance: external governance 4, 22, 24, 213 (neighborhood Europeanization 5–6, 20, 34); good governance 9, 74, 219
GUAM (Georgia, Ukraine, Azerbaijan, Moldova) 71
Gurgenidze, Lado 159
Gurgenidze, Vladimir 115
GYLA (Georgian Young Lawyers' Association) 113, 121, 123

Hanf, Theodor 94, 98
Heritage Foundation: Economic Freedom Index 27, 44, 75, 79, 101
human trafficking 22, 47, 48, 67; 1980 Hague Convention on Civil Aspects of International Child Abduction 47, 68; interdependence 58–9, 60; *see also* JLS

Index

hybrid regime 15, 28, 30, 32, 39, 79, 87, 91, 216; *see also* semi-democratic regime

ICAO (International Civil Aviation Organization) 132
ICHD (International Center for Human Development) 133
IDP (internally displaced person) 46, 81, 104, 105, 118, 146
IEA (International Energy Agency) 73
ILO (International Labour Organization) 127, 133, 134
IMF (International Monetary Fund) 5, 37, 72–3, 86, 169, 195, 201
incentive *see* external incentive; policy conditionality
INOGATE (Interstate Oil and Gas Transportation to Europe) 70, 82, 83, 162, 168
institutional context 23–5, 207; ENC 3, 7, 10, 14, 16; ENP, compliance 25; explaining variation in compliance patterns 66–74, 100; institutional setting hypothesis 25, 213; internationalization of external rules 23, 24–5, 72–4, 213; rule codification 66–8, 73, 100, 213; CIS 24; energy policy 70–2; JLS 68–70; institutionalization hypothesis 23–4, 73, 213;
interdependence 3, 7, 56–63, 207; asymmetric interdependence 6, 20–1, 22, 216, 219; definition 20; economic interdependence 57, 101; ENC, interdependence with EU/Russia 3, 7, 14, 16; energy: policy interdependence 22; ENP, compliance 23; EU 56–7, 101; interdependence hypothesis 23, 63, 100, 213; measurement of 21–2; policy divergence and 22–3; symmetric interdependence 22, 59, 216; *see also* energy interdependence; JLS, interdependence; Russia and interdependence
IO (international organization) 30, 38, 133
IOM (International Organization for Migration) 72, 107, 109, 110, 115; Armenia 72, 126, 127, 130, 133, 138, 140; Georgia 107, 109, 110, 115, 118
Iranian–Armenian gas pipeline 86, 177–80, 184
IRENA (International Renewable Energy Agency) 73

Itera 162–3, 178, 179; *see also* Russia
Ivanishvili, Bidzina 41, 93, 96–7, 113, 188, 189–90, 191; *see also* GD

Jacoby, Wade 34
JLS (Justice, Liberty and Security) 2, 7, 22, 42, 46–9, 102, 208; Armenia 47, 57–60, 64–5, 68, 69, 72, 79, 81, 213; CIS 46–7, 69–70, 72, 85; CSTO 46, 47; ENP Action Plans 46, 47, 67, 69, 81, 84; ENP, shallow/non-compliance 64; EU/Russia cooperation 48–9; EU/Russia policy convergence 46–8, 49, 55, 63, 71, 99, 102, 144, 213; Georgia 47, 57–60, 64, 65, 67, 68, 69, 72, 81; PCA 46, 47, 48, 67, 69; Road Map for the Common Space on Freedom, Security and Justice 48, 49; terrorism 46, 47, 48, 67; *see also* drug trafficking; human trafficking; JLS, compliance; JLS, interdependence; migration management; money laundering; organized crime
JLS, compliance patterns 63–6, 79, 99; capacity building 81–2; institutionalization 68–70; internationalization 72; policy conditionality 84–5; rule codification 67–8; *see also* JLS
JLS, interdependence 22, 57–60; asymmetric interdependence 22; asymmetric interdependence disfavoring EU 57–9; asymmetric interdependence favoring Russia 42, 57, 60; drug trafficking 59, 60; organized crime 59, 60; symmetric interdependence 22, 59; *see also* JLS

Kavtaradze, Gia 120
Keohane, Robert O. 21, 44
KfW (German Development Bank–Kreditanstalt für Wiederaufbau) 73, 82, 158, 160, 161
King, Nigel 44
Kocharyan, Robert 11, 88–90, 91, 98; 2003 presidential election 40; energy diversification 169, 170, 175, 179, 180; migration management 124, 129, 130, 134–5, 138, 140

Langbein, Julia 7, 34, 212
Lavenex, Sandra 19, 26
Levitsky, Steven 21
Liberty Institute 92, 101
Lisbon Treaty 61, 128

Margvelashvili, Giorgi 41, 97
Menz, Wolfgang 44
Merabishvili, Vano 92, 121
methodology 10, 19, 36–9, 43–4; case studies 10, 39–42; data 19, 21, 22, 26–7, 30, 37–8; interviewing 37–8, 44; macro/micro-level analyses 10, 36–7; policies and time frame 42–3; problematization 38, 43
migration management 11, 46, 49, 64–5, 67, 102, 140–4; 1951 Geneva Convention 46, 67; 1967 Protocol 46, 67; asylum and refugees 46, 67, 72; border management 46, 49, 64, 72, 81, 102; capacity building 11, 143–4; CIS 46–7; CSTO 47, 132; deportation 32, 85; ENP Action Plans 2, 11, 103, 104, 115; ENP, full compliance 11, 140; ENP, shallow compliance 64, 102, 142; EU mobility partnerships 84, 109, 137; external incentives 11, 143; illegal migration 22, 46–7, 48, 81, 103; migrant worker 32, 60, 85, 197; National Action Plans on Migration and Asylum 11, 103, 104; PCA 103; policy conditionality 84–5, 142, 143–4; policy, polity, politics misfits 103–106; preferential fit 11, 140, 142, 143; preferential misfit 11, 142, 143–4; remittances 22, 58, 59, 60, 115; socialization 11, 120, 132, 143, 212; Söderköping/Budapest/Prague processes 69, 81; *see also* Armenian migration management; data protection; document security; Georgian migration management; JLS; readmission; Russia and migration management; visa facilitation; visa liberalization
Millennium Challenge Corporation 73
Moldova 2, 13, 216; AA 12, 185, 196–9, 203, 205 (preferential fit 196, 198, 199; Russian sanctions and the speeding up of EU integration 12, 186, 196, 197–8, 199, 204, 215–16); AEI 196, 197, 198–9; corruption 197, 198–9; DP 197, 198, 199; LDP 196, 197, 198; political crisis 1, 185, 196, 197, 198–9, 219; visa facilitation 111; visa liberalization 109, 116, 196, 197; VLAP 109; *see also* AA
money laundering 22, 46, 48, 59; CIS 46; *see also* JLS
Moneyval 22, 46, 69

Nalbandian, Edward 127–8
NATO (North Atlantic Treaty Organization) 165, 191
neighborhood Europeanization 5, 45; agency-centered framework 27–36, 45, 206–207; CEEC 29; 'convergence' 17–18; definition 10; 'enclaves of Europeanization' 8; ENP Action Plans 10; 'external governance' approach 5–6, 20, 34; 'external incentives' model 5; furthering the domestic agenda 4, 7, 32; 'preferential fit/policy conditionality' interplay 186, 188, 207; scholarship on 4–8; rationalist institutionalism 14, 15–17, 23–4, 28, 37, 206; Russia 6–7, 207; *see also* ENP; EU policy transfer
NGO (non-governmental organization) 12, 30, 38, 72, 101, 117, 133
NIF (Neighborhood Investment Facility) 82, 155, 158
Nodia, Ghia 94, 98
Nogaideli, Zurab 96, 154
Nye, Joseph S. 21, 44

Open Society Foundation Georgia 109
organized crime 22, 46, 47, 48, 49, 57, 59, 64, 69, 72; CIS 47; interdependence 59, 60; Second Protocol to the European Convention on Mutual Assistance in Criminal Matters 47, 68; *see also* JLS
Orinats Yerkir 89, 90
OSCE (Organization for Security and Co-operation in Europe) 56, 110, 130, 133; action plan to combat human trafficking 67; action plans on organized crime 47, 72; OSCE Minsk group 57

Pamuk, Yasemin 34
Patarkatishvili, Badri 93, 94
PCA (Partnership and Cooperation Agreements) 27, 43, 46, 68, 69; Armenia 19, 51, 150; energy diversification 52, 150, 151, 157; energy policy 50, 52, 53, 68, 70; Georgia 19, 51, 150; JLS 46, 47, 48, 67, 69; migration management 103; readmission 48, 108
PEEREA (Energy Charter Protocol on Energy Efficiency and Related Environmental Aspects) 51
policy conditionality 31, 33, 209–10, 212, 214, 216, 218; 'conditionality-lite' 6,

Index 271

31; energy policy 85–7 (Armenian energy diversification 173, 175–6, 210); ENP, full compliance 3–4, 14, 31, 32; ENP, non-compliance with 4, 32; ENP, shallow compliance 3–4, 32, 207, 209; EU 3, 31, 84, 85–6; explaining variation in compliance patterns 11, 66, 83–7, 100, 188; IMF 86; incentivize merely cosmetic, rather than profound domestic changes 4, 207, 209; JLS 84–5; migration management 84–5, 142, 143–4 (Armenia 131–2; Georgia 107–108, 110, 111–12, 114, 120, 142, 143–4, 218); rivaling policy conditionality 188; Russia 85, 86; World Bank 86; *see also* EU policy transfer; 'preferential fit/policy conditionality' interplay; Russia, rivaling policy conditionality; sanction

policy convergence/divergence 45–55, 212; CIS/CSTO 23; energy, EU/Russia policy divergence 49, 52–3, 54–5, 63, 99, 149, 183, 213; interdependence and policy divergence 22–3; JLS, EU/Russia policy convergence 46–8, 49, 55, 63, 71, 99, 102, 144, 213

Poroshenko, Petro 200, 202

preferential fit 27–30, 33; AA 12, 187, 204, 208–209, 215; Armenia 87–91 (AA 191–3, 204; energy diversification 180, 183; migration management 124–5, 127, 128–9, 132, 138); capacity building 35, 211–12; definition 29, 187, 207; domestic actor empowerment 28; ENP, full compliance 14, 27, 209; ENP, shallow compliance 3–4, 187; explaining variation in compliance patterns 66, 87–99, 100, 188, 208; Georgia 87, 91–8 (AA 189, 191; energy diversification 11, 157, 164, 167, 168, 180, 182, 183); measurement of 29–30; migration management 11, 140, 142, 143; Moldova and the AA 196, 198, 199; *see also* agency; EU policy transfer; 'preferential fit/policy conditionality' interplay; preferential misfit

'preferential fit/policy conditionality' interplay 31–2; AA 9, 12, 185–6, 188, 203, 204, 207; energy diversification 157, 183; ENP compliance 3–4, 32–3, 207–208, 210, 214; EU policy transfer 14, 27, 35–6, 37; Georgian migration management 120; neighborhood Europeanization 186, 188, 207; *see also* policy conditionality; preferential fit

preferential misfit 27–8, 210; adaptation costs 28, 29; Armenian energy diversification 177; capacity building 36, 211; ENP, non-compliance 4, 26, 36, 209; Georgian energy diversification 161–2, 181–2; migration management 11, 142, 143–4 (Armenia 140; Georgia 116, 120, 123, 142, 143–4); policy conditionality 32, 188; *see also* preferential fit

Prodi, Romano 1, 41, 206

Putin, Vladimir 36, 43, 95, 179, 190, 193

rationalist institutionalism 14, 15–17, 23–4, 28, 37, 206; compliance 19–20; preferences over outcomes 15–16, 23

readmission 72, 102, 103; Armenia 11, 65, 102, 103, 124–9, 140–1; conclusion of readmission agreements 11, 46, 47, 103, 104; document security 104; EU readmission agreement 108; EU/Russia readmission and visa facilitation agreement 49, 107; Georgia 81, 103–104, 106–10, 142, 143–4, 212, 218 (implementation of 106–107, 108–10, 142, 209); illegal migration 103; PCA 48, 108; policy and politics misfits 103–104; third country national/stateless person 103–104, 108; UN Universal Declaration of Human Rights 103; visa facilitation 49, 84; *see also* migration management

regime, domestic compatibility 26–7; *see also* authoritarian regime; democracy; hybrid regime; semi-democratic regime

rule of law 27, 74, 75, 79, 89, 100, 214; *see also* domestic compatibility

Russia 2, 6; approach to the neighborhood as a form of coercion 33; authoritarian regime 40, 41; capacity building 35, 80, 81–2, 83 (CIS agreements 36, 81); domestic compatibility with 25, 79, 214; economic potential 56; energy policy 50–1, 52–3, 83, 86–7, 211–12, 213; as external actor/foreign policy agent 4, 7, 16, 18, 23, 43; impact on EU policy transfer in the ENC 6–7, 42, 208–10, 214, 215, 219; military capacity 56–7, 92, 93, 98, 193–4; neglect of Russia in the study on accession Europeanization 5;

neighborhood Europeanization 6–7, 207; state capacity 77–9; a structural force 7; Ukraine 7, 215–16 (rivaling policy conditionality 201–202, 204; war 1, 2, 33, 185, 203, 216); visa-free regime 59, 85, 102; *see also the entries below for* Russia; Armenian energy diversification and Russia; EU/Russia rivalry; Gazprom; Georgian energy diversification and Russia; UES

Russia and the AA 12; an 'active saboteur' 188; incentives 188; interdependence with Russia 204; sanctions 12, 201, 204 (rivaling policy conditionality 191, 193–4, 196, 201–202, 204; speeding up EU integration 12, 186, 190–1, 196, 197–8, 199, 201, 204); *see also* AA

Russia and interdependence 7, 56–7, 212, 213, 215; AA 204; ENC 6, 21, 56–7; energy, asymmetric interdependence favoring Russia 42, 61–3, 149, 162, 184, 213; JLS, asymmetric interdependence favoring Russia 42, 57, 60; migration management 57–8, 59–60; *see also* interdependence

Russia and migration management 85; Armenia 126–7, 138, 140, 142, 144 (Compatriots Program 11, 136–7, 143); Georgia, passportization as negative incentive 11, 107, 110, 111, 114, 116, 120, 142, 211; impact on non-compliance with ENP 144; interdependence with Russia 57–8, 59–60; negative incentives 142–3; *see also* migration management

Russia, rivaling policy conditionality 3, 4, 9, 11, 31, 209, 214; absence of, as condition for full compliance with EU policies 4, 209; Armenia and the AA 191, 193–4, 196, 204; Armenian energy diversification 176–7, 178–80, 182, 210; Georgian energy diversification 162–4, 167, 168, 182, 210; Ukraine and the AA 201–202, 204; *see also* policy conditionality; Russian constraining effects on EU policy transfer

Russian constraining effects on EU policy transfer 1–2, 7, 8, 18, 206, 214, 215; interdependence with Russia in policy areas 10; Eurasian integration 2, 13; sanctions 2, 3, 4, 8, 12, 32, 85, 86, 142–3, 201, 204; *see also* EU policy transfer; Russia, rivaling policy conditionality

Russian supportive effects on EU policy transfer 4, 7, 8; AA, negative incentives facilitate EU integration 12, 186, 190–1, 196, 197–8, 199, 201, 204; energy diversification, enabling compliance with ENP 183; negative incentives facilitating reform 8, 9, 12, 32–3, 86, 87, 107, 110, 111, 114, 153–5, 156, 157, 165–6, 170–1, 173, 181, 188, 207, 211, 214, 215–16; *see also* EU policy transfer

Saakashvili, Mikheil 11, 79, 91–8, 99, 189–90, 209; authoritarian tendencies 41; energy diversification 153–4, 155–6, 157, 158, 164, 166–7, 168, 182, 184; liberalism 75, 106, 115; migration management 106, 107, 114, 115, 119, 123, 141; *see also* UNM

sanction 16, 32; EU 83; Russia 2, 3, 4, 8, 12, 32, 85, 86, 142–3, 201, 204; *see also* external incentives; Russia, rivaling policy conditionality; Russian supportive effects on EU policy transfer

Sargsyan, Serzh 11, 41, 88, 89, 90, 98; AA 192–3, 194–5; migration management 129, 130, 134–5, 136, 140

Sargsyan, Tigran 129, 135, 136–7, 192, 194, 195

Sargsyan, Vazgen 88, 89, 91

Scharpf, Fritz 15

Schimmelfennig, Frank 19, 26, 31

Sedelmeier, Ulrich 31

semi-democratic regime 1, 15, 28, 215; ENC 2, 206, 219; EU policy transfer 2, 3, 208; hybrid regime 30, 39–41, 87, 215, 216; *see also* authoritarian regime; democracy; hybrid regime

Shevardnadze, Eduard 12, 79, 91–5, 98, 99, 101, 106, 209; energy diversification 12, 152–3, 155, 156, 157, 162, 163, 164, 168, 181–2

Shevardnadze, Nugzar 93

SIPRI (Stockholm International Peace Research Institute) 21, 101

socialization 5, 212; capacity building 34, 80; energy diversification 12, 161–2, 168, 177, 180; ENP 6, 7; migration management 11, 120, 132, 143, 212

South Ossetia 56, 91, 93, 96, 101, 107, 191

'spheres of influence' 8, 45

state: sovereignty 2, 67, 187, 196, 205, 216 (energy policy 29, 35, 215; JLS 29, 35, 43, 215); state capacity 26, 27, 77–9, 100, 212, 214
Stefes, Christoph 87

TACIS (Technical Assistance to the Commonwealth of Independent States) 36, 80, 81, 82, 183; Armenian energy diversification 169, 173, 175, 176; Georgian energy diversification 155, 157; Georgian migration management 120, 123
TAIEX (technical assistance and information exchange instrument) 34, 81, 83, 115, 116, 120, 126, 130, 133
Ter-Petrosyan, Levon 88, 89, 90, 91, 136; energy diversification 169, 170, 171, 173
terrorism 46, 47, 48, 67, 85, 129, 130, 165
TIG (Targeted Initiative Georgia) 101, 109, 110, 117, 119, 144
TRACECA (Transport Corridor Europe–Caucasus–Asia) 162, 168
Trans-Caspian Pipeline System 61
Transparency International 37, 156, 158, 168
Tsarukyan, Gagik 90, 195
Twinning 34, 81, 83, 137
Tymoshenko, Yulia 200, 201–202

UES (Unified Energy System) 50, 62, 86, 155, 172, 174
Ukraine 2, 12, 199–203, 205, 216, 219; AA/DCFTA 12, 100, 185, 199–205; external rivalry 202, 203, 204, 205; multiple incentives 200–202; capacity building 34; CIS 6, 203; corruption 200–201; CU 201; energy policy 51, 55; ENP 6; EU market rules 2; political instability 185, 202–203, 205; Russia 7, 215–16 (rivaling policy conditionality 201–202, 204; war 1, 2, 33, 185, 203, 216); visa facilitation 111; visa liberalization 109, 116; VLAP 109
UN (United Nations): 1948 Universal Declaration of Human Rights 103; 1988 UN Convention against Illicit Traffic in Narcotic Drugs 47, 67; 2000 UN Convention on Transnational Organized Crime 47, 64, 67; 2001 Protocol against the Illicit Manufacturing of and Trafficking in Firearms 47, 64

UNDP (UN Development Programme) 46, 110, 129, 160
UNHCR (UN High Commissioner for Refugees) 72, 134
UNM (United National Movement) 91, 94–5, 97, 145, 160, 161, 167, 189–90; biometric passports and election code 112–13; 'witch hunts' against 41; *see also* Saakashvili, Mikheil
USA (United States of America) 5, 22, 25, 73; Georgian energy diversification 12, 163, 164, 168, 182, 210
USAID (US Agency for International Development) 110, 130; Armenian energy diversification 170, 171, 174, 183; Georgian energy diversification 155, 159, 160, 161, 183

veto player: domestic veto player 6, 28, 31; intra-elite/ intra-governmental veto player 87, 99, 133–4, 208; non-governmental veto player 29, 208
visa facilitation 31, 49; Armenia 42, 81, 127–8, 137; Council of the European Union: Common Approach on Visa Facilitation 84; EU policy conditionality 84; EU/Russia readmission and visa facilitation agreement 49, 107; Georgia 42, 81, 107–108, 110, 111, 116, 121, 128, 142, 211, 218; Moldova 111; readmission 49, 84; Ukraine 111
visa liberalization 3, 31, 84, 87; Armenia 42, 125, 128, 131, 137; EaP 84, 116, 122, 128; Georgia 42, 109, 114, 116, 119, 123, 142, 190, 209, 218; Moldova 109, 116, 196, 197; Russia 116–17, 122; Ukraine 109, 116; VLAP 109, 114, 116, 119, 122
Voronin, Vladimir 196, 197

Way, Lucan A. 21, 216
World Bank 5, 21, 22, 72–3; Governance Indicators 27, 74, 75, 77, 78, 79; migration database 22
WTO (World Trade Organization) 22

Yanukovych, Victor 185, 199–203, 204, 216, 219
Yeganyan, Gagik 124–5, 127, 135
Yerkrapah 88, 89, 91

Zhvania, Zurab 93, 94–5, 96, 106, 163–4, 166